The Gang

The Gang

Coleridge, the Hutchinsons
& the Wordsworths in 1802

John Worthen

Yale University Press
New Haven and London

remembering F. M. W.
(a book he would have liked)

Designed by Adam Freudenheim

Printed in Great Britain

Library of Congress Cataloging-in-Publication Data
Worthen, John.
The gang: Coleridge, the Hutchinsons and the Wordsworths in 1802/John Worthen.
p. cm.
Includes bibliographical references and index.
ISBN 0-300-08819-1 (cloth: alk. paper)
1. Coleridge, Samuel Taylor, 1772–1834 – Friends and associates. 2. Wordsworth, William,
1770–1850 – Friends and associates. 3. Wordsworth, Dorothy, 1771–1855 – Friends and associ-
ates. 4. Hutchinson, Sara, 1775–1835 – Friends and associates. 5. Wordsworth, William,
1770–1850 – Marriage. 7. Poets, English – 19th century – Biography. 8. Coleridge, Samuel
Taylor, 1772–1834. 9. Wordsworth, William, 1770–1850. 10. Hutchinson family. I. Title.
PR4483.W6 2001   821'.709 – dc21 [B]   00-043802

A catalogue record for this book is available from the British Library.
10 9 8 7 6 5 4 3 2 1

GANG. *n.s.* [from the verb.] A number herding together; a troop; a company; a tribe; a herd. It is seldom used but in contempt or abhorrence.
Oh, you panderly rascals! there's a knot, a *gang*, a pack, a conspiracy against me. *Shakes. Merry Wives of Windsor.*
As a *gang* of thieves were robbing a house, a mastiff fell a barking. *L'Estrange, Fable* 21.
Admitted in among the *gang*,
He acts and talks as they befriend him. *Prior.*

(Johnson's *Dictionary of the English Language* 1755)

. . . no French Affair, but a mischiefuous gang of disaffected Englishmen . . .

James Walsh, Government spy, 15 August 1797

A Night or two after a worse Rogue there came,
The head of the Gang, one Wordsworth by name . . .

Coleridge, 'A Soliloquy of the full Moon', April 1802

Contents

List of Illustrations

Preface

What would a biography be like which managed to include everything surviving of a life? Every document, letter and journal entry? Every encounter, known movement, illustration? Every moment of which a record survived?

The impossible-sounding job has in fact been done. Every single document relating to Shakespeare's life appeared in facsimile in Schoenbaum's *William Shakespeare: Records and Images*: there are many books which provide nothing but biographical documents.[1] And Mark L. Reed's two monumental *Chronologies* record every detail of Wordsworth's life up to his middle years (though not, of course, the contents of his letters or other writings).[2] But only in the case of a person with relatively few surviving life records are such compilations possible. Reed never published any further volumes of his *Chronologies*, while Schoenbaum published a book which presented the same facts about Shakespeare without the documents. He wrote, that is, a biography as the term is normally understood.[3]

What we might call the *total* biography of an ordinary life takes us into the imaginative world of Jose Luis Borges. In 'Funes the Memorious', Ireneo Funes is in the frightening situation of forgetting nothing: 'Two or three times he had reconstructed an entire day; he never once erred or faltered, but each reconstruction had itself taken an entire day.'[4] As, of course, it would have to. 'On Exactitude in Science' describes some map-makers' attempts to provide their country with larger, better maps: 'the map of a single Province occupied the entirety of a City, and the map of the Empire, the entirety of a Province.'[5] In time, however, 'those Unconscionable Maps no longer satisfied'. The cartographers 'struck a Map of the Empire whose size was that of the Empire, and which coincided point for point with it'. However, 'The following Generations . . . saw that that vast Map was Useless, and . . . delivered it up to the Inclemencies of Sun and Winters. In the Deserts of the West, still today, there are Tattered Ruins of that Map, inhabited by Animals and Beggars . . .'.[6] The total[7] map is like the reconstructed day, or the biography aiming at totality. All are interminable, all are useless.

And yet . . . there is an instinct in all of us that biographies which are not in some sense complete cannot tell us what people's lives are like. If we miss things out on the grounds that they are unimportant, or because we have not space to include them, or because they do not fit the story we are trying to tell, then all we do is conceal our prejudices.

A good example of this appears in the early biographical documentation of the Wordsworth circle. William Knight published the very first edition of Dorothy Wordsworth's journals in 1897, but announced that it would not be desirable to print them 'in extenso . . . All the Journals contain numerous trivial details'. He would, instead, provide 'samples of these details . . . but there is no need to record all the cases in which his sister wrote, "To-day I mended William's shirts," or "William gathered sticks," or "I went in search of eggs," etc. etc.'[8] He insisted, however, that 'Nothing is omitted of any literary or bio-graphical value.' For him, the triviality of the 'everyday' had nothing to do with biography. In Dorothy's third Grasmere journal-notebook (covering the period 14 February to 8 July 1802) appears the first record of Wordsworth at work on the poem which became his 'Immortality Ode'. Knight's version of the day highlights that significant beginning: 'Saturday. A divine morning. At breakfast William wrote part of an ode. . . . We sate all day in the orchard.'[9] Sitting in the orchard all day is thus a response to the achievement of the poem. Perhaps Wordsworth recited what he had written. But he and Dorothy retreat to recover and rejoice.

The entry Dorothy Wordsworth actually made was rather longer: 'Saturday. A divine morning. At Breakfast Wm wrote part of an Ode. Mr Oliff sent the dung and Wm went to work in the garden. We sate all day in the orchard.'[10] This time, the retreat to the orchard responds to another kind of work. It is a rest from the digging (and perhaps from the smell of the newly dug ground). Knight was too conscious of the intimate and comic juxtaposition of the arrival of the *Ode* and the arrival of the dung to allow the latter into the journal.

But a biography should take seriously what he objects to. For one thing, the entry puts the writing of a poem firmly into the context of a life with other concerns than the writing of poetry. Although autumn would be a more normal time to dig in dung, Dorothy saw it being spread in the fields in mid-April, and gardens need fertilizer to grow vegetables successfully. Looking back from his crops of peas, beans and potatoes later in the year, Wordsworth's garden work on 27 March might well have seemed to him as important as the production, on the same day, of part of a poem.[11]

For dung will not wait for a poem to be finished. If, as seems probable, it was matured horse dung, it sits and stinks until put to good use. It is even pos-sible that the real-life Mr Olive and his very real dung played the role which the certainly fictitious Person from Porlock played in 1798, when Coleridge's drugged and dreamy creation of 'Kubla Khan' was interrupted.[12] But there are no complaints in Dorothy Wordsworth's journal, as there are when visitors interrupted her brother's writing. Even though the poem may not have been expected, the dung certainly was. Mr Olive had offered it ten days earlier, and Wordsworth had been to see him the previous afternoon, presumably to arrange delivery.[13] Dung takes priority over a poem, especially as its arrival had been carefully timed; the Wordsworths were going away the following day. It is not advisable to plant peas or potatoes (or indeed anything) in newly manured ground; if Wordsworth wished to get his potatoes under way by the start of May, as he probably would, the dung would best be dug in before they left. (He dug 'a little' in the garden the day after they got back,[14] presumably readying it for planting.) For people as poor as the Wordsworths, food they could grow themselves was important. At different times the Town End garden produced runner and French beans, peas, kidney beans, spinach, potatoes, carrots, broccoli, onions, turnips, rhubarb, apples and pears.[15]

I think we should be especially interested in the way in which the composition of a poem of the High Romantic period, one intensely concerned with the ideal life of the mind, can also be seen in the context of the pressing concerns of the every day. But of course we can only do that if the dung is allowed to play a fertilising role in the biographical account. If, for example, we look at the *Ode* for a moment: very clearly, like a number of Wordsworth's poems from 1802, it is centred on the ways in which human beings live in the natural world. Natural things rejoice, flower and grow, and the human being as a child shares such unalloyed joy 'Of splendour in the grass, of glory in the flower'.[16] Later, the adult remains aware of the natural world as extraordinarily beautiful, but is no longer an intimate, unthinking part of it. Adults must be caring and careful; they no longer lose themselves in the natural world. Flowers and grass are no longer direct experiences of nature; dung has (as it were) to be dug in, for flowers and vegetables to flourish. The simple, extraordinary splendour has departed; but – this is the *Ode*'s paradox – a relation with the natural world established in early childhood will set a pattern for the whole of the rest of one's life. That had been Wordsworth's subject in poem after poem during this spring of 1802.

Any biography of Wordsworth, I would say, needs to incorporate not only the poem but the dung, and such ideas of nature, as well as Dorothy, Mr Olive, the digging, the orchard, the sitting all day. It would be hard, indeed, to see which could be missed out without lessening our understanding of the Wordsworths at this particular moment. It would be a good idea for a biography, just for once, to include all that it is possible to include, rather than to start from the point of view that selection and shaping are the biographer's first principles; while it would also be sensible to make the biography, so far as possible, of all the people in the group, not just of a central figure chosen (as Knight would have chosen him) for his 'literary value'.

II

I mentioned in passing the other reason why the dung had to be dug in immediately. The Wordsworths were leaving Town End the following day to go and stay with friends; first with the Coleridges in Keswick for a week, then William would be going over to Bishops Middleham to stay with the Hutchinsons, who lived on the other side of England in north Yorkshire. Dorothy would stay with other friends, the Clarksons, in Eusemere for ten days, waiting for her brother to come back. In particular Wordsworth would have wanted to see the eldest Hutchinson sister Mary, to whom he would be getting married later in the year: she was housekeeping for her farmer brother George at Bishop Middleham. (The second sister Sara was with her brother Tom, who was farming at Gallow Hill near Brompton.) When Wordsworth returned he and Dorothy would then walk home to Grasmere; they would be away for the best part of three weeks.

Should not a biography be a biography of all these other people too? Writing a biography of Wordsworth during these three weeks obviously involves writing one of Dorothy (and vice versa); but why should it marginalise the people with whom they were so intimate? Everything Wordsworth wrote about nature and children in his *Ode* was part of an uninterrupted conversation with Coleridge, whose own poetry written this spring addressed identical issues; but everything Wordsworth wrote about children was also an implicit conversation with Mary Hutchinson, as well as an ongoing reminiscence shared with Dorothy: over and over again during the spring of 1802 his poems recreated their common childhood. What is more, on Sunday 4 April, after Dorothy and Wordsworth had got to Keswick, and after Dorothy had 'repeated his verses',[17] Coleridge would work on the poem which became *Dejection: An Ode*. This revolved around the lives of eight beings who obsessed, fascinated and haunted him: Coleridge himself, his wife Sarah,[18] their two children Hartley and Derwent (aged 5 and 1½), his friends Wordsworth and Dorothy – all of them, of course, in the house on the evening of 4 April – and the two sisters, Mary and Sara Hutchinson. All eight were in Coleridge's poem: they knew each other intimately, and the adults constantly thought of each other as sisters and brothers: they found themselves addressed in the poem as 'O Friends, most dear, most true'.[19]

To use a convenient term of Coleridge's own critical and poetical vocabulary, he was writing a 'Conversation Poem', addressed to and concerned with this group of family and friends who were in constant contact with each other. This is true of both its texts (I shall here refer to it as the *Letter* in its long form, and *Dejection* in its short form). Not only did Coleridge address all the group personally at points, but he carried on several different conversations with them; and, like his 1798 conversation poem 'This Lime-Tree Bower my Prison' (which also started with the exclamation 'Well . . .'[20]) the 1802 poem is made up of the reflections of the individual momentarily abandoned by the very friends whom the poetry spends so much time addressing. The *Letter* was in one form actually written to one of the six adults of the group, Sara Hutchinson: she is 'O Sister! O Beloved!', 'Sister & Friend', 'A Sister of my Choice'. In another – or perhaps, rather worryingly, practically the same form, with just the name changed – it was a poem addressed to Wordsworth as 'Brother', and at least part of it was sent to him. In yet another form, it was an untitled manuscript copied out by Mary Hutchinson. In yet another form it was a piece of poetry focused upon Wordsworth's forthcoming marriage to Mary, which Coleridge had known about since around 22 February 1802. On 4 October 1802 – Wordsworth's and Mary's wedding day – it would appear in the *Morning Post*, six months to the day after the date inscribed in its title:[21] the date was the anniversary of Coleridge's own marriage in 1795 to Sarah Fricker, as well (he believed) as the anniversary of the death of his father in 1781.[22]

When Wordsworth got back to the Clarksons on 13 April 1802, just nine days after the Sunday which Coleridge had commemorated in his poem's title, he would find a letter containing 'verses' which had arrived from Coleridge earlier in the day. It was probably his first sight of the poem as it then existed, though it would also have been natural for Coleridge to have repeated aloud what was written, while walking along the road towards the Clarksons house with the Wordsworths on the morning of Monday the 5th. We know too little about the part which the Clarksons may have played in all these exchanges, but we do know that they were particularly concerned about Coleridge's state of mind, health and marriage this spring. (Mrs Clarkson actually woke Dorothy up when the letter from Coleridge arrived on the 13th, showing how important she thought it might be.) And the first thing Wordsworth did, the evening they got back to Grasmere, was to send Coleridge a letter thanking him for his poetry, and enclosing his own two most recent poems. One had been written only that day, during the walk with Dorothy; the other had been written on his journey back from seeing Mary, who was also sent a copy.

III

A detailed biography of the Wordsworths, the Coleridges and the Hutchinsons, covering a brief period, is therefore a good way of describing the lives led by people who wrote such poetry, recited it to each other, sent it to each other, copied it for each other, and who lived in such an extraordinarily intimate way. Thomas McFarland thought 'The Significant Group' was an idea which should help us understand Romantic poetry.[23] I would like to develop the idea into biography itself: a form of writing which has traditionally concentrated upon the lives of one or two individuals at a time.

There are a number of reasons why the biography of individuals – especially these individuals – may not be a good way to proceed. One reason was foreshadowed by George Eliot, when she wrote so tellingly in *Middlemarch* about the normally selfish individual seeing him or herself as a 'supreme self', around whose life and actions the rest of the world apparently falls into place – so that, in her brilliant image, scratches made wholly at random on a mirror fall into concentric circles around a central source of illumination.[24] She was in effect describing the technique of modern scholarly biography and nearly all popular biography, which remains stubbornly nineteenth-century in its hero- or heroine-worshipping concentration on the life of the individual. Lip-service only is paid to the fact that the biographical subject was always the member of surrounding and overlapping groups of other people, alive and dead. Modern biography at times seems to have learned almost nothing from history, sociology, or even psychology, all of which constantly stress the impossibility of telling any kind of truth about individuals divorced from the impinging lives and histories of other individuals. We write biographies of individuals as islands: we live as part of the main.[25]

The other reason is that scholarly biography of Wordsworth and Coleridge has been bedevilled by a need to concentrate defensively upon the person about whom the biography is being written. Actions are interpreted, justified, explained (and explained away) from the point of view of the central figure: it is the others who behave badly, unless the writer is engaged in such a piece of work as Norman Fruman's notorious book on Coleridge, which sought to make Wordsworth by far the stronger, more moral and more creative figure of the two.[26] The practice of elevating one figure over the other has dominated Coleridge and Wordsworth biography for decades; to some extent because the very closeness of the two writers was later wrecked by savage disagreement. Interpreting one of them sympathetically almost inevitably means showing the other in a bad light.[27]

The problems of writing coherent biography of a single individual are nowhere better exemplified than by the way in which events have been described which took place in the autumn of 1800. Richard Holmes, a passionate defender of Coleridge, locates his 'emergent feelings of rivalry with Wordsworth' at this point, and gives an account of how Coleridge's poem 'Christabel' came to be excluded from the second edition of *Lyrical Ballads*, which Coleridge and Wordsworth put together in 1800. He concludes that 'The rejection of "Christabel" seems to have been a wholly unexpected blow for Coleridge'.[28] His account is similar to that which Thomas McFarland had offered in *Romanticism and the Forms of Ruin*, which states that 'Not only did Wordsworth manage to keep "Christabel" from being published in *Lyrical Ballads*' but that it was an act of 'critical ineptitude'.[29] Molly Lefebure, in her Sarah Coleridge biography *The Bondage of Love*, also savagely attacked Wordsworth for his 'dismissal' of Coleridge as a poet, and concluded: 'Clearly, Wordsworth had no conception of the trauma he had inflicted upon Coleridge'.[30] So far as these three commentators are concerned, Wordsworth took a stupid decision, and Coleridge was the helpless (and damaged) victim.[31]

All three are drawing on the authoritative edition of Coleridge's letters, which states unequivocally of Coleridge that 'after a tremendous expenditure of creative energy, he succeeded in composing Part II of *Christabel*, before Wordsworth determined not to include it'.[32] But they carry the attack on Wordsworth still further, into accusations of a 'lack of generosity'[33] to his old friend. Holmes describes how, at the end of October 1800, Coleridge experienced 'a complete writing-block', and – like Lefebure – he links the block to the damage Coleridge suffered from the rejection of 'Christabel'. Lefebure goes further and states that Wordsworth's behaviour to Coleridge 'contributed significantly to . . . the moment when, poised as he already was on the verge of destruction by opium, he had his feet (metaphorically speaking) knocked from under him'. Both Holmes and Lefebure are repeating a charge which Stephen Parrish had made years earlier, in a passage quoted by McFarland.[34] They all write from the point of view of defenders of Coleridge; and this makes them critical of Wordsworth.

The evidence for all their statements are some remarks in Coleridge's correspondence, and Dorothy Wordsworth's journal describing Coleridge's visit to Town End. The complete record of the visit in the journal is as follows:

> Saturday October 4th 1800. . . . Coleridge came in while we were at dinner very wet. – We talked till 12 o clock – he had sate up all the night before writing Essays for the newspaper [the *Morning Post*]. – His youngest child [Derwent] had been very ill in convulsion fits. Exceedingly delighted with the 2nd part of Christabel.

> Sunday Morning 5th October. Coleridge read a 2nd time Christabel – we had increasing pleasure. A delicious morning. Wm & I were employed all the morning in writing an addition to the preface. Wm went to bed very ill after working after dinner – Coleridge & I walked to Ambleside after dark with the letter. Returned to tea at 9 o'clock. Wm still in bed & very ill. Silver How in both lakes.

> Monday [6 October]. A rainy day – Coleridge intending to go but did not get off. We walked after dinner to Rydale. After tea read The Pedlar. Determined not to print Christabel with the LB.

> Tuesday [7 October]. Coleridge went off at 11 o clock – I went as far as Mr Simpson's returned with Mary. She drank tea here. I was very ill in the Evening at the Simpsons – went to bed – supped there. Returned with Miss S & Mrs J – heavy showers. Found Wm at home. I was still weak & unwell – went to bed immediately.[35]

Holmes concludes, after noting the decision not to print 'Christabel' on the 6th, 'There is no further comment. Coleridge left the next day, and Dorothy, "weak and unwell" herself, went to bed early. One can conclude that it had been a stressful visit for all of them.'[36] One would be most unwise to reach that conclusion. The Wordsworths' illnesses were frequent, and they regularly went to bed during the day – or early to bed. To link Dorothy's illness of the evening of the 7th with the 'Christabel' decision taken 24 hours earlier looks wilful. And what about Wordsworth's illness of the 5th? A premonition of guilt?

Holmes's version of what 'had happened' is in fact a rhetorical attack on Wordsworth:

> What had happened was clear: Wordsworth, from a position of apparent weakness, had ruthlessly come to dominate the terms of the collaboration. Having used Coleridge – even, one might think, having exploited him – as advisor and editor, drawing him up to the Lakes for that very purpose, he had entirely imposed his own vision of the collection on the final text . . . Coleridge had submitted himself to Wordsworth in the most humiliating and damaging way; while Wordsworth had shown extraordinary insensitivity to the effect that this rejection would have on Coleridge's powers and self-confidence.[37]

A biographer of Coleridge, writing the usual kind of combative contemporary biography, probably feels that he must present the omission of 'Christabel' from *Lyrical Ballads* like that.[38] What is extraordinary to me is that Holmes's powerful language ('ruthlessly come to dominate', 'the most humiliating and damaging way') should be based on a brief journal entry, a few notes of illness, and the idea that at the end of the month Coleridge *may* have suffered one of his numerous failures to write what was required of him. It should be said that the evidence for the 'writing block' so important to Lefebure and Holmes is a passage in one of Coleridge's notebooks describing – in the third-person – a man who 'knew not what to do'.[39] Coleridge himself wrote a wide-ranging and highly intelligent letter to Josiah Wedgwood the following day, as unblocked as it is possible to imagine; and at the start of October he had provided Stuart with only two out of five essays on Agriculture, Rents and Riots which he had faithfully promised.[40]

And, anyway, should the very great pleasure which both the Wordsworths took in the poem, and which Dorothy twice stresses, play no part in how we understand what happened?

Even more significant than such arguments, however, is Coleridge's own statement to Josiah Wedgwood of 1 November: 'I proceeded successfully – till my poem grew so long & in Wordsworth's opinion so impressive, that he rejected it from his volume as disproportionate both in size & merit, & as discordant in it's character'.[41] This version of its 'rejection' is quite different. It suggests that the poem was too good, too long, too different for *Lyrical Ballads*. Coleridge is flattered by the praise and understands the reasons, although it would be right to recognise that a letter to Wedgwood (a patron keen to see Coleridge's work getting into print, as a return for his philanthropic investment) is also likely to put the best possible interpretation on events.

But those who read the episode as Wordsworth's ruthless exploitation of poor Coleridge have another problem: the aftermath. The friendship between the two men continued, rich and untroubled. As his letter to Wedgwood shows, Coleridge felt no resentment about what had happened on 6 October. He did not feel dominated, or exploited, humiliated or damaged. Instead, he justified the change of policy in letters to his friends.[42] He continued to write prose for the *Morning Post*. And he continued to work on the *Lyrical Ballads* volume editorially; he even copied out for the printer the first 200 lines of Wordsworth's poem 'Michael', the item replacing 'Christabel'. This was either superhuman forgivingness or masochism for someone 'exploited' and 'humiliated' as Holmes presents him.[43] All Holmes can say to explain this remarkable behaviour is that 'Coleridge was slow to admit all this to himself'. That is, the subject of the biography *did* feel what the biographer tells us he must have felt, in spite of the evidence to the contrary. He was just rather slow in getting round to it (it took him years, in fact): whereas we readers have been in on the truth from the start. Holmes needs to escape the fact that the whole structure of exploitation and humiliation which he has erected has no foundation, while everything which Coleridge actually did and said and wrote showed him committed to the idea of a 'Christabel'-less *Lyrical Ballads*,[44] and undamaged by the decision.

But if we look at a Wordsworth biographer examining the rejection of 'Christabel', we find Mary Moorman taking – with equal absurdity – exactly the opposite point of view. In the first place, she emphasises Wordsworth's later criticism of the poem – that the second part 'creates an expectation [of an end], and the daylight . . . divests the persons of much of their charm', [45] despite the fact that Wordsworth's reaction at the time seems to have been unbounded admiration: she then comments that 'the soundness of Wordsworth's criticism [of 'Christabel'] will be felt by most people'; and lastly, she gives a brief account of how the decision to omit the poem was reached: 'After two days of discussion and deliberation they came to a unanimous decision "not to print Christabel with the L.B." It was a sensible decision.'[46] Not only was it objectively sensible to omit 'Christabel', the decision to do so was – after a two days' discussion – 'unanimous' – something apparently demonstrated in the quotation she gives. But there weren't two days of discussion: if Coleridge had left as planned, no decision might even have been taken (it looks like a sudden, spontaneously arising idea). And the sentence from Dorothy Wordsworth's journal is wholly ambiguous: 'After tea read The Pedlar. Determined not to print Christabel with the LB.' Who did the determining, it is impossible to say. Perhaps all three of them; perhaps two. But, if so, which two?

Mary Moorman's account leaves Wordsworth in the unassailable position of demonstrating critical acumen ('most people' will agree with him) and absolute fairness (the decision was taken with the total agreement of his friend). Holmes sees Wordsworth as personally rejecting the poem and bringing terrible trouble on to his helpless and exploited friend. Lefebure believes that Wordsworth destroyed Coleridge's ability to function either as a man or as a poet. McFarland thinks Wordsworth stupid, ungenerous and personally insensitive. But none of these versions of the facts will suffice; a desire to make your own biographical subject the one who behaved best contaminates all of them, and the extreme position taken by each writer merely confirms that we have very little evidence to go on, so that what exists can be read in more than one way.

Above all, it is the desire of biographers and scholars to make dramatically challenging narrative out of this barely-recorded incident which gets them into such trouble. Yet 'balance' may not be the ideal solution either. A more recent Wordsworth biographer, Stephen Gill, criticises Wordsworth for being high-handed in dealing with 'Christabel', and suggests that Wordsworth's behaviour may well have led not only to Coleridge's failure to supply any of the 'Poems on the Naming of Places' planned around the 6th, but also to Coleridge's lack of confidence. To that extent, he agrees with Holmes and Lefebure. However, Gill justifies Wordsworth's behaviour by an extraordinary attack on Coleridge: 'Wordsworth's treatment of Coleridge over *Lyrical Ballads* 1800 was certainly unfeeling. It was due in part to the fact that Coleridge was maddening . . . especially as Coleridge was once again using his, Wordsworth's, poetry to fulfil his obligations to Stuart.'[47] So if Wordsworth was being unfeeling, it was because (on the one hand) Coleridge was being impossible and (on the other) because in this case Coleridge was actually the one doing the exploitation, by passing off his friend's work as his own.

There is very little evidence and very few facts to justify any of these assured statements about fairness and exploitation, unanimous agreement and unfeeling treatment, passing off someone else's work as your own, secret or unadmitted resentment, trauma and conscience-inflicted illness. There are certain coincidences of timing (because x happened *after* y, it is therefore possible that x happened *because* of y). There is the usual pressing need for each biographer to link together disparately surviving pieces of evidence in order to construct a seamless and convincing narrative in which people do things clearly, decisively and dramatically. Holmes, Griggs, McFarland, Lefebure and Moorman are all clearly prejudiced; and in spite of Gill's attempt at balance (a balance which seems fairer to Coleridge than it is to Wordsworth), he nonetheless wishes to justify Wordsworth for behaving badly by showing that Coleridge was behaving even more badly; and he effectively charges Coleridge with stealing Wordsworth's poetry.

IV

This last matter is worth pursuing, as it takes us further into some of the problems of writing fairly or accurately about these people. The *Morning Post* printed a number of poems in the autumn of 1800 which were in part, or completely, Wordsworth's own. 'The Mad Monk' appeared on 13 October. On the 14th appeared 'The Solitude of Binnorie', originally written by Wordsworth, but heavily revised and with an introductory note by Coleridge. The following week, on 21 October, appeared the 'Inscription for a Seat by the Road Side Halfway up a Steep Hill, Facing South': a maddeningly precise title which is either a parody of Wordsworth or one utterly characteristic of him: the poem was certainly originally his. Wordsworth's 'Alcaeus to Sappho' appeared on 24 November. Stuart regularly printed poetry by Coleridge (and paid him a guinea a week for it) but far less by Wordsworth; it would not be until 1803 that he started to print Wordsworth's poems regularly.[48]

I shall discuss 'The Mad Monk' later.[49] A number of explanations can be given for the appearance of the 'Solitude of Binnorie', the 'Inscription for a Seat' and 'Alcaeus to Sappho'. In the first place, Coleridge never claimed any of these poems as his own; the second actually appeared over the signature 'VENTIFRONS' (meaning 'Windy-Brow', where Wordsworth and Dorothy had spent some months in 1794). But presumably Coleridge was paid for the poems, as part of his series of compositions. However, to earn money from Stuart by printing a thoroughly characteristic piece of Wordsworth's poetry (and two utterly uncharacteristic pieces of his early verse, revised) may well have struck both Coleridge and Wordsworth as a nice idea. Coleridge and Wordsworth were seeing each other constantly – they were still working on the final arrangement of *Lyrical Ballads* – and Wordsworth knew all about his friend's work for the *Morning Post*. When Coleridge originally came over on 4 October, the Wordsworths heard how he 'had sate up all the night before writing Essays for the newspaper': and Coleridge would actually send 'Alcaeus to Sappho' to Stuart on 7 October after returning to Keswick from Grasmere, having presumably brought a copy with him.[50] Again, the new *Lyrical Ballads* was supposed to include a section entitled 'Poems on the Naming of Places', and on either 6 or 7 October Wordsworth told their publisher Cottle that Coleridge had already 'furnished me with a few of those Poems'.[51] Wordsworth was, however, trying to convince Cottle that the volume was ready in spite of the changes (like the removal of 'Christabel') currently being made. By the following week, the details of the new group of poems had been worked out: a letter to Biggs and Cottle included the note (in Coleridge's hand) that 'The poems beginning at "It was an April Morning" are to have a separate Title page and advertisement. The Title Page to be Poems on the Naming of Places. The Advertisement as follows . . . '[52] And he gave the text. The appearance of one of those promised poems in the *Morning Post* might well have struck both men as proof that the poems for the section existed, as well as being an advertisement for the volume to which Cottle would certainly not have objected.

At some point, Wordsworth wrote a 'Motto Intended for Poems on the Naming of Places',[53] though he never published it, and on 13 October Dorothy recorded that she had 'copied poems on the naming of places',[54] almost certainly meaning some of her brother's poems. However, Coleridge proved (as so often) too busy to play his part as planned. Dorothy recorded that on the 17th, when he was back in Keswick but sending letters over to Grasmere almost daily, he 'had done nothing for the LB – Working hard for Stuart'.[55] Wordsworth must have supplied the 'Inscription for a Seat' poem for the 21st (incidentally – but perhaps not incidentally – Coleridge's birthday: it may even have been sent up to Keswick as a very practical twenty-eighth birthday present). There was no possibility of resentment, and certainly no theft. Indeed, the day after the poem had appeared, the 22nd, 'Coleridge came in to dinner. He had done nothing. We were very merry.'[56] It sounds as if the 'doing nothing' which Coleridge had successfully accomplished was the cause of the merriment they shared. This particularly cheerful day ended with Coleridge once more reading 'Christabel' aloud to them and to a mutual acquaintance passing through Grasmere, John Stoddart. The poem was clearly not a bone of contention.

We simply do not know exactly how the 'The Mad Monk', 'The Solitude of Binnorie' or the 'Inscription for a Seat' got into the *Morning Post*, any more than we know how 'Christabel' came out of the *Lyrical Ballads*; we know about 'Alcaeus to Sappho' because of the chance survival of part of a letter. All we can say is that the decisions arose out of work done jointly. The second poem was introduced by a paragraph certainly written by Coleridge; the third would have advertised a proposed joint development in the new *Lyrical Ballads*. Dorothy may well have copied all four poems out from original Wordsworth manuscripts; all appeared anonymously. The only thing which the poems' publication are clearly *not* are cases of theft which might be thought to justify bad behaviour by an ill-used person towards an even-worse-behaving person.

But such publication is also only comprehensible following the most scrupulous examination of all the facts. Whatever their innermost feelings about each other may have been, Wordsworth and Coleridge were working together extremely closely. The removal of 'Christabel' from *Lyrical Ballads* and the publication of 'The Mad Monk', 'The Solitude of Binnorie', the 'Inscription on a Seat' and 'Alcaeus to Sappho', rather than being examples of what Coleridge could or should have resented about Wordsworth, or Wordsworth should have resented about Coleridge, may well be examples of how they reached agreement with each other, supported each other, and trusted each other. But McFarland, Holmes and Lefebure blame Wordsworth for behaviour which left Coleridge stricken; Moorman presents him as someone who certainly knew best; and Gill blames Coleridge for behaviour which Wordsworth had every right to resent. All these writers find their own interpretations more interesting than the facts; none is prepared to look at the relationships within the group.

It must be possible to write better biography than this. What is needed is biography which takes the writing of all the people concerned (diarists, housekeepers, letter writers and copyists as well as poets) as seriously as it does conversations and ideas; one which looks not only at Wordsworth from Coleridge's point of view, or vice versa, but at all their relationships. In a matter as delicate and difficult as biography, the biographer must not be allowed to transform what is often a tiny amount of surviving material into a narrative (grand or otherwise) which links the known points as if they were necessarily the important points.[57] The only thing to do is to consider everything that is known in the confusion which the activities of several lives have given it: and to say, if necessary, what is incomprehensible about it. There is often a great deal to be gained by simply going through the events of every day, day by day, and seeing what (if anything) links with what, and who (if anybody) with whom, though normal narrative may not always result. I shall do that where surviving letters and poems – and Dorothy Wordsworth's diaries – allow me to do so. The materials are, fortunately, not so extensive as to risk the production of one of Borges's totalising maps.[58]

But there is another reason apart from the practical for doing this. This is a biography not only of individuals but of arguments and ideas (and poems and letters and journal entries). The Romantic period is to us a site of vivid experience lying at the threshold of our own era and which for that reason has become fascinating to us. These people seem to be having experiences very much as we do, which is often not true of people who lived just a few decades earlier. They are fascinated by the ways their minds work: some of Coleridge's notebook entries resemble stream-of-consciousness fiction: some of Dorothy's journal entries are compressed poetry: Wordsworth is constantly intrigued by his (and Dorothy's) own lives as children, as well as by Coleridge's children. He found the key to their subsequent lives in the way the child survived – and did not survive – into the adult; while the subjects of childhood and children constantly affected all the others in the group too.[59]

Furthermore, we do not now separate poetry from biography any more than Wordsworth himself did, when (probably late in 1802) he was working on the 'Prospectus' to *The Recluse*.[60] He was trying – like any biographer – to distinguish 'Inherent things from casual, what is fixd / From fleeting', so that his poetry 'may live, & be / Even as a light hung up in heaven to chear / The world in times to come'.[61] You cannot change the world; but you can light it, and you can cheer it. One way of doing this is to 'mingle humbler matter' with serious reflections, and, above all,

	. . . with the thing
65	Contemplated describe the mind & man
	Contemplating & who he was & what
	The transitory being that beheld
	This vision, when & where and how he lived
	With all his little realities of life
70	In part a Fellow citizen, in part
	A fugitive, and a borderer of his age . . .[62]

If you are a good writer, you represent (re-present) what the mind is like which does the contemplating, not just what the mind contemplates. This is why the Romantic period is so important to us. The biographer, like the poet, is

concerned with the 'humbler matter' Wordsworth describes; the biographer
also presents 'when & where and how he lived / With all his little realities of
life', and the experiences with which we are concerned are those of lives on the
borders of their age. The adults on whom I shall concentrate were, all of them,
living and loving and arguing and corresponding as a group of good,
respectable citizens, and simultaneously living lives on the edge of the civilised
and respectable.

Very little new will now be discovered about their lives, individually; the
biographical record is probably almost complete. But part of our consciousness
as readers, for better or worse, is to inhabit the biographical record which
grows out of the poetry, the journals, the essays, the letters. The biographical
record is, I would say, inseparable from our awareness of the works: and by
'works' I mean not only the poems which the poets in the group wrote, but all
the tasks with which they were engaged. This includes journals, poems, notebooks, letters, gardens, relationships – and children. Children were the centre
of all their lives, this spring. It was either late in March or early in April 1802
– exactly when Coleridge was working on his extraordinary *Letter* mourning the end of his marriage – that he and Sarah Coleridge conceived their
daughter Sara, to be born just before Christmas 1802;[63] it was late in March
that Wordsworth resolved to see his own illegitimate child Caroline, born to
Annette Vallon in France in 1792;[64] it was in August that he and Dorothy saw
her; and it would be in October that he and Mary Wordsworth (as she by then
was) conceived their first child John, to be born in June 1803.

V

I shall assume throughout that the idea of the group is crucial if we are to
understand this period, these poems and these people. But there are distinctions to be made. A number of families living in the Lake District saw a
good deal of each other: in particular the Wordsworths, the Coleridges, the
Wilkinsons, the Clarksons and the Lloyds; others, such as the Beaumonts, were
regular visitors. They all tended to acquire each others' friends.

Within such friendships, however, we can detect another, more central and
more tightly-knit group, in which Mary and Sara Hutchinson, 100 miles away,
were closer to Coleridge and to the Wordsworths than the latter were even to
their good friends the Clarksons at the head of Ullswater, only 15 miles away;
and in which Coleridge was often closer to the Wordsworths in Grasmere than
he was to his own wife in Keswick. This, of course, was one of the problems
which beset them. I have, so far, barely mentioned Sarah Coleridge. Coleridge's
loyalty to the others in this alternative family at times ran directly contrary to
his loyalty to his wife and children, and he would end by in effect sacrificing
his marriage for the unconventional family grouping offered by the
Wordsworths and the Hutchinsons: only to discover that that family, too, left

him isolated and unhappy, especially when Wordsworth's marriage and his growing family started to take precedence over his friend.

That, however, was some way off. In 1802, Coleridge was still endeavouring to be a man happy with his children (if not with his wife) while remaining loyal to his 'other' family: one undefined by actual family ties but interestingly aware of itself as a group: the two Hutchinson sisters, Wordsworth and Dorothy, and Coleridge himself (sometimes supplemented, in memory, by the Wordsworths' brother John): sisters and brothers all.

They literally had sisters and brothers, of course: Dorothy was constantly aware, in her own life, of the way she relied 'and have ever had reason to rely, upon the affection of my Brothers and their regard for my happiness . . . '.[65] The Hutchinson sisters all lived with and kept house for their brothers;[66] and when Mary Hutchinson finally left home to marry Wordsworth, it would be her loss of her immediate family of which Dorothy was naturally most aware: 'Poor Mary was much agitated when she parted from her Brothers & Sisters & her home.'[67] The fact that Coleridge had lost his sister, and did not get on very well with any of his real brothers, would certainly have attracted him to this alternative family, where the words 'sister' and 'brother' had a special meaning. Whereas 'sister' has for centuries meant 'one who is reckoned as, or fills the place of, a sister', Robert Burns, as late as 1795, is credited with first using the word 'brother' in a similar way: 'Said affectionately of one regarded or treated as a brother; one who fills the place of a brother'.[68] When Wordsworth wrote about Grasmere as the right place for him and Dorothy to live, he too was very aware of wanting it be a place for them all, sisters and brothers affectionately alike:

> Already with a Stranger whom we love
865   Deeply, a Stranger of our Father's house . . .
> . . . and others whom we love
> Will seek us also, Sisters of our hearts,
870   And one, like them, a Brother of our hearts
> Philosopher and Poet . . .[69]

That is, John Wordsworth, Mary and Sara Hutchinson, and Coleridge. When Coleridge was thinking about the poem which would become the *Letter*, he also planned 'A lively picture of a man, disappointed in marriage, & endeavoring to make a compensation to himself by virtuous & tender & brotherly friendship with an amiable Woman . . .'.[70] The friendship would be 'brotherly' – fraternal, kind, affectionate – not only because it would *not* come between a man and his marriage, but because brotherly relations would ideally involve the same kind of friendship, 'of our hearts'. Coleridge would, naturally, address Wordsworth as 'Brother & Friend of my devoutest Choice';[71] but he would use exactly the same language when addressing Sara Hutchinson.

> Sister & Friend of my devoutest Choice! . . .
> A very Friend! A Sister of my Choice –[72]

When Dorothy thought of Mary Hutchinson, it would of course be as 'O Mary, my dear Sister!': but not just because they would shortly be sisters-in-law. She was a sister long before Wordsworth would marry her: a sister of our hearts, one of the group.[73]

They had been thinking of themselves as a group for a long time. Dorothy, Wordsworth and Coleridge, in 1798, had called themselves the Concern – 'a commercial or manufacturing establishment', in their case presumably for the manufacture of books of poetry – and Coleridge was still thinking of them as that in 1805, after John's death, when he mourned the fact that John would now never 'settle in your native Hills, and be verily one of the Concern. –'[74] He would coin another word in 1805, following John's death: 'Ἐηορεητασ' – Enopentas, the five in one: Dorothy, William, Mary, Sara and STC himself. In 1800, Wordsworth had himself called them 'many into one incorporate', and thought about them as 'one family'; and it is interesting that he should also have developed a comparable language – 'the set' – for his three brothers, Dorothy and himself.[75] Back in 1797, a government spy had described Wordsworth, Dorothy and Coleridge as a 'gang'.[76] By a nice coincidence, late in April 1802 Coleridge claimed Wordsworth as 'the head of the Gang', presumably meaning the gang of poets.[77] He thus suggested both the original meaning of 'gang' (labourers or workmen who went about together: in their case, working on poems rather than canals), as well as the 'depreciatory' meaning 'associated with criminal societies': for 'gang' was a word – as Dr Johnson put it in 1755 – 'seldom used but in contempt or abhorrence'. It is however as 'the gang' that we might well think of this group of people in the first part of 1802: as a borderline, fugitive, family: a working group of sisters and brothers. And they were, literally, 'of a gang': inhabiting the same society, having the same interests.[78]

In Part I, I examine the pre-history of the events of 1802, and then each of the three families, the Wordsworths, Coleridges and Hutchinsons: their friendships, partnerships, situations. In Part II I look in detail at how the central group lived between March and July, particularly in their awareness of Wordsworth's forthcoming marriage to Mary Hutchinson, and the particular concerns they all had with children. Part III describes the summer of 1802, including the preparations for the Wordsworth marriage, and ends with the wedding itself on 4 October. The Epilogue looks forward a year to the ways in which relationships between the characters changed during 1803, but ends up concentrating on a single day (11 January 1803) in the lives of the central group.

Part I
Pre-History

Chapter One

Many into One Incorporate

The Wordsworths and the Coleridges had elected to live in what was – for middle-class people, especially writers, at the turn of the nineteenth century – an extraordinary place: far from publishers, libraries, learning, the metropolis, society, friends. The journey to London took two or three days of expensive and (in winter) extremely uncomfortable travel. Even for Wordsworth and Coleridge to get to each other by walking between Keswick and Grasmere meant a journey of about fourteen miles by the road which went over Dunmail Raise (Dorothy, like contemporary maps, called it 'the Rays'); it took more than four hours to walk uninterruptedly between the two houses on a good day.[1] Whether it was sensible even to undertake the journey would depend on the weather and the condition of the road; and (particularly in winter), with a stop along the way, trudging through the mud would take them all the hours of daylight.[2]

They had chosen, however, to surround themselves with the mountains, lakes, fields and woods which actually formed the subject of Wordsworth's poetry, and at crucial times did so for Coleridge too. Nature was a subject of overwhelming interest to them. This does not of course mean that they agreed about it. In 1802 Coleridge cared too much about the Christian divinity, and Wordsworth too little, for full agreement to be possible. Major differences between what Coleridge would write about Nature in *Dejection*, and what – by 1804, at least – Wordsworth would be saying about it in his *Ode* show that they disagreed profoundly. But they both wrote directly about the importance of Nature for the people they were, had been, and were involved with, and they drove each other into realising what they believed.[3] And Nature was also the constant topic of their exchange with the group.

For this group of people constantly addressed themselves to the natural world, in their poems, in their philosophical attitudes and in the everyday relations of gardens, cooking, weather, view and walk. There is no better way of seeing this than in their constant habit of naming places, and by looking at what they made of the place which – certainly for Dorothy, Wordsworth, Coleridge and Mary Hutchinson, and probably too for Sara Hutchinson – became the centre of their joint existence: Grasmere.

II

Grasmere had not of course been just a lucky discovery. Wordsworth had been
there as a boy:

> At sight of this seclusion I forgot
> My haste for hasty had my footsteps been,
> As boyish my pursuits . . .
20 > Long did I halt I could have made it even
> My business & my errand so to halt
> For rest of body 'twas a perfect place
> All that luxurious nature could desire
> But tempting to the Spirit . . .[4]

In April 1794, when he and Dorothy 'first began our pilgrimage together',
they had stayed a night at Robert Newton's inn on the corner by the
church; they had walked up from Kendal and Ambleside and over White
Moss, to drop down into Grasmere Vale itself. Dorothy remembered how
'it was just at sunset. There was a rich yellow light on the waters & the
Islands were reflected there'.[5] They were looking at the view which years
later she would regularly recall in her Grasmere journal. Wordsworth never
forgot the stream (it may even have been the one running down beside the
house they finally occupied) where they drank as they came down into the
valley:

> . . . when first,
10 > Two glad Foot-travellers in sun & shower
> My Love & I came hither while thanks burst
> Out of our hearts to God for that good hour
> Eating a Traveller's meal in Shady Bower
> We from that blessed water slaked our thirst.[6]

They would have walked past the house at Town End, at the extreme southern
end of the hamlet, where they came to live five years later: in 1794 it may still
have been *The Dove and Olive Branch* inn.[7]

Wordsworth returned to Grasmere at the start of November 1799. He came
over from the Hutchinson farm at Sockburn in Yorkshire, where he had left
Dorothy, Mary and Sara, together with their sister Joanna and their brothers
Tom, George and Jack; and he came with his brother John as well as with
Coleridge (Sarah Coleridge and Hartley being still down in Somerset).[8] The
ostensible point of the journey was for Wordsworth to look for a house in the
area for himself and Dorothy, but another reason may well have been the fact
that Wordsworth and Mary Hutchinson knew that one day they would marry.

He would therefore have been looking for a home not just for Dorothy and himself – or for John, whom they believed would also make his home with them when not at sea – but for the long-term future, in which he would be married and have children. This 'small abiding-place of many men'[9] was, ideally, to be

> A termination and a last retreat
> A Centre, come from wheresoe'er you will[10]

– whether you came from Somerset, or from Sockburn, or from the centre-less life which both Wordsworth and Dorothy had been leading since 1794. The Coleridges would come up from Somerset to live near them: Wordsworth gave his friend an extensive tour of the region while they were there, to ensure that he began to become familiar with it. The fact that Coleridge and Wordsworth walked up to Keswick after finding the house in Grasmere shows, too, that they were looking for a house near a town which – in such a region – would have been necessary to convince Sarah Coleridge that she could indeed move up to the Lakes. And they found one 'that was being built and was to be let this midsummer'.[11] From the very start, then, Wordsworth's choice of the place to live was involved with the plans and hopes of the rest of the group. In 1804, Mary and Sara's brother Tom would also come to the region, to work a farm near the Clarksons at the head of Ullswater, meaning that not only Sara Hutchinson but her sister Joanna would become regular visitors to Grasmere.

Wordsworth and Dorothy came over together at the end of December; again, they travelled from Sockburn, this time accompanied part of the way by George Hutchinson, as far as Leyburn, and on foot thereafter. Molly Fisher (who lived just across the road from the house at Town End, and worked for them for 2s a week) had lit fires in the house for a fortnight before they arrived, and never forget her first sight of Dorothy 'in t'laal striped gown and tlaal straw Bonnet'. The house (much later known – not by the Wordsworths – as 'Dove Cottage'[12]) would prove too small for the very long-term, but for two people was an excellent starting point: the place where he and Dorothy could bring the others together, in what had (appropriately) been an inn for nearly two hundred years, in what they now thought of as 'unity':

> A Whole without dependence or defect
> Made for itself and happy in itsef
> 170   Perfect Contentment Unity entire.[13]

Although 'the Rooms are so small', it offered a good deal of accommodation: in the summer of 1800 it would sleep five adults and a child.[14] John actually offered Wordsworth £40 to build a house in Grasmere, and although Wordsworth opted for the existing house, John's offer was another kind of blessing. What Stephen Gill has called the Wordsworths' 'hesitant but inexorable movement back to the Lake District' was complete, though I think it was by no means an accident that 'Coleridge was won over at the same time . . .'[15] It was part of their shared belief in each other, and in their joint activity, that he should be.

Being together in this place became seriously important for them. Visits from the group were constant, and one visitor stayed on with them when Wordsworth married Mary in October 1802. (Sara would eventually also make her home with the Wordsworths.) Wordsworth would write about this visiting and staying in *Home at Grasmere*:

> Such is our wealth: O Vale of Peace we are
> And must be, with Gods will, a happy band[16]

Grasmere was where, despite 'the quietness / Of this sublime retirement', he would 'boldly say that solitude is not / Where these things are':

> Society is here:
> The true community the noblest Frame
> Of many into one incorporate

That was a way of defining the group politically, and radically, as well as socially; as John Turner has pointed out, 'This is an enthusiasm in which the idealisms of pastoral and classical republicanism blend, not to picture the truth of common day but to give voice to an aspiration delighted to find that, after all, it may breathe the air of common day'.[17] Above all it was an enthusiasm about how they could think of themselves as a group.

As a way, however, of keeping the group together even when they were separated, the Wordsworths started to celebrate places in their own immediate location by naming them after the people who came to Town End, and whom they loved. Naming places was a habit Wordsworth may well have known from his own childhood in the Lakes, and the Hutchinsons certainly knew it too. It was on a visit to them that Coleridge first encountered it: 'In the North every Brook, every Crag, almost every Field has a name as a proof of greater Independence and a society more approaching in their Laws and Habits to Nature.'[18] Dorothy Wordsworth records a number of names in her journal which may have been those she was told, or may have been those which she and Wordsworth themselves gave to the features they noticed, while Coleridge's notebooks are peppered by the names he was scribbling down, whether from the lips of Wordsworth during his first tour of the region in November 1799, or while out walking with someone else – like John Ponsonby, his host in Ennerdale in August 1802 – or whether he was simply reading the map he had drawn to take with him when walking and climbing.[19]

But naming places was also a practice totally in keeping with their relationship as a group.[20] The Wordsworths' first year in Grasmere was 1800. John Wordsworth came for a visit which lasted from January (only a month after Dorothy and Wordsworth had themselves arrived) to the end of September; and during that time Mary Hutchinson also came to stay for six weeks between February and April[21]; while the Coleridges (with the four-year-old Hartley) arrived in June (Sarah Coleridge six months pregnant with Derwent) and stayed with the Wordsworths in Grasmere for a month before going on to their house in Keswick. So – apart from Sara Hutchinson – within six months they had all been there, and Sara came over in November for a four-month visit.

By 1 August 1800, the Wordsworths had taken to calling a little spit of land at the foot of Grasmere lake Mary Point; it would be partnered by Sara's Eminence, named after her sister when she came to stay in the winter. (In June 1802, Coleridge would go 'to S & M points' for a walk.)[22] By October 1800, too, Coleridge had his own 'seat' in the neighbourhood; when he was over for a visit on the 22nd, Dorothy noted how 'C and I went to look at the prospect from his seat'.[23] They constantly extended their range of named places. It was not just John's tragic death in February 1805 which made memories of his one and only stay in Grasmere so important: his sister and brother were naming things after him soon after he left them in 1800. The first reference in Dorothy's journal to 'John's Firgrove' appears in April 1801, and she mentions it twice in November 1801. Leading to it – of course – was 'John's path',[24] while one of the Wordsworths' favourite walks was the half-mile from Town End up to 'John's Grove'.[25] When they took that walk, there was a gate beside the road, offering the view over Grasmere which Dorothy had first seen in 1794 and described in November 1801: 'the whole scene impressive, the mountains indistinct the Lake calm & partly ruffled – large Island, a sweet sound of water falling into the quiet Lake.'[26] They christened it 'Sara's Gate': Sara Hutchinson had regularly taken that walk with them, and stood and admired that view, during her own first visit to Grasmere from November 1800 to March 1801. In April 1801, Wordsworth and Dorothy wrote to Mary Hutchinson how

> this gate was always a favorite station of ours; we love it far more now on Saras account. You know that it commands a beautiful prospect; Sara carved her cypher upon one of its bars and we call it her gate. We will find out another place for your cypher, but you must come and fix upon the place yourself.[27]

For another aspect of the naming was the actual – at times the ritual – inscription of the person's name or initials on the object named. Wordsworth would write in *Home at Grasmere* how, after only a few weeks in the valley, he

had begun 'Already to inscribe upon my heart'[28] his feelings for the place
and its inhabitants: but the group would cut literal inscriptions on rocks and
trees. I shall discuss later the extraordinary energy they all put into cutting
their initials on what they originally called Sara's Rock (just Sara's initials
had first been inscribed), half way between Grasmere and Keswick.[29] But
other objects were inscribed too: for example, while staying with Catherine
Clarkson at Eusemere in April 1802, Dorothy 'marked our names on a tree'[30]
(she probably meant her name and Wordsworth's). And there was 'Mary's
Stone', inscribed during her first visit: 'We sate by the roadside at the foot of
the lake close to Mary's dear name which she had cut herself upon the
stone. William employed [sic] cut at it with his knife to make it plainer.'[31]
This rock was still known by local people as 'Wordsworth's Seat' at the end of
the nineteenth century. Yet another Hutchinson sister had her own rock: eighteen months after the younger sister Joanna had first visited Grasmere,
Wordsworth cut her name on a rock, and also wrote his poem 'To Joanna' about
it. And there were at least two further places connected with Sara Hutchinson
besides her Rock: the seat started on 26 March 1801 on White Moss Common,
when Sara herself laid the first stone, but which was not complete until 10
October 1801, when Wordsworth and Dorothy and Coleridge finally finished
it – we find the Wordsworths sitting on it in March 1802 – and the so-called
Sopha of Sods, built at Windy Brow near Keswick on 13 August 1800.[32] This
would be the subject of a poem written by Wordsworth but published by
Coleridge, and it would be referred to as Sara's own particular place in
Coleridge's *Letter*:

> And yet far rather, in my present mood,
> I would that thou'dst been sitting all this while
> Upon the sod-built seat of Camomile –[33]

We know about most of these locations because Dorothy happened to mention
them in her journal. There must have been others to which she never referred.
But the naming of places had become part of their everyday lives. When that
sudden gap opened up in the second edition of *Lyrical Ballads* in October 1800,
Wordsworth and Coleridge quite naturally proposed to fill it with a section
called 'Poems on the Naming of Places'.[34]

Many of the walks they took also involved discovering, inhabiting, re-
visiting, and making places their own. On 23 April 1802, for example,
Wordsworth, Dorothy and Coleridge were looking for a place to sit down
while out walking, because 'The sun shone & we were lazy'; they were
only about a mile from the Town End house, in fact, at the foot of Nab
Scar at Rydal. But seats were one of their ways of making a place their own,
where they would sit together. They were not looking for a 'prospect' or a
view, as twenty-first-century tourists might be looking: a landscape to escape

other human beings. The Wordsworths, Hutchinsons and Coleridge wanted a place to be together in. Coleridge was leading the way on this occasion, and 'pitched upon several places but we could not be all of one mind respecting sun and shade so we pushed on to the Foot of the Scar'. They left Wordsworth 'sitting on the stones feasting with silence – & C and I sate down upon a rock Seat – a Couch it might be under the Bower of William's Eglantine'.[35] Wordsworth thus had no seat; but when they went back down to him, they found that 'He had made himself a seat in the crumbly ground'. Coleridge however remains determined to find something more their own – and he does:

> we found him in a Bower, the sweetest that was ever seen – the Rock on one side is very high & all covered with ivy which hung loosely about & bore bunches of brown berries . . . at the top of the Rock there is another spot – it is scarce a Bower, a little parlour, one not *enclosed* by walls but shaped out for a resting place by the rocks & the ground rising about it. It had a sweet moss carpet – We resolved to go & plant flowers in both these places tomorrow. We wished for Mary & Sara. Dined late.[36]

Their resolution at the end of the day's walking and clambering is characteristic. They plan to revisit: they will improve what they have found: and they will remember those who were not there. The Good Place is committed to the absent, whose bower it will become; it is dedicated to the future as much as to the present.[37]

It would be too easy to dismiss such activity as the transient pleasure of a group of educated and high-spirited people who could afford to spend their days clambering round the Lake District, naming things. They were engaged in what we might now call emotional mapping: identifying the ways in which they belonged both to each other and to the place. The good lives they were determined to live, they would define as lives maintained in contact with the needs and feelings of the others, in a place as beautiful and as rich as possible in shared feelings. Wordsworth and his sister had, after all, known this particular country since childhood, though they had also lived away from it for a long time: but it had multifarious links with their past. Now possessed of their own place in it, they were the ones bringing the others into it, and creating new memories and new links. What Wordsworth and Dorothy brought forward from childhood, the others were now discovering, in a place where they could (in one way) be children together. It would be wrong to ignore this but also wrong to denigrate it.

> No where, (or is it fancy) can be found
> The one sensation that is here; tis here

Here as it found its way into my heart
In childhood . . .[38]

The Hutchinsons and Wordsworths were linked by their situation as orphans,
while Coleridge was regularly looking for and enraged by the father figures he
encountered. The group centred on Grasmere and Keswick, if at one level children, were children growing up into the possession of adult selves and the
emotional recreation and repossession of their world.

III

Sarah Coleridge has continued as the individual most significantly missing
from almost all the inter-relatedness of these family groups. The fact that
she did not join in the activities of the others does not however mean that
she was uninterested in what they did. She got Wordsworth to recite his
poems when he went up to Keswick on 4 March: the fact that he became
'a little fatigued' while doing so suggests some kind of social event.[39]
And when Coleridge reported to Southey in July his disagreements
with Wordsworth's 1802 version of the Preface to *Lyrical Ballads*, and
commented on the 'extreme elaborations and almost constrainedness of the
diction' (in contrast with the poems' plainness) he noted that Sarah Coleridge
had 'said with some acuteness, that she wished all that Part of the Preface to
have been in Blank Verse—& vice versa &c'.[40] It is possible, of course, that her
interest in Wordsworth's work was a way of pointing out to her husband how
much more productive his friend was being. But she was reading what
Wordsworth wrote.

However, the fact that Coleridge was a writer was one reason why he quarrelled so much with her. Writers working at home have a peculiar
need of what, on the last day of 1801, Coleridge nostalgically called 'domestic
Tranquillity':[41] returning to Keswick in March, 'scarce a day passed without
such a scene of discord between me & Mrs Coleridge, as quite incapacitated
me . . .'[42] The mutual accusations of Greta Hall also meant that Sarah was a
good deal less involved in his writing than she had once been, and a significant
part of his output in 1802 would be of a kind which he had actively to
prevent her from reading. One of the reasons for the dual existence of the
Dejection poetry was so that the longer version, addressed to Sara Hutchinson,
although accessible to the group, could remain hidden from Sarah Coleridge.
Coleridge had long adopted the habit of putting things into his notebooks
either in Latin or in his own system of cipher when he wanted to keep them
from his wife (she was the only possible reader of his notebooks most of the
time, so the encodings must have been to keep things from her). How he kept
the *Letter* or 'A Day Dream' (or, later, 'To Asra') from her we do not know;
sending copies, even the only existing copies, to his friends would have been

one way. It is even possible that that was how the *Letter* and 'To Asra' (inserted into a manuscript given to Sara Hutchinson in 1804) continued to exist. The poems published in the *Morning Post*, like *Dejection* and 'The Day-Dream', would have been available to Sarah, along with the minor poems published in September and October 1802: themselves perhaps a public justification for Coleridge's writing during a year when the most important poems had to remain secret.

But it is unlikely that he would have shared with Sarah his anxiety as a writer. A man who could write to his wife – as he did on 22 November 1802 – that 'it is without any feeling of Pride in myself, to say – that in sex, acquirements, and in the quantity and quality of natural endowments whether of Feeling, or of Intellect, you are the Inferior',[43] is not likely to have allowed her to see the personal distress which at times he showed his men friends: 'I can say with strict truth, that the happiest half-hours, I have had, were when all of a sudden, as I have been sitting alone in my Study, I have burst into Tears.—'[44] His depression, however, had more than one cause. He was aware that the promises he had been making to produce work had started to fall on deaf ears. What would Tom Poole have made of Coleridge's remark, on 19 February 1802, that 'You may be assured, that in a very short time the first sheet of my metaphysical work will go to the Press.—'[45] Poole had heard that before. Coleridge, in the period 1800–1802, constantly made promises he could not keep. He would, for example, tell William Sotheby in July 1802 that he could send him a translation of the first book of Gessner's poem *Der Erste Schiffer* whenever it was needed: but he had probably translated only a few lines. He told Southey at the end of July that in a few weeks he would be sending a book to the press about Greek translation: and then he would be working on a book 'Concerning Tythes & Church Establishment'; he would also 'shortly' be producing two volumes of essays on (and selections from) British poets.[46] None of these even got written, let alone published.

What looks like brimming optimism ('you spawn plans like a herring' commented Southey[47]) actually demonstrates that anxiety. By 1802, he needed constantly to talk and plan and promise, to stop himself considering his actual position. An extraordinary letter he wrote to William Godwin on 22 January 1802, for example, shows how clear he could be about the extent to which he lacked 'the self-impelling self-directing Principle' to write.[48] This was not simply another guilty self-accusation; he knew he did not write as he could and should. During the winter of 1801–2 in London he was supposed to be working for the *Morning Post* and 'reading in the old Libraries for my curious metaphysical Work—'.[49] He did as little as possible of the first (spending three weeks in Somerset) and very little of the second.[50] He knew that this would lead him into profound self-dislike: 'in the consciousness of this Truth I lose a larger portion of Self-estimation than those, who know me imperfectly, would easily believe—'[51] He could be wickedly self-critical; years earlier, in 1795, he had told Southey 'The Truth is – You sate down and wrote – I used to saunter about and think what I should write.'[52] Having such highly intelligent insights into what he was doing (or not doing) meant, however, that he would usually continue to do it (or not do it). As he would tell Southey in July 1802, 'my worst Self-delusion is, a compleat Self-knowledge, so mixed with intellectual complacency, that my q[uick]ness to see & readiness to acknowledge my faults is too often frustrated by the small pain, which the sight of them give[s] me, & the consequent slowness to amend them.'[53] He was, again, as worried about his health, and mystified by it, as anyone could be whose future depended upon what he could earn by his writing; but he also understood, to an extraordinary degree, the way in which 'this very ill-health is as much an effect as a cause of this want of steadiness & self-command'.[54] He believed that he got ill by indulging himself (which meant alcohol and opium: the alcohol – usually brandy – being necessary to keep the opium on his stomach). But the more he worried about dosing himself, the more he needed to do so, to stop himself worrying.

He recorded in a letter to Daniel Stuart what his capacity for self-contempt meant: 'my taste in judging is far, far more perfect than my power to execute – and I do nothing, but almost instantly it's defects & sillinesses come upon my mind, and haunt me, till I am completely disgusted with my performance ...'[55] His confidence as a writer was at times terrifyingly low, as he had revealed to William Godwin in January 1802: 'As an *Author*, at all events, I have neither Vanity nor ambition – I think meanly of all, that I have done; and if ever I hope proudly of my future Self, this Hot Fit is uniformly followed & punished by Languor, & Despondency – or rather, by lazy & unhoping Indifference.'[56] But although 'I have neither Vanity nor ambition' is a worrying admission for a writer, it is also a self-dramatising remark. Coleridge is proud of nothing, he has nothing to look forward to, nothing to hope for. Yet the eloquence with which he denounces himself also contradicts any real need there might be for him to denounce himself. His self-criticism in his letters to Godwin and Stuart is never simply critical. He dramatises both his failures and his ideas, and is wonderfully witty about them; but he is still not able to turn them into the books for which he has both ideas and contracts. Conversation was his greatest relief of all and became a kind of compulsion. It offered him an escape from the abysses of self-doubt: he once remarked that 'The stimulus of Conversation suspends the terror that haunts my mind'.[57] In talk, too, he could dramatise himself to his heart's content; and the group's existence meant that he had a circle of people always ready to listen and admire. Letter-writing was important, too, for exactly the same reasons, even if the long letters he would (for example) write to Sotheby in 1802 would constantly promise achievements he was unable to fulfil.

The anxious side of him as a writer was probably the one he took to the Wordsworths, however, knowing that they would always listen sympathetically. Until his return from his Malta journey of 1804–6 he was absolutely sure of Dorothy's sisterly love and sympathy, and Wordsworth's brotherly love and intense belief in him: Dorothy's journal and letters constantly stress his unhappiness, just as her brother's letters stress his ability. He needed the Wordsworths as a family which would accept the very worst about him (up until 1807 they always did) and who would still love him.[58] He cast Mary and Sara Hutchinson in the role of sisters who would do the same: the loving and beloved sister was someone to whom he always responded.

IV

Wordsworth's writing in 1802, however, although (like his friend's) read by all those in the group, was in its own way as worrying a subject as Coleridge's. Coleridge at least had an income independent of his writing; he had many connections with the literary world, and Stuart at the *Morning Post* was prepared to print (and pay for) anything he wrote, in prose or verse. He could actually afford to let publishers down, and fail to do the things he promised his friends. In 1802, he and Wordsworth both wrote some of the most famous poems of their lives. *Dejection*, the *Immortality Ode*, 'The Leech-gatherer'. But Wordsworth would only have been known for the publication of a single sonnet.[59] Of the two of them, Coleridge was by far the better known and more highly-regarded writer. Wordsworth was extremely obscure (his 'reputation . . . hitherto *sectarian*' as Coleridge would put it in January 1803[60]): no one published his work unless he specifically pushed it into print. All he had published, in his whole life, were relatively short poems; he published no new volume between 1800 and 1807, and few individual poems. To make matters worse, he was now preparing to marry a woman as poor as he was.

However, he continued (with customary dedication, obstinacy and determination) to work on poetry as he always had. At the start of 1802 he had three long poems under way ('The Pedlar', *Home at Grasmere*, and the 'Poem to Coleridge'); and in the spring, as I shall show, he wrote far more lyrics than usual. But he published none of them: he seems to have worked with almost no consciousness of the literary marketplace. His existence as a writer thus depended to an extraordinary extent on the community he had helped create around him. I pointed out above our problems with understanding how 'Christabel' came to be excluded from the second edition of *Lyrical Ballads*, and the ways in which the collaborative relationship between Wordsworth and Coleridge operated.[61] One possibility I did not mention was that Coleridge may consciously have been excluding himself (and may have been happy to be excluded) from a publication which he could see his friend needed far more than he did. It may not have been masochism but friendship which saw him work so hard for a volume from which his own most recent contribution was now omitted.

It was Hazlitt who noted how, when Wordsworth was in company with Coleridge, he exhibited 'a convulsive inclination to laughter about the mouth, a good deal at variance with the solemn, stately expression of the rest of his face';[62] and when Wordsworth introduced Coleridge to his old friends the Clarksons in 1799, Catherine Clarkson observed how Wordsworth 'seems very fond of C. laughing at all his jokes & taking all opportunities of shewing him off'. But it was not just that Coleridge could make Wordsworth laugh (which rather few people did) but that Coleridge remained a model of playfulness and boyishness; especially delightful to a man who – though he revered the idea of childhood – had himself grown up rather early. Wordsworth found Coleridge as man and writer 'marvellous' (to use his own later word);[63] it was not just the young poet Thomas Chatterton who lay behind Wordsworth's creation of the 'marvellous boy' of his poem 'Resolution and Independence' in May 1802.[64] It was Coleridge himself as marvellous boy whom Wordsworth and Dorothy loved, feared for and eventually mourned; they were brotherly and sisterly towards his follies, endlessly concerned about his illnesses and problems, always supportive of his schemes, constantly fearful of his future.[65]

For his part Coleridge gave them his brilliance, his learning, his conversation; he made them laugh, and made them a family when he was with them. He seems to have kept them young, too, when they might have grown crotchety in their early thirties. For their part, they liked to see him as the boy he liked to be: as Wordsworth would write in May 1802, 'Noisy he was, and gamesome as a boy'.[66] Dorothy had written in her first letter to Mary Hutchinson after meeting him, back in 1797: 'He is a wonderful man. His conversation teems with soul, mind, and spirit. Then he is so benevolent, so good tempered and cheerful, and, like William, interests himself so much in every little trifle.'[67] That last detail was repeated in Wordsworth's 1800 poem 'A Character', which described a person paying 'attention full ten times as much as there needs';[68] while in the 'Stanzas' he wrote about Coleridge in the summer of 1802 he singled out his microscope: 'Glasses he had, which little things display, / The beetle panoplied in gems and gold, / A mailèd angel on a battle day'.[69] They could both lose themselves for hours in the smallest things. Coleridge admired Wordsworth as an elder brother (only two years older but never really *young*) just as he responded to Dorothy as a beloved sister; he teased them, played with them both, needed them badly. He saw in Wordsworth, of course, precisely the stability and sense of direction which he himself lacked; he envied him, admired him, loved him.

The stresses caused by their joint publication of the 1798 and 1800 editions of *Lyrical Ballads* have obscured the very remarkable fact of their collaboration, not just in including poems they had both written (Wordsworth's part in 'The Rime of the Ancyent Marinere' has been documented[70]) but in attempting to create (in 1798) a body of work which would go together; and then, in 1800, a book which would significantly advance Wordsworth's reputation. Trying to distinguish the contribution of one from the work of the other is to ignore how they worked. Coleridge wrote how the Preface to the 1800 *Lyrical Ballads* 'so arose out of Conversations, so frequent, that with few exceptions we could scarcely either of us perhaps positively say, which first started any particular Thought . . .'[71] Coleridge was perfectly clear about his disagreements with Wordsworth – for example, over metre: '*metre itself* implies a *passion* . . . and tho' I stated this to Wordsworth, & he has in some sort stated it in his preface, yet he has [not] done justice to it, nor has he in my opinion sufficiently answered it'.[72] Coleridge commented that 'we have had lately some little controversy on this subject—& we begin to suspect, that there is, somewhere or other, a *radical* Difference [in our] opinions'. Yet he followed this up with a quotation from St Augustine about how sweet it is to spice general agreements with your friends with rare disagreements;[73] and to Southey, a fortnight later, he would write that although it was 'a radical Difference' yet 'I need not say, that any diversity of opinion on the subject between . . . Wordsworth and myself, can only be small, taken in a *practical* point of view.'[74] They disagreed: what could be more natural? Another and major difference between them was that Wordsworth managed to write down what emerged from their talk, while Coleridge did not. It was nevertheless *joint* work, for all the differences which emerged out of it.

Coleridge biographers are in general so anti-Wordsworth that they try to shake Coleridge free of his friendship with Wordsworth whenever they can. One of the problems with keeping a biography accurate is when large quantities of material are missing. There was a tremendous correspondence between Keswick and Grasmere between 1800 and 1803. But it has almost entirely vanished; so that surviving letters to other people take on a peculiar importance. Holmes notes the start of Coleridge's extensive correspondence with William Sotheby in the summer of 1802; if we forget the enormous correspondence between Coleridge and the Wordsworths, we may be tempted to do what Holmes does, and see the correspondence with Sotheby as a kind of escape from the Wordsworths ('spontaneous, relaxed, highly intelligent, and above all, perhaps, outside the Wordsworthian sphere of influence').[75] There is nothing in the record which suggests that Coleridge's feelings for the Wordsworths had diminished in any way. On the contrary, Coleridge's description of going to their house at Town End while they were away in August is affectionate to the last degree.[76]

We can however take the idea of working in common a stage further, and link it with the ideas which Coleridge and the two Wordsworths

regularly had about living together or – at least – close enough to work as
partners. Sharing a house or living near to each other was something in
which Coleridge, Wordsworth and Dorothy had believed from the very start
of their acquaintance, in June 1797. Coleridge had actually met Wordsworth
in March 1797, when it turned out that they liked each other and admired
each others' poetry; but there was no sign then of that extraordinary
partnership which started during Coleridge's visit to the Wordsworths in
Racedown on 6 June. Coleridge came to stay for ten days, but in the
event stayed (depending on how one calculates) either for three weeks, or for
nearly seven years. For when he returned to Sarah and Hartley in Nether
Stowey on 2 July, the Wordsworths almost immediately went with him. By 17
July they had given up their rent-free house at Racedown and taken an expensive house at Alfoxden, precisely so that they could all be together. And until
Coleridge went to Malta in 1804, all their living was centred on each other,
whether in Somerset, Germany or the Lake District. At times, their collaborative projects were so extensive that – although they were not actually living
under the same roof – they might as well have been; the work in 1798 to
prepare the first *Lyrical Ballads* and the joint work in the autumn of 1800 to
prepare the second are such times. The idea of a joint household, however,
outlived the idea of adjacent households, and perhaps outlived the friendship
itself.

What made the idea of an actual joint household impossible either in
the short or the long term was the fact that Sarah Coleridge did not want
such a thing, and nor did any of the other three want it with her. This
became clear probably only in 1800, and though the six or – depending on the
birth of the Coleridge children – seven, or eight of them lived together when
it was sensible to do so (for example, in the summer of 1800, when the
Coleridges were waiting to move into Greta Hall) they never did so for
very long.

There was, of course, in the ideas of common life between the Wordsworths,
Hutchinsons and Coleridge a degree of literary and intellectual fashion.
To some extent they were responding to ideas of living demonstrated in
Bernardin de St Pierre's novel *Paul et Virginie*, which affected a generation
with its version of small groups of people living a rural life outside society,
cutting their names on rocks and naming places. Feeding into the idea
of common living were also ideas left over from pantisocratic theories of
equality in the group belonging to the early 1790s with which Coleridge had
been so deeply involved. All these things Sarah Coleridge seems either to
have ignored or at best tolerated. However, the Hutchinsons and Wordsworths
and Coleridge could also work through and overcome their various
orphan syndromes by finding new and better ways to live as family and
extra-family groups. There were also additional benefits. Coleridge could
escape the intimacy of a life lived on the terms his wife demanded; the

Hutchinsons got away from the pressures of their own small family groupings on their farms; the Wordsworths could also escape a way of life which at times was deeply claustrophobic. The house at Town End (such a centre today of cheerful tourist industry, all year round) was horribly isolated in winter, in particular when Coleridge was in London. For all their love for the place, at times the Wordsworths just ran away. Dorothy wrote towards the end of February 1802 that 'We have been staying a month, just after Christmas at Mr Clarkson's . . . and one of the Miss Hutchinsons has spent seven weeks of this winter with us, so we have not been much in solitude'.[77] That is, they had not been alone together in the house at Town End. We should not look for any of these particular needs to be the main reason for people in the group sharing writing, houses, children, siblings and families. All were contributory factors. And things sometimes went wrong between them. But – given the conditions of shared life which they established – Coleridge and Wordsworth seem to have worked together as writers and thinkers in ways we are still trying to understand;[78] Dorothy played a fascinating but often underestimated role as partner in their common literary life: the two Hutchinson sisters were crucial as readers, copyists and letter writers. They supplied endless support and belief: they were an audience for the work of the poets, but they also made up (with their own extended family of sisters and brothers) just the kind of extra family grouping which the 'true community' needed.

V

But not everything is clear, even in such a summary. We still do not know, for example, exactly what Sara Hutchinson was doing when she inscribed poems by Wordsworth and Coleridge in a small notebook and created a treasure-trove of early versions of their poetry: and we do not know exactly was happening when Dorothy made copies of Wordsworth's poems, and sent them across the Pennines to the Hutchinsons. I will end this chapter by considering three objects, surviving by chance, which can, in very practical ways, illuminate the joint activity and community of these writers and partners during the spring of 1802.

The first is a (now) water-stained piece of good quality paper[79] bearing the writing of Coleridge, Dorothy, Wordsworth and Mary Wordsworth. Coleridge originally used it for a fair copy of his poem 'The Full Moon in a Passion'; this occupied the front (recto) of the sheet and came halfway down the back (verso). The lower part of the verso remained blank. Because the poem contained many extremely short lines, there also remained a good deal of blank space on both sides of the sheet, on the right hand side; and in an age when paper was expensive and sometimes in short supply, it was natural to re-use it – especially good quality paper. Coleridge apparently wrote the poem in April 1802, and may have given the sheet to the Wordsworths when he saw them at the start of the month; alternatively, he may have given them (or made them) a copy when he came to visit them between the 20th and the 25th. (It contains no marks suggesting that he sent it by carrier.)[80]

What the Wordsworths did with the sheet was to fold it twice, to make a kind of booklet of four pages. Dorothy then used it to make a copy of Wordsworth's poem 'The Tinker'; she inscribed this on the lower half of the verso, which up to now had been completely blank. The poem had been written between 27 and 29 April, and her copy probably dates from soon after that. She then turned to the one other completely blank quarter page of the booklet – on the top right of the recto – and into that space she copied Wordsworth's poem 'Foresight', which he had written on 27 April. Again, her copy seems to have been made very soon after the poem's completion. It is therefore probable that the sheet had thus far been re-used by the end of April, or very early in May.

All three poems now on it also appeared in Sara Hutchinson's notebook; but her copies have slightly different texts. We can therefore be certain that this particular sheet did not go across to Gallow Hill to become the source of Sara's copies. Still *other* copies, made by Coleridge and Dorothy (or by Wordsworth himself), must have been sent, containing their own textual variants. This usefully reminds us just how many different copies of all these poems were being made, at different times, by these sisters and brothers.

We can however discover a little more about the history of this particular sheet by observing that the one remaining area of blank space was used by Wordsworth to draft stanza seven of his poem 'A Farewell'. He composed this towards the end of May 1802; and the draft seems to come from a very early stage of composition.[81] This shows that, after Dorothy had made her copies on it, the sheet stayed in Town End with the Wordsworths; and at some stage – certainly after 4 October 1802 – Mary Hutchinson (now Mary Wordsworth) initialled a brief note on it: 'This spoiled leaf is the original of a printed Poem, in the hand writing of the author. S. T. Coleridge M W'.[82] When she arrived in Town End in October 1802, the sheet was still there, probably kept for the sake of Coleridge's poem. That, at least, is what Mary thought worth recording. The survival of the sheet also serves to remind us that Coleridge gave the Wordsworths copies of his poems, just as Wordsworth gave and sent Coleridge copies of *his* poems; that the Hutchinsons saw copies of nearly all these poems being written and copied over in the Lake District; and that Dorothy, in particular, was responsible for a vast amount of copying of her brother's work. The sheet – to use phrases which Wordsworth himself used this spring – is a kind of 'Bible' of the past: 'dead times revive in thee'.[83] The whole sheet appeared as follows (italics replace text missing from the now damaged sheet):

The Full Moon in a Passion.

Vexation! Vexation! Nought left in its' station!
Now as Heaven is my Lot, they're the Pests of the Nation!
With Clinkum or Blankum
Whereever they can come
O they are the Chaps for a rare Botheration!
With Fun, Jeering,
  Conjuring,
  Sky-staring,
  Lowngering,
And all to the tune of Transmogrification –
  Those muttering
  Spluttering
  Ventriloquogusty
  Poets
  With no Hats
  Or Hats that are rusty!
And me they all spite, an unfortunate Wight –
And the very first moment that I came to light
A Rascal hight Voss, the more be his Scandal,
Turn'd me into a sickle with never a Handle.
A Night or two after a worse Rogue there came,
The head of the Gang, one Wordsworth by name, –
Ho! what's in the Wind? Tis the Voice of a Wizard.
I saw him look at me most terribly blue;
He was hunting for witch-rhymes from great A to Izzard;
*And soon as he'*d found them, made no more ado,
But chang'd me at once to a little Canoe.
*From this strange En*chantment uncharm'd by degrees
I began to take courage & hop'd for some Ease,
When one Coleridge, a Raff of the self same Banditti
Past by – & intending no doubt to be witty
(*Because I'd th'*ill-fortune his taste to displease)
He turn'd up his Nose,
*And in pitif*ul Prose
Made me into the half of a small Cheshire Cheese.
Well, a night or two past, it was wind, rain & hail –
I went safely abroad in a thick cloak & veil;
But the very first evening he saw me again,
The last mentioned witch-wolf popp'd out of his Den –
I was testing a moment on the bare edge of Naddle –
I fancy, the sight of me turn'd his brain's addle!
  For what was I now?
  A compleat Barly-mow!
And when I climb'd higher, no leave did he beg,
But chang'd me at once to an Ostrich's Egg.
But now, fate be praisd! in contempt of the Loon,
I am I myself I, the jolly full moon!
But yet my heart's fluttering!
For I heard the Rogue muttering –
He was hulking and skulking by the skirt of the Wood,
When lightly and brightly a tiptoe I stood
On the long level Line of a table-topp'd Cloud
What a capital Skittleground! quoth he aloud –

Ann that work of yours I'm
⟨That is work which⟩ I am rueing
Do as Charles & I are doing
Strawberry blossoms one & all
We must spare them! here are many
Look at it the flower is small
Small & low though fair as any
Do not touch it. – Summers two
I am older ann than you
Pull the primrose Sister Ann
Pull as many as you can
These are daisies take your fill
Pansies & the Cuckow flower
Of the lofty Daffodil
Make your bed & make your bower
Fill your Lap & fill your bosom
Spare the little Strawberry blossom

Primroses the spring may love them
Summer knows but little of them
Violets do What they will
Wither'd on the ground must lie
Daisies must be daisies still
Daisies they must live & die
Fill your lap & fill your bosom
Only spare the strawberry blossom

And wish'd from his Heart nine Nine-pins to see
In size and in brightness proportion'd to me.
So I fear'd from my soul
That he'd make me a bowl –
But in spite of his spite
This was more than his might –
And still, Fate be prais'd, in contempt of the Loon,
I am I myself I, the Jolly full Moon.

     So here's Botheration,
     To those Pests of the Nation,
     Those fun jeering,
     Conjuring,
     Sky-staring,
     Lowngering,
Vagrants, that nothing can leave in its station –
     Those muttering,
     Spluttering,
     Ventriloquo-gusty
     Poets
     With no Hats
     Or Hats that are rusty. –

the best
a living eye
lad in its primrose vest
ke a starry sky
st leaves the hedge did
beauty lie
little sparrow built its nest
be gone in its mortal
Some thing stay must stay to tell us of the
rest.

Who leads a happy life
If it's not the merry Tinker
Not too old to have a Wife
Not too much a thinker
Through the meadows, over stiles,
Where there are no measured miles,
Ever gay he finds his way
Among the lonely houses
Right before the Farmer's door
Down he sits; his brows he knits
     Then his hammer he rouzes
     Batter batter batter
     He begins to clatter
And while the work is going on
Right good ale he bowzes;
And when it is done away he is gone
And in his scarlet coat
     With a merry note
     He sings the sun to bed
And without making a pother
Finds some place or other
     For his own careless head.

This spoiled leaf
is the original of a
printed Poem, in
the hand writing of the
author. S. T.
Coleridge
M W

With a light soul to cover him
And sorrow & care blow over him
Whether he's up or a bed.

When in the Wo*ods the little Fowls*
Begin their *merry-making*
Again th*e jolly Tinker bowls*
Forth wit*h small leave-taking*
Through the *valley, up the hill*
He can't go wrong *go where he will*
Tricks he has *twenty*
And pastimes in *plenty*
He's the terror of *boys*
In the midst of their noise
When the market maiden
Bringing home her lading
Hath passed him in a nook with his
With his
With his outlandish look,
And visage grim & sooty,
Bumming, bumming, bumming.
What is that that's coming?
Silly maid as ever was
She thinks that she & all she has
Will be the Tinker's booty
Not doubting of her dread
Like a Bullfinch black & red
The tinker shakes his head,
Laughing laughing laughing,
as if he would laugh himself dead
& thus with work or none

VI

Because so much of Dorothy's copying has now vanished, we must make a particular effort to understand the role she was playing. The sheet I have just described is, in fact, one of only four extant examples of the copying she did this spring and summer of 1802.[84] But if we look at her journal, we find constant entries of the kind 'All the morning I was busy copying poems', 'Writing all the morning for William'.[85] From this spring of 1802, we find 'I left Wm & while he was absent wrote out poems' and 'I copied Wm's poems for Coleridge'.[86] Back in June 1801, she had asked her lawyer brother Richard for '6 quires [144 sheets] of the largest size writing paper, for rough draughts'; she needed more on 9 February 1802.[87] If we look just at what she did between the middle of February and the middle of March, we find the following:

10 February	I was writing out the Poem [*The Pedlar*] as we hope for a final writing . . .
12 February	I recopied the Pedlar . . .
12 February	I almost finished writing The Pedlar, but poor William wore himself & me out with Labour.
20 February	After Tea I wrote the first part of Peter Bell . . .
21 February	I wrote the 2nd prologue to Peter Bell . . . After dinner I wrote the 1st Prologue . . .
3 March	I was so unlucky as to propose to rewrite The Pedlar . . . I wrote in the afternoon . . .
4 March	We had a deal to do . . . poems to put in order for writing . . .
6 March	I wrote the Pedlar & finished it before I went to Mr Simpsons . . .
7 March	I stitched up the Pedlar – wrote out Ruth . . .
8 March	. . . rewrote in the Evening the alterations of Ruth . . .
14 March	Mr Simpson came in just as he was finishing the Poem. After he was gone I wrote it down & the other poems . . .[88]

Just as with the letters she wrote, she did not record everything she copied (not one of the four surviving examples of her copying is mentioned in her journal), so this February–March list is only a selection of the work she was doing. But, just to give some estimate of how much even this selection involved, 'The Pedlar' in its July 1802 form was 280 lines long, and the February version not probably much shorter. James Butler suggests that Dorothy first copied it in December 1801, then again between 10–14 February 1802, then again early in March, and then yet again in July. The four copyings together probably amounted to over 1,000 lines of poetry.[89] 'Ruth' was 258 lines long: the first part of 'Peter Bell' 339 lines long, its second prologue 190 lines long. Dorothy was perhaps only noting the longer items she copied. But – once again – not a single line of any of this copying survives. Without it, however, Wordsworth could hardly have survived as a poet.

But it was not even just a question of women like Dorothy, Sara and Mary making fair copies. Very frequently, the copies were made to transmit the poem to its immediate audience – the others in the group. My second example is a fragment of paper, only discovered in 1977: one of only two survivors of what during this spring was an almost daily intercourse of letters (and, from the Wordsworths, poems) sent to the Hutchinsons.[90] The fragment contains four of the eight stanzas of 'To the Cuckow', in Wordsworth's writing, on one side, and on the other side, also in his hand, an extra stanza for 'To a Butterfly', a poem previously sent to them.[91] This is probably why the fragment was preserved; the rest of the page being discarded (along with other drafts) during the work of making clean copies in which Wordsworth, Dorothy, Mary and Sara jointly engaged to create *Poems, in Two Volumes* between 1804 and 1806. The unused stanza, however, was kept. It is ironical that the only existing example of a copy of a poem actually sent to the Hutchinsons should be in Wordsworth's hand rather than Dorothy's, but that may even be why it was preserved. Authors' manuscripts are always more valued than the manuscripts of copyists.

There is however yet more writing on the surviving fragment; what looks at first like the fragment of a letter from Dorothy Wordsworth turns out to be an almost complete letter, squeezed in at the bottom of the right hand side of the paper, sideways to the poetry drafts on the front and back. So the letter counts as Dorothy's, even if the copies are not.

The fragment has been cut from the bottom of a sheet of paper very similar to that used for a letter Wordsworth wrote to Coleridge on 16 April 1802; it may have been written shortly afterwards.[92] The original two-stanza poem 'To a Butterfly' had been composed on 14 March and 'To the Cuckow' had been written 23–6 March, but Wordsworth had written 'a conclusion to the poem of the Butterfly' on 20 April.[93] It seems more than likely that he wrote the extra stanza as part of that 'conclusion'. If the Hutchinsons already had the first two stanzas, sent across to them sometime since the middle of March, the probable date for this letter to them would be sometime in the last ten days of April.[94] The original page would have looked like this:

[?space for poems or letter]

To the Cuckow.

O blithe New-comer I have heard!
I hear thee and rejoice:
O Cuckow shall I call thee bird,
Or but a wandering voice?

While I am lying on the grass
I hear thy hollow shout
From hill to hill it seems to pass,
About and all about.

To me no Babbler with a tale
Of sunshine and of flowers,
Thou tellest, Cuckow in the vale
Of visionary hours.

Thrice welcome, darling of the Spring!
Ev'n yet thou art to me
No Bird, but an invisible thing,
A Voice, a Mystery.

[?space for rest of 'To the Cuckow']

[space for frank, postmark etc]

[Miss Hutchinson
Gallow Hill
near Wykeham
Malton
Yorkshire]

[space for text]

Lines to be added to the Po

I knew not then that it was so –
It was a thing I *could* not know
Now, Butterfly, I read in thee
Much of that tender history
Kind Creature! see him how he roves
About my head; of her
My own sweet Friend, of gardens groves
Meadows with flowers, & early loves,
A dear Remembrancer.

ear friends I love
ou dearly – I
cannot express how
glad I am that we
shall see you before
we go to France

The letter's references to '[D]ear friends', and to seeing them shortly, demonstrates that the sheet was originally addressed to both Mary and Sara Hutchinson; we do not know the Hutchinsons' movements in the summer of 1802, though by mid-June they were both at Gallow Hill, and were still there in July.[95]

The brief note from Dorothy shows that the sheet *had* originally been (at least in part) a letter; we cannot however tell whether the part now missing had contained more poetry, or some poetry and a letter from Wordsworth, or simply a letter from Wordsworth. The fact that only four of the eight cuckoo stanzas survive however shows that the verso originally contained the rest of the poem. Assuming that 'To the Cuckow' was completed on the now missing upper portion of the verso, there would have been room below it for another poem or part of the poem before the blank portion in the middle of the sheet needed to form the outside of the letter and to bear the address and postmark, before the sheet was concluded with the extra stanza of 'To a Butterfly' and Dorothy squeezed her note into the last remaining area of blank space at the bottom of the page. There would also have been room for a few more lines in the extra space alongside the letter's wafer or seal. On the missing part of the recto, there would have been room for roughly thirty lines of a letter, or of poetry (or both), above the four stanzas of 'To the Cuckow'; descenders of two characters on the right hand side of the fragment show that every part of the sheet had indeed been filled, as was normal practice when using a medium as expensive as the postal system.

It is today an insignificant-looking scrap of paper; but it serves the vital function of reminding us how important it was to Wordsworth to get his poems into the hands of the Hutchinsons. He did not save money by waiting until he saw them. Nor did he send his poetry by carrier (or pedlar). He wanted them to have it soon after it was finished, and to comment on it: he certainly got comments on 'The Leech-Gatherer' in June, as one of the few surviving letters to them demonstrates. We should probably imagine the Hutchinsons sending a regular stream of such letters containing comments, responding to the letters with poems. Coleridge is the one now famous for his verse *Letter*, but Wordsworth and Dorothy sent far more actual letters with poems in them. I shall say more below about how the Hutchinsons probably responded to this particular poem.[96]

It is clear that, at this stage, Wordsworth's audience was Dorothy, Coleridge and the Hutchinsons; and we can perhaps add Sarah Coleridge, while it seems likely that he would also have read his poetry to the Clarksons. He did not however publish a book of poems between 1800 and *Poems, in Two Volumes* in 1807; this fragment of paper helps us see one of the ways in which he survived as a poet.[97]

VII

The third item taking us to the heart of their existence as a group is a note-book of poems compiled by Sara Hutchinson, to which her own contribution is usually taken for granted.[98] But the notebook is an example of how the Hutchinson sisters played their own crucial part in the common enterprise in which this extra-family group was engaged during these years; and the context in which it was created offers us some of its meaning. Copying was a very practical way in which the work of the individual was subsumed into the enterprise of all of them; and it is an important example of the work which a non-creative member, and a female member with a housekeeping job, would do.

Sara Hutchinson inscribed poems into a small notebook about four-and-a-half inches wide by seven inches tall, with a flexible cover of originally red, now brown, leather over cardboard; the price – 1/2 (i.e. one shilling and twopence) – is recorded in ink on the front endpaper. This was a rather expensive notebook, designed to be kept and valued. At one end of the book there are eleven poems by Coleridge, and at the other, twenty-five by Wordsworth. Forty-one blank pages appear between the two sections of poems, and a few are interspersed among the poems themselves.[99] At the same end of the book as the price mark – the end from which Coleridge's poems begin – Sara wrote 'Sarah Hutchinson's Poets –' and added an elaborate scrolled line beneath it: she was naming her collection. The book continues with ten poems by Coleridge which Sara inscribed, while Coleridge himself added the eleventh.[100] The first poem in the book is the splendid *jeu d'esprit* 'A Soliloquy of the full Moon' which Coleridge had written out on the sheet of paper which he gave to the Wordsworths: 'affectionate, facetious, thoroughly frivolous'.[101] He never included it in his Poetical Works.

At some stage – perhaps more than once – Coleridge had the notebook in his own hands, and made some corrections and additions. To the third poem, 'Tranquillity – an Ode', he added ten lines, and made one alteration.[102] In the fifth poem, 'Inscription', Coleridge made another alteration. The eleventh poem is entirely in his hand but was almost certainly entered very much later; perhaps as late as 1808.

Coleridge wrote the first two poems in the spring of 1802, so that Sara inserted them sometime after that, presumably from copies which Coleridge sent across the Pennines. Four of the first five poems had some direct link with Sara herself. I discuss below 'The Language of Birds'; 'Tranquillity' recalls the 'mossy seat' which was actually built up for Sara near Grasmere;[103] the 'Ode After Bathing' records Coleridge's visit to the Hutchinsons in August 1801 when he went swimming at Scarborough with Sara's brother Tom. And the 'Inscription for a Fountain on a Heath' uses the image of the small pulse of water under sand which Coleridge had discovered in August 1801, and linked with Sara and the others.[104]

All this suggests that Sara was, at some point after April 1802, compiling in the first part of the book her own collection of unpublished Coleridge work. Most of it was presumably sent to her in letters or (in the case of 'Tranquillity: An Ode' and 'Ode after Bathing') possibly existed as fair copies which Coleridge had given her when visiting Bishop Middleham and Gallow Hill during July and August 1801. 'Inscription on a jutting Stone, over a Spring' (written in September 1801) could either have been sent to Sara in a letter or have been brought in person by Coleridge in March 1802. Coleridge wrote the sixth poem she inserted, 'The Picture', in the summer of 1802 and a copy must have been sent in a letter. But by the time it was inscribed, the use of the book seems to have changed; and a blank leaf separates it from the preceding poems.[105]

What is most striking, of course, is that only one of the poems mentioning Sara by name, or arguably written to her, is included. Early in April Coleridge was writing his verse *Letter* both to Sara and about her; and yet, although at some stage that poem was seen by Mary Hutchinson (who transcribed it), no copy appears in Sara's collection; nor is there a copy of the poem 'The Day-dream' which may have accompanied the *Letter* when Mary transcribed it,[106] a poem drawing on Coleridge's memories of Sara and Mary. Nor is the most significant poem Coleridge wrote to Sara, 'To Asra', included: he gave her a copy in 1803 or 1804. Coleridge also wrote 'A Day Dream' late in March 1802 and 'The Keepsake' by September, and it is hard to believe that he did not send Sara copies; but only the second appears in the notebook.

A natural conclusion would be that either she was censoring its contents, or that it was a record more public than private of Coleridge's poems: or perhaps both. That she was making a public record may be confirmed by the fact that, shortly after she had begun to transcribe Coleridge's work, she also copied in Wordsworth's poems, over a period of two or three months during the early summer of 1802: one batch around 7 May, perhaps, another around 8 June, a third sometime later. Perhaps she only added the title *Sarah Hutchinson's Poets* (a reference to the anthology *A Complete Edition of the Poets of Great Britain* compiled by Dr Robert Anderson, popularly known as *Anderson's Poets*) when she began to transcribe the poems by Wordsworth.[107] But what she created allows us to understand what he was doing as a poet during this marvellous spring better than any other document.

Like Coleridge's, Wordsworth's poems would have arrived at Gallow Hill either written into letters (as on the sheet described above) or on separate sheets included in letters to Sara or Mary. The originals were presumably either destroyed with the letters, or – if kept – may have been used, revised and then burned during the compilation in 1806 of *Poems, in Two Volumes*.[108] But Sara Hutchinson preserved an astonishingly rich compilation of what Wordsworth managed to finish and he and Dorothy to copy that spring: twenty-five poems out of a total of around forty, while of course we cannot be certain that a copy of every poem was even sent to Gallow Hill, or reached Sara via Mary. She was in one sense making permanent what was essentially ephemeral. At times, both the Wordsworths and Coleridge turned their work into small self-sewn book-lets: Coleridge's own handwritten copy of the *Letter* is in just such a handmade booklet, while Dorothy records making a booklet ('I worked hard, got the backs pasted the writing finished, & all quite trim') for the *Pedlar* of February 1802.[109] One reason was so as to preserve the copy better than a single loose leaf (or in the case of longer poems, leaves) of paper would preserve it; I described above the fate of the single loose sheet of paper of Coleridge's *The Full Moon in a Passion*, as it found itself re-used.[110] Another reason was doubt-less so that the copy could be passed from person to person, around the group: be literally a 'booklet', when no printed form was available. Poems in booklet form suggest the audience which was going to use them.[111]

We might think of Sara's leather-bound notebook as serving the same func-tion, but making the perishable a great deal less perishable, more effectively than hand-sewn booklets ever could. It is of course possible that Coleridge and Wordsworth had asked her to keep copies for their own future use. She was well known to them as a copyist: the previous year, John Wordsworth had been grateful for 'two large & ful [sic] sheets of poetry unpublish'd of W^m & copied by Sara'.[112] Three of the poems she included in her notebook never in fact became part of the canon of either of them: 'A Soliloquy' appeared in no collection during Coleridge's lifetime, and two linked short poems by Wordsworth – 'These chairs they have no words' and 'I have thoughts that are fed by the sun' – were not printed until 1947.[113] But Sara copied all three of these poems into her collection. Until the Wordsworth poems were copied again in 1804 (some of them from this actual manuscript of Sara's) hers may well have been the only copy in existence: the only text which kept them alive, so to speak.

The Coleridge and Wordsworth poems were, then – as the title says – *Sarah Hutchinson's Poets*: possessed and preserved, inscribed and stored, available to the gang (a word of course occurring in the very first poem in her book – 'A Soliloquy'). Both poets were brought together in the handwriting of another person in the group, just as had happened to their work during the compilation of the two *Lyrical Ballads* publications and – in a different way – in the pages of Dorothy's journal.

What, then, was the job of the copyist of Wordsworth's and Coleridge's work, in these years? Wordsworth seems to have found almost all aspects of writing difficult; he groaned over the agonies of new composition and invari-ably became ill. As Dorothy had noted in September 1800, 'he writes with so much feeling and agitation that it brings on a sense of pain and internal weak-ness about his left side and stomach, which now often makes it impossible fo [sic] him to when he is in mind and feelings in such a state that he could do it without difficulty.'[114] He himself, in October 1803, described his 'aversion from writing' as 'little less than madness': 'during the last three [y]ears I have never had a pen in my hand for five minutes, [b]efore my whole frame becomes one bundle of uneasiness, [a] perspiration starts out all over me, and my chest is [o]ppressed in a manner which I can not describe.'[115] He also found re-working old compositions painful; and he even disliked making copies of his own work. This last was, at least, a job which others could do, and Dorothy, Mary and Sara Hutchinson ended up doing a vast amount of it for him. Coleridge was far more ready to copy his own work at this stage; but, for example, in the work which had created the 2nd edition of *Lyrical Ballads* in the summer of 1800, Dorothy ended up as main copyist for the enterprise. Most of the long letters to Biggs and Cottle about detailed textual corrections, however, include the handwriting of all three of them, with Coleridge writing out detailed corrections for poems by himself and by Wordsworth, Wordsworth doing the same for poems by himself and by Coleridge, and Dorothy doing the same for them both. And the final poem of the volume – Wordsworth's 'Michael' – was sent to the publisher with its first 216 lines copied by Coleridge, and the remainder by Sara Hutchinson.[116]

The fact is that the poets – and the group – depended upon the work of the women who transcribed, copied, re-copied and preserved for posterity. It was, for example, because Sara Hutchinson copied out the lengthy journal letters which Coleridge wrote on his walking tour 1–6 August 1802 that we know so much about those particular days: the original letters (which may have gone back to Coleridge, or to the Wordsworths, or to some other reader) are lost. She had done the same in 1801; John Wordsworth had thanked Dorothy for her letter 'with Sara's Copy of Letters & you must give her my kind kind love and thanks to her'.[117] It is possible that Sara copied the August 1802 letters because Coleridge had asked her to: more likely that she copied them to ensure their survival when sending the originals on to people whose travelling address was uncertain. Her sister Joanna did the same in 1803: while staying at Town End with her sister Mary, she copied those letters of Mrs Clarkson to Dorothy which arrived while Wordsworth and Dorothy were away, before Mary sent on the originals (which in fact never caught up with them).[118] And back in 1798, Dorothy had been responsible for copying a letter from Coleridge to Charles Lamb which Coleridge needed to preserve.[119] The women who made copies of hundreds of lines of poetry, who wrote vast numbers of letters of their own and copied pages of letters from other people, actually made the remote and highly unusual lives of these poets possible; they were an integral part of a creative group. They obviously commented on what they copied, too; when Sara Hutchinson told Wordsworth what she thought of his poem 'Beggars' which she transcribed in the spring of 1802, her 'feelings upon the Mother, and the Boys with the Butterfly' were (in Wordsworth's astonishing phrase) 'an affair of whole continents of moral sympathy'.[120] That was why he needed her as a copyist: not just for usefulness, but as a sympathetic reader and a loving sister.

Chapter Two

Wordsworths: 1 March

On 1 March 1802, William and Dorothy Wordsworth had been living in their house at Town End for two years and three months. Coleridge was on his way back from London; he had been spending the winter in lodgings near Covent Garden, working as a journalist for the newspaper the *Morning Post*. Sarah Coleridge, up at Greta Hall with the children, had had to cope without him over the winter, though the income he gained in London was a help. At Gallow Hill Farm, near Scarborough in Yorkshire, where Coleridge was currently headed, Sara Hutchinson was living with her brother Tom, for whom she and her elder sister Mary had at different times been housekeeping since the middle of 1800. Sara had remarked that 'the country is very pleasant – the farm good & the house very convenient'.[1] At Bishop Middleham, 50 miles away to the north–west in County Durham, Mary (known all her life as an excellent household manager) was housekeeping for her brother George on his farm.

The 'modest partners' of the gang[2] were thus scattered over northern England; and yet they maintained an extraordinary, familial intimacy. This was partly because of the visits they paid to each other, but very largely because of the letters they sent. On the last day of February, for example, Dorothy had started a letter to Sara Hutchinson; on 1 March she would finish it, write a letter to Mary Hutchinson, and start another letter to Sara, while she and Wordsworth would receive letters from both Sara and Mary, and Wordsworth would write to Coleridge: Wordsworth probably reading the letters which Dorothy wrote, she probably reading his.

How could they afford to do this? In 1802, a letter of a single folded sheet cost its recipient one shilling. It was another matter if you were lucky enough to acquire a sheet already franked; or if you were able to involve a Member of Parliament in the matter (by using their address), as their letters went free. But letters from the Wordsworths to the Hutchinsons were expensive. Letters to and from Coleridge after he had moved up to the Lakes in June 1800 were cheaper; they went via the carrier Fletcher, who left his cart in a shed just across the road in Town End. If the Wordsworths put a letter under the shed door at night, it would be taken up to Keswick early the following day. Letters came from Coleridge the same way. But the rest of the post had to be paid for at the full rate; the total would be allowed to mount up and they would pay the bill at intervals.[3] Post from Yorkshire or County Durham seems to have taken two or three days to arrive. But they never seem to have written less to each other because of the costs, or to have complained about what came.[4]

It is striking how much of the daily life of the Wordsworths in Grasmere revolved around the business of writing, walking to the post, receiving and reading letters. The first day of March, for example, was (according to Dorothy's journal),

> A fine pleasant day, we walked to Rydale. I went on before for the letters, brought 2 from M & S.H. – we climbed over the wall & read them under the shelter of a mossy rock. We met Mrs Lloyd in going – Mrs Olliffs child ill. The Catkins are beautiful in the hedges. The ivy is very green. Robert Newton's Paddock is greenish – that is all we see of spring. Finished & sent off the Letter to Sara & wrote to Mary. Wrote again to Sara, & William wrote to Coleridge. Mrs Lloyd called when I was in bed.[5]

This entry helpfully suggests a number of patterns in the Wordsworths' joint life. In the first place, neither Dorothy nor Wordsworth has a job (though both work extremely hard); when the sun shines they go out in the morning, when it rains they go out in the afternoon. Their hours are neither the early hours of working country people, nor the regular hours of working urban people, nor even the well-ordered hours of respectable middle-class people. They stay up all night when they choose ('We sate together talking till the first dawning of Day') or when visitors suddenly arrive bringing news. When, for example, William and John returned from Yorkshire in June 1800, 'We did not go to bed till 4 o clock in the morning'. When Coleridge comes over in mid-March 1802 'Wm & I sate up till 4 o clock'.[6] If they sleep badly – 'William has got no sleep. It is after 11 & he is still in bed' – or are just back from a journey (journeys on foot or on horseback, of the kind they made, were very tiring) they stay in bed in the mornings: 'William did not rise till dinner time'. They normally eat dinner around 3.00 p.m., whereas 'the custom of all the lower order of people in this country' was to 'dine at 12 o'clock' and to be 'in bed at 9'.[7] But if they are ill – as Wordsworth and Dorothy both often are, Wordsworth particularly when writing, with pains in his side and head – then they go to bed in the middle of the day; and then they get up and go on with life.

Wordsworth is a little over five foot ten inches tall, 'rather a fineish man in build . . . tall and lish'. He is 'what you might call a varra practical-eyed man, a man as seemed to see aw that was stirrin'.'[8] But he wasn't just an observer. Coming over Grisedale pass with Dorothy in February, walking home from the Clarksons at Eusemere, they had found themselves closed in by low cloud and mist, at about 2,000 feet, and had lost their path in the snow: but Wordsworth knew his mountain well enough to get back on to the path and then safely down: 'thanks to William's skill we knew it long before we could see our way before us'.[9] He walks and skates, rows and rides. Dorothy is skinny and small, deeply tanned, but tough and wiry: extremely alert, with piercing eyes but bad teeth. They are very poor by the standards of their family, class and education. Dorothy has no income at all, but is given presents of money by three of her brothers, while Wordsworth gives her a home. Wordsworth receives something over £40 a year from an annuity purchased after he had been left money in the mid-1790s. They spend £5 a year on rent, a further £5 4s. on their servant Molly Ashburner. A new gown for Dorothy would cost 12s.; a shift, 5s. 10d.; a pair of stockings 1s. 3d. Wordsworth asks his lawyer brother Richard and his friend Basil Montagu for cast-off clothes: 'any clothes of your own which you can spare'. A box containing shirts and a pair of pantaloons had arrived on 1 February; Dorothy works 'putting the linen into repair' the following day, works on the shirts from Montagu a couple of days later, and on 14 February Wordsworth wears the trousers. They eat the food of the poor, oats rather than flour (Wordsworth has oat broth – thin porridge – for breakfast: the present of a barrel of 'the best american flour' in June 1801 had been 'most acceptable'). Their only real luxuries are postage and tea from London; they hope that their brother John will send them a 'Box of Tea'.[10]

On 1 March, they walk to Rydale for the post. It is a mile and a half from Town End; but they often walk to Ambleside (a round trip of six miles) and get their post a day earlier than it will arrive in Rydale. They can easily walk twenty or more miles in a day when they choose. On their triumphant journey over the Pennines to Grasmere in December 1799, when they came to take possession of their promised land, they had covered twenty-one miles on one day, and the following day 'walked the next ten miles, by the watch over a high mountain road, thanks to the wind that drove behind us and the good road, in two hours and a quarter'.[11]

Another pattern: Dorothy goes ahead to get the mail. Wordsworth presumably walks more slowly: he may well be writing a poem in his head, and reciting it aloud as he walks: 'He was yan as keppit his heäd down and eyes upo' t'ground, and mumbling to hissel'.[12] He preferred to compose out of doors when he could, to the rhythm of his own walking; at one stage he even planned to dedicate his 1807 collection of poems to the path in the Town End orchard:

> Orchard Pathway, to and fro
> Ever with thee, did I go,
> Weaving verses, a huge store!
> These, and many hundreds more . . .[13]

He worked there all year round; only a fortnight after this 1 March entry, he would go 'up into the orchard' to escape a visitor '& wrote a part of The Emigrant Mother'.[14]

On the previous day, 28 February, however, something dreadful had happened to the (indoor) work on his poem 'The Pedlar'. Dorothy recorded 'disaster Pedlar' in the margin of her journal, suggesting a late addition to an entry written earlier. It has been suggested that the revision had become so heavy that the page was no longer readable,[15] but it is hard to imagine a sheet so covered with writing that *nothing* could be deciphered. It sounds more as if an accident had occurred to the fair copy which Dorothy had already written out and (in her usual way) constructed as a booklet, and which Wordsworth had subsequently revised. Either it had got soaked in ink, or the wrong booklet had been burnt – with the immediate and horrible realisation that what had been destroyed was the corrected draft, not the superseded one, and that the poem had thus regressed in a moment to its previous state.[16] They did burn discarded drafts; on 9 November 1800 Dorothy recorded 'burnt the sheepfold', a draft of the poem which would become 'Michael'.[17] Open fires would have added the pleasure of seeing superseded drafts blazing away to nothing, while simultaneously giving light which – in winter – would illuminate the new draft: but not if the wrong pages had been burned.

Whatever disaster it had been, to a poem which always seems to have been a struggle, Wordsworth might well have been walking more slowly than Dorothy on the morning of the 1st; planning what to do, recovering lines and revisions previously made, not wanting to get as far as Rydale village itself, where he might have to stand and talk to an acquaintance. A neighbour almost fifty years later remembered how 'He'd gang t'other side o' t' road rather than pass a man as exed questions a deal'.[18] He holds back; Dorothy gets the mail.

But then, another utterly characteristic action. Where a respectable couple would have gone home, given their hats and coats to the servant, sat down and read their letters (or more likely still, would have sent the servant to get the mail in the first place), Wordsworth and Dorothy climb a wall to get out of the wind, unfold the sheets and read their letters sitting on the ground. Sitting down, lying down and sleeping, reading together outdoors, were all as common to them as writing or reading or walking or living – but not sleeping – together.

Country people, however, drew their own conclusions. In Germany in the winter of 1798–9, the Wordsworths' greatest problem besides keeping warm had been to meet people; and according to Coleridge, in Germany at the same time (but not in Goslar), this was because 'Sister is considered as only a name for Mistress'.[19] But England was no better. In Somerset in 1797, the local doctor denouncing Wordsworth to the Home Office (the report which led to the arrival of the spy denouncing them as a 'mischiefuous gang') had noted that Wordsworth 'has no wife with him, but only a woman who passes for his Sister', while in the Grasmere district,

there was an unnatural tale current . . . of Wordsworth having been intimate with his own sister – The reason for this story having birth seemed to be that Wordsworth was very much in the habit of taking long rambles among the mountains, & romantic scenes near his habitation – his sister, who is also a great walker used very frequently to accompany him . . . It is Wordsworth's custom whenever he meets or parts with any of the female part of his own relations to kiss them – This he has frequently done when he has met his sister on her rambles or parted from her and that on roads or on mountains, or elsewhere, without heeding whether he were observed or not . . . and this simple fact . . . has been made up into the abominable accusation bruited about, to his prejudice amongst his coarse-minded neighbours.[20]

So when Dorothy rejoined her brother and perhaps got a kiss – a fortnight earlier, his mouth had been 'very cold when he kissed me',[21] and he would have been pleased on the 1st that there were letters from both Hutchinson sisters – and they vanished over the wall together – local people would have drawn their own conclusions.

To me it seems so improbable that Wordsworth and Dorothy would ever have had sexual relations that the point must not be laboured; but the idea that their relationship was in some way (or ways) incestuous has been constantly hinted at.[22] In the first place, nearly all the evidence of the details of the relationship come from Dorothy's own journal, where – all unconsciously – she provided language and behaviour which a post-Freudian age finds sexual:

> William's head bad after Mr S was gone I petted him on the carpet . . .
> O the Darling! here is one of his bitten apples! I can hardly find it in
>   my heart to throw it into the fire.
> I slept in Wm's bed, & I slept badly, for my thoughts were full of William.
> After dinner we made a pillow of my shoulder, I read to him
>   & my Beloved slept.[23]

If, however, she had been attempting to conceal the nature of her relationship (for incest, ma'am, is a crime), she would have been a good deal more careful.[24] It is precisely because she was *not* trying to conceal it that the 'evidence' stands out. When Coleridge first saw her, in June 1797, what struck him was how non-sexual she was. He quoted his own 'Vision of the Maid of Orleans' (later 'The Destiny of Nations'), in which he compared Joan of Arc with the Virgin Huntress Diana: 'her most innocent soul / Out beams so brightly, that who saw would say, / Guilt was a thing impossible in her'.[25] I think it most unlikely that, even in winter, sister and brother ever occupied the same bed. We have evidence that even though the house at Town End could be extremely cold in winter, and sleeping in the same bed (thoroughly wrapped up in layers of night shirt and night gown) might have seemed seem the most obvious thing to do, all the same they did not: Dorothy wore instead 'all the clothes I could find'. Although their relationship was physically intimate (when Wordsworth got back after a long ride 'he looked delightfully, but it was a sort of flushing in his face', Dorothy noted), there was nothing sexual about it.[26]

II

It had not just been over a wall that the Wordsworth pair vanished that morning. It was into 'the shelter of a mossy rock'. Not just shelter; not just the shelter of a rock. Dorothy is describing the details, as when she distinguishes the green of the ivy – 'very green' – from the grass just poking through in 'Robert Newton's Paddock': 'greenish – that is all we see of spring'.[27] Wordsworth had perhaps been composing that morning already; Dorothy will probably write this episode into her journal in the late afternoon or evening. Her journal is another aspect of her loving role in the relationship; she observes, remembers, creates a body of memories which, as I shall show below, are at times drawn upon for poems. She has been described as 'a mere cataloguer of irrelevant detail, a person strangely fixated on the minutiae around her',[28] but that is a townee's complaint. The detail in her entries responds to the complexity of the natural world which she had trained herself to observe and to describe.

Today we are in the slightly odd position of knowing more about Dorothy Wordsworth's experiences than those of any of the others in the group.[29] In 1798, or 1800, or 1802 it would have been the other way about: she was the one who would have been harder to know, the small, unobtrusive, at times almost invisible one, among loquacious and cheerful companions like Coleridge and Sara Hutchinson, and quieter but impressive ones like Wordsworth and Mary. But while Coleridge's everyday talk, knowledge, wit and profundity have (from this period, at least) vanished beyond recall, and Sara Hutchinson's high spirits exist only by reputation, Dorothy's small records of daily life survive.

But is that what the journals are? A record of pies baked, walks taken, visits paid: letters written and received: poems started and finished? We need to disentangle her journals' overlapping functions because, in them, the extraordinary nature of the mutual reliance of these people becomes clear as nowhere else. It has become fashionable to claim for her journals and letters the status of work which is as independent and personal to Dorothy as their poems were to Wordsworth or Coleridge.[30] I suggest that it is by seeing the journals and letters in the context of the group as a whole that we can understand their full significance: the same is true of the poems which the men wrote.

Dorothy kept a number of journals, and they seem to have had rather different functions. She started her first in Alfoxden in the early spring of 1798; she began the second, a travel journal, on the German trip of 1798–9. She wrote the third, famously, in Grasmere between 1800 and 1803: and then she wrote an extensive account of the trip to Scotland she made with Wordsworth and Coleridge in the summer of 1803, though this was explicitly 'not a journal, *for we took no notes,* but *recollections* of our tour in the form of a journal'.[31] There are also later journals, of trips to the Continent in 1820, Scotland again in 1822, and the Isle of Man in 1828. The record of the German trip is only a fragment;

the 1803 Scottish tour journal is another kind of production altogether; the later journals, although lengthy and full of *aperçus*, occupy another world of emotion. But even the Alfoxden and Grasmere journals seem to have had different functions, and seem to have been started – and stopped – for very different reasons. Although it lies chronologically out of the scope of the rest of this book, the Alfoxden journal tells us so much about Dorothy's relationship with Coleridge and Wordsworth that we must return to the spring of 1798 to look at it.

Dorothy started it on 20 January 1798, but it survives only in the form of William Knight's transcription for his 1897 edition. As I noted in the Preface, Knight was an enemy of the trivial, and he also deleted things which he thought showed people in an unfortunate light – in particular, their illnesses. The only independent survival of any of the Alfoxden journal is a four sentence transcript of its opening by Wordsworth. This, however, at least shows us that the Alfoxden journal started exactly as Knight printed it; we must simply be cautious in conclusions we draw about its differences from its successors. However, the focus of the Alfoxden journal (at least to start with) appears quite different. During January and February 1798, Dorothy hardly mentioned visits, letters or people encountered; she was writing a nature journal of what could be seen and heard in their North Somerset locality. The journal is completely impersonal until the fourth day of entries; 'we' are then only included in the course of an observation about the sound of the sea – a noise 'distinctly heard on the tops of the hills, which we could never hear in summer. We attribute this partly to the bareness of the trees, but chiefly to the absence of the singing of birds . . .'[32] Not a single name appears in the first five days' entries (inconceivable in the Grasmere journal), and even 'William' makes no appearance until January 29th (equally impossible in the Grasmere journal). Journeys are only recorded for the sake of observations made on them, and those are nearly all of nature: exceptions (the 'pink and blue' clothes of the 'lasses' on 4 February) stand out. An indoor detail given on 2 February – 'The room smoked so that we were obliged to quit it' – is unique in the diary up to that point. Dorothy was writing a diary of the world outside.

Every day is covered; there is obviously a certain self-discipline at work, so that entries are made even after 'Upon the whole an uninteresting evening' (27 January), 'an uninteresting evening' (30 January) or when 'We saw nothing very new, or interesting' (7 February). As the weeks go by, she includes some very short entries and after three months had obviously abandoned the journal's primary function as nature observation. The entries for 28–31 March, obviously made in retrospect, represent no more than duty being done.

> *28th.* – Hung out the linen.
> *29th.* – Coleridge dined with us.
> *30th.* – Walked I know not where.
> *31st.* – Walked.

The strictness which governed what she allowed herself to include also relaxed as the weeks went by. At the beginning of March, she started an entry 'William and I drank tea at Coleridge's', in just the style common in the Grasmere journal, but such comparative triviality is explained by the entry's continuation: 'A cloudy sky. Observed nothing particularly interesting – the distant prospect obscured.' With nothing else to include, she could allow herself the record of tea at Nether Stowey.

But why was she writing a journal? That depends partly upon its function – and its presumed readers. We can be certain that Dorothy's purpose was not scientific as, say, Gilbert White's nature observations of the 1770s had been scientific: there are no measurements of temperature, no careful records of the arrival of migrating birds. But if we ask who read Dorothy's journal, we are carried a little further. The audience at Alfoxden would have been Wordsworth and Coleridge; and though there is no record of either of them actually reading the little book, the presumptive evidence that they did is very strong: and even if they did not do so, the journal could still have been 'for' them.

There has naturally been some speculation about why Dorothy started a journal. Gittings and Manton suggest that the Wordsworths had just heard that they would not be allowed to stay at Alfoxden beyond the early summer of 1798 and that Dorothy therefore started to record the things which made life there so very attractive. But they had actually known since September 1797 that their time at Alfoxden was limited.[33] The immediate cause is more likely to have been the fact that Coleridge had left Nether Stowey on 12 January for at least a fortnight – and perhaps longer – and that, without him and his ever-flowing series of reactions to their everyday experience, both Dorothy and Wordsworth would have felt a gap in their lives. The journal may well have been started to ensure that they went on seeing, without him, what he always made so memorable: and it would also enable *him* to see what they had been experiencing, when he came back. But we still need to ask why that meant (in the first instance, at least) a nature journal.

It had been Coleridge who had written the previous July of Dorothy: 'Her information various – her eye watchful in minutest observation of nature – and her taste a perfect electrometer – it bends, protrudes, and draws in, at subtlest beauties & most recondite faults.'[34] Such language, it has been suggested, makes Dorothy (like Coleridge) a poet-as-child-of-nature. But it is her astonishing responsiveness, not her naturalness, which Coleridge singles out; and his admiration can be further explained if we look at the notebooks which he had himself been keeping since 1794. It is striking how very little description of the natural world appears in them during those early years. There are scientific observations, certainly – how candles light a face, or how they burn[35] – but the observations of nature are always used to point a moral or sharpen a reflection. 'Smooth, shining and deceitful as thin ice. . . . Discontent mild as an infant low-plaining in its sleep.'[36] That last might have been occasioned by Hartley as a baby: but the point is to characterise discontent, not the baby.

At a date around late 1797 or early 1798, Coleridge began to put genuine observations of the natural world into his notebooks. He notes, for example, 'Broad-branching pollards with broad-branching head' in what might actually be a line of poetry, but which has a sharp observation implicit in it; and in the first of a number of entries which can be securely dated to the early spring of 1798, 'The subtle snow in every breeze rose curling from the Grove, like pillars of cottage smoke.'[37] It is unlikely to be a coincidence that such entries are simultaneous with the commencement of Dorothy's first journal. It seems extremely likely, to put it no more strongly, that her notebook was conceived as her own exemplary account of how to look at the world. It would ensure that the principles and language of every day observation and experience would be preserved. Coleridge had been full of praise for Dorothy's sensitivity and capacity for observation; the journal would make the very best use of her talent. A visitor to Coleridge in the summer of 1797 had noted, beside the 'musing tenant' of Alfoxden manor – Wordsworth – the 'maid / Of ardent eye'.[38] Dorothy's eye was animated by the desire to respond and to feel, and regularly applied itself to the observation of things in letters, for example; but at the start of 1798 she seems to have set herself to create a sober, accurate record of nature's characteristics, and its capacity to move human beings.

Coleridge's role as provoker and audience may even explain an oddity for which neither an error in Knight's transcription nor a series of misdatings by Dorothy can really account:[39] the fact that although Coleridge only apparently returned to Nether Stowey on 9 February, she recorded on the 3rd 'Walked with Coleridge over the hills', on the 4th 'Walked a great part of the way to Stowey with Coleridge' and on the 5th 'Walked to Stowey with Coleridge'. It is possible that Coleridge actually got back a week earlier than he preferred to tell people; it is even possible that – as on other occasions – he had preferred not to return directly to his own home, as duty demanded, but had gone to stay with the Wordsworths for a few days when he was supposed to be somewhere else: so that he really was a companion on Dorothy's walks. But it is also possible that she was 'walking with Coleridge' even when he was physically still in Bristol. It was to show him the world that she took his walks, looked at the world to see what he would have seen, and then wrote down the things they would both have noted. His presence – close or distant – was one of the things that made Dorothy write as she did. The Alfoxden journal constantly takes walks with Coleridge, and often we cannot tell whether Wordsworth is with them or not.

Wordsworth's copying out of the first four sentences of the journal, however, suggests that he too recognised in it a profoundly important language of observation. Nature, not only heaven, lies about us, and not just in our infancy:[40] and the Alfoxden journal was a way of constantly affirming in detail its presence and its power. What Dorothy was doing was recording the everyday in a form in which Wordsworth could, if he wished, start to recover it. And the same applied to Coleridge.

This may been why her journal fairly quickly came to share things which can be found in both Coleridge's and Wordsworth's own writing. After mentioning tea at Coleridge's on 7 March, and noting down the fact that there was nothing else worth noting, she added a sentence which echoes down the centuries: 'One only leaf upon the top of a tree – the sole remaining leaf – danced round and round like a rag blown by the wind.' Coleridge's *Christabel* contains the lines

> There is not wind enough to twirl
> The one red leaf, the last of its clan,
> That dances as often as dance it can,
> Hanging so light, and hanging so high,
> On the topmost twig that looks up at the sky.[41]

It seems rather unlikely that Coleridge would have written those lines had he not either read Dorothy's journal, or been out with the Wordsworths and shared the observation, or heard her – or Wordsworth – make the observation, or himself have made the observation, which Dorothy wrote down and which he subsequently used in *Christabel*. It is particularly interesting that we cannot *know* the sequence of what actually occurred; simple assertion ('Coleridge, too, depended for language on Dorothy's journal, as the evidence of *Christabel* shows') cannot replace the uncertainty which it is our duty to record.[42] Dorothy's references to the horned moon on 21st and 23rd March are, for example, possibly indebted to the 'hornéd moon' in *The Rime of the Ancyent Marinere*,[43] which Coleridge was writing and which the Wordsworths were reading as it was being written; unless – that is – Dorothy first made the observation, and Coleridge wrote it down: or Wordsworth first said it, and both the others remembered it.

These coincidences (or non-coincidences) however reveal that at least at times Dorothy *was* writing for, with and around the poets around her; was playing her part as an acute observer of the natural world. She saw floating threads from spiders' webs, and called them 'restless' on 8 February. Coleridge wrote of 'restless gossameres' in *The Rime of the Ancyent Marinere*.[44] She noted how the moon looked on 25 January when she and Wordsworth were on their way to Thomas Poole's house while Coleridge was still away: 'At once the clouds seemed to cleave asunder, and left her in the middle of a black-blue vault. She sailed along, followed by multitudes of stars, small, and bright, and sharp.' Wordsworth wrote about the moon in his poem 'A Night-Piece', describing how

> There, in a black-blue vault she sails along,
> Followed by multitudes of stars, that, small

And sharp, and bright, along the dark abyss
Drive as she drives . . .

Again it does not matter who wrote first; it is *their* language which they record. And, perhaps most significantly of all, Dorothy noted how, one stormy evening on a walk to Stowey a week later, on 31 January, 'the moon immensely large, the sky scattered over with clouds. These soon closed in, contracting the dimensions of the moon without concealing her.' Coleridge was probably away at this date but he would, soon afterwards, do two significant things. He would write in *Christabel* how

The moon is behind, and at the full:
And yet she looks both small and dull.

and he would himself make the notebook entry

Behind the thin
Grey cloud that cover'd but not hid the sky
The round full moon look'd small —[45]

It is not even the language which is shared in that last triple coincidence: the only word actually in common is 'moon' and Dorothy does not use the words 'small' or 'hid' or 'behind'. The very fact that we cannot demonstrate obligation confirms that we are confronting a shared habit of mind. Walking with Coleridge regularly revealed this. Two years later, for example, in October 1800, when he was staying in Grasmere, he and Dorothy went for an evening walk which must have taken them to Rydal Water and to Grasmere (Wordsworth had gone to bed). Dorothy noted simply: 'Silver How in both lakes'. Coleridge made an entry in his own notebook: 'Silver How casts its shadow in two Lakes'.[46] Commentators like Gittings and Manton have been concerned with the question of authority (who was first responsible for the observation) and indebtedness (who only heard or read it), and conclude that, in such cases, 'The debt . . . is practically impossible to determine . . . It can only be said that in literature as well as life, this was a time of the most intensely shared sympathy.'[47] I would rather say that the 'debt' is impossible to determine because it is not of 'debt' that we should be thinking. Dorothy is using her journal to record language which is simultaneously being used and discussed by the two poets; they admire her gifts of observation and language, and in some instances draw upon her journal, just as she will constantly draw upon the conversations which all three of them were having. It is absurd to try and determine who originated a phrase. The 'coincidences' pay tribute to the habits of minute observation in which they believed, which they encouraged in each other, and in which they participated whether together or apart.

What links all the observations is not coincidence in the sense of chance, but the coincidence of minds consciously working in similar ways. It would not even have been necessary for Wordsworth to have read Dorothy's journal to have written his poem 'A Night-Piece'; he was there when the original observation was made, and he may well have helped form the phrasing in the journal, as much as the journal formed the phrasing of his poetry. Rather than thinking of the Alfoxden journal as a practical resource – a kind of bottom-drawer stock of observations – it is probably more accurate to see it as something which Dorothy knew was her particular contribution to the joint enterprise of their writing lives that first spring spent, in 1798. The two poets would have believed in it as an enterprise as much as they probably asked to borrow it, to copy bits out.

The Alfoxden journal ends when the three of them temporarily go in different directions at the end of May. It is notoriously difficult to keep up the habits of home when away, but the journal had actually been flagging for weeks. Out of twenty-four days between the end of April and the middle of May, Dorothy only made entries on six. But the ending of the journal exactly corresponded with the breaking up of the winter's period of intense companionship. They were now actually *working* together, on *Lyrical Ballads*, where Dorothy did most of the transcription. That was where her writing now went.

III

The Grasmere journal is very different. Dorothy began it on 14 May 1800, the day her brothers John and William left Grasmere to travel across to the Hutchinsons. It is immediately about *her* experience, though it is also for them to read when they come back, to see what she had been doing. Its potential audience would have been limited to Wordsworth and to any of the group who came to stay at Town End: Coleridge, John Wordsworth, the Hutchinson sisters. But this time there is no actual record of anyone except Wordsworth being involved with the progress of the journal.

In the middle of the long first day's entry, however, she considers why she is writing it: and this, of course, is also addressed to the person reading the journal: 'I resolved to write a journal of the time till W. & J. return, & I set about keeping my resolve because I will not quarrel with myself, & because I shall give Wm Pleasure by it when he comes home again.'[48] Giving Wordsworth pleasure is one thing; not quarrelling with yourself is harder to understand. It may simply mean 'because I don't intend to change my mind'. But it also sounds as if the journal were being written to occupy the mind, to come between it and the quarrels it might otherwise be having. The crucial quarrel would have been with the fact that William and John had gone to see the Hutchinsons: Dorothy's sense of being abandoned is very strong in these first

few entries. She has barely got John and Wordsworth on the road with cold
pork in their pockets before she is saying what it means to her:

> My heart was so full that I could hardly speak to W when I gave him a farewell
> kiss. I sate a long time upon a stone at the margin of the lake, & after a flood of
> tears my heart was easier. The lake looked to me I knew not why dull and
> melancholy, the weltering on the shores seemed a heavy sound. I walked as long
> as I could amongst the stones of the shore.

So as not to go back to the empty house; so as to remain where she had been
happy with Wordsworth; so as not to register the parting as having happened:
so as to be an unfeeling stone herself. Not quarrelling with yourself means
getting out of the cycle of reproach (for which you reproach yourself), anger
(which you are angry for feeling) and self-denigration (because you are abandoned) which Wordsworth's attachment to Mary provoked in her.

The same happens on the following days. On Friday the 16th, her third day
alone, Dorothy records starting a letter 'to Mary Hutchinson' – the full name
confirming that the name is *not* yet 'Mary Wordsworth', nor simply 'dear
Mary'. Dorothy then goes for a walk:

> Grasmere was very solemn in the last glimpse of twilight it calls home the heart
> to quietness. I had been very melancholy in my walk back. I had many of the
> saddest thoughts & I could not keep the tears within me. But when I came to
> Grasmere I felt that it did me good. I finished my letter to MH. – ate hasty
> pudding, & went to bed.[49]

The journal entries, like the walks, are exercises in self-healing. She also writes
tiny self-reflecting poems: after a day of entries detailing the mundane events
of life, she ends 'The Skobby sate quietly in its nest rocked by the winds &
beaten by the rain.'[50] So is she to herself. There is nothing here for Coleridge
to read and admire, though he may have read and would have admired. It is her
life as abandoned woman (when Wordsworth is away) and of partnered woman
(when he has returned) that she records: the diary of an ideal life which she also
knows she will shortly lose. She and Coleridge had very many experiences in
common, which may be why she was so touched by the joys and disasters of
his life. The profoundest feeling of all they shared, however, was probably the
mutual sense of being abandoned by Wordsworth when (in October 1802) he
got married.

By the spring of 1802 (to come home to the subject of this book) her journal
had become a kind of lyrical gatherer-in of the events of what she knew would
be the last spring of her life as her brother's partner. Did Wordsworth read it,
however? In 1933, Ernest de Selincourt (doubtless thinking of the 14 May 1800
entry) wrote that she made her journal entries for her brother 'at his suggestion,
and for his special pleasure'.[51] Pamela Woof is cautionary: 'W's reading or

listening to passages was probably sporadic: he never, for instance, filled in the words of the inscription that he had seen on a decayed house in Borrowdale, though D left space in the Journal for at least 12 words . . .'[52] The fact that Wordsworth did not often – or even ever – *read* her journal is, however, no evidence that he did not wish it to be kept, or make suggestions for entries, or rely on it to be there if he wanted it, to check a detail. It was Dorothy's writing discipline, as poetry was his; her reading to him from it was one of the bonds between them.

The interplay between the language of Dorothy's journal and her brother's poems went on. But the events of everyday life as Dorothy records them offer significant insights – or even potential narratives – which might become poems. The skobby on its nest might have been one. And Wordsworth seems more than once to have used Dorothy as the first recorder of observations which he knew were important. I will discuss later her description of the leech-gatherer they met in 1800;[53] her description of the daffodils they saw together on 15 April 1802 has long been celebrated as an example of how Wordsworth drew upon her journal. She had made the entry a day or two after the original experience: its very length suggests a conscious set-piece.

> . . . as we went along there were more & yet more & at last under the boughs of the trees, we saw that there was a long belt of them along the shore, about the breadth of a country turnpike road. I never saw daffodils so beautiful they grew among the mossy stones about & about them, some rested their heads upon these stones as on a pillow for weariness & the rest tossed & reeled & danced & seemed as if they verily laughed with the wind that blew upon them over the Lake, they looked so gay ever glancing ever changing. This wind blew directly over the Lake to them. There was here & there a little knot & a few stragglers a few yards higher up but they were so few as not to disturb the simplicity & unity & life of that one busy highway.[54]

Dorothy's journal entry would remain as a moment captured, with the language of the moment preserved, so that her brother could later come back to it. The journal, in fact, offers us an opportunity to see what Wordsworth's famous phrase 'emotion recollected in tranquillity' actually meant in practice. The phrase referred not just to the activity of the mind of the poet, but to the actual physical process of writing. Poetry, in the words of the 1800 'Preface' to the *Lyrical Ballads*,

> takes its origin from emotion recollected in tranquillity: the emotion is contemplated till by a species of reaction the tranquillity gradually disappears, and an emotion, similar[55] to that which was before the subject of contemplation, is gradually produced, and does itself actually exist in the mind. In this mood, successful composition generally begins . . .[56]

Dorothy's journal was frequently the place where the emotion could be contemplated, with some of the original language provoked by the experience; and thus recovered, and the poem started. He saw – she saw – and in their discussion of what they saw, a language developed, some of which she wrote down. Later, he could use her journal as a way of starting the process of feeling again.[57] In this case it took him two years to write the poem. He actually used remarkably little of his sister's description:

> I wandered lonely as a Cloud
> That floats on high o'er Vales and Hills,
> When all at once I saw a crowd
> A host of dancing daffodils
> 5   Along the Lake, beneath the trees,
> Ten thousand dancing in the breeze
>
> The waves beside them danced, but they
> Outdid the sparkling waves in glee: –
> A Poet could not but be gay
> 10   In such a laughing company:
> I gaz'd – and gaz'd – but little thought
> What wealth the shew to me had brought:
>
> For oft when on my couch I lie
> In vacant or in pensive mood,
> 15   They flash upon that inward eye
> Which is the bliss of solitude,
> And then my heart with pleasure fills,
> And dances with the Daffodils.[58]

The poem moves its centre of attention away from what dominates the journal entry – the broad road of flowers, 'that one busy highway' – to what they do in recollection. He may even have recognised this, because in 1815 he added an extra stanza with the lines 'Continuous as the stars that shine / And twinkle on the milky way, / They stretched in never-ending line / Along the margin of a bay: / Ten thousand saw I at a glance, / Tossing their heads in sprightly dance.' The details about the line and the continuity were exactly those Dorothy had originally stressed: he may well have looked at the journal again.

All Wordsworth took from the journal in 1804, however, were the words 'along the shore' (making it 'Along the Lake'), the fact of 'under the trees' (turning it into 'beneath the trees'), and the words 'laugh' and 'danced': that last word perhaps more important than the rest put together. Did he need to read (or to hear Dorothy reading) the entry to write such a poem? Probably not. But the *language* of dance mattered, and without it there would have been no poem. The poet probably knew that there was a poem there, somewhere. For a couple of years, he did not address himself to it; though the odd 1802 poem 'The

Barberry-Tree' seems to have derived something either from the original experience beside Ullswater, or from Dorothy's journal entry, or from both: that was where the language of dance seems to have gone to, in 1802.[59] But eventually a memory of the original moment, with the journal entry serving as a kind of memory, is consulted; the memory brings back the emotion; and Wordsworth is able to write the poem because he feels he has got back into the original experience. In this case it seems quite likely that the emotion included the feeling of (and probably the actual word) dance. Wordsworth's wife Mary would be responsible for two lines in the poem (ll. 15–16) though she had not been present at the original experience: but she too was one of the group.

And although the journal might here seem to have functioned as a kind of memory bank, the poem points out that if memory itself does not hold the experience, then the experience has played no part in your life, and so was probably not important: certainly not worth a poem.

On one occasion, we can be quite sure that a journal entry was made to preserve something for Wordsworth. On 30 January 1802,[60] while shaving in the morning, Wordsworth asked Dorothy 'to set down the story of Barbara Wilkinsons Turtle Dove' in her journal, and her entry immediately includes it. He presumably thought he might use the anecdote, and wanted her to record it, presumably fairly soon after hearing it.[61]

But a similar apparently deliberate inclusion of a description, several days after it had happened, had occurred back in June 1800. On 10 June, Dorothy's journal had carried the usual day's entry, concluding with a description of what she and Wordsworth did in the evening (they had gone to Ambleside, and on their return found that John Wordsworth had gone to bed), but then it includes a complete reminiscence of an event a fortnight earlier: 'On Tuesday, May 27th, a very tall woman, tall much beyond the measure of tall women, called at the door . . .'[62] The entry for 27 May – written while Wordsworth was away in Yorkshire with John between 14 May and 7 June – contains, however, no mention of this caller. It seems almost certain that Dorothy told her brother about the woman when he got back (quite possibly during their evening walk to Ambleside and back on the 10th) and that he then asked her to record it, which she did, with considerable care.[63]

And this encounter Wordsworth did use, nearly two years later, in the spring of 1802: Dorothy's journal for 13 March records how 'William finished Alice Fell, & then he wrote the Poem of the Beggar woman taken from a Woman whom I had seen in May – (now nearly 2 years ago) when John & he were at Gallow Hill – I sate with him at Intervals all the morning, took down his stanzas &c'. They had walked to Rydale after dinner for letters, but Wordsworth was still working on his poem; along the road he 'got warmed with the subject & had half cast the Poem'.[64] The journal entry, however, proved as troublesome as it was helpful. Later in the day, after tea, Wordsworth asked to hear the entry as originally written, which suggests that up to now he may have been working from memory and imagination: 'I read to William that account of the little Boys belonging to the tall woman & an unlucky thing it was for he could not escape from those very words, & so he could not write the poem, he left it unfinished & went tired to Bed.'[65] The tyranny of someone else's words (even Dorothy's) was too strong. The language had, however, never been Wordsworth's own (he had not been there to share it or develop it on the original occasion) and he could not possess the episode for himself. The following morning, however, before getting up to a late breakfast (and before seeing Dorothy), he 'finished the Beggar Boys'.[66] Dorothy copied it out later that morning. Without her, the poem might never have been written at all; but it was also important that Wordsworth managed, one way or another, to find his own emotional response.

On at least one occasion Dorothy's journal entry was probably made subsequent to the poem which her brother wrote: but, once again, precedence seems entirely unimportant. The entry for 16 April 1802 – probably inscribed late that night, or the following day – records how she briefly left Wordsworth on his own at the foot of Brothers Water:

> When I returned I found William writing a poem descriptive of the sights & sounds we saw and heard. There was the gentle flowing of the stream, the glittering lively lake, green fields without a living creature to be seen on them, behind us, a flat pasture with 42 cattle feeding, to our left the road leading to the hamlet, no smoke there, the sun shone on the bare roofs.[67]

When she says she 'found him writing a poem', she means that he was working on one in his head; it was not his habit to transcribe until a fairly late stage in the process. It seems, therefore, that he told her what he was doing: whose particular observations were they, then, which went into the finished poem?

> The cock is crowing,
> The stream is flowing,
> The small birds twitter,
> The Lake doth glitter,
> 5   The green field sleeps in the sun;
>
> The Horse and his Marrow
> Drag the plough and the harrow,
> The cattle are grazing,
> Their heads never raising,
> 10   There are forty feeding like one.
>
> Like an army defeated
> The snow hath retreated,
> And now doth fare ill

On the top of the bare hill;
15 The Plough-boy is whooping – anon – anon:

There's joy in the mountains,
There's life in the fountains,
Small clouds are sailing,
Blue sky prevailing;
20 The rain is over and gone![68]

Because they were on the road at the time, the poem was not actually 'written' for some hours; but Wordsworth and Dorothy habitually recited his poetry as they walked along (she had been repeating his new poem 'The Glow-worm' to herself on her own brief walk).[69] She noted in her journal that 'William finished his poem before we got to the foot of Kirkstone'. From 'the Bridge near the foot of Brother's Water',[70] where he 'wrote' it, to the foot of Kirkstone pass, is a distance of about a mile and three-quarters: a strolling time of some 30–40 minutes, for the repetition and improvement of the poem: with Dorothy obviously playing her part.

When they got home that evening, one of Dorothy's jobs was to transcribe the poem; she inserted it into her brother's letter to Coleridge, and its first stanza into her own letter to Mary Hutchinson: she does not seem to have made her own journal entry until later.[71] On the other hand, the journal entry stands as a piece of description in its own right: the poem's 'forty' cattle become a precisely counted '42'.

This is the point made by John O. Hayden about another 1802 poem ('Composed after a Journey across the Hambleton Hills') which Wordsworth wrote on – or probably about – 4 October 1802, his wedding day.[72] Lines 5–10 of the poem run:

5 The western sky did recompence us well
With Grecian Temple, Minaret, and Bower
And in one part a Minster with its Tower
Substantially distinct – a place for bell
Or clock to toll from: many a glorious pile
10 Did we behold . . .[73]

This poem shares a good deal of the description in Dorothy's journal, which records how

far far off us, in the western sky, we saw the shapes of Castles, Ruins among groves, a great, spreading wood, rocks, & single trees, a minster with its tower unusually distinct, minarets in another quarter, & a round Grecian Temple also – the colours of the sky of a bright grey & the forms of a sober grey, with a dome.[74]

Hayden comments: 'it is now thought that the poem and journal entry probably derived from the conversation during the time in question'.[75] 'Conversation' is a slightly odd word to use, but he is right to include the third person in
the carriage: Mary Wordsworth, as she had now been for around nine hours.
What she contributed may be as important as what anyone else said, although
her name is on neither journal entry nor poem. The poem makes the 'shapes' a
good deal more dramatic; the journal entry calls them 'sober grey' and the sky
'bright grey', while in the poem 'Many a glorious pile / Did we behold'. The
journal entry is, perhaps appropriately for Dorothy recording this day, also
rather more ominous, with its 'Ruins among groves, a great, spreading wood,
rocks, & single trees'. Dorothy is seeing things which will not be seen again:
'But there's a Tree, of many, one, / A single Field which I have looked upon, /
Both of them speak of something that is gone'. There is also a hint of the
grimmest of the 'Lucy' poems of 1799: Lucy dead and rolled around with
'rocks and stones and trees'. The married man's poem, however, shows that
westward, look, the land is bright.[76]

Once again, precedence is not the point, though biographers of individuals
always stand up for the importance of their own subject. In cases such as these
it is the interplay which matters: the fact that the language of reminiscence, loss
and decision was in common between Wordsworth and Dorothy, and was now
being shared by Mary Wordsworth, so that, in fact, the only thing the coach
journey produced was something joint.

Similarly, Coleridge was a writer for all of them. On 22 March 1802,
Wordsworth and Dorothy were both thinking a lot about him, recently
returned from Gallow Hill (and deeply distressed) as he was: he had stayed
with them over the weekend. Dorothy wrote in her journal how 'We talked a
good deal about C & other interesting things';[77] and when she went on to
describe their quiet evening at home, it was to the language of 'Frost at Midnight' that she turned, while regretting that no letter from its author had come.
It is an entry written in real-time, noting the events of the moment. Her brother
'is now reading Ben Jonson I am going to read German it is about 10 o clock,
a quiet night. The fire flutters & the watch ticks I hear nothing else save the
Breathings of my Beloved & he now & then pushes his book forward & turns
over a leaf . . . No letter from C.'[78] In Coleridge's poem, of course, the word
'flutter' had had a peculiar significance:

> the thin blue flame
> Lies on my low burnt fire, and quivers not;
> Only that film, which fluttered on the grate,
> Still flutters there, the sole unquiet thing.[79]

The *Morning Post* printing had had an explanatory footnote: 'In all parts of the
kingdom these films are called *strangers* and supposed to portend the arrival of
some absent friend'. Coleridge was certainly an absent friend, much worried

over and mourned for. So too was Mary Hutchinson (they had been talking that evening of Wordsworth's plans to marry her).

But Dorothy's engagement with Coleridge did not end there. It had been 'My cradled infant' who had come to dominate 'Frost at Midnight', and his 'gentle breathings' which characterised him (l. 45). Dorothy has no child beside her, but she too has her beloved, for whom she is both happy and anxious; and it is his plural (and capitalised) 'Breathings' which she records. Thus is Coleridge with them both, that quiet evening in March 1802.[80]

IV

It is not, however, just as a diarist that Dorothy Wordsworth should be celebrated, although it is the only way in which, today, she is really visible (or audible). In 1802, her letter writing would have been a far more time-consuming and equally important part of her life. On 1 March (to go back to the beginning), she gets a letter from Sara and another from Mary: she finishes her letter to Sara and has it sent, writes a letter to Mary, and starts another letter to Sara.

Was that an exceptional day, or a normal one? Remarks in her journal – combined with the letters which *do* survive – help us estimate the total number of letters she wrote. Not every surviving letter was mentioned in the journal, while very few of the letters which she records writing actually survive. But the journal and the surviving letters indicate that she and Wordsworth together wrote at least four letters to Coleridge during March and six during April; and that she and Wordsworth together wrote at least five letters each to Mary and Sara Hutchinson during March, and two each to them during April. Dorothy was personally responsible for the majority of these letters; Wordsworth hated letter-writing, being 'the most lazy and impatient Letter writer in the world': 'partly from a weakness in my stomach and digestion and partly from certain habits of mind I do not write any letters unless upon business not ev[en] to my dearest Friends. Except during absence from my own family I ha[ve] not written five letters of friendship during the last five years.'[81] By that definition, in the summer of 1802 Mary and Sara were both of 'my own family', as was Coleridge. And if we consider the number of letters which we know left Town End, it would probably be safest to double Dorothy's figures, and then regard the total as a considerable underestimate. Dorothy would perhaps have written twenty to twenty-five letters during March, and twenty during April, to Coleridge and Sara and Mary combined. If they received roughly as many as they sent, which is likely, this figure is confirmed by the fact that they had to pay for around thirty letters which arrived between the start of December and the end of January, when they were away from home for three weeks.[82] The figures are sufficiently close to suggest that, when at home, Dorothy probably wrote a letter a day: and we should not forget that she maintained correspondences with a number of other people too. It would in fact be surprising if she did not write at least thirty letters a month. We can do a sudden spot check in June, when Dorothy was anxious that she was not being a good correspondent (she had been ill): she wrote to Sara and Mary only on the 5th, the 8th, the 10th and the 14th.[83] Her letter writing on 1 March, then, looks perfectly normal.

But only two letters survive, out of the total of around sixty she probably wrote in the course of March and April: one to her brother Richard and one to Mary Hutchinson. The fact that so few of her letters survive massively reduces our understanding of the central part she was playing in the life of the group. She was, in her letters, constantly bringing them all together. Even when Wordsworth went away for a couple of days – in the week starting on Monday March 1st he would visit Sarah Coleridge from Thursday to (she imagined) the following Monday – she wrote to him in Keswick on the Thursday and the Friday. It is easy to underestimate (or forget) the creativity which attends such regular letter writing; one scholar unwisely remarked recently that she 'wrote relatively little'.[84] She probably wrote a great deal more than her brother and Coleridge combined.

Very rarely, purely by chance, we are able to gain an insight into the role played by her letter writing, and to compare it with the journal she was writing at the same time. One such occasion is the evening of 16th April 1802. She and Wordsworth got home in the twilight (around half past six at night) – almost too dark to see how the garden had developed over the preceding three weeks. Presumably they ate something, and heard gossip from the neighbours. And then they got to work. Dorothy first wrote a long letter to Mary Hutchinson describing their journey and safe arrival (they would neither of them have sent a letter on either of the previous days, while on the road from the Clarksons); at the end of her letter she transcribed the first stanza of the poem written at Brother's Water earlier in the day. While she was writing to Mary, Wordsworth was sitting beside her in front of the fire writing to Coleridge. They then swapped over letters, so that Dorothy wrote the whole of the same poem into the letter to Coleridge, while Wordsworth wrote the second stanza into the letter to Mary, and himself added a note. The sequence in Dorothy's letter to Mary starting with the departure to Eusemere, and ending with the arrival in Grasmere, occupied some 682 words.

At some stage either the same evening or the following day – most likely after the letters[85] – Dorothy wrote a long journal entry (some 1,390 words, so more than double the length of the passage in the letter) about the journey, which covered very much the same sequence of subjects as her letter to Mary, but very differently. The passage in the journal about the daffodils which would later matter so much to Wordsworth has no counterpart in the letter. The letter however lists what they ate for supper, Mary obviously wanting to know that William had eaten well: but as the first part of the letter dwells on Mary's terrible thinness, as reported by Wordsworth, the list also becomes a kind of exemplary meal. The journal notes the kinds of flower they found on the journey: the letter does not. The journal entry records that William found books at the inn, and names three of them (Wordsworth might have wanted a note of that); the letter does not mention them. The journal describes the scene at Brother's Water in as much detail as the poem William would write, as well as twice mentioning the poem; the letter mentions only the fact that William wrote the poem.

The journal was thus being written as part of that mutual insight into nature and the language of experience, and into the possibility of its becoming poetry, upon which William depended. The letter was written to reassure Mary that they both (but in particular William) were well, to give her a quick résumé of what they were doing, and to ensure that she knew the local gossip (the fact that at the Olives' sale things had been overpriced, so that they had not missed anything), as well as the more significant things to do with the house at Town End to which she would herself soon be coming (the fact that Aggy Ashburner was lame, and how Molly was and how well she had kept the house while they were away[86]).

But if the letters Dorothy wrote were all similarly detailed, sensitive and reassuring, as well as lengthy (the whole letter to Mary was almost exactly the length of the journal entry), then Dorothy was writing *for* her correspondents in ways which ensured that they shared an extensive knowledge of what was happening, and were being kept up to date about things in which they had an interest. And, of course, as I showed in Chapter One, the copying of poems (and the inclusion of them in letters) was another major piece of her work.

Our perception of Dorothy's role at the centre of these lives has, however, been hugely diminished by the loss of almost all the letters she wrote. If that is true for Dorothy, it is even more true of Mary and Sara Hutchinson, and of John Wordsworth. At least Dorothy's journal survives, to remind us of one of her roles; and the two poets have their poems, often in multiple drafts and variants, as evidence of their writing; while relatively more of their letters survive, too, since the letters of such people have always been regarded as important objects in their own right. But the colossal correspondence going on between at least three of the gang is now (like an iceberg) almost invisible; we must simply recognise it as a fact. The massive volumes of the correspondence of Sara Hutchinson and Mary Hutchinson contain not a single surviving letter from 1802, though (again) we know that both sent a total of at least seven each during March and April and – again – it would probably be best to multiply that by two and regard the result as an underestimate. Each of them probably wrote at least fifteen to twenty letters in the course of the two months, to Dorothy and William Wordsworth alone, and of course many more still to their brothers, sisters and cousins.[87] As well as being responsible for a good deal of the households' actual work (in particular the cooking, sewing, mending and washing[88]) these women constantly corresponded; and this enabled the scattered households to be dedicated to each other far more closely than we can now see without making a great effort of historical recreation.

V

To what address, then, did Wordsworth send his own letter to Coleridge of 1 March? And why did he write to him?

Coleridge, they believed, was on the point of leaving London (he had actually left the day before); but the Wordsworths seem to have got caught up in a small and unconvincing deception which accompanied his departure. We do not know when he decided not to return direct to Sarah Coleridge and Keswick from London, but during the last week of February he told his wife that Sara Hutchinson would probably be going over to Grasmere shortly, for the Wordsworth wedding, and that he would therefore make a diversion in his own route back in order to assist her on the journey over: 'If it be decided, that Sarah is to come to Grasmere, I shall return by York, which will be but a few miles out of the way, & bring her / .'[89] The Wordsworths, however, who would have been putting Sara up, knew nothing about an impending visit – let alone about Wordsworth's impending wedding – until the 26th, when they also got a letter from Coleridge. This nails the untruth. Of all these people, Sara Hutchinson was renowned for not making promises to visit which she did not keep, or making plans which she subsequently changed. She herself once noted: 'William would vouch for the perfection of my character on this point. He always says that when Sara fixes to come you may be *sure of* her.'[90] She was currently at Gallow Hill with her brother Tom, and her sister Mary was also there on a visit from Middleham; this alone suggests why Sara would have had absolutely no intention of going to Grasmere. On the 26th, however, Dorothy had recorded that they had had letters from Mary Hutchinson and Coleridge, and that the Coleridge letter had baffled them: 'a short one from C. We were perplexed about Saras coming. I wrote to Mary. Wm closed his letter to Montagu, & wrote to Calvert & to Mrs Coleridge.'[91] Presumably Coleridge had spun them the same tale he had told his wife, to help explain his diversion into Yorkshire, and the consequent delay in his return to Keswick. A further refinement would a little later explain why his journey from London would have to be diverted not just as far as York but into a visit to Gallow Hill itself. It is hard to see his letter to the Wordsworths as anything else than an attempt to cover his tracks. The fact that Wordsworth immediately wrote to Sarah Coleridge also suggests that he had been asked to do so: there is no other record of his ever writing to her. Presumably Coleridge had written something to the effect 'I'm delayed and will probably have to go direct to Gallow Hill to collect Sara, to bring her over: since I shall be late back, could you possibly – good friend as you are – go over to Keswick for a couple of days?' At all events, Coleridge was still supposed to be home by the middle of March, perhaps even as early as the 7th;[92] but Wordsworth arranged to go over to Keswick on the 4th, when Coleridge would certainly not be there. Something was being arranged for Sarah Coleridge with which Wordsworth was helping; on the 23rd (when Coleridge was still in London) they had been waiting for the arrival of 'papers from Mrs Coleridge'.[93]

But when Wordsworth wrote to Coleridge on the 1st – and he would have written to Gallow Hill – he presumably said something like 'surprised to hear you went to Gallow Hill, but do give Mary (and Sara) my love: you must have misunderstood about the wedding, it won't be for months; but my dear friend of course I shall go up to Keswick, as you requested: I shall go on Thursday'. And of course he did.

Chapter Three

Coleridges: 2 March

Coleridge could not of course hope to keep a visit to Gallow Hill a secret, however much he might attempt to conceal his movements and get home only a few days later than expected.[1] But why was he covering his tracks?

He had for some time been delaying going home to Keswick. Things were seriously wrong with his marriage; he appears to have been apprehensive of falling back into the cycles of anger and mutual recrimination which had soured life at Greta Hall during the previous autumn, before he had gone down to London. Suffice it to say that his immediate provocation to go to Gallow Hill was an exchange of letters he had had with Sara Hutchinson. In the *Letter* he would describe sending her a letter which left her 'weak and pale with Sickness, Grief and Pain'.[2] Two years later, on the anniversary of her reply, he wrote in his notebook: 'Rickman's, Tuesday Night, Feb. 21. 1804, 11 oclock / the day of the Receipt of that heart-wringing Letter from Sara, that put Despair into my Heart, and not merely as a Lodger, I fear, but as a Tenant for Life.'[3] We have no idea what she had written to him; but if he had made some kind of appeal to her to love him, as seems likely, she had obviously rejected it, while revealing herself agonised by what he had said. He left London for Yorkshire exactly a week later, on Sunday 28 February; it had probably taken him that long to escape his obligations to Stuart and the *Morning Post* (he was still leaving five days earlier than originally arranged).

What has been assumed to be his love for Sara Hutchinson has, however, been allowed to colour our whole picture of the needs of a man with a failing marriage; and I wish to spend this chapter looking at the Coleridge marriage as it existed at the start of 1802. Sarah Fricker, brown-ringleted, vivacious, full-figured, had married Coleridge in October 1795; Coleridge 'pale and thin, has a wide mouth, thick lips, and not very good teeth, longish loose-growing half-curling rough black hair'. Dorothy Wordsworth described his eyes as 'large and full, not dark but grey . . . He has fine dark eye-brows, and an overhanging forehead'.[4] The Coleridges' son Hartley had been born in September 1796, Derwent in September 1800, and her daughter Sara would be born in December 1802; her son Berkeley, born in May 1798, had died in February 1799.[5] The fact that so little has yet appeared in this book about Sarah Coleridge is an indication of how much on the periphery of the others's lives she was: to the extent that she was, now, paradoxically, on the periphery of Coleridge's life as well.

There were many reasons for this. For six years and more, Coleridge and she had lived through the whole gamut of problems of the unsalaried and undisciplined man supporting a wife and a growing family; even with the £150 a year guaranteed by the philanthropic Tom and Josiah Wedgwood from 1798 onwards, the Coleridges still had constant money problems. Coleridge had been ill a great deal in the winter of 1800, and remained so during the spring and early summer of 1801: 'Nine dreary months – and oh me! Have I had even a fortnight's full and continuous health?' he had written at the start of July 1801.[6] Wordsworth (to whom Coleridge owed £20) commented to Tom Poole (to whom Coleridge owed over £50) that 'this has rendered it impossible for him to earn any thing, and his sickness has also been expensive'.[7] The following winter, when Coleridge had been in London working for the *Morning Post*, just as he had done in 1799–1800, had in part been planned as a way of helping their financial situation, though it is also clear that by the autumn of 1801 he increasingly wanted to spend time away from home.

It needs to be said that there is no indication in the record before 1800 of any major problems between the two Coleridges. Coleridge had known for years that he and Sarah were very different, and that 'we cannot be happy in all respects'; but over the years things had generally been getting better, rather than worse, in the marriage, so that in spite of the fact that they disagreed rather comically about where to live early in 1800, for example ('that situation which suits my wife does not suit me, and what suits me does not suit my wife'), he could write only a few days later that 'nunc vero (ut omnia mitescunt) tranquillus, imo, animo grato! ['now (as everything mellows) I am content, indeed, thankful!']'[8] But with Coleridge's months of illness from the winter of 1800 to the summer of 1801, his increasing inability to get down to any of the projects to which he knew he should be devoting himself, and the money problems which his illness (and that inability) compounded, relations between the couple deteriorated. It seems that – as is usual in such cases – they quarrelled and had rows, and that there were then quite long periods of relative calm. They had a particularly bad patch in the spring and early summer of 1801, for example, and then Coleridge went away for a month. They seem to have had another fearsome time in the autumn, when Coleridge decided he must go away for the winter, either down to Somerset or to London. Dorothy Wordsworth's journal shows that at this point he spent a lot of time in Grasmere with them, suggesting that he was unhappy at home, but also ensuring that he would pile up resentment at home for his obvious preference for being with the Wordsworths. He went back to Keswick on 10th October after a visit to Grasmere, for example, but came back less than a week later, on the 15th, and stayed until the 19th, before going home again. He returned to Grasmere on 6 November for another three-day visit, and then Dorothy, Mary Hutchinson and Wordsworth went back to Keswick with him on the 9th (his last day before he had arranged to leave for London). It looks as if he wanted his friends there as a buffer between himself and Sarah; and Dorothy's journal shows that she was very worried about him.[9] There was then a reasonably friendly correspondence between Coleridge and Sarah, to judge by the surviving fragments of his letters. Not living together solved some of their problems.

But it is not just bad temper and rows we are considering. What exactly Sarah Coleridge felt about her husband at this stage we do not know, but Coleridge himself was sure by the autumn of 1801 that he could no longer live happily with her. His difficulties with himself were growing larger with the years, however, and as I suggested above, one of the largest was – simply – what sort of a writer he ought to be, and what kind of work he should be doing.[10] He was fairly sure, after 1800, that he would not be a poet (and indeed wrote relatively little poetry after that year). He did *not* want primarily to write political journalism, although he was extremely good at it. He did believe that he should be dedicating himself to some major piece of work; but as the years went by, he still did not know exactly what that work should be. His vagueness can be judged by his deprecating reference to 'my curious metaphysical Work' to Tom Poole in December 1801;[11] the gap between what he – and others – expected of him, and what he actually did, grew wider and wider as time went by, which he found demoralising. He experienced his failure both emotionally (letting down his friends and supporters) and financially (a number of publishers had given him advances for books which he was not writing). His constant illnesses (opium related, as I shall suggest below), his unhappiness, his procrastinations, his inability to do anything which might satisfy himself, or anyone else, grew steadily worse; he would remark in September 1801 'I confess, I have written nothing that I value myself *at all*'.[12] And it seems that Sarah got blamed, to some degree; and (obviously) in her turn blamed him for the money worries, for ignoring her, and for his behaviour during his periods of tortured unhappiness. By the autumn of 1801, they were thoroughly miserable together.

This did not mean, however, that Coleridge wanted to divorce Sarah, or to set up another establishment with his children, apart from her. He never even considered either of those quintessentially modern solutions. He did not believe that a marriage could be ended: 'deeply am I convinced of it's indissolubleness'. Nor did he believe in taking the children away from Sarah, 'that she should be a Widow & they Orphans'.[13] Nor did he have an affair with another woman. All he could contemplate was living apart from Sarah, and doing his best 'in the earnest desire to provide for her & [the]m'. He saw a life of unhappiness and difficulties stretching ahead of him, with periods of release and loneliness (as during the winter of 1801–2) when he was in London. In the verse *Letter*, thinking of some particularly bad times in the relationship, he would describe

> . . . those habitual Ills,
> That wear out Life, where two unequal minds
> Meet in one House, and two discordant Wills –

But as that poem would go on to point out, succinctly and with complete clarity,

> This leaves me, where it finds,
> Past cure and past Complaint![14]

There was no cure: and no point in complaining. But, as he would put it in October 1802, 'the less I loved my wife, the more dear & necessary did my children seem to me'.[15] He would have to live as separated a life as he could, seeing the children when he could: and finding the family he so badly craved in other, sisterly and brotherly relationships.

All his life he had had problems with sisters and brothers. He was the youngest of nine children; his eldest brothers he hardly knew, the brother closest to him (Frank) he both loved and quarrelled with savagely, and Frank was sent off as a cadet to India at just the time when Coleridge's father John died, leaving Sam at the age of nine deeply bereft. Two other brothers died while he was young; he ended up in an uneasy relationship with just one of them, the clergyman and headmaster George. His only sister of an age near his own, Nancy, to whom he was very close as a child, had died at the age of twenty-five in 1791, when Coleridge was nineteen; Coleridge wrote one poem about the moment he was told that she was fatally ill ('How are ye gone, whom most my soul held dear!') and another soon afterwards which started 'I too a sister had! too cruel death!'[16] It is clear that in Wordsworth and Dorothy, he had found a relationship both complementary to, and offering something different from, his marriage.

Complaints about Sarah do not bulk especially large in surviving letters between 1796 and 1801, but they are not the kinds of things which are likely to have been preserved. There seems to have been no call for them before 1800, anyway, while what Coleridge called 'Indifference' is an undramatic subject. Endurable time for both the Coleridges, in the early stages of their marriage's breakdown, was marked by her finding ways of coping with his distance from her (the distance seems have been one of the methods he used to evade her anger), and by his finding ways of deflecting her anger with him. Who started these patterns of behaviour, or who was primarily responsible for them, is of course quite undiscoverable and probably unimportant. It is clear that she continued to be fond of him, in spite of the distance he was attempting to put between them, and the anger she felt with him. For his part, it seems that increasingly he could not bear being with her.

It was not until their spectacular rows started that there was actually much for him to complain of. In October 1802 he would give his patron Tom Wedgwood a dramatic account of developments during the past year: these carefully-turned sentences refer to the later part of 1801 and the first half of 1802, and are Coleridge's reasons why he had been unable to repay his patron's generosity with actual intellectual production: 'Ill tempered Speeches sent after me when I went out of the House, ill-tempered Speeches on my return, my friends received with freezing looks, the least opposition or contradiction occasioning screams of passion, & the sentiments, which I held most base, ostentatiously avowed . . .'[17] Apart from the usual irritations shown by two people determined to find fault with each other, the line about 'my friends' – undoubtedly a reference to the Wordsworths – helps us to understand how and why things were coming to a head. So far as Sarah Coleridge was concerned, the growing Coleridge family demanded attendance, provision and loyalty, all of which Coleridge was increasingly unwilling to give. She naturally fastened on his relationships with his friends, to blame him for his absences and failures.

We can see this clearly in an extraordinary notebook entry which Coleridge made in September 1801. It shows him attempting to analyse for the very first time Sarah's liability to anger, and to search out its cause. He traced it back to what he thought were her problems with her sense of self. It is worth looking hard at this, not because what it says about Sarah is true, but because it takes us into the problems of the whole relationship, and it also reveals Coleridge's sheer intelligence, as well as his wonderful slipperiness of mind. The entry begins in mid-sentence, following a deletion:

> coldness perhaps & paralysis in all *tangible* ideas & sensations – all that forms *real Self* – hence <the Slave of her> she creates her own self in a field of Vision & Hearing, at a distance, by her own ears & eyes – & hence becomes the willing Slave of the Ears & Eyes of others – Nothing affects her with pain or pleasure as it is but only as other people will *say it is* – nay by an habitual absence of *reality* in her affections I have had an hundred instances that the being beloved, or the not being beloved, is a thing indifferent; but the *notion* – of not being beloved – that wounds her pride deeply.[18]

To Coleridge, Sarah has a problem with her 'real self', and so relies upon what others say about her – and is thus the victim of what she hears and sees. She does not experience what he calls 'pain or pleasure as it is': she only *responds*. Again, I must stress that this is not necessarily a true account; it is probably extremely biased. But it shows Coleridge attempting to locate the problem of the relationship not in their own power struggles, but within the world of their acquaintance, and their disagreements about the kinds of people they wanted (and wanted their children) to be close to.

It is an analysis which brilliantly pre-dates a good deal of twentieth-century thinking about the problems of self-esteem. It also, however, places the analyst himself outside the circle of those much affected by 'other people'. He is one who can be a rebel and social non-conformist, one who – unlike Sarah – has no need to bother about common judgement.

Coleridge reaches the remarkable conclusion that Sarah's anger is not in fact a proof of the strength of her feelings (which she and most people today would probably still claim) but just the opposite. People angry in her way do *not* 'feel much <u>within</u>, & <u>deeply</u>': their anger is a response to the 'others' who are capable of affecting them so much.

> genuine Anger, which is made up of *Fear & animal Courage,* will be found in those most, who most hang upon the opinions of others, & to whom these opinions are of the most importance – *Sailors* are very often angry – so Verse-makers who are not Poets, are angered, irritable – Le Grice, a Wit almost a genius, was a very angry Man –. George Hutchinson.[19]

Coleridge had met Sara Hutchinson's younger brother at Sockburn in 1799, and had lived in his house during July and August 1801: he was 'a young farmer' who 'makes very droll verses in the northern dialect & in the metre of Burns, & is a great Humourist'.[20] He had also clearly demonstrated another side, too, in the summer of 1801. The example of the sailors is clearly spurious; Coleridge is having trouble identifying people who 'most hang upon the opinions of others'. But he very much wants to show how anger is a powerful but paralysing response to the situations created by our relationships. His real aim is to identify Sarah's anger as caused by her incapacity to relate to the world around her. Anger, in this analysis, is not so much a psychological problem as a psycho-social one. *Real* feelings are not just violent moments in a life but – he uses the words several times – 'tangible' or 'tactual'. That is what makes them different from mere 'appetites'. Those are 'always *local* in the body itself an object of sight or visual idea not to mention the immediateness of their application to some distinct separate, visible part of some other Body external to theirs.'[21] Coleridge has got his argument back on course. Sarah's attachment to the forms of society, her fixation on appearances, and her willingness to be governed by social conventions, are part of the same complex of attitudes which make her both angry and desperate to be found attractive. He is able to conclude that Sarah has no centre of self, no real feelings of her own; instead she has what we would call neurotic needs to be loved and admired.

This conclusion tells us as much about Coleridge as it does about Sarah. He himself implicitly has a centre of self, he stands aloof from common judgement, he is unaffected by the world's conventional valuations. *His* anger is a product of real feelings, *hers* is a by-product of her need to be admired. He has found a way of getting round the disturbing quality of her anger – the fact that it might be caused by something in *him*. The way of thinking he develops here makes it, strictly, *her* problem. The entry also reveals how little he was prepared to think his way into the problems a woman in the male world of 1801 might have with sustaining a sense of self.

Phrases have been extracted from this entry to show Coleridge blaming Sarah Coleridge for 'sexual frigidity',[22] and to accuse Coleridge himself of having changed a great deal from the young man who had been so profoundly attracted by her in 1795. But although there certainly is an unthinking male sexual snobbery about the charge that Sarah is 'uncommonly <u>cold</u> in her feelings of animal Love', that point is almost incidental. What Coleridge is really writing about is the problems he believed Sarah had with relationships with the world outside herself; and what he cannot bear is the way she allows herself to be subjected to conventional judgements.

II

Sarah Coleridge had certainly begun to express strong objections to the Wordsworths. In December 1802, Coleridge would appeal to her: 'how much of our common Love & Happiness depends on your loving those whom I love, – why should I repeat?'[23] What she appears to have objected to in the Wordsworths was not (as has been suggested) their tolerance of Coleridge's opium addiction, for which there is no evidence,[24] but something much more basic: their unconventionality, their refusal to behave according to the demands of their social position, and the fact that Coleridge was constantly going to see them. This is why Coleridge's long analysis of Sarah is important. It describes not only how he believed Sarah reacted to others, but it also shows him positioning himself as one who shares the Wordsworths' attitudes; he is as unconventional, as uncaring of 'other people', as they are.

But from Sarah's point of view, the Wordsworths were not only constantly taking her husband away from her and his family; they were people who paid far too little attention to rank and propriety. They either ignored or laughed at conventions of behaviour in dress, visiting, regular hours and regular meals; they walked about like tramps, by day and by night. As early as 1794, Dorothy's aunt Mrs Christopher Crackanthorpe had been complaining about her niece's habits of 'rambling about the country on foot', travelling without a chaperone, and placing herself in an 'exposed situation'. Dorothy herself described the 'employments' of her life in Grasmere as 'not very various yet they are irregular. We walk [every] day and at all times of the day'.[25] Wordsworth's habits of composition out loud, on the move, and of vanishing up to the orchard to escape visitors, were – to a person conscious of good manners – probably matched in offensiveness only by Dorothy's readiness to interview passing tramps about their lives, to invite them in for a meal and a talk; and then go for a walk at midnight, by herself. The Wordsworths' constant demonstrations of freedom, in thought, word and deed, directly conflicted with Sarah's code of good manners and belief in respectability.[26]

From the point of view of any normal, class-conscious middle-class person, two things in particular about the Wordsworths – their dress, and their outdoor behaviour – would have seemed suspicious. As late as 1828, when Wordsworth was reasonably prosperous, and a sight to be looked out for by tourists, a

stranger thought he looked 'more like a mountain farmer than a "lakes poet".
His whole air was unrefined and unprepossessing'.[27] A local butcher remarked
– again, comparatively late in Wordsworth's life – that he was not only 'quite
pläinly dressed' but actually 'poorly dressed, ya mun saay, at the best o' times'.[28]
Back in 1802, when he was extremely poor, he would most of the time have
been a great deal shabbier (in spite of his nearly-new pantaloons from London).
But the Wordsworths' unconventional dress and behaviour were also the badge
of their difference. We can guess how Sarah Coleridge – or Mrs Crackanthorpe
– would have responded to the Wordsworths vanishing over the wall on 1
March to read their letters, sitting on the ground. Thomas De Quincey tells a
fascinating anecdote of the Coleridges and Wordsworths out for a walk
together – sometime between 1797 and 1802 – returning 'drenched with rain'.
Dorothy 'with a laughing gaiety, and evidently unconscious of any liberty
she was taking . . . would run up to Mrs Coleridge's wardrobe, array herself,
without leave asked, in Mrs Coleridge's dresses, and make herself merry
with her own unceremoniousness and Mrs Coleridge's gravity.'[29] Dorothy,
according to this account, saw her own behaviour as one of 'the natural privi-
leges of friendship': friendship defined, of course, on her terms. (She would
warn the Hutchinsons, on her way to them in July 1802, that 'I shall bring very
few clothes. I shall trust to Sara's wardrobe', and 'I intend to take one of Sara's
white gowns with me into France'.[30]) But it seems rather unlikely that she was
genuinely 'unconscious of any liberty she was taking' when borrowing clothes
from Sarah Coleridge. Her sensitivity to others was phenomenal, and if Sarah
had viewed such behaviour with 'gravity' then Dorothy would certainly have
noticed it. If the anecdote is true, then Dorothy's behaviour seems a kind of
challenge deliberately made to a person believed over-concerned with trifles
and foolishly small minded. The person challenged will of course get very
angry. And Sarah Coleridge, in the De Quincey account, 'viewed such free-
doms with a far different eye'. What made it especially difficult for her was, of
course, the attitude of her husband, who – according to De Quincey – did not
stick up for her: 'it barbed the arrow to her womanly feelings, that Coleridge
treated any sallies of resentment which might sometimes escape her as narrow
mindedness'.[31]

There was, of course, a world of difference between the Coleridges' life at
Greta Hall at £40 a year, and life in the Wordsworths' unnamed ex-inn at £5 a
year,[32] just as there was between the Wordsworths' income of between £40 and
£50 a year, and Coleridge's £150 a year from the Wedgwoods, plus what he
managed to earn in addition. Coleridge however shared at least something of
his wife's taste: his description of himself as someone enjoying fashionable
London in February 1802 reveals the dandy as one of the roles he enjoyed
playing. On the other hand, as early as 1797 he had declared himself proudly
'a genuine Sans culotte, my veins uncontaminated with one drop of Gentility';[33] there was no one like Coleridge for standing up for ease and freedom
as against constraint and conventionality, which his habits of climbing and

wandering, and his love for the Wordsworths, of course exemplified. When particularly angry with Sarah in November 1802, he made a statement of his own beliefs about such things directed at what he found most irritating about her. This letter has been seen as part of a quarrel with his wife over Sara Hutchinson, though the surviving fragment of it is clearly not that. Coleridge loved, he insisted,

> warm Rooms, comfortable fires, & food, books, natural scenery, music &c; but I do not care what *binding* the Books have, whether they are dusty or clean – & I *dislike* fine furniture, handsome cloathes, & all the ordinary symbols & appendages of artificial superiority – or what is called, *Gentility*. In the same Spirit, I dislike, at least I seldom like, Gentlemen, gentlemanly manners, &c. I have no Pride, as far as Pride means a desire to be *thought* highly of by others . . .[34]

Such an attack on *Gentility* in 1802 was a way both of defending the Wordsworths against Sarah, and of showing how much her 'desire to be *thought* highly of by others' annoyed him. The Wordsworths notoriously lacked 'all the ordinary symbols & appendages of artificial superiority' but they were also independent of – and contemptuous of – what Coleridge had called, earlier in the letter, the 'advantages of external fortune'. This letter is the angriest surviving letter from Coleridge to Sarah, and it is significant that it should have accused her of snobbery and superficiality. He wrote to her again in January 1803 to show that he understood how 'remote' she felt from the Wordsworths, even though he went on to defend his friendship with them.

> You are a good woman with a pleasing person & a healthy understanding – superior certainly to nine women in ten, of our own rank, or the rank above us . . . Depend on it, my dear Wife! that the more you sympathize with me in my kind manners & kind feelings to those of Grasmere, the more I shall be likely to sympathize with you in your opinions respecting their faults & imperfections. I am no Idolater at present; & I solemnly assure you, that if I prefer many parts of *their* characters, opinions, feelings, & habits to the same parts of your's, I do likewise prefer much, very much of your character to their's – Of course, I speak *chiefly* of Dorothy & William – because Mrs Wordsworth & her Sister are far less remote from you than they . . .[35]

She had known the Wordsworths for six years, had lived with them, seen them constantly. Yet they were still 'remote' to her. The Hutchinsons, however, were more Sarah Coleridge's kind of people; even if not well off, they were at least genteel.

Given her objections to the Wordsworths, it is the more remarkable that Sarah Coleridge was, for so long, apparently prepared to listen patiently to her husband's schemes for living with them. In February 1802, for example, she received a letter from him suggesting that within a few months they should all move together to the south of France: 'Wordsworth . . . Mary, & Dorothy will be our companions, & neighbours . . . About July we shall all set sail from Liverpool to Bordeux &c —'.[36] She may have been confident that nothing would come of the plan (nothing did). But she had obviously had to accept such plans, which at least once *had* turned into reality. In 1800, she had found herself transported to the Lake District (where she had never been and knew no one) simply so that her husband could have regular access to the Wordsworths. The move up to the Lakes involved, for certain, a considerable sacrifice to her; even Dorothy Wordsworth, that most devoted of partners, would not be budged when it came to deciding where she, Mary and Wordsworth would settle after her brother's marriage to Mary ('I made a vow that we would not leave this Country for G Hill'[37]). Sarah's family were all down in the south-west of England, and confronted by her imminent move up to the Lakes in 1800, were 'much against our removing to such a distance'. But she was prepared to make the sacrifice: the distance from her family 'was the only objection on my part'. Things were cheaper in the north, and the Keswick house would be a good deal better than the Somerset house had been. She explained how, in Greta Hall, they were 'most delightfully situated, we have a large and very convenient house furnished with every article of comfort (but without elegance) and we are to pay a very moderate rent.'[38] The fact that the house was so large and comfortable (and relatively inexpensive, for its size and situation) was certainly one reason which helped Coleridge convince her they should move. Another advantage of Greta Hall was its closeness to Keswick: it 'combines all possible advantages both for his wife and himself, *she* likes to be near a Town, *he* in the country'.[39] And, having moved there, she stayed on in Greta Hall even when it turned out to be (in winter, according to Dorothy) 'miserably cold and ill-built'[40] and continued to do so after 1806, when her marriage to Coleridge effectively came to an end. (She lived there until 1830.)

A letter she wrote to her ultra-respectable sister-in-law Mrs George Coleridge in September 1800, however, allows us to see things precisely from her point of view. Although it describes the decision to move to the Lakes, and gives many details of the move, it only mentions the Wordsworths in passing, as having helped them to secure the house. The fact that they had actually moved entirely for the sake of being near Town End (Wordsworth was certain that Coleridge had 'come down' to the Lakes 'on my account'[41]), and the fact that she and Hartley and Coleridge had spent three weeks living in Town End before moving into Greta Hall, at no point get into the letter. Instead Sarah lists the attractions of the 'neighbours and acquaintances', without (again) mentioning the Wordsworths:

> Since our arrival the neighbouring families have most of them visited us: A Colonel Peachy who lives in the Summer in a very beautiful house on an island in the Lake Derwent Water – it is just opposite to our house about a mile across;

a Mr Spedding and his wife and her unmarried sisters, all young persons, seem to be an agreeable family – and they live here all the year. The Revd Mr Wilkinson; Mr Losh etc – all of whose visits Samuel has returned . . .[42]

It may be that she simply took the Wordsworths for granted, as she knew them so well. On the other hand, they were not people whose visits anyone would 'return', and it is *that* kind of 'respectable & neighbourly acquaintance' she seems to have valued.[43] Dorothy included a satirical account in her journal of meeting one of those respectable neighbours in December 1801, near Keswick: Miss Barcroft, on horseback, 'had not seen Mrs C "The weather has been such as to preclude all intercourse between neighbours" '.[44] That was not language which the Wordsworths would ever have used, nor the kind of friendship in which they believed. At that very moment, in spite of rain, hail and snow, they were walking fourteen miles up to Keswick to see their friends.

It may well only have been after she got to the Lake District, however, that Sarah Coleridge discovered how very odd and (to her) awkward the Wordsworths were: or what it was like to feel neglected when Coleridge was visiting them. During their period in Somerset together, the Wordsworths had actually been living in an extremely superior house (at £23 a year), and she may have felt that the responsibilities of being the tenants of Alfoxden Manor had rubbed off on them. The house in Town End was very different. To Sarah Coleridge it would have been an inn, with decades of candle-grease and tobacco smoke still thick on the walls.[45] There is no record of her spending another night there after Christmas 1800. On their very first visit, in the summer of 1800, she, Coleridge and Hartley had shared the tiny house with Dorothy, Wordsworth and John Wordsworth; at Christmas, John had been replaced by Sara Hutchinson, and Sarah had (in addition) her three-month-old baby Derwent with her.

While never a friend of the Wordsworths, Sarah Coleridge was however pre-pared (in the summer of 1802) to invite them to live in the other half of Greta Hall. That would to her doubtless have seemed appropriate to their new situation, with Wordsworth marrying Mary, and doubtless children to follow. She may also have thought that the change into upmarket accommodation would do them good: while such a move would at least stop Coleridge gallivanting down the fourteen miles to Town End every other day. If that did not suit them, she was happy to assist them in finding accommodation in a house nearby, as they had helped her to find a house. She probably believed that the marriage would at least to some extent conventionalise the Wordsworths, and make them more acceptable neighbours. Mary (and Sara) were not so 'remote' from gentility, after all, as Wordsworth and Dorothy.

But during the years 1801–2, things often seem to have been awkward. When the Wordsworths and Mary Hutchinson stayed overnight at Greta Hall in November 1801, for example, and Dorothy's journal record makes no reference to Sarah Coleridge at all (she was probably over in Eusemere with her children) 'We enjoyed ourselves in the study & were *at home*. Supped at Mr Jacksons. Mary & I sate in C's room a while.'[46] The following morning, 'Poor C left us', and we *know* why he is 'poor'. Dorothy makes the point that it is only in Coleridge's room that they are *at home*: obviously not elsewhere, nor in other ways. Things had been much worse during a visit to Greta Hall for eight days in the spring of 1801, when Coleridge was ill and could not get down to Grasmere. Dorothy then noted how 'We should have stayed longer at Keswick but . . . we are never comfortable there after the first 2 or 3 days'.[47] She wrote Mary Hutchinson a letter about the visit which, during an extremely long description of Coleridge and his illness, ignores Sarah's existence. When she does get round to mentioning Sarah, it is only to show irritation. She starts off cheerfully 'Mrs C. is in excellent health' – but as the letter has been about Coleridge's serious illness, that is almost a reproach. Dorothy goes on: 'She is indeed a bad nurse for C., but she has several great merits'. Dorothy fails, however, to say what those merits are. All she says is that Sarah is 'very much to be pitied, for when one party is ill matched the other necessarily must be so too.'

She then tries once more to describe Sarah's 'merits' but again does nothing but list her faults: 'She would have made a very good wife to many another man, but for Coleridge!! Her radical fault is want of sensibility and what can such a woman be to Coleridge?' Then comes the final put down: Sarah is really good for nothing except breast-feeding the seven-month old Derwent. Dorothy is shocked at how long she spends on it:

> She is an excellent nurse to her sucking children (I mean to the best of her skill, for she employs her time often foolishly enough about them). Derwent is a sweet lovely Fatty – she suckles him entirely – he has no other food. She is to be sure a sad fiddle faddler.[48] From about ½ past 10 on Sunday morning till two she did nothing but wash and dress her 2 children and herself, and was just ready for dinner. No doubt she suckled Derwent pretty often during that time.

The Sunday had been the eighth day of the Wordsworths' stay, and patience was clearly running out. But never did a childless woman reveal more clearly the narrowness of her sympathy. One hopes that Mary – preparing to marry Wordsworth – realised from such a letter what she in turn would have to put up with in Dorothy.[49] What Dorothy was actually most irritated by, perhaps, was the time-wasting; she herself would have done some gardening, walked to Rydale to collect the letters, written letters of her own, and done some copying for Wordsworth, all in the time it takes Sarah to get her children ready for dinner. And, worst of all, Sarah actually seems to *enjoy* breast-feeding!

III

Molly Lefebure's biography of Sarah Coleridge was an attempt to show how Sarah was, in effect, reviled and marginalised by the Wordsworths, and that the dismissive way in which she was treated by almost everyone from 1797 onwards arose from the Wordsworths' attempts to get Coleridge away from her, and from Coleridge's own unprincipled damning of her character. Lefebure sets the situation out very differently: that Sarah Coleridge was a strong-minded, intelligent woman who found herself landed with an opium-riddled and emotionally untrustworthy husband; that Coleridge could not stand her independence and went crying to the Wordsworths about how awful she was: and that they not only accepted this version of her but actually did their best to end the marriage.[50] It comes as a shock to realise that not only is no source given for such a claim, but that no source could be given; there is no evidence to support it.[51] It is, to be sure, extremely hard to see Sarah Coleridge except through the eyes of her husband or of Dorothy Wordsworth; but that is not because we foolishly accept biased evidence. It is because they are the two who left the bulk of the evidence about her. It is certainly right to overturn an unthinking acceptance of all that Dorothy had to say about Sarah Coleridge. She disliked her thoroughly, and hardly ever let slip an opportunity to show it; writing to Mary on 16 April about an exceptionally kind fellow guest at the Patterdale inn, for example, Dorothy commented 'She did more for me than Mrs Coleridge would do for her own sister under like circumstances'.[52] (It is striking how a *sister* is, for Dorothy, the most intimate of all relations.) And it is also true that anyone partnered with – let alone married to – Coleridge would have had a most difficult time: of that there can be no doubt. In daily life he was such an extraordinary mixture of the brilliant and the damaged, the clear-sighted and the self-deceiving, the energetic and the procrastinating. But above all his egotism, or (to put it another way) his inability to deal with the world except as it could minister to his supreme self, made him a frustrating companion. He was, however, the most wonderfully talented man, in so many ways that one is left speechless at his sheer capacity, range and humanity.

We are not however confronting the evidence of good behaviour or bad behaviour on either side. There is nothing wrong with believing polite, kind, well-ordered and cheerful behaviour preferable to unchecked liberty and doing what you want, when you want to. There is nothing wrong with preferring the latter, either. The problem only arises when the differences infiltrate a marriage, and people quarrel about them all the time. We are observing the problems of people who cannot get on together without constantly bringing up their differences, as opposed to those who are able to overcome their differences and not simply become irritable with each other for being unlike themselves. The differences between Sarah Coleridge and Coleridge ended up in their eventual separation; the differences between Sarah and the Wordsworths grew to a point where they made everyday life seriously difficult, after they had only spent a short time together.

The Coleridge marriage effectively foundered on Coleridge's need to be part of the alternative family group, rather than married to Sarah. What relation, then, did Sarah Coleridge have with the Significant (or family) group? For most of their marriage, Sarah Coleridge had no real interest in the Wordsworths (or in the Hutchinsons), though visits could be paid and the habits of friendship maintained. The Coleridges' move to Keswick in the summer of 1800 was fatal for their marriage. Sarah found herself either left out of her husband's intimacy with the Wordsworths, or standing well clear of it: both left her angry and resentful. She had never been inclined to participate in the joint activities which mattered so much to the others. We can see this in a very simple way. Her handwriting never appears on any of the poetry manuscripts which circulated between the rest of the group, in contrast with Mary Hutchinson (both before and after her marriage), Sara Hutchinson and Dorothy. Even Coleridge played his part over *Lyrical Ballads*.

It cannot simply have been devotion to her children that held Sarah back, either from working as a transcriber of manuscripts or as a walking and exploring companion. We know that Dorothy could be an excellent child minder and substitute parent, and that she was happy to play that role for her friends; in Alfoxden, the Wordsworths cared for Basil Montagu's five-year-old son Basil, and in the spring of 1801, while Coleridge was ill, Hartley Coleridge was sent down to live with the Wordsworths for a period while he went to school in Grasmere, though the experiment (significantly) does not seem to have been repeated. When the Wordsworths visited the Coleridges, it was natural for Dorothy to help with the children: on 2 April 1802, for example, she and Wordsworth 'sate all morning in the field I nursed Derwent', and in December 1801 she and Mary Hutchinson had had the children to look after while Sarah Coleridge was out: 'we drank tea by ourselves, the children playing about us'.[53] But the Wordsworths' beliefs about children also conflicted with how Sarah brought her own children up, and probably horrified her. Back in 1796 at Racedown, while looking after Basil Montagu, Dorothy had articulated the Wordsworth system of child care for a five-year-old: 'He is quite metamorphosed from a shivering half starved plant, to a lusty, blooming fearless boy. He dreads neither cold nor rain. He has played frequently an hour or two without appearing sensible that the rain was pouring down upon him or the wind blowing about him.'[54] The Wordsworths' son John, one month old in July 1803, would be 'already very much sunburnt' from being out of doors so much; and when Sarah's daughter Sara stayed with the Wordsworths in 1808, Coleridge would claim that she 'became rosier and hardier' away from her mother (obviously from being outdoors in all weathers). He insisted that his son Derwent, too, became 'more manly and less timid'.[55] The point being made was that children brought up by Sarah Coleridge were softer, gentler, genteeler (and paler).

What mattered more to Sarah Coleridge than the activities of the group –
writing, observation, copying, constant walking and talking – were visits to
(and the companionship of) sensible neighbours, a good house, decent clothes
and the loving upbringing of the children at home (not straggling over the
countryside in the rain). In 1807, even Coleridge himself acknowledged –
among Sarah's 'excellent qualities' – 'attention to her children'. She was not
interested in alternative families and chose to remain outside; but her distance
from the others is also invaluable in helping us understand how very odd they
were.

No one can be an arbiter in a dispute between a husband and a wife
when every piece of existing information about the relationship survives
arbitrarily and – in a sense – inconsequentially. What matters is simply that
we should try and understand the terms of their arguments, and that we
should so far as possible identify what appear to have been the fault lines in
their relationship. We should probably also accept that it is easier to know
things about Coleridge than about Sarah; there is simply more surviving material, so that we are always liable to be biased in seeing things from his point of
view.

Coleridge himself had a near fatal capacity for abstract thinking, and for
losing himself in his own contemplations, to the exclusion of everything else
(responsibility, fairness, devotion, action). As he himself wrote in January 1802,
from London, a month before setting out for Gallow Hill:

> partly from an unhealthy & reverie-like vividness of *Thoughts*, & (pardon the
> pedantry of the phrase) a diminished Impressibility from *Things*, my ideas,
> wishes, & feelings are to a diseased degree disconnected from *motion & action*.
> In plain & natural English, I am a dreaming & therefore an indolent man –. I am
> a Starling self-incaged, & always in the Moult, & my whole Note is, Tomorrow,
> & tomorrow, & tomorrow.[56]

Even such insights are not trustworthy, of course. Coleridge is writing this to a
friend who has every reason to feel annoyed by Coleridge's failure to answer
his letters. After the abstractions of the first sentence – which show how unem-
barrassed he really is by the unhealthiness of the habits he condemns – comes
the wonderful simplicity of the 'natural English' revealing what he *really* is.
Who could be seriously angry with a man who admitted his dreaminess and
laziness so cheerfully?

The last sentence of the quotation in particular shows how Coleridge would
use his capacity for ludicrous self-image to charm his way out of people's
annoyance with him. Not only is the caged starling a lovely image for the
entrapped self – still chirruping furiously – but 'always in the Moult' gives it
just the necessary touch of grotesqueness to inhabit any reaction in his reader
except that of delight. We have to remember that the procrastination actually
meant that he constantly let people down and hurt them, Sarah Coleridge

probably more than anybody. She could not depend upon him: for money, for being there when she wanted him, for the sake of the children. It was not just a matter of Coleridge being wonderfully funny about his failures to be responsible. But, of course, being Coleridge he was able to be perfectly clear about this himself, as he showed in 1814:

> . . . in *exact proportion* to the *importance* and *urgency* of any Duty was it, as of a fatal necessity, sure to be neglected . . . In exact proportion, as I *loved* any person or persons more than others, & would have sacrificed my Life for them, were *they* sure to be the most barbarously mistreated by silence, absence, or breach of promise. —[57]

Even in that, there is a worrying use of the passive voice – as if these things somehow just happened, rather than being behaviour for which he was responsible. By his unhappy mid-thirties however, from 1806 onwards, self-pity made him incapable of sustaining even such insights except in laughter which would also allow him to ignore the very insights he had reached; and he preferred to accuse anyone and everyone ('Cruelly have I been *treated* by almost every one') rather than find himself guilty of anything worse than what he himself called his 'tenderness of Heart', his 'disinterested Enthusiasm for others' and his 'eager Spirit of Self-sacrifice'.[58] That grotesque baulking at insight was, however, still some years away.

All I can point to with certainty from the period 1801–2 is Coleridge's extremely analytical writing about his wife, as about himself. He is less interested in how people actually behave than in finding ways of blaming them for it; while the blaming regularly seems to have replaced the need to *do* anything – about them, or about himself. When faced by the necessities of – for example – earning money, or fulfilling his obligations, or being responsible for the situation of his family, then his pattern was to abstract himself and to operate in a detachment as complete as he could make it: and to blame those who made him feel guilty. This left Sarah Coleridge helpless and angry, but also enabled him to see her as the one who shouted and quarrelled and made his life impossible: the one who upset him so badly that (as a result of her anger) he now *genuinely* could not do anything.[59] Quarrels with her 'incapacitated me for any worthy exertion of my faculties by degrading me in my own estimation. I found my temper injured, and daily more so.'[60]

With this kind of analysis directed at her, no wonder that Sarah felt blamed when she did not feel abandoned: and the fact that the relationship (for whatever reason) had slipped into this pattern of recrimination, anger and self-justification ensured that the situation got worse. The more Sarah felt she was wriggling on the pin of his analysis – as opposed to being warmed by his charm and his sympathy – the angrier she probably was, and the more both she and he would feel unloved. The more he went away and spent time with the Wordsworths, telling himself that he had to do that just to protect himself, the more she would blame them, and resent his going. There were clearly many such vicious circles in their relationship. But what Coleridge was trying to puzzle out also shows his extraordinary capacity for understanding; we should not just dismiss it as a wordy (or opium-riddled) attempt to justify himself.[61]

IV

In our relief at no longer needing to be shocked at an addiction, we are in danger of forgetting some crucial facts about opium. Not until 1824 were withdrawal symptoms comprehended; while the side effects of opium's regular use, and the complex nature of addiction itself, were not understood either.[62] As a result, the sweats, the swelling of limbs, the rise in blood pressure and temperature, the irregularity of the bowels, that followed the use of opium, were often assumed to mark the recurrence or a new development of the disease that the drug had been used to alleviate if not to cure. To the patient there naturally seemed no recourse but to revert again to the drug.[63]

That, in its turn, confirmed the addiction and increased the unpleasantness of the side effects. Coleridge had been taking opium and laudanum irregularly for several years without apparently linking its use with the 'rheumatic disease' from which he had started to suffer. He had fallen into an especially severe and vicious cycle of illness and recovery during the winter of 1800–1, without of course knowing what he was suffering from. If, however, he stopped taking the opium, then he suffered again, even more badly. He and his doctor were baffled; the illnesses went on and on, continually developing new forms. He had 'rheumatic fevers, swollen leg joints, boils, agonising nephritic pains, and a swollen testicle diagnosed as a hydrocele': to this list could be added 'bad eyes, swoln Eyelids', 'pains in the calves of my legs', '*frantic* Itching', and ulcers on the Scrotum.[64] He would find himself suddenly better: and then ill again. 'He is apparently quite well one day, and the next the fit comes on him again with as much violence as ever', Wordsworth noted: 'I am seldom in health three days together', he himself had complained in April 1801.[65] And of course only opium, taken to relieve his sufferings, could alleviate the illness, but – naturally – reinforced the addiction. He finally treated the apparent rheumatism with a new medicine, which he had read about in a medical journal: the so-called 'Kendal Black Drop' – and 'it worked miracles'.[66] He was well within days. This was, however, an especially strong tincture of opium in vegetable acids; so that when it was cut down or withdrawn, the pains and illnesses broke out again in new forms, worse than ever. He described to Tom Poole the 'terrible' pains in his back 'which almost alternated with the stomach fits': and, too, '– The Disgust, the Loathing, that followed these Fits & no doubt in part too the use of the Brandy & Laudanum which they rendered necessary – this Disgust, Despondency, & utter Prostration of Strength, & the strange sensibility to every change in the atmosphere even while in my bed –'[67] Again, in 1803, suffering from 'Bowel & Stomach attacks frequent and alarming', his only solution was 'an Ounce of crude opium, & 9 ounces of Laudanum'.[68] The man writing this has very little idea of addiction: or of side effects: or of withdrawal symptoms. Brandy and laudanum are simply 'necessary'. In 1814, he recalled that as late as 1803 'I yet remained ignorant that the direful sufferings, I so complained of, were the mere effects of Opium'. As he referred in April 1816 to '15 years habit', a date around 1801 for his addiction would seem probably right.[69]

The actual addiction, which has been so poetically written about (it 'combined with his metaphysics to carry him away into clouds of unknowing'[70]) probably mattered rather less to Coleridge, his friends and his family in these early years than the painful and frequently self-hating episodes of depression which accompanied the side effects of the addiction and the withdrawal. Although he suffered 'unsightly swellings of my knees, & dismal affections of my stomach & head' he also knew that what he suffered as 'mere *pain* is almost incredible; but that is a trifle compared with the gloom of my Circumstances'.[71] The massive doses of opium he would take in 1813–14, for example, would be genuinely life-threatening (he was ingesting from 4–5 ounces to 'near a pint' – nearly 20 fluid ounces – of laudanum a day, as well as 'great quantities' of alcohol), and even when under some control (as under the Gillman regime which followed) he was still taking 'four tea-spoonfuls' a day.[72] In the period 1801–2, the addiction was almost the least thing that he suffered. He did have terrible dreams; but he had always had bad dreams. And he could, fortunately, afford to buy the opium, even when using Black Drop, which cost 'eleven shillings for a phial of four ounces'. The ounce of opium and nine ounces of Laudanum mentioned above would cost him 'half a guinea', so about the same.[73] But at least his addiction did not reduce his family to starvation. That may sound small compensation, but is important in a catastrophe of this magnitude.

There is no evidence that his addiction was responsible for his failure to fulfil his intellectual or literary potential, or for the various catastrophes of his life (the loss of so many friendships and so much good will over the years: the break-up of his marriage: the fact that he lost touch with his children). These disasters were all under way before he became addicted, and continued down to the 1820s, when his addiction was at least under a kind of control. Opium was not to blame for his procrastination, though it first dulled the pain of guilt, and then sharpened the accusations of self-indulgence which increased the guilt ten-fold: 'It is not my bodily Pain – but the gloom & distresses of those around me for whom I ought to be labouring & cannot. –'[74] He would write into his notebook the following year, as again he linked the failure with the pain: 'This is Oct. 19. 1803. Wed. Morn. tomorrow my Birth Day, 31 years of age! – O me! my very heart dies! – This year has been one painful Dream/I have done nothing! – ' In 1832 he would describe opium as the 'Poison, which for more than 30 years has been the guilt, debasement and misery of my Existence.'[75]

The physical consequences and side effects of the addiction, and of his various attempts to free himself of the habit, were, however, very serious. He suffered from the kind of ill health for the rest of his life which was the direct consequence of (on the one hand) addiction and (on the other) withdrawal from the opium habit; in particular he suffered from constant stomach trouble. (He would leave instructions in 1834 for an autopsy which would show the world what he had been suffering from: it showed almost nothing except a dreadfully enlarged heart.) At times his crippling ill health reduced him to a pitiful condition, as in the spring of 1801: 'He was sitting in the parlour, and looked dreadfully pale and weak. He was very, very unwell . . . ill all over, back, and stomach and limbs and so weak as that he changed colour whenever he exerted himself . . . he was never quite well for more than an hour together during the whole time we were there . . .'[76] At other times it was simply sufficiently bad to come between him and the determination he needed, to do what he wanted. From 1801, Coleridge was a chronic invalid who was at times perfectly well. For a long time, he could not know what had happened to his health, though his experiences during the winter of 1800 and the spring and summer of 1801 seem by 1802 to have led to his discovery of some kind of uneasy equilibrium in how much opium he took, and how much he cut back, so that at least he was not confined to bed half the time. He doubtless became an expert on draught and dosage; Dorothy would refer to him as 'our physician Coleridge'. By 1816, and probably a good deal earlier, he could be precise about what his body required: 'No sixty hours have yet passed without my having taking [taken?] Laudanum'.[77]

The moral consequences of addiction to someone as self-reflective and intelligent as Coleridge – guilt, fears of hypochondria, self-blame, depression – were, anyway, as bad as or worse than the physical consequences of withdrawal. He wrote in July 1801 how 'nausea & giddiness are far worse than pain – for they insult & threaten the steadiness of our moral Being – & there is one thing yet more deplorable than these – it is the direful Thought of being inactive & useless.'[78] He was an expert on the links between the mind and the body: he knew his own capacity for self-reproach, and the fact that he would also repress it – but he also became aware of how repression took a physical toll. He noticed how, the more he forced away his attention 'from any inward distress, the worse it becomes after – and what I keep out of my mind or rather *keep down* in a state of under-consciousness, is sure to act meanwhile with its whole power of poison on my Body.'[79] He knew that his depressing idea of himself as someone hopelessly weak-willed and useless was very damaging. It could be turned to comedy; but the comic self-revelation was likely, in its turn, to become yet another self-lacerating evasion of reality. His self-respect was, as a consequence, fatally damaged; and the kinds of self-belief which were going to be crucial to someone whose talents did not exactly fit any profession or employment, but who needed to make his own kind of career, were pulverised by depression, guilt and self-disgust.

Because of his opium habit, in almost every way tendencies already latent in Coleridge were encouraged, and potential catastrophes enacted. He became more trapped within abstract thought, more selfish, more detached, more emotionally needy (and greedy) as a consequence of what he undoubtedly suffered, physically and in terms of guilt, depression and self-blame; less able to cope, less able to concentrate, more likely to live by his wits than by his talents. His intelligence was quite undamaged; but his abilities to cope with the consequences of being intelligent were very badly damaged.

His capacity for the searching and awkward analysis of the feelings of others, too, was – at least in 1802 – matched by his ability to be horribly honest about himself. This is what makes these early analyses of himself interesting rather than self-indulgent. The verse *Letter* which he would write in the spring of 1802 suggests, for example, how he sometimes felt about the very children whom he told himself he loved so dearly, and who usually seemed one of the saving graces of his existence:

> Those little Angel children (woe is me!)
> There have been hours, when feeling how they bind
> And pluck out the wing-feathers of my mind,
> 280   Turning my Error to Necessity,
> I have half-wished, they never had been born,
> THAT – *seldom*; but sad Thought they always bring . . .[80]

It cannot have been so seldom, or so fragmentary a half-wish, if he articulated it in a poem centred on his crucial relationships (he would repeat it, almost word for word, four years later.[81]) The children damaged Coleridge, he felt, because his worries about supporting them, and caring for them, meant that he could neither think nor act as he wanted to. In effect, the children plucked the feathers which would have allowed his mind to soar.[82] There is no point in disputing whether this might be true (though it certainly sounds like the identification of yet another set of beings to blame for his depression). The point is that Coleridge felt at times quite unreasonably angry with his children, and with the fact that he had conceived them; and, quite unfairly, he blamed them for the way his life and intellectual career had gone. His original 'Error' of marrying had turned into the 'Necessity' of supporting the family he had created.

Such resentment is, of course, perfectly compatible with loving his children, as he certainly did. But loving to play with them and to stir them up to mischief and wildness, loving to be with them as a child himself – which the record shows him doing[83] – was not incompatible with a desire to put them out of his mind whenever he wished, so that he could retreat to his study and do the reading he wanted to do, and (ideally) the writing he knew he ought to be doing. (He explicitly wanted a house with 'a Study out [of] the noise of Women & children', and found it in Greta Hall.[84]) There are complex elements of blame at work here; self-criticism for having been attracted to his wife, and self-blame for sleeping with her, matched by unreasoning anger that she should have attracted him, conceived children, and thus damaged him and his future so irretrievably. He preferred to regard her childbearing as something autonomous: 'I have too much reason to suspect that she is breeding again / an event, which was to have been deprecated',[85] he would remark coolly in 1802.

Coleridge's thinking about children impinges on a great deal of the writing which both he and Wordsworth would do this spring, and operates as a kind of constant sub-text to Dorothy Wordsworth's own feelings about her brother's impending marriage. Wordsworth too wanted children, and there is glee in Coleridge's mention to his brother-in-law of Wordsworth's return to Grasmere after his marriage as *'one of us'*.[86] From Dorothy's point of view, it would however be as *one of them*: her brother clearly wanted a wife and children more than he wanted *her*. As I suggested above, Dorothy had a lot in common with Coleridge, especially in the winter and spring 1801–2. Their dependence on Wordsworth meant that their lives were enormously enriched, whilst they also both felt let down by his need for Mary. Dorothy managed to overcame this feeling, intelligently and loyally and heroically; it is less clear that Coleridge did. One way of thinking about his long-drawn-out fantasy about Sara Hutchinson is not just to see it as a determined parallel to his friend's courtship of and marriage to her sister Mary, but as a way of getting an unmarried sister for himself. Perhaps significantly, it had been just a week before he left for Yorkshire at the end of February 1802 that he had heard the news that Wordsworth would be marrying Mary some time that year: the news came almost simultaneously with the 'heart-wringing' letter from Sara.

It is hard to know what he thought would result from his March 1802 visit to Gallow Hill. He could congratulate Mary on her forthcoming marriage, and could apologise to Sara for having made her so miserable, before making his inevitable return to the obligations, constraints and passions of Greta Hall. He may well have hoped (men do) that Sara would turn out to love him after all, and that that would solve all his problems. But if, as seems likely, she was still upset, even ill in bed, because of what he had written to her, then (as he would put it in his *Letter*) he would simply want to 'sit beside thy Bed' and 'press thy aking Head' and 'bring thee Health again—/ (At least to hope, to try)'.[87] And he would be able to fantasise about what life would have been like if – like Wordsworth – he had been partnered by a Hutchinson sister. Going to see the Hutchinsons, too, meant that he could postpone the realities of home for another fortnight.

On 2 March 1802 Coleridge arrived at Gallow Hill.

Chapter Four

Hutchinsons: 11 and 12 March

What has been of primary fascination to biography, however, is not Coleridge's guilt about a miserable Sara Hutchinson, but his passionate love for her. 'If they were ever to have become lovers, it would surely have been now' says Richard Holmes, about Gallow Hill in March 1802.[1] What had happened between them up to this point?

Coleridge had first met Sara in the autumn of 1799. The Wordsworths had been living for six months at Sockburn on Tees in County Durham with their old friends the Hutchinsons, whom they had known since childhood (the Hutchinson sisters and brothers – like the Wordsworths, orphaned early – were about to separate to live on the rented farms they were occupying in 1802); and in late October 1799 Coleridge arrived with the publisher Cottle. They only stayed one night, and the next day Coleridge and Wordsworth travelled across to Grasmere, as I described above;[2] but something about that first visit to Sockburn – which may have been no more than the extreme warmth and friendliness of the family, and the convenient closeness of the house to the coaching route – made Coleridge go back within a month. He may have been attracted to Sara, but there is no evidence for it; we cannot even be sure that Sara was there in October 1799,[3] and – anyway – the person Coleridge particularly remembered from this first visit was Mary. (He addressed her, but not Sara, in the letter he sent to Sockburn around 10 November 1799, during the visit to Grasmere.) Four years later, thinking of his first visit to Sockburn, he wrote 'O dear Mary never shall I forget your manners.'[4]

Anyway; he went back to Sockburn (this time without Wordsworth) late in November 1799, and while there or shortly afterwards made the following entries in his notebook:

Print of the Blackwall Ox, of Darlington – so spot-sprigged / Print, how interesting – viewed in all moods, unconsciously distinctly, semiconsciously, with vacant, with swimming eyes – a thing of nature thro' the perpetual action of the Feelings! – O God! when I now think how perishable Things, how imperishable Ideas – what a proof of My Immortality – What is Forgetfulness? –

May not Time in Association be made <u>serviceable</u> & evidence Likeness/.

The long Entrancement of a True-love's Kiss.[5]

The point about the print appears to be how the extremely artificial and *un*natural Ox becomes oddly *natural* in recollection, because of the way it is altered by the feelings of those who look at it: and how imperishable feelings are, in contrast with an extremely perishable print (foxed all over). The next entry relates to the same point about 'Time in Association'; the third entry is a bit of confirmatory evidence – a kiss may be momentary but its *entrancement* (in memory) will last far longer.

In 1803, Coleridge went back to these records of the events of 1799 and recreated them in a new notebook entry; they now appeared very differently.

> Print of the Darlington Ox, sprigged with Spots. – Viewed in all moods, consciously, uncons. semiconsc. – with vacant, with swimming eyes – made a Thing of Nature by the repeated action of the Feelings. O Heaven when I think how perishable Things, how imperishable Thoughts seem to be! – For what is Forgetfulness? ++ Renew the state of affection or bodily Feeling, same or similar – sometimes dimly similar/ and instantly the trains of forgotten Thought rise from their living catacombs! – Old men, & Infancy/and Opium, probably by its narcotic effect on the whole seminal organization, in a large Dose, or after long use, produces the same effect on the visual, & passive memory/. ++ so far was written in my b. pocket [book] Nov. 25th 1799 – Monday Afternoon, the Sun shining in upon the Print, in beautiful Lights – & I just about to take Leave of Mary – & having just before taken leave of Sara. – I did not then know Mary's & William's attachment/ The lingering Bliss, The long entrancement of a True-love Kiss.
>
> Nov. 24th – the Sunday – Conundrums & Puns & Stories & Laughter – with Jack Hutchinson – Stood up round the Fire, et Sarae manum a tergo longum in tempus prensabam, and tunc temporis, tunc primum, amor me levi spiculo, venenato, eheu! & insanabili, &c.[6]

That last, completely new entry recreated events he remembered of the previous evening in company with the eldest Hutchinson brother. The Latin was to protect the entry against his wife's understanding it; they were still living together in 1803.

The Ox print is now triggering off memories of his meeting with the two women. In a wonderful phrase, he describes how 'trains of forgotten Thought' can 'rise from their living catacombs!'[7] He also emphasises the dates, as he always tended to do with days he saw as turning points. It is of course quite unclear whether the kiss mentioned here is being linked with Sara, or Mary, or was (now) itself now a re-working of a phrase appearing in his own poem 'The Keepsake' which he had finished in September 1802 ('the entrancement of that maiden kiss'[8]), or whether it was simply a repetition of the original idea of the imperishable enshrined in the transitory.

The fact, however, that both Coleridge and we read these entries knowing that he loved Sara Hutchinson changes them completely. We read them for the evidence of his love; and when he re-read them in 1803, he re-wrote them in the knowledge that he was devoted to her. It seems likely that the much less explicit 1799 entries were adapted to this new knowledge: the undramatic past gently manipulated into epiphanic and symbolic significance. The new pieces of recollection – the events round the fire side, the pressing of the hand – do not have the significance of the actual entries from 1799: not because Coleridge was a liar or had a bad memory, but because he so badly needed in 1803 to make sense, to himself, of the things which had been happening to him over the last couple of years. The same is even more true of a note he made in the period 1808–10, when (perhaps significantly) he recalled a different first crucial moment with Sara: 'Whether from that morning on which I sate beside you on the Sopha in the Drawing Room at Sockburn, I have not manifestly <u>loved</u> you – whether <u>you</u> have seen or known any wavering <u>in</u> <u>my</u> <u>reverence</u> of <u>you</u> . . .'[9] From 1802 onwards, he clung to his love for Sara Hutchinson as the most important thing in his life;[10] and he went on re-creating (and adding epiphanic significance to) its crucial moments. His actual feelings in 1799 are therefore especially important.

Biographers and scholars however assume that the 1803 notebook versions are authentic accounts of 1799. Griggs, discussing November 1799, calls the 1803 entry 'A notebook entry of that date'; Holmes ascribes to Coleridge's memory of standing round the fire 'all the accidental quality of truth', and refers to Coleridge on his return visit in November 'in an oasis of happiness, flirting with everyone'.[11] Nothing in the 1799 entries could lead to such a conclusion. I suggest that what we have to do, here as elsewhere, is to try to keep distinct actual events (so far as we know them) from the overlays of interpretation (especially Coleridge's own interpretation) which affect how we read them.

The fact that Coleridge actually saw nothing of Mary Hutchinson for the next seven months, and nothing of Sara for nearly a year, strongly suggests that although he may have found both attractive (and not forgetting the sofa-sitting, the hand-taking and – four years after the event – deciding that this was the moment when he had been pricked with love's dart), he had no idea of an attachment either to Mary or to Sara. The one poem he wrote at this stage which might be thought to have some link with the Hutchinsons – his 'Introduction to the Tale of the Dark Ladie' – is by no means a love poem to Sara, although it has a Sockburn background and setting. There is a nice image of a woman, in Coleridge's best cod-Medieval style, next to a recumbent statue in Sockburn church:

> She lean'd against a grey stone rudely carv'd,
> The statue of an arméd Knight:
> 15   She lean'd in melancholy mood
> Amid the lingering light.[12]

The narrator tells his 'Genevieve' the story of a knight who rescues a lady but goes mad; this moves her to tears and she embraces him:

> I saw her bosom heave and swell,
>   Heave and swell with inward sighs –
> I could not choose but love to see
>   Her gentle bosom rise.[13]

And so he wins her heart, and her, and marries her. But although it has been assumed that the poem is a declaration of love to Sara,[14] there is no evidence for this. It is a poem which haunted its generation (Keats wrote *La Belle Dame Sans Merci* because of it), but I can imagine Sara reading it and no more identifying herself with the woman in it than she would have identified the finely sculpted fourteenth-century carving in Sockburn church with the poem's 'rudely carv'd' stone. The real-life Sara Hutchinson – 'a little over five feet in height, rather plain-featured', with 'a delicately fair skin and a profusion of light brown hair' – sounds in her surviving letters far too down-to-earth a woman to have thought much of embraces in a ruined church at twilight, offered by a man telling stories of going mad.

The biographical attempt to create a sequence of 'Asra poems' which Coleridge is supposed to have been writing to Sara from 1799 onwards has led to some extensive misdating (and over-interpretation) of individual poems.[15] Not until 1802 did Coleridge start to write poems addressing Sara Hutchinson directly, and attempts to find such poems written earlier than that are doomed to failure.[16] Again, a crucial notebook entry of March or April 1800 may be connected either with Sarah Coleridge or with Sara Hutchinson: it runs 'Mr Coleridge A little of Sara's Hair in this pocket'.[17] Biographers assume that it refers to a romantic 'keepsake' of auburn hair appearing in the poem 'The Picture' which Coleridge would write eighteen months later.[18] The entry appears however to record someone drawing Coleridge's attention to what was in the pocket, not to a 'keepsake'; and neither Sarah Coleridge nor any servant in Somerset would have known Sara Hutchinson's name, let alone what her hair was like, at that date (Sarah would meet her for the first time in November 1800). The entry simply cannot be interpreted as biographers wish to.[19] The lack of evidence of any relationship between Coleridge and Sara Hutchinson at this stage – the lack of any certain reference to her in Coleridge's notebooks, for example, or in his surviving correspondence – should probably lead to the conclusion that although he found her attractive, he was not in love with her. Biographers who scent romance, however, will not be put off by a simple lack of evidence: references to the crucial role of Sara Hutchinson in Coleridge's life appear everywhere.[20]

II

We need to put Coleridge's relationship with the Hutchinson family beside Wordsworth's. By 1799, Wordsworth had known Mary (and probably Sara) for twelve years. Dorothy Wordsworth had been at school with the Hutchinson sisters, and when she came to Penrith in 1787 she renewed her friendship with them: they were living with their grandfather because, like the Wordsworths, their parents had died when they were children. Like the Wordsworths, too, they had almost no income beside what they earned. When Wordsworth came over to see her, he too met the Hutchinsons. Biographers following *The Prelude* of 1805 – with its reference to 'the blessèd time of early love' – have dated his 'love for Mary' as early as 1787,[21] but there is no sign of his having any desire to marry her, or any passion for her, for a long time afterwards. The actual events of 1787 also seem to have very far from 'blessèd' except in recollection.[22] Mary, to judge by reports dating from a good deal later, was 'neither handsome nor even comely' – she was 'a tallish young woman', all her life thin, certain, dedicated: 'the pläinest woman in these parts, – for aw the warld the bettermer part of an auld farm-body'. But she was distinguished by 'sweetness all but angelic' and 'sunny benignity'.[23] It has been suggested that when Wordsworth wrote his poem 'Beauty and Moonlight' he was thinking of her,[24] but this is the usual attempt by biographers to manufacture material where none exists.

The Wordsworths went on seeing the Hutchinsons at intervals. In 1796–7 Mary had come to stay with Wordsworth and Dorothy in Racedown for seven months, and years later, Wordsworth let himself fantasise about how things might then have developed

> ... if you had but taken the road through Bristol when you left Racedown; in which case I should certainly have accompanied you as far as Bristol; or further, perhaps: and then I thought ... you would have walked on Northwards with me at your side, till unable to part from each other ... I fancied that we should have seen so deeply into each others hearts, and been so fondly locked in each others arms, that we should have braved the worst and parted no more.[25]

The phrase 'seen so deeply into each others hearts' tells us, perhaps, rather more than 'braved the worst' or the pleasant fantasy. They had, after all, been living in the same house for seven months when Mary made her journey northwards. Why would a shared journey have made such a difference, except that Dorothy would no longer be acting as chaperone? Neither of them had any money on which they could support the other or a family, and they would both have felt that this was sufficient reason not to marry; the early summer of 1797 showed Wordsworth that he was actually in the middle of a financial crisis.[26] But they were also both far more likely to bury their feelings than to express them. It is striking that when Coleridge – Wordsworth's closest friend – first met Mary in October 1799, he had no idea of Wordsworth's particular attachment to her. This suggests that it is possible that Wordsworth barely did, either. If Wordsworth and Mary had really been able to see 'deeply into each others hearts' in 1797, then they might have 'braved the worst'. But the fact is that they did not; and probably could not.

When the Wordsworths came back from Germany in the summer of 1799, they had nowhere to go, and it was natural that the Hutchinsons (now all living together near Sockburn) should offer them the same hospitality which the Wordsworths had showed Mary two years earlier. The difference this time was that, after a few months, Wordsworth would set out to find a house where he and Dorothy could settle; and it seems possible (in the characteristic inching forward manner in which he and Mary conducted their relationship) that he may well have done so hoping that – *if* he and Mary married – then this would be the house to which they would come. And, as I showed above, as soon as they were settled in Grasmere, reciprocal visits from the Hutchinson sisters started. Only then, perhaps, did Mary and Wordsworth actually start to express (as opposed to feel) 'early love'. But it was not until this period of visits by the Hutchinson sisters – Mary between February and April 1800, Sara between November 1800 and March 1801, Mary from October 1801 to January 1802 – that Coleridge began to see very much of them. The road from Durham or Yorkshire naturally took them first to Penrith, where an aunt lived,[27] and from there it was a convenient journey to Keswick; visits to Grasmere via Greta Hall became common as soon as the Coleridges had moved in. Mary, for example, stayed at Greta Hall for two weeks before Coleridge walked her down to Grasmere on 6 November 1801;[28] Sara stayed at Keswick in November 1800, on her way to Grasmere, and subsequently went back to stay there at least once; and she would do the same in January 1803, at the end of a visit to Grasmere.[29] She thus began to see a good deal more of Coleridge: we know for example that while Coleridge was ill, one afternoon in the early spring of 1801, he spent some time reading out part of the Introduction to Bartram's *Travels* to her, 'when William & Dorothy had gone out to walk';[30] this was almost certainly in Keswick.

It was during this period, too, that Coleridge seems to have played a leading part in initiating that series of outdoor memorials to people in the group, in which the Wordsworths and he participated during the rest of their time in Grasmere.[31] It is possible that Coleridge found that he was falling in love with Sara: the (alas) envenomed scratch at last becoming a poisoned wound. On the other hand, he very well may not; such projects as the start on Sara's seat in April 1801 and its completion in October 1801 were joint ventures with the Wordsworths, not demonstrations of love.

Biographers and critics, however, are determined to seize on a date for Coleridge falling in love, as if such a thing must have been triggered by a particular (if now irrecoverable) event. Griggs asserts that it was in the winter of 1800–1 and Dekker goes along with him;[32] Whalley prefers the autumn of 1799; Chambers contends that the summer of 1801 was the most likely time, while Ruoff regards 1800–1 as 'the time . . . of the early, and apparently happiest, days of his love for Sara Hutchinson'.[33] Holmes gives the title 'Lover' to the chapter in which he charts Coleridge's life in 1801 but also refers to the winter of 1800–1 in Grasmere as the time when 'the good-humoured flirtations of Sockburn changed into something far more intimate and serious';[34] Lefebure plumps for 'the spring of 1801' for the time when his feelings 'were suddenly changed into hopeless infatuation; "the abrupt creation of a moment"'.[35] Parrish prefers a scatter-gun approach and suggests that Coleridge was 'wounded . . . by love's poisoned and incurable sting' in 1799 (thus accepting the 1803 notebook entry as true of 1799, and agreeing with Whalley), opines that 'the love took firm hold during Sara's winter stay . . . 1800–1' (thus agreeing with Griggs, Dekker, Holmes and Lefebure), while remarking that 'the love' became serious during 'Coleridge's visit to her family in the summer of 1801' (thus agreeing with Chambers).[36]

Not one of these commentators has, of course, any evidence for the date assigned. They depend upon hypothetical dates assigned to poems hypothesised to be written to Sara.

Coleridge was however ill a great deal in the spring of 1801, which is probably why Sara went to stay with the Coleridges in Keswick for a while (she could help with the children). Dorothy remembered how, on the visit which she and Wordsworth paid just after Sara left, Coleridge 'was sitting in the parlour, and looked dreadfully pale and weak. He was very, very unwell in the way that Sara can describe to you – ill all over, back, and stomach and limbs and so weak as that he changed colour whenever he exerted himself at all.'[37] This illness of the spring of 1801 showed Coleridge deep into the side effects and the withdrawal symptoms of opium addiction: 'Swoln Knees, & knotty Fingers, a loathy Stomach, & a dizzy head.'[38] Sara Hutchinson was obviously welcome at Greta Hall; Sarah Coleridge had no reason to be suspicious or jealous of her, and may well have preferred her to the Wordsworths, especially Dorothy, as a visitor. Coleridge must, incidentally, have felt himself particularly unattractive in such a state of health; he was certainly 'at times an object of moral Disgust to my own Mind'.[39]

In July 1801, Wordsworth insisted that Coleridge's illnesses meant that 'he has been confined to his *bed* one may say, the half of the last ten months: this has rendered it impossible for him to earn anything'.[40] The consequences of his illnesses were even more dramatic than that: although it was predictable that Dorothy Wordsworth would see Sarah Coleridge as 'indeed a bad nurse for C.',[41] illness and its treatment very often clarify and sharpen the attitudes of partners to each other. And the Coleridges' real marital troubles seem to have started in the spring and summer of 1801: but not apparently because of Sara Hutchinson. The surviving record shows that Coleridge's problems with his marriage came first, and the development of his feelings for Sara Hutchinson either in consequence, or some time afterwards.

There is, too, not a single piece of evidence that at this stage (or at any other) Coleridge contemplated an affair with Sara: not with her, not with anybody. He found Sara – or, more exactly, Sara and Mary – wonderfully sisterly and mothering, but also found himself thoroughly *safe* with them too. Mary was (he now knew) deeply attached to Wordsworth; and Sara was a thoroughly level-headed woman (unlike – the interior monologue might have gone – his wife), but also very entertaining; quick witted, vivacious, full of those animal spirits in which he found his wife so lacking (but then Sara had not had three children); intelligent, unintellectual. And although she had no children, she was very happy *with* children. He had seen her with the children of her brother Jack at Sockburn in 1799, and it is probably not an accident that the first three scraps of correspondence with her to survive are wholly about the sayings and doings of Hartley and Derwent, while the fully surviving letters to her from 1802 also all have long passages about the children in them.[42] His verse *Letter* would characterise her as 'nested with the Darlings of her Love'.[43]

A development which may have been significant took place in the summer of 1801. Having been laid up for months, Coleridge achieved some kind of balance between overdosing on opium and cutting back too severely on it; as a result he suddenly felt well again. For some time he had wanted to consult books (especially Duns Scotus) in Durham Cathedral Library: George Hutchinson's farm at Bishop Middleham was only eight miles south of Durham, and Sara Hutchinson was currently there. How far that last fact encouraged Coleridge to go, and how far it was simply an incidental bonus, we cannot tell. He went over to Bishop Middleham for the second half of July 1801; he then remarked about Sara, in a letter, 'the woman is so very good a woman, that I have seldom indeed seen the like of her'.[44] It sounds almost as if he were appreciating her for the first time, suggesting that she had *not* been the real reason for his visit. On the other hand, he was writing to his wife's brother-in-law, and would have had to be discreet if he had really been attracted to Sara.[45] He was not yet completely well, however: he still had inflamed joints, and boils, and consulted a doctor who recommended 'horse-exercises and warm sea-bathing'. Coleridge followed the advice exactly: he saw himself this summer as 'rambling after Health, or at least alleviation of Sickness',[46] and probably thought this a convenient excuse for extending a library visit to more than a month away from home. He 'took the opportunity of riding with Sara Hutchinson to her brother Tom's house: Gallow Hill was some sixty miles away, two days ride. The journey has been presented as being made with Sara 'together on horseback'.[47] This is unlikely; two horses would have been the only sensible way for two people to have made such a journey, unless they took turns in walking and riding. At Gallow Hill (where they arrived on 31 July) Coleridge stayed for the first nine days of August. We know almost nothing about what happened there: I shall discuss the little we do know at the start of the next section. The only poems which recreate Coleridge in Yorkshire this August are the cheerful but, as Holmes points out, essentially formal poem 'On Re-Visiting the Sea-Shore', about sea-bathing, and another splendid *jeu d'esprit* verse letter written to Joanna Hutchinson and a friend of hers after he had returned to Bishop Middleham, where he stayed until the last week of August. Sara Hutchinson however helped him by copying out a very long extract from St Thomas Aquinas into his notebook, from one of the books he had borrowed from the Durham library.[48]

After the prolonged illnesses of the spring, it had obviously been a cheerful summer, though his joints remained bad (he even underwent a day's immersion in sulphur baths on returning from Gallow Hill: 'And then I *did* smell – aye, I smelt, by old Davy, / Like a Pole Cat serv'd up in an addle-egg gravy'[49]); but the length of time he had spent away from home was perhaps the most significant fact. And – again – he had done almost nothing (there had been only one book by Scotus in the library). He also timed his return home to coincide with a visit to Keswick from Southey and his wife Edith. It looks as if he was doing his best to spend as little time as possible alone with Sarah; what he told himself he wanted was 'deep tranquillity':[50] exactly what he could not get at home. Perhaps significantly, he wrote out the long analysis of Sarah discussed above almost immediately after getting back from Bishop Middleham: it looks like a response to being back with her (and with her sister).[51]

By the time he left Keswick again, in November, the truth could not be flinched from. 'If my wife loved me, and I my wife, half as well as we both love our children, I should be the happiest man alive – but this is not – will not be! –'[52] But even that puts too cheerful a complexion on things. By the time he left for London, he was going through some kind of crisis, and was extremely unwell again. Dorothy Wordsworth was in a state of very great anxiety; she was always concerned about him, but nowhere else was she more worried:

> Poor C left us ... every sight & every sound reminded me of him dear dear fellow – of his many walks to us by day & by night – of all dear things. I was melancholy and could not talk, but at last I eased my heart by weeping – nervous blubbering says William. It is not so – O how many, many reasons have I to be anxious for him.[53]

The addiction was now a constant presence, with its attendant joint and bowel and digestion problems – but not the only problem. He seems now to have been deeply depressed.

In the almost total absence of documentary evidence, we cannot assign feelings to dates; but it is possible that what for Coleridge – even as late as July 1801 – had been no more than a warm attraction to Sara Hutchinson was becoming, by the winter of that year, more serious; not because *she* was feeling differently, but because *he* was. He did not see her between the end of August 1801 and the start of March 1802, but entries in his notebook addressed to an otherwise unknown 'you' and 'her' suggest that it was Sara who was now on his mind: 'By thinking of different parts of her Dress I can at times recall her face – but not so vividly as when it comes of itself – & therefore I have ceased to try it.' And, 'As I have been falling to sleep, the Thought of you has come upon so strongly, that I have opened my eyes as if to look at you –'[54] The fact that in September 1801 he asked Daniel Stuart to send Sara (a 'very dear Friend') the *Morning Post* for the period while his work was appearing there is probably less significant than the fact that he couched his request as stemming as much from Wordsworth as from himself. There is some covering of tracks here.[55]

And yet it is still hard to judge how important such feelings were, in the context of all the problems of his life. His marriage increasingly filled him with anxiety and despair, his frequent illnesses made him desperate, and Sara Hutchinson may well have found herself thrust in (to start with) as the answer to his problems, only (in the end) to be yet another cause of them. Whereas she seems originally to have occupied the role of the beloved sister, with whom he could enjoy both tenderness and flirtation, by February 1802 he was sure he needed her badly, primarily I suspect because she apparently offered him the rest, warmth and contentment (the 'tranquillity') he so much desired. To judge however by her 'heart-wringing' letter of 21 February 1802, this development seems to have horrified her rather than delighted her; there is nothing in the surviving record to suggest that she actually responded to him in any way at all.[56]

Coleridge biography however always makes a good deal of what is believed to be an incident (or series of incidents) which occurred (or may have occurred) at Gallow Hill during the August 1801 visit. The fact that we are so uncertain shows how tenuous our biographical grasp is on these things: our ignorance is why the so-called 'Asra poems' have to be pressed into service for a potential insight into the 'moments of erotic paradise' which Coleridge experienced: 'It was only in the Asra poems that he was able to record directly the secret paradise of Gallow Hill'.[57] Holmes refers to 'a number of rapturous incidents' which took place there. Whalley however believes that the first 'incident' took place at Town End, and only 'the second incident' at Gallow Hill, as late as March 1802.[58]

But nothing is 'recorded' (serious word) in those poems; and language which discusses or describes 'incident' is misleading. The only evidence comes from two of Coleridge's notebook entries (one made in 1801, one in 1810) and from three poems: 'A Day Dream', 'The Day-Dream' and the *Letter*.[59] If we view these passages dispassionately, they look very unlike a record of 'incidents' indeed.

In the 1801 notebook entry (which Coleridge probably inserted between 15 and 18 September, about five weeks after leaving Gallow Hill), there is a description of firelight or candlelight – or of darkness and then light – in a room, and of a couch or sofa: the narrator is intensely aware of a woman beside him or (perhaps) lying on him, and it is the extraordinary awareness which is the point. Even in darkness, the narrator can still *see* the woman's face. The entry starts enigmatically; it is not clear what or who was pressed to 'my bosom'.

Prest to my bosom & felt there – it was quite dark. I looked intensely toward her face – & sometimes I <u>saw</u> it – so vivid was the spectrum, that it had almost all its natural sense of <u>distance</u> & <u>outness</u> – except indeed that, feeling & all, I felt her as <u>part</u> of my being – twas all spectral – But when I could not absolutely <u>see</u> her, no effort of fancy could bring out even the least resemblance of her face. – ⟨sopha⟩ Lazy Bed – Green [?marone/marine] – the fits of L & D from the Candle going out in the Socket. – Power of association – that last Image how lovely to me now –[60]

Nowhere, of course, is there any indication of who the woman is, or where Coleridge might have had this experience, but Gallow Hill is obviously possible, as is George Hutchinson's house near Durham, if indeed it was Sara of whom Coleridge was thinking (it might just as well be Mary).[61] The last phrase ('how lovely to me now') suggests an experience some time back, only recently valued properly. To turn this into an 'incident' as Holmes does – for example, 'lying on the sofa in the kitchen in the firelight, with Asra's body pressing a "brooding warmth" against his breast'[62] – is to recompose it completely.

The next passage, from the poem 'The Day-Dream' (published in October 1802 and probably written that year) does the opposite, by stressing how much the narrator can actually *see*:

> My Mouth half-open like a witless Man,
> I saw the Couch, I saw the quiet Room,
> The heaving Shadows & the fire-light Gloom . . .
> Across my chest there liv'd a weight so warm
> As if some bird had taken shelter there;
> And lo! upon the Couch a Woman's Form!
> Thine, Sara! thine! . . .[63]

This shows that Sara – on the couch – is *not* the same 'weight so warm' which the narrator feels across his chest. On the other hand, this is poetry, not reportage; we are aware of desires, and a moment's vivid awareness, but not of events.

In the next passage, from 'A Day Dream',[64] the feeling of weight is repeated, but the crucial difference is that three people, not two, are involved.

> For dearly, Asra! love I thee!
> This brooding warmth across my breast,
> This depth of tranquil bliss – ah, me!
> Fount, tree and shed are gone, I know not whither,
> But in one quiet room we three are still together.
>
> The shadows dance upon the wall,
> By the still dancing fire-flames made;

And now they slumber, moveless all!
And now they melt to one deep shade!
But not from me shall this mild darkness steal thee:
I dream thee with mine eyes, and at my heart I feel thee![65]

The elements of fantasy seem far more powerful than those of memory: the crucial presence is *dreamt*, not remembered. Magnuson, nonetheless, refers to 'an evening with Mary and Sara described in "A Day Dream" '.[66] Yet there never *was* a time (before December 1802) when Coleridge, Mary, Sara, Wordsworth and Dorothy were together, as they are about to be in this poem: 'Our sister and our friend will both be here tomorrow'.[67] Coleridge clearly delighted in *making* such conjunctions for the group. Another appears in his notebook from March-April 1802 as 'Poem on this night on Helvellin / William & Dorothy & Mary / – Sara & I –', which may well be 'A Day Dream' transferred to another setting.[68]

The fourth passage, from the *Letter*, reproduces elements of the same setting, but with many differences. There is no lying *across* the breast this time, no weight: the narrator, by contrast, is himself at rest supported by the woman. The man's head is in one woman's lap while the other woman's eyelashes brush his cheek: and this time, the eroticism is transformed into extraordinary tranquillity.

It was as calm as this, – the happy Night
100   When Mary, Thou and I, together were,
The low-decaying Fire our only Light,
And listen'd to the stillness of the Air!
O that affectionate and blameless Maid,
Dear Mary! – on her Lap my Head she lay'd –
105   Her Hand was on my Brow
          Even as my own is now;
And on my Cheek I felt thy Eye-lash play –[69]

Whatever is being created here, it bears very little relationship to the previous passages. The final passage dates from 1810, and in it Coleridge is showing to his own satisfaction how certain trains of thought inevitably stir up other trains: the 'you' in this passage is undoubtedly Sara Hutchinson. The same three people are in the firelight, but apparently seated, with children in the room, and a dog.

(. . . I inevitably by some link or other return to you, or (say rather) bring some fuel of thought to the ceaseless Yearning for you at my Inmost, which like a steady fire attracts constantly the air which constantly feeds it) I began . . . to pass rapidly as in a catalogue thro' the Images only, exclusive of the thousand Thoughts that possess the same force, which never fail instantly to awake into vivider flame the for ever and ever Feeling of you – The fire / Mary, you, & I at Gallow-Hill/ – or if flamy, reflected in children's round faces – ah whose children? – a dog – that dog whose restless eyes oft catching the light of the fire used to watch your face, as you leaned your head on your hand and arm, & your feet on the *fender* . . .[70]

But even this passage only shows that by 1810 Coleridge was certain that his love for Sara Hutchinson was (and had for years been) the centre of his existence.

The point would seem to be that what biographers and critics treat as biographical source material simply isn't. The poetry passages do not have the kind of relation to each other which might characterise re-workings of 'a series of rapturous incidents'; and to bring them into the kind of close relationship which biography needs, one has to ignore everything contradictory of such a reading. As its title states, 'The Day-Dream' offers a fancy, not a reality – the weight of the woman turns out to be imagined, not real. 'A Day Dream' – the title again significant – has as its original setting 'a fountain . . . A willow and a ruinèd hut', and is explicitly set in 'June'.[71] Such material is intensely *poetic*, and there is no test which enables one to determine what might be poetry, and what incident, in such constructions. The two prose passages obviously refer to different occasions. The one clear thing – I would say – is that such material is not anecdotal. It cannot be used to describe *events* in a biography.

The language of fire, of darkness, of rest, of weight, of softness and touch, and all their interlinked associations, haunted Coleridge for ten years. That is why such passages matter to biographers: not because something happened one day, or one evening, of which we can now recover the truth. What the last – notebook – piece shows is that the flame and the darkness were for Coleridge *reflections* of, emblems of, an idea of extraordinary intimacy (and tranquillity) with women. *Of course* Coleridge used flame and fire in the poetry written about and around Sara and Mary; such words related to the brevity of his times with them, to the warmth of feelings of being at home in the company of tenderness, with the stillness of night-time being the context of such feelings. A touch: a face seen in extraordinary vividness: the sense of warmth and weight: the sense of three people together (brother and sisters rather than any kind of lovers), perfectly happy. The images suggest what attractions Coleridge may have found in the company of the Hutchinson sisters, but not how either he or they behaved.

For they tell us, significantly, absolutely nothing about the feelings of either woman; and nothing about things said or exchanged. It was how such feelings stayed with him in memory that mattered, especially in 1810. The recreating power of memory was what he kept writing about, not the facts of an incident.

But it may well have been going over and over the same feelings which helped convince him that he was deeply in love with Sara (or, more precisely, with Asra, his recreated version of her); the memories cannot tell us *what* made him fall in love with her, or when. And they tell us absolutely nothing about her at all. He made a horribly self-pitying notebook entry in 1808 which spilled out the whole fantasy life which he had been living for (he claims) '~~10~~ years', but which was then probably nearer six or seven.

> O SARA! SARA! – What have you done in <u>deceiving</u> him who for ~~10~~ years did so love you as never woman was beloved! in body, in soul, in brain, in heart, in hope, in fear, in prospect, in retrospect –! Not he alone in the vulgar meaning of <u>he</u>, but every living atom that composed him was wedded & faithful to you / Every single thought, every image, every perception, was no sooner itself, than it became <u>you</u> by some wish that you saw it & felt it or had – or by some recollection that it suggested – some way or other it always became a symbol of <u>you</u> –[72]

One must simply repeat that there is not a shred of evidence either that this was what Coleridge felt in 1801 or even in 1802, nor that Sara ever responded to any of this in any way except with pity and (for as long as she could bear it) with compassion. What Coleridge did, or Sara did, or what she thought, or what he thought, or what his wife did or thought, are now lost to us; and as a result biographers have had to do a good deal of creative manipulation – as with the flame and darkness passages I just discussed. This has not however stopped biographers referring to 'their love', to her 'protestations of devotion', to her problems being 'in love with a married man', or to their eventual mutual 'renunciation' of their love.[73]

It has, furthermore, been stated as a fact that Sarah Coleridge was jealous of Sara Hutchinson, and sent her an anonymous letter in the autumn of 1801; but no evidence exists. The same biographer asserts that this anonymous letter provoked Coleridge's determination to leave his wife, and that the Wordsworths also did their best to persuade him to do so: but, again, there is no evidence for this.[74] Every biographical account agrees that in November 1802 Sarah Coleridge was jealous about the way her husband met Sara Hutchinson in Penrith on his journey to London; but there is actually not a scrap of evidence that Sarah Coleridge reacted to the meeting with 'barely suppressed fury' (as Holmes puts it) or that as a result there was 'a long and angry exchange of letters between Coleridge and Sarah, which continued through November and December'.[75] There were two angry letters, but the disagreement seems to have been over Coleridge's extravagance with money, coupled with the usual quarrel about the Wordsworths. All these manipulations have been caused by the fact that biographers wish for evidence, seek it where they may, and create it if it does not exist.

If we stick to the facts, however, we can say that Coleridge was particularly miserable in London in the winter of 1801–2; on 6 December a letter from him arrived in Grasmere (where Mary Hutchinson still was) and Dorothy noted that 'It was a sad melancholy letter & prevented us all from sleeping'.[76] Only two days earlier they had received a letter from him written 'in good spirits'; so something appears to have suddenly occurred: probably another bout of illness. On 19 December he sent Sara his copy of *Bartram's Travels*, perhaps as a Christmas present, but also to remind her of how he had read to her from it, a year earlier:[77] and it was around this date that he also sketched out an idea for a piece of writing addressing itself to his situation (about a man wanting a 'virtuous & tender & brotherly friendship with an amiable Woman') which sounds very like a preliminary idea for the *Letter*, and which I discuss below.[78]

By the end of January, things were even worse. Up in Grasmere they had 'A heart-rending letter from Coleridge – we were as sad as we could be'.[79] They even discussed the idea of Wordsworth 'going up to London himself'; given that Wordsworth had not been in London since the summer of 1799, that would have been a dramatic step.[80] It would however be quite wrong to assume that the depression from which Coleridge was suffering was the consequence of his love for Sara Hutchinson. He had always been liable to fall into what he himself called 'dejection', and between the autumn of 1801 and the spring of 1802 he was at times deeply depressed. Some combination of the physical effects of his addiction (and withdrawal), his feelings about himself as worthless, his unhappiness in marriage, his sense of failure in his writing and in the rest of his life and – now – a self-destructive attraction to Sara, would have been its components.

When, however, Coleridge decided to go to Gallow Hill on his way back to Keswick, certain kinds of evidence do again start to enter the biographical record; though, once more, of a very enigmatic kind. In London between November and February, he had made a notebook entry which announced 'Miss Sara Hutcheson's new gospel – alias – Honesty.'[81] This may suggest that Sara – in the role of a particularly tight-lipped Miss Hutcheson – had told him by letter that she would not be a party to anything inconsistent with honesty. Everything was going to be above board: she would not allow him to do or say or write anything which he could not tell his wife about. One of the few things about which we can be reasonably certain is that, while in London and miserable himself, Coleridge made Sara very unhappy indeed by letter. He was certainly thinking very precisely about sending kisses around this time: a notebook entry runs 'Word of mouth – exp[ression]. for a kiss in a Letter –', while on 4 December the Wordsworths had had a letter from her which Dorothy specifically recorded as 'written in good spirits' but in a letter to them which arrived on the 13th, and was probably posted on the 11th, she had written 'in bad spirits about C'.[82] We know that Coleridge himself was in a particularly bad state exactly then, writing his 'sad melancholy letter' to the Wordsworths;[83] and this suggests that Sara had also received some such 'complaining' letter from him. Coleridge himself wrote in his own *Letter* how at some stage he had sent 'from afar both Pain and Sorrow thither':

> I wrote thee that complaining Scroll
> Which even to bodily sickness bruis'd thy Soul!
> And yet thou blam'st thyself alone! and yet
> Forbidd'st me all Regret.

At some point, according to the *Letter*, she had been made 'weak and pale with Sickness, Grief and Pain', whilst still refusing to blame *him*.[84]

This may mean that – in some way – she had responded to him, and then desperately wished she hadn't. On the other hand, there is nothing anywhere in the whole biographical record incompatible with the idea of Coleridge being in love with Sara Hutchinson while she never responded to him for one moment in any way at all, except by blaming herself profoundly for attracting him, and writing miserably back to him – as she would to a man she very much liked and admired, who was making an embarrassing fool of himself and upsetting her badly – that he must not wish he did *not* feel like this. That is a possibility which we must always keep in mind, though it would of course seriously reduce the pleasure of biographers (and readers) if we concluded that it was probably the truth.

The date of 21 February was important to Coleridge; I pointed out above that two years later he made an entry in his notebook commemorating 'the day of the Receipt of that heart-wringing Letter from Sara . . .'[85] That almost certainly makes 21 February 1802 the day when he heard how ill Sara was, as a consequence of what he had written to her. Eight days later he left London and travelled to Gallow Hill. He arrived there on Tuesday 2 March, and stayed for 10 days; he left on Saturday the 13th.

Knowing how Sara felt about Coleridge is the most difficult part of all these relationships. He could be the most enchanting and playful companion; the copy of his fantasy moon poem which she transcribed into her notebook in the spring of 1802 shows that she not only made copies of his serious work, but that he gave her the fantasy too. At least one of his notebook entries from his March 1802 visit to Gallow Hill shows how he enjoyed her *bons mots*: 'N.B. 3 Cats, Black, White: & Black & White / i.e. Hell, Heaven, & this Life. March 8, 1802. Gallow Hill – S.H.'[86] But even Sara's response to Coleridge as a man she *may* possibly have been attracted to – and her insistence on 'honesty' suggests that she may well *not* have been – is a very long way indeed from the sexual relationship which Holmes invents for her and Coleridge. Every surviving piece of material suggests that the relationship existed in Coleridge's head far more vividly than it did anywhere else; but Holmes assumes that – because Coleridge fantasised about Sara in a particular way – then she responded in that way. This leads Holmes to suggest about Coleridge's visit to Gallow Hill in March 1802:

> If they were ever to have become lovers, it would surely have been now, after the four months' absence from Greta Hall, the long soul-searching, and the pas-

sionate correspondence. It is impossible to know what intimacies took place, though the 'Letter' is full of physical tenderness and what can only be described as Asra's generous bedded warmth and maternal body-heat . . .[87]

There is however no record of 'soul-searching'; and 'the passionate correspondence' between them exists only in Holmes's sexually-determined imagination of it. He quotes 'An expressive fragment of his correspondence with her' which 'survives from this period':[88] 'If I have not heard from you very recently, and if the last letter had not happened to be full of explicit love and feeling, then I conjure up shadows into substances – and am miserable.'[89] But this is taken from one of Coleridge's notebooks: there is no surviving fragment of correspondence at all. What is more, the entry (which belongs to the autumn of 1803, not to the spring of 1802) consists of Coleridge's fantasies about Sara; it concludes, '– the Tale grows pleasanter – & at length you come to me / you are by my bed side, in some lonely Inn, where I lie deserted – there you have found me – there you are weeping over me! – Dear, dear, Woman!'[90] In the 'Tale' Coleridge is telling himself about what Sara *might* have said or done, he wonders whether he may not be 'turning shadows into substances'. He has to ask himself whether what he imagines hearing from her was *not*, after all, full of explicit love and feeling. The only really certain thing about the entry is that, by 1803, Coleridge felt miserable about not being loved, and sometimes invented things to comfort himself. We learn from it nothing about what Sara felt, or did, or wrote, in 1801 or 1802. The 'correspondence' is as much a biographer's fantasy as the bedded warmth, which Holmes says 'can only be described' as showing Sara's bedded warmth and maternal body-heat. What he means is that he himself wants to describe it like that, and accordingly embeds the word 'bed' in his sentence. The lines from the *Letter* do nothing to support his description:

> Thou being innocent and full of Love
> And nested with the Darlings of thy Love
> And feeling in thy Soul, Heart, Lips, and Arms
> Even what the conjugal and Mother Dove
> That borrows genial warmth from these, she warms,
> Feels in her thrill'd wings, blessedly outspread![91]

Coleridge can only be referring – in so far as the lines refer to the real-life Sara Hutchinson – to her *capacity* for extending love which, as I suggested above, is maternal love to her 'darlings', those nested with her, meaning her sisters Joanna and Mary, and – perhaps – her brother Jack's children (Coleridge's 1810 Notebook entry shows that he linked her presence in the firelit room with children). And in this poem, of all poems, children play a very significant role.

Anyway, having enjoyed tantalising his readers with the possibilities of Coleridge and Sara in bed together, Holmes then declares his belief in their 'sexual innocence'.[92] It would be more accurate to say 'non-sexual innocence'. Instead, he introduces a footnote about Coleridge's fantasies from 1803 about being cushioned on a large-breasted woman which have nothing to do with the matter at all, except that they throw a suggestive sexuality over the whole matter of the relationship between Coleridge and Sara.

However, he then suggests that, having got almost to the stage of sexual relations, 'Certainly what Coleridge agreed with Asra during those days at Gallow Hill was a form of renunciation.'[93] But there is no evidence of that either. There had been, so far as we know, no 'intimacies' between Sara and Coleridge, nor had their relationship ever been shaped by the sexual except (just possibly) by Coleridge's shaping spirit of imagination, and (without question) by the lusts of his biographer.[94] Nor is there any evidence of 'renunciation' (which – of course – implies having done something worth renouncing). Holmes's word 'Certainly' does duty for a complete lack of certainty. All we might note is that the arrangement of names in Dorothy's journal on 6 March, recording two letters sent to Gallow Hill, may show how the Wordsworths were now tending to think of Coleridge ('a letter to Mary H also to Coleridge & Sara').[95]

By no means always an accurate recorder of things in his notebooks, Coleridge however kept a meticulous note of date and place in most of the entries which concerned himself and Sara during this March 1802 visit to Gallow Hill. He marked out its significant moments like memorials. Of the five entries he made mentioning Sara during the visit itself, four are precisely dated. At least three of them, however, are incomprehensible. The first one reads, 'March 7, 1802. Calfskin Coat – Ward's promise, item. Moleskin Sara Mary cut hers open more wraps.'[96] Something about coats; something perhaps about the softness of Moleskin being appropriate for Sara (just possibly involving a sense of skin and touch); something about opening and exposing, and then covering, at the breast; we can understand no more, and even those suggestions may be wrong.[97] The following day came Sara's joke about the cats: at least comprehensible. And then another thoroughly enigmatic entry, this time undated: 'Wordsworth & [?M] – S & Coler. – Little Boy seeking me – N.B. poems –'[98] This suggests that discussion at Gallow Hill of the impending wedding of Wordsworth and Mary led him to set down Sara and himself as the missing (but complementary) partnership. There is also a recurrent theme in Coleridge's writing of the lost child;[99] part of Coleridge himself, as he doubtless knew. He may here be recording a dream in which he was pursued by a child (for example, his own son Hartley), just as Sara was obviously *not* pursuing him. He could develop this idea in poetry. In the spring of 1802, he would write two poems ('The Language of Birds' and 'The Day-Dream') in which a small boy's search makes demands on the adult to tell more of the truth than is customarily told. He sent 'The Language of Birds' to Sara.

The next entry is one of the most baffling of all, in spite of its precise memorializing and special characteristics. Kathleen Coburn comments that it is 'A *very* large and clear entry, obviously marking something of importance'.

> Gallow Hill, Thursday March 11th, 1802
> S. T. Coleridge
> Sara
>   SarHa[100]

Coleridge feels the same delight in patterning Sara as part of his own life as in the other entries. But then – a recollection of how her name sounded when spoken with a gulp? or a sudden indrawn breath? of surprise, of unhappiness, of loss?[101] The puzzle is not to be solved. The final entry, however, offers an overview of the whole visit: 'Friday, March 12th / '& wept aloud.' – you made me feel uncomfortable / Saturday, March 13th, left Gallow Hill on the Mail, in a violent storm of snow & Wind – Sunday slept at Scotch Corner / Arrived at Gallow Hill, March[2nd], Tuesday, 1802 –'[102] The visit is thus finally rounded up into its own neatly constructed epitaph. There were tears and an unidentified quotation on the Friday, but Holmes is wrong to say that the entry records how Coleridge himself "wept aloud" on parting.[103] It may be so; it may have been her: it may just be a quotation. The other phrase which gets written down – 'you made me feel uncomfortable' – is rather more likely to be Sara's explanation of what his attentions did to her. That would certainly have been a burr in the mind, the kind of remark which one cannot forget. Between the 11th and the 12th, Coleridge's expressions of love for Sara (if that is what they were) may have been explicitly rejected (which would be consistent with her having written some kind of heart-wringing rejection to him on 21 February).

Again, he could not help contrasting what had happened to him and what was happening to Mary Hutchinson and Wordsworth. He would be left with eight years of regret, at exactly the time when Wordsworth's relationship with Mary was going from strength to strength: 'A blessed Marriage for him & for her it has been!' Coleridge would note enviously in 1808 – to continue, sourly: 'But O! wedded Happiness is the intensest sort of Prosperity, & all Prosperity, I find, hardens the Heart – and happy people become so very prudent & far-sighted'.[104] What would come out of his feeling for Sara, so far as he was concerned, however – and especially so far as we are concerned – would be two poems; the *Letter* and *Dejection*. When every feeling and every tear had gone, his words would remain.

And so Coleridge, sadder but not I think wiser, returns to wife and children in Keswick, although he fails to note the fact in his notebook entry about leaving and travelling: he is more concerned to enclose the Gallow Hill visit in its own small island of time, in the dated, memorialized notebook entries. He must have had a dreadful journey back over the Pennines: he left on the Saturday in a 'violent storm of snow & Wind' – a day Dorothy recorded, over in Grasmere, as being 'as cold as ever it has been all winter very hard frost'.

Saturday had continued 'terribly cold we had 2 or 3 brisk hail showers', while the Sunday was sunny 'yet it was extremely cold'.[105] Coleridge had only got as far as Scotch Corner by the Sunday night, and would have reached Keswick cold and cramped and probably exhausted after three and a half days travelling in coaches and waiting about at inns; he would not have been out of bed very early on the Wednesday.[106] There would have been some explaining to do, about where he had been, and why, and with whom, and why for so long, and why – after all – Sara was not coming across for the Wordsworth wedding; and why he himself would be going off again, to see the Wordsworths, in only a couple of days' time.[107] (That can hardly have helped things.)

IV

Running in tandem with these new directions of feeling in Coleridge was, of course, Wordsworth's own attachment to Mary Hutchinson. Sometime during the winter of 1801–2 this had become a decision to marry. Coleridge had urged Wordsworth to the decision, which *may* well have been taken around 6–9 November 1801 while Mary Hutchinson was with them and Coleridge had also come to stay in Grasmere before going to London. Coleridge was very far from well (Dorothy was desperately anxious about him, as described above); in an anguished notebook entry in 1808, he recalled how 'in my bed I – then ill – continued talking with [Wordsworth] the whole night till the Dawn of the Day, urging him to conclude on marrying [Mary Hutchinson]'.[108] The notes of parallels between himself and Wordsworth which Coleridge created at various times[109] show how natural it was for him to follow this particular line of thought, and it looks as if – as soon as Wordsworth was certain to marry Mary – Coleridge became serious about his love for Sara.

This should not surprise us; it is another one of the things which may become more natural if we think about these people not so much as individuals but as an alternative family group. Holmes says of the spring of 1802 that Wordsworth's forthcoming marriage with Mary Hutchinson provoked 'terrible feelings of jealousy and despondency' in Coleridge; but, again, there is no evidence until some notebook entries made very much later, probably in 1808 but conceivably in 1810, when all the conditions of Coleridge's life had changed.[110]

It is typical of our state of biographical knowledge that we do not know exactly why or when Wordsworth and Mary decided to get married; but that may (anyway) be to focus on the wrong thing. In spite of Coleridge's desire to be the one responsible, there may have been no 'decision' in the simple sense. The fact that they *would* get married seems to have been one of those pieces of knowledge which they and their families had shared for a couple of years at least – the only question being exactly when. In November 1801, Wordsworth would be thirty-two in four months time: Mary was just four months younger.

Coleridge's 'urging' before he left may however have led directly to Wordsworth's proposal; Molly Fisher was 'very witty with Mary' the following Monday, the 16th, when Dorothy recorded her comment 'there's no thing like a gay auld man for behaving weel to a young wife'.[111] Wordsworth and Mary were the same age, and an older man might well have been more doting. A decision to marry may also have led to another important development. While Mary was still at Town End, Wordsworth wrote to his brother Richard (*c.* 21 November 1801), wanting to know how much money he and Dorothy 'have received from you since the beginning of December two years back. We wish to know exactly what we have spent during this time ...' As eldest son, Richard was administrator of his father's estate, and there-fore in effect in charge of his family's financial affairs. Wordsworth appears to be trying to work out his financial situation, and to calculate how much money of her own Dorothy would need to live without her brother's financial support.[112]

If this is true, then one thing Wordsworth and Mary had obviously *not* decided to wait for was any solution to the Wordsworths' seventeen-year fight to recover the money which their father had died being owed by Sir James Lowther (the Earl of Lonsdale) and the Lowther estate. Back in 1797 it might have seemed that the legal process would probably settle the matter, leaving the Wordsworths decently off. But the legal process had got nowhere and there seemed no chance of ever recovering the money. With the death of Sir James on 24 May 1802, and the decision in June 1802 of his heir to make good his debts, everything would change; and the Wordsworths finally got their money, with some of the accumulated interest, in 1803. Wordsworth and Mary would have been heartened by this unexpected blessing on their decision to go ahead with the marriage; but in the period November 1801 to March 1802, they could only have counted on an income of around £70 a year (£40–£50 from Wordsworth and around £23 from Mary).[113]

Wordsworth and Mary had last been together on 22 January 1802, when – after a three month stay in Grasmere, Keswick and Eusemere paralleling that of Sara the previous year – Mary had gone back to her Monkhouse relations in Penrith, on the way back to Middleham. Wordsworth had then only seen her 'for a couple of hours'[114] on 15 February when he had ridden up from Grasmere to Eamont Bridge to catch her on her way home to County Durham. For that 'couple of hours' he spent most of three winter days travelling, covering around 25 miles on horseback from Grasmere to Eusemere to stay with the Clarksons on the 14th (the road over the Kirkstone pass, in snow, being especially difficult), and then walking 10 miles up to Eamont to see Mary on the 15th. He and Mary would doubtless have walked on together to join up with the mail coach from Penrith to Middleham, before Wordsworth walked back to spend a second night with the Clarksons, He must then have ridden almost all day on the 16th, covering 30 miles or so, travelling round by Keswick for the longer (but safer) journey home to Grasmere. The massive journey for such a short time with Mary suggests that they may well have had something crucial to settle, at no matter what cost in time on the road. And in retrospect it looks as if this brief time with Mary was decisive for their marriage later in the year. A letter went off to Coleridge in London from the Wordsworths on 19 February which told him the decision: Wordsworth would have been sure to tell Coleridge before almost anyone. Wordsworth also got 'a very long' letter from Mary on the 24th and the same day wrote to Annette Vallon,[115] to whom he would also have felt obliged to tell the news at once. On the same day, however, Coleridge would cheekily use the fact that Wordsworth would be getting married as part of his own excuse for going to Gallow Hill without attracting comment.

Part II
Joy and Melancholy

Chapter Five

Animating the Child: 14 to 26 March

Around 11 March, just as Coleridge at Gallow Hill was making those agonised, dated entries about Sara in his notebook, Wordsworth suddenly began to write new poems. Three of them were short narrative poems about poor or travelling people, of a kind he had written before, but one of them was a new kind of poem altogether. On Sunday the 14th – that bitterly cold day when Coleridge was travelling back across the north of England towards Keswick –

> while we were at Breakfast that is (for I had breakfasted) he, with his Basin of Broth before him untouched & a little plate of Bread & butter he wrote the Poem to a Butterfly! – He ate not a morsel, nor put on his stockings but sate with his shirt neck unbuttoned, & his waistcoat open while he did it. The thought first came upon him as we were talking about the pleasure we both always feel at the sight of a Butterfly.[1]

Their talk may well have been precisely focused by the mention of a butterfly in one of Dorothy's journal entries (for 27 May 1800) which she had read out to Wordsworth the previous evening, while he was at work on his poem 'Beggars'. The journal entry recalled 'two boys . . . one about 10 the other about 8 years old at play chasing a butterfly', and the poem had borrowed the incident.[2] Now Wordsworth wrote a lyric poem which reached back into his own childhood.

Dorothy's description of him is, however, particularly striking. She shows him (literally) unbuttoned, unstockinged, waistcoat open: caught by the poem in the middle of dressing, about to eat. When the poem demands, then the conventional adult has to attend to it, even on a cold morning. But he is not the Romantic poet, collar open and hair tousled as inspiration floods through him. He sits beside his simple breakfast in his parlour, and cannot in fact *be* the properly dressed or conventional adult: he is caught up by memory, no more properly dressed (or breakfasted) than a schoolboy. Dorothy would like to scold him for not eating his porridge (doubtless growing cold), but she is also entranced at the arrival of 'To a Butterfly'.

His previous writing about children had tended to be in narrative, blank-verse poetry; he had been struggling since December with his poem *The Pedlar*. But the previous Tuesday had seen what was – for the moment, at least – work and revision on the *Pedlar* satisfactorily completed, though he would return to it in July.[3] The contrast between that intractable poem (which had occupied him for three years, on and off) and writing this little poem at breakfast, all at once, can be imagined. What is more, the poem initiated the sudden opening up of what feels like a previously closed-off past. 'To a Butterfly' was a poem which involved Dorothy too; her delight with the way he wrote it, just there in front of her, was linked with the way it reanimated their common childhood.

> Stay near me! do not take thy flight!
> A little moment stay in sight!
> Much reading do I find in thee;
> Thou Bible of my infancy!
> 5 Float near me – do not yet depart!
> Dead times revive in thee;
> Thou bring'st gay creature as thou art,
> A solemn image to my heart,
> My Father's family!
>
> 10 O! pleasant, pleasant, were the days
> The time when in our childish plays,
> My sister Dorothy and I
> Together chased the Butterfly.
> A very hunter I did rush
> 15 Upon the prey: – with leaps and springs
> I followed on from brake to bush:
> – But she, God love her! fear'd to brush
> The dust from off his wings.[4]

This spring of 1802, so important for both Wordsworth and Coleridge in the development of lengthy, narrative and *conversational* poems, was also the time when Wordsworth developed a new kind of simple, autobiographical lyric poetry about childhood.

But it would, too, be a time when Coleridge was thinking about children, when Sarah Coleridge was doubtless very conscious of getting pregnant again, when Mary Hutchinson would have been thinking about her future as a wife and mother, when Sara Hutchinson and Dorothy were both directly confronted with their fate as childless women. One of the new elements in the February–March work on *The Pedlar* had been what Sara had told Wordsworth about her own childhood experience of James Patrick, the autodidact pedlar of Penrith (a letter from her which they had received on 27 January had contained 'a most interesting account of Mr Patrick'.[5]) The little girl of ten who hears the stories of his early life had obviously been drawn from Sara herself:

> There was a little Girl ten years of age
> But tiny for her years a pretty dwarf

> Fair-hair'd, fair-fac'd, & though of stature small
> In heart as forward as a lusty child . . .

The Pedlar had also – in this February–March 1802 form – included an Introductory passage about the upbringing of the Pedlar himself.[6]

Wordsworth's poetry had regularly drawn on the experiences of Dorothy or himself as children; but it was now pointing up the contrast between the wild and unthinking child – 'lusty', like the little girl in *The Pedlar*, immersed in the pleasures of its own self-contained existence – and the way in which the adult, detached from experience, looks and feels. The very form of the new poem about the butterfly (the lyric, with its brief re-creation of special moments) raised the question of what (if anything) could be carried over to adulthood from the state of childhood. How did the adult now reanimate the experience and write the poem? The butterfly – utterly transient, absolutely frail – functions, paradoxically, as a means of preserving the past. It brings back crucial facts about the child, as a family bible does names and dates. The child Dorothy here, however, is more like an adult: thoughtful, caring, knowing the transience of the butterfly, like the poem in being aware of the transience of childhood. The 'I' figure, however, intent as he is on seizure and grasping, is aware of nothing except the chase. A child will not normally realise things about itself while *being* itself: a few weeks later Wordsworth tried out on the Hutchinsons the extra stanza for the poem starting 'I knew not then that it was so'.[7] But they would probably have agreed that the stanza was not necessary: it simply reminded Wordsworth – and his reader – that the child *could* not be aware of the significance of such an experience. And the reader already knew that.

There is clearly an intense nostalgia for childhood in such poetry; yet the reader, like the narrator, is located entirely in a present in which such things are only memories. But there is an underlying question about how such experiences may have led you to being the person you now are. Wordsworth on that Sunday morning in March 1802 was both the unbuttoned and careless child, lost in the chase (of language, poetry and recollection, and of the child he had once been) as well as the *other* child, anxious about transience and loss. He himself went through both those states of feeling during the rest of the day. After the poem's miraculous, immediate creation at breakfast (captured, as it were, with a sudden swoop of the net) it became something requiring a great deal of hard, considered work. Dorothy transcribed it '& the other poems & I read them all over to him'; they went for a walk; the sun shone 'yet it was extremely cold'.[8] They had dinner, probably at about 3 p.m., and then Wordsworth went back to bed, yet could not sleep; afterwards they 'sate comfortably by the fire'. But then came anxiety, cares and trouble. They sat 'till he began to try to alter the butterfly, & tired himself he went to bed tired'.[9] He was still working at the poem ten days later.

It is extraordinary, however, not just how much work went into these simple poems, but how completely the idea of the child and of childish experience was coming to dominate Wordsworth's writing. The children in the poem 'Beggars' which he had written the previous day had been – in every sense – 'wild': liars and emotional blackmailers, both of them. Yet their chasing of the butterfly reminds the reader that they are also just children: amoral, not immoral. The very next poem on which Wordsworth worked – 'Once in a lonely hamlet I sojourned' (later 'The Emigrant Mother') – continued thinking of the child and its upbringing. A Frenchwoman nurses and takes care of a child (not her own) and talks to it as if it *were* her own; her own real child is away in France, being brought up by others. Although we know that Wordsworth was working on the poem during 16–17 March in the orchard at Grasmere, his own later recollection of it placed it in another context altogether: 'If I am not mistaken, the lines were composed at Sockburn when I was on a visit to Mary and her brother'.[10] He *was* mistaken, but the link is important. He had been thinking of Mary as a potential mother; while he himself was both a *real* father as well as the emigrant father of his illegitimate French child Caroline Vallon. 'Once in a lonely hamlet I sojourned' shows that the way he looked at children related not just to his own experience as a child but – since 1792 – to the thought of his own child, growing up in France.[11]

Dorothy's own feelings about herself and her beloved (who was however neither her child nor her partner) got into the day's diary entry. In the poem, the woman thinks how her child 'knows't the pillow of my breast'; Dorothy goes to the orchard while Wordsworth is finishing the poem '& walked backwards & forwards in the Orchard till dinner time – he read me his poem. I broiled Beefsteaks. After dinner we made a pillow of my shoulder, I read to him & my Beloved slept'.[12] The poem and journal share the same language. One of Wordsworth's constant endeavours was to locate the child within himself; at times like this it is clear how Dorothy helped him. The poem went on writing itself, however, in ways that outstripped her. He got up and

> We walked backwards & forwards between Home & Olliffs till I was tired William kindled & began to write the poem. We carried Cloaks into the orchard & sate there a while there I left him & he nearly finished the poem. I was tired to death & went to bed before him – he came down to me & read the Poem to me in bed –[13]

So she is, now, the child, tucked up in bed and read to, at the end of an exhausting day.

The next day – Thursday the 18th – Wordsworth went somewhere for a day and a night; he probably walked up to Keswick so that he and Coleridge could have a good talk together while walking back together to Grasmere the following day – and, of course, in that way he was able to get news of Gallow Hill and of Mary twenty-four hours earlier. On Friday the 19th, late in the afternoon, Coleridge arrives, eyes swollen from the wind; Dorothy feels 'much affected with the sight of him – he seemed half Stupefied'. Wordsworth comes in half an hour later (he had probably been down to Rydale for the post), and argues with Coleridge about Ben Jonson; Coleridge goes to bed late, but Wordsworth and Dorothy stay up till 4 in the morning: 'My spirits were agitated very much.'[14] Back in February, Dorothy had read Wordsworth some of Jonson's short poems, and only ten days earlier, on 9 March, Wordsworth had been 'reading in Ben Jonson – he read me a beautiful poem on Love'. Was it that poem and its version of love about which they now disputed?

> Since you must go, and I must bid farewell,
> Hear, mistress, your departing servant tell
> What is it like: and do not think they can
> Be idle words, though of a parting man?
> It is as if a night should shade noon-day,
> Or that the sun was here, but forc'd away . . .[15]

There are of course many candidates for a poem by Jonson about love; and *Anderson's Poets* (of which the Wordsworths had a copy) printed most of Jonson's poetry. This is simply one poem which would have been appropriate.[16]

But it was not perhaps only the disagreement about Jonson which stirred up Dorothy's feelings so badly: nor even the fact that Coleridge was attracted to a woman to whom he was not married. The really upsetting thing – from the point of view of both Dorothy and of the biographer of Coleridge – was the way in which Coleridge reacted to these experiences. Years later he would tell himself that he had been deeply in love; yet even his sonnet 'To Asra' (written some time between 1802 and 1804, and probably towards the end of that period) is more concerned to wish Asra a happy life than to describe her response to him: as if the narrator knows very well that his feelings could not make her happy. It starts off by saying that the two states 'mutual Love' and 'Happiness' are almost indistinguishable. But it then spends seven lines describing the feelings welling up in the narrator, without in any way suggesting how Asra might respond. The narrator's final wish is that he could 'transmute' his loving feelings into 'one rich Dower / Of 'Happy Life' for her. The 'mutual Love' so indistinguishable from 'Happiness' turns out not to be mutual at all, and feelings need to be transmuted *into* Happiness for the beloved to enjoy them; while the wedding dower which the narrator promises Asra is, significantly, for her to enjoy on her own rather than with him. It is an oddly incoherent poem behind its rather old-fashioned formal wit, but may – in that way – respond to the complexity of Coleridge's situation. He knew he could not impose his love on Sara if *she* did not respond. And we have no insight into her point of view at all. Their only mutuality is in silence.

It is the single Coleridge poem which might be called a love poem to Sara, but her feelings are as absent from it as they are from every other part of the record. One conclusion might be that, although he came to love her deeply, she did not love him at all. But her feelings remain as mysterious as Mary's for Wordsworth. The latter couple at least married and became passionate about each other, so we can retrospectively imagine just a little of the process of their love.[17] What is most vivid in the record of Coleridge and Sara is not passion, or mutual love, or anything mutual at all, but his dejection. His feelings for Sara always tend to be accompanied by breakdowns of his health, as though both he and his whole future were being hopelessly damaged by what he was going through: 'as if a night should shade noone day'. It was a standing joke between the Wordsworths and Coleridge that a letter from him would contain nothing but complaints ('Oh, for one letter of perfect uncomplainingness!' Dorothy had sighed in May 1801.[18]) How we judge the unhappiness he was experiencing in the middle of March 1802 will however depend very much upon whose biography we are reading.

Seeing things from the point of view of the Hutchinsons and Wordsworths as well as of Coleridge, however, it immediately seems likely that what agitates Dorothy on 18 February may not have been the state of Coleridge's marriage, or his career as a writer; it may not even have been his feelings for Sara Hutchinson. It may well have been a discussion which, within three days, had resolved itself into the decision that Wordsworth would see Annette Vallon and Caroline before he married Mary. Did Coleridge – fresh from the politics and gossip of London – bring with him the news that not just letters but actual travel to and from France would very soon again be possible for English citizens following the Treaty of Amiens, which was formally to be signed on 25 March? It had been a subject of intense debate in Parliament during January and February. However, we cannot know exactly what agitated Dorothy on the evening of 19 February; all we can do is point to the coincidence of the writing of the 'Emigrant Mother' poem, Coleridge's arrival in a state of real unhappiness, the plan to see Annette and Caroline, and Dorothy's conflicting feelings about both her brother's marriage and Coleridge's situation.

But, at all events, they went on thinking about children. The following evening, the Saturday, with Coleridge still in the house, 'after supper we talked about various things – Christening the Children &c &c went to bed at 12 o clock'. Only one of Coleridge's children had been christened; he had been a Unitarian, and eighteen months later would exclaim, just before the christening (at the age of seven) of Hartley, 'o with what reluctance & *distaste* have I permitted this ⟨silly⟩ unchristian, & in its spirit & consequences anti-christian Foolery to be performed . . .'[19] But what about Wordsworth's children? His daughter in France, brought up as a Catholic? The children he now might well be hoping for, with Mary? (Their children would indeed be christened, and Coleridge would stand godfather for the first.)

Coleridge went back on the Sunday; they couldn't get a horse for him, so he had to walk, but they only went the first half-mile with him, up to the Swan inn. The reason, for certain, was that they had themselves planned to go up to

Keswick in the next couple of days. And, too, it was now Wordsworth's turn to be 'very unwell': in spite of which 'We had a sweet and tender conversation. I wrote to Mary & Sara.'[20] A 'sweet and tender' conversation sounds like a brother reassuring his sister that she is still loved in spite of Mary, in spite of Annette . . . and that (of course) she must go and see Annette and Caroline with him, because he could not possibly go on his own.

The following day's post brought matters to a head: '2 letters from Sara H. & one from poor Annette'. Since the negotiations for the peace had started, letters had started to get through: their first letter from France seems to have been delivered in December 1801.[21] Thereafter, there was a regular – even extensive – correspondence between Annette and the Wordsworths (Dorothy, of course, had never even seen Annette).[22] The decision Dorothy and Wordsworth took on the evening of the day when Annette's letter came was a striking one. They would go to France and they would see Annette and Caroline. But the decision was a complex one too, as Dorothy's journal entry suggests: the day that the letter from 'poor Annette' arrived, 'We talked about C & other interesting things we resolved to see Annette, & that Wm should go to Mary. We wrote to Coleridge not to expect us till Thursday or Friday.'[23]

II

Biographers have in general taken this decision 'to see Annette' for granted. But seeing an ex-mistress after ten years is always strange; though seeing her before you get married is perhaps less odd, especially as there was a child involved – and the window of opportunity for a visit had suddenly opened. Seeing the child may well have been more important to Wordsworth than seeing the mistress, though biographers are more interested in the latter, as (naturally) Dorothy was too when she made 'Annette' the visit's focus. But there is nearly always an element in biographical writing which dictates that – because we know *what* happened next – then it is clear *why* it happened next. Gill says that Wordsworth 'was eager to see Annette while travel to France was still possible, and to meet his daughter. By introducing Annette and Caroline to Dorothy, moreover, he would at last be able to include her in one part of his life she had not shared.'[24] All that may be true; but it makes the visit sound normal and natural, and entirely the consequence of Wordsworth's own decision. Gill also says that it was only in April that Wordsworth told Mary 'that he was determined to see Annette before their marriage'. That *may* be true. But Gill makes it sound as if Wordsworth simply decided that he would go (for no reason apart from eagerness), and that he then told Mary his decision, presumably also telling her that they would not be getting married until he had been to France; and that as Dorothy had somehow been excluded from that part of his life which involved Annette, so he now wanted to include her.

None of these 'reasons' is necessarily or even probably true; all are narrative strategies for a biographer. Dorothy had always been thoroughly involved with Annette and Caroline, and was as little excluded as anyone could be, though doubtless curious to see what Annette was actually like; while Mary Hutchinson (as Mary Moorman suggests) may well have been party to the decision from the start: Moorman actually makes Wordsworth's February visit to Mary 'chiefly' so that they could 'discourse about Annette'.[25] Of this – again – we have no evidence. We have in fact no knowledge either of Wordsworth's eagerness to see Annette, or of his lack of it; and the range of possibilities is as usual narrowed by the fact that it is Wordsworth's biographers who write about these things.

It seems to me a good deal more likely that Annette initiated the idea of the visit; that it was she who insisted that Wordsworth must see her and Caroline while they could. She would actually have wanted two very specific kinds of reassurance. Firstly, she would have wanted to ensure that Wordsworth's marriage to Mary would not mean the end of his financial responsibility for Caroline. We do not know what arrangements he had entered into for the support of Caroline at this stage, but when she got married in 1816 he settled £30 a year on her, commuted to a lump sum of £400 in 1835. It seems unlikely that – poor as the Wordsworths were in these years – Wordsworth had failed to send money when he could: and it seems probable that one reason for seeing them this summer would be so that he could give Annette money he could not get safely into her hands in any other way, as well as to reassure her of his continuing responsibility, in spite of his impending marriage.

The other kind of reassurance would have been of a rather different kind. Annette would badly have wanted to hear that, although Wordsworth was getting married, he would not be claiming as his own the child who was still legally his to command. Because Caroline was illegitimate, under French law of that period she had no legal relationship with her mother. The thought of this would have scared Annette, in spite of Wordsworth's reassurances. She would have wanted to establish some legal relationship, now that it was certain Wordsworth was not going to marry her. This reason for the journey to Calais has not been allowed the significance it deserves. Coleridge was one of the very few people to know all about the Calais trip: and *he* believed that while the Wordsworths were there, 'Dear little Caroline' might become 'a ward of Annette'.[26] If the Wordsworths' visit to France were going to achieve that, it can only have been because Wordsworth was going to appear, presumably in front of a lawyer, and either sign or make a declaration of some kind, which would make Annette legally Caroline's guardian.

Annette might not have been able to marry Wordsworth, as she would probably have preferred, but she could at least ensure that he resigned Caroline to her. And that would not have been an appeal he would have wanted to resist. Hence perhaps the 'poor Annette' of Dorothy's journal entry of Monday the 22nd: Annette was not the one able to insist upon Wordsworth making such a move, although she probably badly wanted it. She may also have been extremely hard up: 'poor' in every sense.

The visit to France before the wedding, therefore, may have been motivated more by duty than by desire. Wordsworth's 'eagerness' to see Annette may or may not have existed; but he was blessed (and cursed) with the kind of sense of duty to which only someone with utterly opposed desires and needs would respond. He would write about himself a couple of years later in his 'Ode to Duty':

25	I, loving freedom and untried;
	No sport of every random gust,
	Yet being to myself a guide,
	Too blindly have reposed my trust:
	Resolv'd that nothing e'er should press
30	Upon my present happiness
	I shov'd unwelcome tasks away
	But thee I now would serve; more strictly if I may.[27]

Seeing Annette and Caroline would certainly 'press / Upon my present happiness'; for that reason too he may have decided to see them. They may have chosen to meet in Calais simply because both parties would have almost the same length of journey (Blois – between Orléans and Tours – to Calais, via Paris, was almost as long a journey as Grasmere to Dover via London).[28] But Mary Hutchinson may also have been concerned that – in case the Treaty of Amiens suddenly collapsed – Wordsworth and Dorothy would be able to get out easily; the last thing a woman about to get married would have wanted was to find her partner stuck in France. Wordsworth, too, may have preferred not to go into the heart of France (a country he now hated and despised) but to remain on the periphery.

Wordsworth, too, *may* have felt (it would have been characteristic of him) that he could not decently get married until he had done something to discharge his old debt of guilt and responsibility. He might not have felt that if the Treaty of Amiens had not opened up the window of opportunity. But it had: and that changed everything. He obviously would not go to see either Annette or Caroline after he was married, with or without his new wife; it would be emotionally stupid either to expect Mary to meet his old mistress or to expect her to hang around waiting while *he* did. But he could probably help Annette financially, and do something about the legal status of Caroline; so he would go.

This was why the decision about France was bound up with the idea that Wordsworth should 'go to Mary'. He needed to talk through with her any money settlement he wanted to make; while they also needed to take some decisions about *when* they would now be marrying and where they would live. There seems to me absolutely no possibility that Wordsworth would have waited a fortnight, keeping Mary in the dark, after making a decision about going to France. Within forty-eight hours of the evening when they 'resolved to see Annette', Dorothy was writing to Mary; while the latter had sent a letter apparently wondering whether she and Wordsworth and Dorothy would be happier living at Grasmere or at Gallow Hill, as it turned out that Tom and Sara Hutchinson would not after all be going to live in Lincolnshire, and – if Wordsworth and Dorothy came over to Gallow Hill to live – that would allow the whole family to stay together . . .

Dorothy would be very firm about this last suggestion, however. 'I made a vow that we would not leave this Country for G Hill'.[29] And the timing really took care of itself, as Mary and Wordsworth probably discovered when they saw each other. If the Wordsworths were going to Calais in the summer, then they could go to the seaside too, to make something of a holiday out of the visit, while Wordsworth did his legal duty; the start of August would be a good time. It would also be prudent to wait several months to ensure that the Treaty really was holding: but 'present happiness' was also extremely important, and not to be endangered. If Mary and Wordsworth were thinking very far ahead, they may also have decided at this stage to acquire a licence which would allow them to get married without the saying of the banns in church, and so allow them to marry as soon as Wordsworth got back. Wordsworth may even have toyed with the idea of getting married on 4 October (Coleridge's wedding day), but at this stage such a date must have looked rather late. If the wedding were small and only family came, then it would not matter if its date were settled nearer the time; and it could also be in the middle of the harvest season (important for a family of farmers: a return visit from the Hutchinsons could only be envisaged 'after Mr Hutchinson's harvest is over'[30]). Wordsworth and Dorothy had financial matters to consult their brother about in London, before the wedding; that meant a visit, which however could also be fitted in around the trip to Calais. Like most decisions, this one almost certainly gradually evolved, rather than simply being *taken* by any one or two individuals.

Was it, then, just coincidence that Wordsworth's writing about children and the past should have been interrupted by a decision to go and see his own daughter, and resign her to her mother? Probably. But events had started to pile up in a way which meant that he was compelled to think about what life had been like before he was a responsible, decision-making adult (if indeed he now was one), as he revisited his past. And if he wanted an idea of what Caroline might now be like, he only needed to think of Dorothy when young: the remembered image of his sister supplying the imagined image of his child.

III

Poems do not wait for arrangements to be made, either. Before Coleridge's arrival from Keswick, poems had been coming to Wordsworth regularly. When he left they started again, though in theory the Wordsworths had only a couple of days at home before going up to Keswick. On Monday the 22nd, however, Dorothy wrote postponing their visit until Thursday or Friday, and she must have written again later in the week putting it off until Sunday the 28th. This gave them more time quietly at home, to think through the whole Annette and Caroline business (it also meant that they would spend less time with Sarah in Greta Hall).

On the day Coleridge left, 'William worked at the Cuckoo poem': he worked at it again on the Friday, while on the Wednesday he revised 'The Butterfly'; and sometime this week he must have written 'The Sparrow's Nest'.[31] All three were summer poems, written long before butterflies or cuckoos or eggs in nests appeared. But they were not forward-looking: they looked back to childhood. The closer to Mary – and to Caroline and Annette – he became, the more Wordsworth turned to Dorothy.

'The Sparrow's Nest' started with one of those beautifully simple invocations – 'Look, five blue eggs are gleaming there' which is both a call to attention in the present moment of the poem, and a direct invitation to memory:

> 5
> I started seeming to espy
> The home and little bed
> The sparrow's dwelling which hard by
> My Father's house in wet or dry
> My sister Dorothy and I
> 10
> Together visited

Becoming aware of the nest means a direct shift to focussing on the home, unheralded, not even necessarily welcome. The poem turns out, however, to be as much about the sister as it is about the moment of recollection:

> She look'd at it as if she fear'd it
> Still wishing dreading to be near it
> Such heart was in my sister when
> A little Prattler among men.

She may have been a chatterbox; but the point is the continuity which she herself creates. She is now 'The blessing of my later years', but she

> Was with me when a Boy:
> She gave me eyes she gave me ears
> And humble cares and delicate fears
> A heart the fountain of sweet tears
> 20
> And love and thought and joy.[32]

It is striking that Wordsworth should have been writing such poetry at exactly the time of his decision 'to go for Mary'. We should not see it simply as his way of reassuring Dorothy that he still loved her. It was a way of reassuring himself that – whatever direction his life was now taking – it still had its roots in child-hood, in an uninterrupted continuity, and that he very badly *needed* the experi-ence of continuity when about to do something which would so radically change 'present happiness'.

'To a Cuckow' had started with the cuckoo's call – an evocative and precise 'hollow shout' – and the fact that the bird is invisible. Both presence and absence are then firmly located not just in an English countryside but in a time of 'visionary hours': a time when something apprehended as a boy goes on recurring to the adult, independent of clock or date, and thus brings together quite different periods of his life.

> The same who in my school-boy days
> I listen'd to, whom I
> Look'd for a thousand thousand ways
> In bush, and tree, & sky
> 20   To seek thee did I often rove
> Through woods & on the green
> And thou wert still a hope a love
> Still long'd for never seen.[33]

What the bird did then – as it still does – was make him feel that the world is not simply substantial but full of the unexplained; of hopes and loves and longings which cannot be pinned down or possessed, but which together make up the 'golden time' which continues to haunt the adult. And – as an adult – he wants it to go on haunting him. What a poem can do is define what the haunting feels like, and say how the adult can recover the child's way of experi-encing things:

> 25   And I can listen to thee yet
> Can lie upon the plain
> And listen till I do beget
> That golden time again.[34]

The adult also knows that he is doing the recreation: *he* begets the golden time.

It was turning out to be an extraordinary week. On the Tuesday, after working at the 'Cuckow' poem in the morning, 'After dinner he slept I read German, & at the closing in of day went to sit in the Orchard – he came to me, & walked backwards & forwards, we talked about C – Wm repeated the poem to me – I left him there & in 20 minutes he came in rather tired with attempt-ing to write – he is now reading Ben Jonson.'[35] There may have been no con-nection; but it sounds as if talking about Coleridge somehow took them back to the poem. They may have been thinking about Hartley; it may have been the way they were increasingly thinking about Coleridge's own childhood as the crucial time when something had gone wrong. This was an insight which the spring and summer would further develop; Coleridge was never far from their minds.

IV

Up in Keswick, Coleridge had been reunited with the children whom he loved so dearly, and who troubled him so much; reunited in that characteristic way which saw him back in Keswick (exhausted) on Tuesday the 16th after his journey from Yorkshire, only to leave again on the Friday. He may have been a loving parent; he was also a terribly absent one.

But we must not underestimate the importance of children to him, either. Wordsworth might write poems about childhood; Coleridge had children around him. Just before leaving London in February, he had written to Sarah, 'O that I were at Keswick with my Darlings! My Hartley / My fat Derwent!'[36] His notebook for the winter shows childhood constantly recurring. Back in November, ten days before leaving for London, the family had commemorated Hartley going into trousers: and Coleridge was very aware of the contrast between the slightly self-conscious pleasure the boy now showed, and what he used to be like: 'Sunday, November 1. 1801. Hartley breeched – dancing to the jingling of the money – but eager & solemn Joy, not his usual whirl-about gladness . . .'[37] On 9 November, in a letter to Southey, he recorded the same event: 'it was an *eager* & solemn gladness, as if he felt it to be an awful aera in his life. – O bless him! bless him! bless him! If my wife loved me, and I my wife, half as well as we both love our children, I should be the happiest man alive – but this is not – will not be! –'[38] While in London, he had written to Sarah very tenderly about the children: he had just been writing about people who

> are subject to sad Caprices in this mortal
> Life. – O my dear Hartley – my Derwent! my
>   ! – The night before last I dreamt
>   them so vividly, that I was quite ill
> in the morning – & wept my eyes red – which
> was good for me.[39]

The paper was deliberately cut and torn, hence the missing words, the second line's gap probably filled with 'I saw'. But it is possible that – rather than writing simply 'the children' in the first gap, as has been suggested – Coleridge inserted the name of the child who had died, Berkeley, which may have been why the paper was mutilated subsequently (it is hard to see why else words should have been removed). Just before leaving Somerset to return to London in mid-January 1802, he had written to Sara Hutchinson with a particularly

touching account of Hartley. A Mr Peach had been staying with their landlord
William Jackson, and had just left; he had possessed a fascinating collection of
china figures, including a bulldog, to which Hartley had become very attached,
and which he had been taking to bed with him at night. Hartley was distraught: 'Mr Jackson saw that the poor Boy's eyes were *full*, & that he could
scarce keep his heart down at the departure of the Bull-dog & the good creature could not stand it, but without saying a word walked into town & brought
back four fourpenny Images, which now take it by turns to sleep in Hartley's
arms.' But that led to its own problems. Sarah Coleridge had been instructing
Hartley in the ten commandments, but found him now having problems with
the second ('Thou shalt not make unto thee any graven image . . . Thou shalt
not bow down thyself to them, nor serve them'): ' "What is the matter, my
Dear? – *I'se afraid, the Lord will be angry with me.*" And what for?' *'Because I've got
four Images, & I take one to bed with me every night. But what* IS *worshipping
Images?'*[40] It is the link between the child's imagination and the adult world of
responsibilities which so fascinates Coleridge, exactly as it would have fascinated Wordsworth. A couple of entries from Coleridge's notebooks probably
record things recalled on the coach journeys up from Somerset to London back
in January; they may be observations or recollections (in which case the 'little
fat thing' is probably Derwent). The first entry reads 'A little fat Thing trotting
along by one's knee-side.' The second, 'Bloody hand had he? School boy made
ideot by cruelty of Schoolmaster'.[41] Back in London at the end of January
Coleridge had written into his notebook a version of a line from his own poem
'The Day Dream' with its powerful tactile memory: 'a playful Tenderness;
Touching the Heart, as with an infant's finger'.[42] And while on the journey
back from Gallow Hill in mid-March he had probably made the peculiar entry
I discussed above ('Wordsworth & [?M] – S & Coler. – Little Boy seeking me –
N.B. poems –')[43]: one of the patterned entries he was so fond of; and included
within it another reference to the 'Day Dream' poem, though it is also tempt-
ing to think of Coleridge speculating about how much of his own self was
involved in the small boy searching for the adult.

I also pointed out how a surprising number of his surviving letters (and
letter fragments) to Sara Hutchinson from 1802 are about children; the subject
was one which would not upset her, as his February letter so obviously had, but
Coleridge was also fascinated by the experience of the six-year-old. However,
the child of Coleridge's descriptions is not just confronted by the adult world,
as all children are, but is *anxious* about it; aware of it as strange, if not incomprehensible: '– Hartley told his Mother, that he was thinking all day – all the
morning, all the day, all the evening – "what it would be, if there were *Nothing*
/ if all the men, & women, & Trees. & grass, and birds & beasts, & the Sky, &
the Ground, were all gone / *Darkness & Coldness* – & nothing to be dark &
cold."' What should a mother say to *that?* Coleridge, in the same letter, did his
own bit of explaining: how Hartley's 'motto from infancy might have been *not
me alone*! [']My Thoughts are my Darlings!' – Hartley's *attachments* are exces-

sively strong – so strong, even to places, that he does not like to go into town – or on a visit / The field, garden, & river bank / His Kitchen & darling Friend – they are enough . . .'[44] His 'darling Friend' – William Jackson's cook and housekeeper Mrs Wilson – was (according to Coleridge) 'a mother to Hartley'.[45] But it also sounds like the classic pattern of a child pursuing whatever security he can find in a life where a great deal worries him; in particular he may have been anxious about his parents. Coleridge was struck – but also a little proud – that the boy did not get on with other children: 'Play fellows are burthensome to him'. But Coleridge saw himself as the exception: 'excepting *me* / because I can understand & sympathize with, his wild fancies – & suggest others of my own.' The child may very well have preferred his father's company when he could get it, and would have made a point of showing that he did: his father was regularly absent for months at a time. But the father was also flattered that the child made an exception of him, finding him sufficiently child-like to be acceptable (which again pleased Coleridge very much). Hartley found his father a delightful if utterly unreliable part of the adult world: remarkable because he never criticised. He offered unconditional love; he did not insist on the ten commandments or formal lessons:

> Some time ago I watched Hartley under the Trees, down by the river – the Birds singing so sweetly above him / & he was evidently lost in thought. I went down, & asked him what his Thoughts were – so he hugged me, & said after a while 'I thought, how I love the sweet Birds, & the Flowers, & Derwent, and Thinking; & how I hate Reading, & being wise, & being Good.'[46]

That was not a reply he would dared have given his mother. But his father was delighted by it, and – having quoted the anecdote – referred to his own poem 'The Foster Mother's Tale', with its 'unteachable' small boy who

> never learnt a prayer, nor told a bead,
> But knew the names of birds, and mock'd their notes
> And whistled, as he were a bird himself . . .[47]

That image of *wildness* was one to which Coleridge himself was deeply attracted, and had been for years – as was Wordsworth. There is no doubt that Coleridge encouraged it in Hartley, as we know he did in his daughter Sara in 1808.[48]

Another image from the summer of 1802 of Hartley being invited to comment on the adult world, and doing his best to live up to his father's expectations, appears in one of the letters to Sara Hutchinson:

> Dear Hartley – ! – I picked up a parcel of old Books at Wilkinson's which he gave me / among them is an old System of Philosophy by some FANTASTIC or other, with a large Print of Sun, Moon, & Stars, Birds, Beasts,

& Fishes – with Adam and Eve, rising out of a Chaos! . . . I asked Hartley what he thought of it – & he said – it is *very* curious! A Sea not in a World, but a World rising out of a Sea! (these were his own unprompted words, & entirely his own idea – There they all are – Adam & all! – Well! I dare say, they stared at one another finely!'[49]

Coleridge is again immensely pleased by the remark. But he also tells the long and fascinating story of Hartley's horror of '*crazy* Peter Crosthwaite', a friend of William Jackson's. Hartley – aged nearly six – had cried and screamed for a quarter of an hour after being confronted with Peter, and had had to be carried out; but eventually he calmed down, and explained to his father that he had been so upset because he could not bear 'things that are not like other things'. Coleridge pointed out that he had been fascinated by a monkey and a dromedary which he had seen in London a couple of years earlier – but Hartley reminded his father that he had, at first, been very frightened of them: '*so he was, poor Fellow! God knows*', recalled Coleridge guiltily. Hartley went on: 'but now I am not frightened at them, <u>because</u> <u>they</u> <u>are</u> <u>like</u> <u>themselves</u> . . . "I mean, I am frightened at men that are not like men / a Monkey is a monkey – & God made the Dromedary – but Peter is a crazy man – he has had a chain upon him!"' That anxiety at a world refusing to be *like itself* is very acutely observed by the child and by the father. The aftermath of the episode, the terror and recovery, is also worth recording:

> – Poor fellow! when he recovered, he spent the whole afternoon in whirling about the Kitchen, & telling Mrs Wilson wild stories of his own extempore composition about mad men and mad animals – all frightful: for tho' he cannot endure the least approximation to a sorrowful Story from another Person, all his own are most fantastically tragical.[50]

Hartley deals with his anxiety by telling stories about it, and so commanding it. He was a precociously clever child, and in some ways terribly like his father; and as all these stories are selected and told *by* his father, they are also reflections on how Coleridge liked his child to be (and was also worried about him being).

It can, then, have been no coincidence that – at some stage this spring or summer – Wordsworth himself wrote the most extraordinary poem about Hartley. The Wordsworths had always seen a lot of him, first of all in Someset, when he was still a baby;[51] and then, of course, the Coleridge family had come to stay with the Wordsworths in the summer of 1800, while on their way to their house at Keswick (Hartley then coming up to four years old). In September 1800 he had been sent down to live with them when his mother was preparing to give birth to his brother Derwent. Dorothy commented: 'he is a sweet companion, always alive and of a delightful temper, I shall find it very difficult to part with him when we have once got him here.'[52] At the start of

May 1801, when he was four-and-a-half, he again came down to live at Town End, probably to attend the school in Grasmere – his education at Greta Hall consisting, apparently, in crawling around the vegetable gardens of Greta Hall with his father, examining ant-heaps.[53] It sounds a young age to leave home to go to school; but he was a precocious child who had (after all) known the Wordsworths all his life. The Wordsworths very much enjoyed having him to stay, anyway, and one of the few surviving letters of the hundreds they sent to Coleridge belongs to the time when Hartley was with them. The only restriction he seems unwittingly to have imposed on them is that they could now only go out for night walks when Molly Fisher (who lived across the road) was in the house; and, this particular evening, they could not both go to the post 'as we have suffered Molly to retire to cover and little Hartley cannot be left'.[54] Little in both senses; a child, but also extremely small, both as a child and as an adult. Dorothy wrote:

> I could talk to you a long time about Hartley. Dear little fellow, he is well and happy. He has slept very quietly at nights ever since you were here only he is long in falling asleep. He talks a great deal about Mrs Wilson. Tell her that I am sure he can never forget her. If he had not been in bed and asleep he would gladly have written her a letter.[55]

Characteristic that the child, of course, would miss the housekeeper and substitute mother Mrs Wilson more than his parents.

He was, in every way, a special child; small, thin, very articulate, and constantly amused, intrigued and intellectually tormented by his father. A series of questions posed by Coleridge in July 1802, ending characteristically with 'What do you mean, Hartley?' would provoke Hartley's response 'Don't ask me so many questions, Papa! I can't bear it.'[56] The Wordsworths would have been duller company but probably less taxing, and they may have thought that they could offer him a more settled and less quarrelsome home than Greta Hall did. He probably spent May–June 1801 with them. The Wordsworths would then have seen him again in November and December, when they visited Keswick: Wordsworth would have seen Hartley on his own visit to Keswick 4–7 March, when he read his poetry aloud, and then again on 18 March, when he went up to Keswick to bring Coleridge back with him the following day.

We do not know when Wordsworth wrote his Hartley poem; it may well have been around 27 March 1802, though June and September 1802 are also possible times.[57] The first stanza, in its earliest surviving state, runs:

To H.C.

Oh Thou whose fancies from afar are brought
Who of thy words dost make a mock apparel
And fittest to unutterable thought

The breeze-like motion and the self-born carol
5   Thou blessed Fairy! that dost float
In such clear water that thy boat
May rather seem
To brood on air than on an earthly stream
Suspended in a stream as clear as sky
10   Where earth and heaven do make one imagry
O happy Vision blessed Child!
Thou art so exquisitely wild
I think of thee with many fears
Of what may be thy lot in future years[58]

The child is adept with language to an extraordinary degree, full of imagination; not exactly 'not of this world', but somehow suspended so that he finds no clear distinction between the fancied and the real. And he is very much to be envied. His childish 'wildness' does not mean he chases butterflies (or tells lies); it is an *exquisite* wildness.

But, interestingly, it is exactly this which makes the narrator worried. Is it possible to be *too* wild a child, so that the transition to being an adult will either be made imperfectly – or (most worryingly of all) not be made at all? The adult like Wordsworth may deeply regret the loss of the period of childhood, but adulthood (with its responsibilities and pains and necessary losses and cares) is thrust remorselessly and inevitably on to the growing child. The adult who somehow remains a child, into adult life, may be profoundly troubled, utterly cast down by care and pain, and thus unable to deal with life (Coleridge *père* would not have been far away from this train of thought). Hartley, anyway, seems a candidate for such a future. The second stanza pursues the idea:

15   I thought of times when pain might be thy guest
Lord of thy house and hospitality
And grief uneasy lover! never rest
But when she sate beneath the touch of thee . . .

And for Hartley, one of two things will happen:

Nature will either end the[e] quite
Or lengthening out thy season of delight
– Preserve for thee by individual right
A young lambs heart among the full-grown flocks

So, miraculously, he *may* somehow remain a child, as an adult; may be a special case, with his own 'individual right', his own young lamb's heart. And looking at him now – as a child – how could one doubt it?

25   What hast thou to do with sorrow
            Or the injuries of to-morrow
            Thou art a dew-drop which the morn brings forth . . .

So one will just have to hope and pray that Hartley will be lucky.

But the image of the dew-drop brings its own inevitable conclusion. Bright, marvellous, sparkling it may be, but it is also

            Ill fitted to sustain untimely shocks
            Or to be along the soiling earth
30   A gem that glitters while it lives
            And no forewarning gives
            But at the touch of wrong without a strife
            Slips in a moment out of life.[59]

It is an extraordinarily ominous and in some ways frightening poem, suggesting that catastrophe and death are the natural consequences of being a child who does not grow up, or an imperfectly adjusted adult; and one wonders what reading it did to Hartley (it was published in a slightly revised form in 1807, when he was eleven).

The most striking thing of all is the poem's psychological insight. One would like to be able to report that Hartley Coleridge, far from being a fragile 'dew-drop', grew fat and prosperous, and gave the poem the lie. But he did not; he had a tragic life, as a failed scholar, failed teacher, occasional poet and genteel, alcoholic vagrant. The Wordsworths went on giving him what support they could. He ended up living in Grasmere, and died in January 1849 at the age of 53, before either Wordsworth or Dorothy. Wordsworth helped with arrangements for the funeral, and declared that Hartley should be buried next to the Wordsworth family graves: 'Let him lie by us, he would have wished it'.[60] The 'us' is the whole Wordsworth and Hutchinson family; Hartley was a child to them all. But how did Wordsworth feel about effectively writing Hartley's epitaph when he was five or six?[61]

The poem however brought to a head Wordsworth's intense thinking about the child's necessary wildness, and its terrible danger too. You wish, perhaps, to bind your life together so that you are the same person as an adult as you were as a child – and yet that is impossible. You have to grow into being an adult, with all the pain which that involves, and to some extent you give up being the child; a barrier grows between you and that childish time. That simply has to happen. It's conceivably far worse if it *doesn't* happen.

'To H. C.' is a painful poem in every sense. It would constantly have reminded them of his father, too; it was knowing Coleridge so well which allowed Wordsworth to see so deeply into the child ('the child is father of the man' was a line he would draft just a couple of days later). The poem about the child was a kind of coded warning to the father.

On Friday the 26th, apart from working on 'The Cuckow' – and writing to Annette, someone else who continued to haunt him out of the past – Wordsworth reworked another (apparently previously drafted) poem, about Silver How, the hill to the south-west, over which the moon rose, which the lakes reflected, and which they could see from their house. No extant poem concerned with Silver How can, however, now be identified among Wordsworth's poetry written in these months.[62] That is slightly odd; every single other piece of writing mentioned in Dorothy's Journal can be identified and in most cases dated. It would, of course, be especially interesting if this unidentified poem (which on the Friday afternoon 'he had been trying without success to alter') had been one describing how – beneath Silver How – 'waters on a starry night / Are beautiful and fair': that is, if it incorporated writing which would acquire a new form in the *Ode* he would work on the next day. The pattern of a poem going badly towards the end of one day, but developing brilliantly the following morning, occurs more than once in the biographical record.[63] All we can say for certain is that the Silver How poem has vanished – or, more likely, became part of another poem – and that last thing at night, another poem supplanted it. 'While I was getting into bed', Dorothy noted, 'he wrote the Rainbow':[64] that is, 'My heart leaps up'.

V

This was the third or fourth poem of this fortnight to concentrate on how the child's experience is – and is not – something which shapes and conditions the adult's experience. With this poem, and with the *Ode*, Wordsworth brought to a climax an intensely creative fortnight. 'My heart leaps up' briefly and hauntingly summed up things which had been said in different ways in both 'The Butterfly' and 'The Cuckow'; but it also tried to see the positive side of what he examined tragically in 'To H. C.'. Wordsworth first called his new poem 'Extempore', as if his writing had, suddenly, crystallised into these few lines. We do not know exactly what the first draft was like, but we do know that Wordsworth tried to revise it in May ('William very nervous – after he was in bed haunted with altering the Rainbow'[65]). But the version he sent to Sara Hutchinson before that attempt at revision is probably quite close to what suddenly emerged on the evening of 26 March.

> My heart leaps up when I behold
> A Rainbow in the sky:
> So was it when my life began,
> So is it, now I am a Man,
> So be it, when I shall grow old
> Or let me die!
> The Child is Father of the man;

5

> And I should wish that all my days may be
> Bound each to each by natural Piety.[66]

The last three lines are a kind of stepping back from the insight of the first six; they may even be a later addition to an 'extempore' opening.[67] The seventh line is a conversation stopper if ever there was one, a question as much as it is an answer. The last two lines are different again: given all this, what effect on my life should it have? I 'should wish': I am not certain, I am not certain that I even want it: I think I do. And where the first six lines are so sharp, hard, crystalline, the last line means what you think it does. 'Piety' – with or without the capital letter which Sara Hutchinson gave it and which Wordsworth gave it again in 1842[68] – is *Pietas*, the respect a child owes its father: as an adult you *respect* the childhood which has brought you up, as a father brings you up. The line is also a challenge to the way you may wish to invoke other kinds of (non-natural) Piety, as in the christening of children, for example, to go back a week.

The child's feelings are where your adult feelings start from; to some considerable extent you still *are* the child you once were. Every time you see a rainbow, you prove it. But the very next poem Wordsworth worked on – within twelve hours – brought all that into question, even more dramatically than 'To H. C.' had done.

During that memorable Friday, Dorothy had spent some time at her customary, crucial work of copying. They had walked up to the Olives after tea, and there 'I left Wm & while he was absent wrote out poems'. Wordsworth was making arrangements for a delivery of dung the following morning, and Dorothy was doubtless making copies for Coleridge, to take with them on the Sunday. When Coleridge wrote to his friend Tom Poole at the start of May, he noted 'I will transcribe 2 pleasing little poems of Wordsworth's –'[69] and included texts of two poems, one of them 'The Butterfly'.[70] It has been suggested that Coleridge disapproved of Wordsworth's output of short poems – we should certainly ask what quantity of disapproval may be contained in that word 'pleasing' – and I shall look at this whole subject below.[71] But Coleridge also clearly liked such poems in one way; and he obviously had nothing new of his own which he wanted to copy out. A long poem he himself was writing that spring was in progress: it too was about pain and loss and childhood, but it was certainly not 'pleasing'.

Chapter Six

The Ode and the Letter: 27 March to 13 April

I discussed in the Preface Dorothy's journal entry for Saturday 27 March: the divine morning, the arrival of part of an ode, the arrival of Mr Olive's dung, the digging, the sitting in the orchard. The following day, Dorothy and Wordsworth walked up to Keswick in pouring rain, and stayed with the Coleridges for a week; and they were there on 4 April, which Coleridge celebrated in the title of the poem he wrote as the *Letter* and published as *Dejection: an Ode.* But what exactly arrived as part of Wordsworth's ode on the morning of Saturday 27 March? And what exactly was Coleridge writing a week later? And what was the relationship between the two poems, as well as between the two poets? All this is surprisingly mysterious, and it is worth disentangling the few available facts, which over the years have – for the sake of convenient narrative – been polished into a kind of burnished orthodoxy. There are in fact two, rather different stories which might be told at this point, in part about the poems, but mostly about the relationships of people in this alternative family group.

Coleridge biographers are generally keen to show their man hostile (with good cause) to Wordsworth; Wordsworth biographers concentrate on Wordsworth's (very proper) efforts to set his friend straight. The first of the stories which it is possible to tell about the two poems recounts how Wordsworth began the first four stanzas of his *Immortality Ode* on 27 March; and how Coleridge – because he did not agree with them – answered them in a poem of his own addressed to Sara Hutchinson, his *Letter*, written on 4 April: a poem which Holmes suggests the Wordsworths 'initially greeted with dismay'; and how Wordsworth, in his turn, seeing that Coleridge's poem 'was a challenge that could only be answered in poetry', made a 'poetic response'[1] to the Coleridge poem with 'The Leech-gatherer', written in May, telling *him* in turn what he was getting wrong; while Coleridge, later in the summer, revised *his* poem into a much briefer public version (*Dejection: an Ode*) which he published on 4 October, and which in its turn 'responds to Wordsworth's "The Leech-Gatherer"'. The story can be summed up as follows: 'It has long been recognised that the first four stanzas of *Intimations*, together with *Dejection* and *The Leech Gatherer*, form a sequence, provoking and answering each other, and showing in the process a widening gap between the two poets . . .'[2]

All that may be true: at any rate, it hardly needs arguing for, as its way of linking together the available pieces of evidence lies behind every extant piece of scholarly, critical and biographical writing about the events of this spring. So, for example, simply confining ourselves to the March–April end of the story, Coleridge's *Letter* as a 'response' to Wordsworth's poem is confidently described: 'That Coleridge begins the verse letter to Sara as a response to the first four stanzas of Wordsworth's "Intimations" is well known . . .'; 'the fair copy of Coleridge's first version of "Dejection" . . . containing what are unquestionably direct responses to lines from the early stanzas of the Ode, bears the date 4 April 1802.'[3] A recent Wordsworth biography not only says that the first four stanzas of the *Ode* were written on 27 March, but even tells us why Wordsworth stopped: 'he abandoned them in despair',[4] presumably grateful for the dung's arrival, so that he could (gloomily, of course) dig it in.

II

It seems however impossible that Coleridge could have written his *Letter* (even in its short form as *Dejection*) 'between sunset and midnight'[5] on Sunday 4 April 1802, in spite of the fact that he would inscribe the date of 4 April 1802 in his fair copy of the *Letter*, and 'Letter written Sunday Evening, April 4' on a version of *Dejection* he made on 19 July 1802. The *Letter* would end up 338 lines long: the longest piece of verse he had written since the second part of *Christabel* in 1800, in fact, over which we know he toiled for months.[6]

The inscribed date is however remarkably similar to those he made elsewhere. He gave the subtitle 'Written on the Christmas Eve of 1794' to his poem 'Religious Musings'; he added 'composed . . . on the last day of that year' to his 1796 poem 'Ode to the Departing Year'; and he gave his poem 'To William Wordsworth' in 1807 the subtitle 'Composed on the Night after his Recitation of a Poem on the Growth of an Individual Mind'. Not one of those claims was literally true. Each of the poems (419 lines, 161 lines and 112 lines long respectively) took a good deal longer than claimed by the date. A single day's or night's inspiration and composition was part of Coleridge's mythology of them. Because he was so interested by spontaneity, he regularly employed such a fiction about work which had taken a great deal longer than a single evening or day to produce; there would have been about five hours and twenty minutes available for such a purpose, early in April.[7] And Dorothy Wordsworth herself actually recorded, of that very evening in Greta Hall, where she and Wordsworth were staying, 'We sate pleasantly enough after supper':[8] they would have had supper sometime between eight o'clock and ten o'clock. It seems therefore probable that Coleridge wrote rather little of the 338 line poem that evening, but spent it (as Dorothy did) 'pleasantly' in company. He would not be seeing the Wordsworths again for several weeks, and for that reason if no other is extremely unlikely to have shut himself away in his study.

The alternative story of the writing of both these poems is – in just that way – both messier and less conclusive. It suggests that the two poets had probably both spent a considerable time, during the past two years, writing two large-scale works, the *Ode* and the *Letter*, and that the sequence of composition in both cases is almost unknowable: except that both probably started earlier, and finished later, than is usually accepted. This story seeks to replace the beautifully shaped orthodox account of a series of poems and responses with one which is a good deal less certain: in which both writers (in so far as they were speaking to each other in their work) sometimes spoke at the same time, because they were actually *closer* to each other than they are in the admonitory orthodox version. An alternative story can, however, give equal weight to all the available facts. And if it leaves holes and gaps – well, that is commonly the nature of surviving evidence, and biography must just accept the fact.

So what might Wordsworth have been writing before the dung arrived? Would we even recognise it if we had it? No extant manuscript of any of the *Ode* can be dated before March 1804; and Wordsworth was a compulsive reviser. It is possible that not a line of the 1804 version of the poem had more than a tenuous relationship with what he was writing in 1802. The orthodox account, however, depends on the text of the start of the poem in March 1804 being to all intents and purposes identical with the text of the poem on 27 March 1802.

One piece of text, however, dating from considerably earlier than 1802 (but published as part of an ode), suggests what an early version of the start might have been like:

> 'There was a time when earth, and sea, and skies,
> 10   The bright green vale and forest's dark recess.
> When all things lay before my eyes
>   In steady loveliness.
> But now I feel on earth's uneasy scene
>   Such motions as will never cease!
> 15   I only ask for peace –
> Then wherefore must I know, that such a time has been?'[9]

We only have to put those lines alongside the opening stanza of the *Ode* as it existed in March 1804 to see the differences and some of the worrying similarities:

> There was a time when meadow, grove and stream
>   The earth, and every common sight
>   To me did seem

Apparell'd in celestial light
5   The glory and the freshness of a dream;
It is not now as it has been of yore,
Turn wheresoee'r I may
By night or day
The things which I have seen, I see them now no more[10]

Whatever Wordsworth was writing on 27 March 1802, it may have been as different from the 1804 *Ode* as is that stanza.

That stanza had appeared in a poem ('The Mad Monk'[11]) published in the *Morning Post* on 13 October 1800 at exactly the time when work was appearing on which Coleridge and Wordsworth had collaborated (three other poems submitted by Coleridge in fact being written by Wordsworth: 'The Solitude of Binnorie', 'Inscription for a Seat by the Road Side Halfway up a Steep Hill, Facing South' and 'Alcaeus to Sappho'[12]).

Various explanations of the 'Mad Monk' lines have been produced,[13] but it remains unresolved whether the *Morning Post* publication was (i) written by Coleridge as a parody of Wordsworth (but how could he be parodying something not yet written?); (ii) written by Coleridge but later seized on by Wordsworth as providing the manner and substance for a poem he himself wanted to write (though all the other examples show the debt being the other way round); (iii) written by Wordsworth and inserted by Coleridge in his poem (odd but possible); or (iv) written by Wordsworth and given to Coleridge to get him out of a problem with a deadline. During October and November 1800 Wordsworth regularly supplied Coleridge with poems when necessary.[14]

But if we accept that Wordsworth *may* originally have written the lines, then a date for some at least of the *Ode* by October 1800 becomes not just a possibility but really rather likely. It is hard to imagine that either Coleridge or Wordsworth could have written the *Morning Post* stanza unless something akin to the opening of the *Ode* already existed. It seems to me most probable that the 'Mad Monk' poem was authorially a joint effort, with Coleridge in his best Gothic vein supplying the effects, and Wordsworth providing the lyric (which appeared in inverted commas). The poem was published only a week after they had been together working on the new edition of *Lyrical Ballads*, one day before a poem certainly by Wordsworth appeared in the *Morning Post*, and six days before another poem appeared there which we can also be certain was written by Wordsworth.[15]

This alternative story would therefore suggest that when Wordsworth worked on his *Ode* in March 1802, the poem was bringing together ideas, language and possibilities which had been circulating in his poetry (and circulating to Coleridge too) for at least eighteen months.

It was thus obviously a different kind of poem from 'The Leech-gatherer'. The latter was fairly quickly written and dispatched to friends: Coleridge, Sara and Mary all saw it in May 1802. The *Ode* however was 'work in progress', rather as the 'poem to Coleridge' (later *The Prelude*), 'The Pedlar' and *Home at Grasmere* were: so that it was not sent around, though Wordsworth *was* in the habit of reading such work aloud to an intimate circle.

The *Ode* might thus best be seen as a work whose material and ideas were under constant discussion between Coleridge and Wordsworth and Dorothy, and at times others, and which was extended and developed over a period. We outsiders get only occasional glimpses of it during that period, as it momentarily breaks the surface before submerging again. Even a phrase as memorable and distinctive as the *Ode*'s 'And fade into the light of common day', can find its parallel in *Home at Grasmere*, written early in 1800 and transcribed in 1802: '. . . finds these the growth of common day.'[16] On the other hand, there is also evidence that what was supposed to have been written *later* (in the period between 1802 and 1804) was actually in progress in the spring of 1802. What Jonathan Wordsworth saw as an 'anticipation' of 'The Ode' in 'The Barberry-Tree' (written around May 1802) –

> And when my trance was ended
> And on my way I tended, . . .
>
> And by the Vision splendid
> Is on his way attended . . .

– may not be an anticipation at all, but (as I shall suggest below) yet another of the parodic versions of Wordsworth's existing styles which accumulated in 'The Barberry-Tree'.[17]

But *differences* between work sharing a common language also abound; where the early 1800 *Home at Grasmere* would remark 'Spring! for this day belongs to thee, rejoice!/ Not upon me alone hath been bestowed', the *Ode* would in 1804 state 'To me alone there came a thought of grief'.[18] But then the *Ode* vanishes again into its own pre-history, until (probably) the appearance of the *Morning Post* stanza in October 1800; it is a gnomic voice coming out of the side of Etna, issuing from some monk or hermit: Wordsworth in Grasmere, perhaps, as portrayed by Coleridge. Its next appearance is in the language of Coleridge's *Letter*, where he shows himself thoroughly aware of the kind of writing Wordsworth was doing:

> These Mountains too, these Vales, these Woods, these Lakes,
> 290   Scenes full of Beauty & of Loftiness
> Where all my Life I fondly hop'd to live –
> I were sunk low indeed, did they <u>no</u> solace give;
> But oft I seem to feel, & evermore I fear,
> They are not to me now the things, which once they were.[19]

That may be Coleridge's echo of what he had heard, or read, in April 1802; it may go back to what he had heard and read in November 1800 – or to any date in between.

Wordsworth's writing of 'My Heart leaps up' on 26 March 1802 seems to have provoked the reappearance of the *Ode* work; in part because it ran clean counter to something the *Ode* had quite likely been saying for some time (that the natural world no longer had the significant impact which once it had had). The following day, Dorothy's journal shows the *Ode* full in view. It appeared again, perhaps, in the double poem 'These chairs they have no words to utter' which Wordsworth was heard repeating in April 1802, a poem which also has links with 'The Mad Monk'. And then, another positive sighting, on the evening of 17 June 1802, when Dorothy noted: 'William added a little to the Ode he is writing'.[20]

To sum up this story, then. Wordsworth may well have written something of his *Ode* – probably concentrating on what the adult can no longer see in the natural world – during 1800: and Coleridge and Dorothy knew all about it. The work would then have remained 'in progress' for a period of eighteen months or so; it is just possible that it was known between him and Dorothy as the 'Silver How poem'. He certainly resumed work on a poem of that name on 26 March 1802, and wrote a conclusion for it; but then struggled with revision 'without success'. The first six lines of his poem 'My Heart leaps up', drafted on the evening of the 26th, may well have been a 'timely utterance' which gave relief to poetry which had hardly moved for eighteen months or so, just as they gave relief to the thoughts of the bleakness of increasing age and incapacity to experience the natural world as fully as before. (We would of course expect such an utterance to *post*-date the poetry it was providing a relief from, rather than to *pre*-date it, as in the orthodox account.) It would also have been natural for the *Ode*, at that point, to have moved into an engagement with the ideas about children which had been so important in Wordsworth's life and writing over the previous fortnight, and which had been central to 'My Heart leaps up'.

However, the child who (at least by the time the poem was finished, in 1803 or 1804), had taken his position at its centre, did not acquire that position simply because 'My Heart leaps up' had propelled him into it. The child occupies a very strange position in the 1804 poem. On the one hand, he is addressed with extravagant titles: 'Thou best Philosopher . . . Mighty Prophet! Seer blest!' This child is not just father of the man: he is grandfather, great-uncle, superior being, close to God, closer still to Nature. But the poem also sees the child as perfectly ordinary: simply optimistic, *not* worrying about death; possessing

> the simple creed
> Of childhood, whether fluttering or at rest
> With new-born hope for ever in his breast,[21]

Readers usually feel rather more at ease with that version of the child than with
the Prophet and Seer. I suggested above how important Hartley Coleridge was
to Wordsworth in 1802; the poem 'To H. C.' is intensely reminiscent of
passages in the 1804 *Ode*. And in that poem a child extremely suggestive of
Hartley plays a significant role as incipient adult, imitating the affairs of adulthood, and being thoroughly disturbing to the watching adult. Why, asks the
1804 *Ode*, does such a child positively thrust himself into adulthood?

> Why with such earnest pains dost thou provoke
> The years to bring the inevitable yoke . . .
> Full soon the soul shall have her earthly freight,
> The world upon thy noble nature seize,
> 130   With all its varieties,
> Heavy as frost, and deep almost as life.[22]

The child, watched over by the despairing adult, will not allow its own childish nature to govern it. 'Heavy as Frost' (and Coleridge's 'Frost at Midnight', in
which the infant Hartley had been safely guarded from frost's effects, is once
again not far away), the world's secret ministry infiltrates the child, and
destroys it *as* a child.

There seems to me rather little coherence in the way such poetry slips from
attitude to attitude towards children. Whether that is a reflection of the conditions of the poem's composition over a period of years, or whether it is because
the poem is being honest to the variety of roles it finds the child occupying, is
not clear. It does however suggest how, over the period 1802–4, Wordsworth
enlarged and extended his understandings of the child in the *Ode*, and found
ways of being honest to all of them; rather as the whole *Ode* is balanced around
a contradiction ('as an adult, you've lost what is most important of all': 'the
adult loses nothing, there is only gain') which I shall discuss at the end of this
Chapter.

III

If it were simply dates and texts we were seeking to establish, then perhaps
none of this would matter very much. But if it is relationships which we wish
to trace, it matters a great deal. I showed above how too little attention has
been paid to the continuing relationship between Wordsworth and Coleridge
after 1798: most critics and biographers have, for their own purposes, sought to
play up the disagreements between the two writers and to locate a particular
time for some kind of a falling *out* of love with each other, with as much
dedication as biographers try to establish when Coleridge fell *in* love with
Sara Hutchinson.[23] Wherever one looks, however, the relationship between
Coleridge and the Wordsworths springs into emotional life. One tiny example:

Coleridge in London in January to February 1802, reading Sir Thomas Browne's *Religio Medici*, came across the sentence 'I love to lose myself in a Mystery, to pursue my reason to an *oh altitudo!*' He scribbled in the margin 'So say I: so does dear W. W.'[24] He naturally thought of his friend as dear; exactly as Wordsworth, writing to him in April 1802, naturally bade *him* 'Farewell, my dear, dear friend', and Dorothy thought about him in November 1801 as 'dear dear fellow'.[25]

Just looking at this crucial week between 27 March and 4 April reveals the opportunities they had for closeness, as well as for discussion of these particular poems. On Sunday the 28th – with the letters to Annette and Mary written, a box of clothes sent on by carrier, decisions about France taken, the garden dug and a poem under way – the Wordsworths walked the fourteen miles up to Keswick. It poured with rain: 'Arrived wet to skin'.[26] Coleridge, however, came to meet them in spite of the weather: 'C was not tired with walking to meet us – I lay down after dinner with a bad head ach.' Coleridge and 'dear W. W.' presumably then spent the evening together: Wordsworth's first chance to tell his friend how the *Ode* was developing.

The following day, Dorothy made some preparations for the next three weeks of travelling, and also talked to Sarah Coleridge. The men went off by themselves, 'to Ormathwaite', a couple of miles away, probably to visit the Rev. Joseph Wilkinson, an old acquaintance. The week would be full of walks, visits, teas and dinners with friends – and, for the Wordsworths, just sitting down outdoors: Dorothy records how they 'sate for some time on the hill'. On the Friday, they 'sate all the morning in the field', Dorothy playing the part of the good guest: 'I nursed Derwent' (just eighteen months old). On the Saturday, however – they may have been waiting for good weather – 'Wm went on to Skiddaw with C': a day's walking and climbing together. On the Sunday there were more walks and visits, and Dorothy 'repeated his verses' to the company: 'We sate pleasantly enough after supper'. There would have been a vast amount of time for Wordsworth and Coleridge to engage in talk, poetry, their common concerns. And, at the end of the week – after that day out with Wordsworth, and after hearing *his* verses – Coleridge wrote something of his new poem: an account of depression, of failure in marriage, of hopeless love, all in the context of the group as a whole.

But to whom was this poetry addressed? This may appear an altogether unnecessary question. Holmes and Gill both call the *Letter* the 'Letter to Sara Hutchinson' in their indexes as well as their texts, while Holmes and Beer actually create a new Coleridge title by calling it that in published editions;[27] Mary Moorman calls it 'the "Letter" in verse to Sara Hutchinson'; Whalley goes so far as to refer to it throughout his book as the *Letter to Asra*; and Griggs included it as a letter to Sara Hutchinson in his edition of Coleridge's *Collected Letters*.[28]

It is worth reminding ourselves that neither of the two authoritative texts has a name inscribed in its title.[29] Given the damage caused by something

Coleridge had written to Sara in January or February 1802, which reduced her to 'bodily Sickness',[30] she may well not have been sent the finished poem at all. (None of it appears in the collection of Coleridge's poems which she herself made.[31]) The narrator of the poem recognises that 'thou art weak & pale with Sickness, Grief, & Pain, / And I – I made thee so!'[32] It is even possible that what she had been sent was some draft of part of the poem. If that were true, then Coleridge would never have considered dispatching a complete poem which would have carried the process a good deal further.

His remark to Thomas Poole on 7 May 1802 that he had – on 4 April – written him a letter in verse, but had not sent it,[33] is usually assumed to be a lie (an excuse for failing to write a real letter); while the fact that the Sotheby text of 19 July has 'Wordsworth' throughout where the Mary Hutchinson and Coleridge copies have 'Sara' is – again – usually taken as a kind of cover-up, an act of self-censorship. But I am suggesting that what existed of the poem may have been on Coleridge's desk, as ideas and fragments and drafts, from December 1801 onwards, at least, and perhaps even earlier: just as Wordsworth's *Ode* had been on *his* work table. And that at different times it had struck him as a letter to Sara, to Poole, to Wordsworth.

There is evidence for a long period of gestation. As early as the autumn of 1800, Coleridge had made a notebook entry describing the sounds of the night wind: 'A trembling Oo! Oo! like a wounded man on a field of battle whose wounds smarted with the cold'. This entry precisely prefigures the *Letter* and *Dejection*:

> 'Tis of a Rushing of an Host in Rout,
> And many Groans from men with smarting Wounds –
> At once they groan with smart, and shudder with the Cold![34]

He did not, at any rate, have exactly *that* experience on the evening of 4 April 1802, storm or no storm. Like any poet, he was using a metaphor (we find him going to Humphry Davy's lectures on science at the Royal Institution in January 1802 'to renew my stock of metaphors'.[35]) Again, in February 1801, another reference to the sound of the wind (this time in a letter to Poole) runs parallel to lines 211–15 of the *Letter* and lines 115–19 of *Dejection*.

Even more strikingly, in the winter of 1801–2 he was obviously contemplating writing several poems about love, one of which very clearly became the *Letter*. He planned

> A lively picture of a man, disappointed in marriage, & endeavoring to make a compensation to himself by virtuous & tender & brotherly friendship with an amiable Woman – the obstacles – the jealousies – the impossibility of it. – Best advice that he should as much as possible withdraw himself from pursuits of morals &c – & devote himself to abstract sciences –[36]

The fact that the narrator of the *Letter* resolves

> . . . to be still & patient all I can;
> And haply by abstruse Research to steal
> From my own Nature all the Natural Man —[37]

suggests how close the winter plan came to the poem as actually written: a relationship with a 'virtuous & tender & brotherly friendship' was perhaps what he still wanted. And then, in March 1802, a notebook entry written almost certainly at Gallow Hill about the appearance of the new leaves on the Larch — 'The Larches in spring push out their separate bundles of Leaves first into green Brushes or Pencils, ⟨then into⟩ which soon then are only small tassels [. . .]'[38] is directly comparable to lines 26–7 of the *Letter* and is very clearly either their source or their fellow. Too early in the year for actual observation in North Yorkshire at the start of March, the observation may in fact go back to something seen and remembered the previous year, and only now written down. He was starting to transcribe into his notebook phrases and fragments he would subsequently use. Between 1 and 13 November 1801, for example, he had made the following entry: 'Health in his cheeks & the Light of honorable Thought in his Eyes —'.[39]

If we set this against what became lines 145–6 in the *Letter*, it is obvious that this tiny piece of the poem has already been 'written' (although differently gendered):

> Health in thy Limbs, and in thy Eyes the Light
> Of Love, and Hope, and honourable Feeling

These examples all serve to remind us that the *Letter* and *Dejection*, like Wordsworth's *Ode*, for all their appearance of being the spontaneous overflow of powerful feelings, and occurring on a particular day, actually had a creative history of metaphor, plan, draft version, and revision.

And although the *Letter* is a poem apparently describing a particular evening, with very clear facts about the weather, the sky, the time and the date, we actually have reason to doubt the literal truth of each one of them. Sunday the 4th was not even the evening of the new moon (that had been two days earlier, on Friday the 2nd). There had however been a spectacular new moon on Friday 5 March, with exactly the phenomenon of 'the old moon in the new moon's arms' which the *Letter* and *Dejection* would describe, and at least two of the group had seen it: Dorothy Wordsworth in Grasmere, and Wordsworth in Keswick (Coleridge himself being over at Gallow Hill, seeing Sara Hutchinson): Sarah Coleridge may have seen it too. It would be interesting to know if the spectacle had also been visible on the other side of the Pennines, at Gallow Hill, where Coleridge had been since 2 March. If he had seen it there, in the company of Sara, it might well have taken on an even more special meaning for him (and for her): and if Mary had seen it too, then all six of the group would have seen it at the same time.

But it is at least worth considering the idea that (whatever the date says) the moon and the storm in the *Letter* and *Dejection* are as likely to have been purely literary events – like the apparent fact of the inscription between twilight and midnight – as events occurring on a particular day.

The date of 4 April in its title suggests, however, that the poem took some important step forward that day; the fact that the Wordsworths were in the house at the time probably had something to do with it: so that Coleridge's poem – or poems – or poetry – turned into yet another of those 'Apologia Pro Vita Sua' pieces of writing which so many of his works are.[40] On this date, it may indeed have taken on the shape of a poem (or possibly even two poems), rather than being a heap of ideas and drafts, and have acquired its shape of a symbolic evening turning to storm and night. It was also epiphany poetry; recording the realisation that his marriage was at an end. It would not be unusual for such a realisation – if that is what it was – to arrive during a visit from two of his closest friends. It is when you see your wife (or husband) with your friends that you ask yourself why you are married to *this* person as opposed to spending more time with *these* people; and house guests are notorious for driving existing tensions between couples up to a new pitch. With the Wordsworths asleep in the house, and a storm raging mentally (if not literally), Coleridge allowed himself to pursue – out of the thinking and anxieties and excitements of the past three years – a way of summing up what he felt.[41]

At this point, one direction it was taking was that of a poem (or a letter) addressed to Poole, probably explaining why Coleridge had done so little for the past two years; focussing upon dejection, too, it could easily have at one time been a letter to Wordsworth, as Coleridge made it in July. Another form may have been that of a poem to Sara Hutchinson, to explain to her why he had been behaving as he had.

The idea of Coleridge's own work in progress taking on the shape of a poem (or poem/letter) to Wordsworth may be reinforced if we consider that Wordsworth would certainly have repeated to him whatever existed of his own *Ode*, during the previous week. It would have been especially interesting if, from the top of Skiddaw the day before, they had been able to look across to the sea to the west: 'Hence in a season of calm weather, / Though inland far we be, / Our souls have sight of that immortal sea, / Which brought us hither . . .'.[42] But sometime around 11 or 12 April (the Wordsworths had left on the 5th) a letter went off to Dorothy Wordsworth from Coleridge which arrived at the Clarksons' house on the afternoon of 13 April: and it contained poetry. It was not until late on the 13th, between 8 and 9 at night, that Wordsworth himself got back. But Mrs Clarkson had clearly considered the letter important: 'Mrs C waked me from sleep with a letter from Coleridge'.[43] If Coleridge had wanted to send a letter to the Wordsworths direct, sending it to them at the Clarksons was obviously the best way: he knew they would be based there until the middle of the month (and that Dorothy would be there the whole time).

Wordsworth's return home from journeys normally cheered her up, and his arrival this time had provoked her to scream aloud when she was told he had arrived,[44] but the following morning things were very different. Whatever was in Coleridge's letter – and it seems to have been partly about his health, partly about his state of mind ('I fear he has his own torments' Dorothy commented[45]) – it had a serious effect on her. Wordsworth slept until early afternoon, following his day-and-a-half's ride over from Yorkshire, leaving Dorothy to walk with Mrs Clarkson. 'I was ill out of spirits – disheartened'. After dinner, later that afternoon, 'Wm & I took a long walk in the rain'.[46] It surprises me that so little attention has been paid to the fact that the letter from Coleridge contained poetry, and that Wordsworth commented on it in the reply he wrote three days later, when he and Dorothy were finally back in Grasmere:

> Now for a word about yourself. I am very sorry indeed you have been poorly. Let us see you as soon as ever you find an inclination to come over. I was much pleased with your verses in Ds letter; there is an admirable simplicity in the language of the first fragment, and I wish there had been more of the 2nd; the fourth line wants mending sadly, in other respects the lines are good.[47]

Coleridge had thus sent at least two 'fragments' of poetry, the second shorter than the first. On two other occasions later in the summer he sent some of the poetry he was working on to his correspondents; and it seems extremely likely that these April fragments, too, had been of the poem which became the *Letter* and *Dejection*. The fragments went to the Wordsworths within eight days of the date at the poem's head, the poem probably far from finished. But the poem-as-letter – in this case a letter to be read by the Wordsworths – had obviously taken a genuine step into existence. Wordsworth himself included two poems in his reply (the two he had himself just written, during his journey back from Yorkshire to Grasmere), but ended his letter 'Farewell, my dear, dear friend': obviously thinking of Coleridge as 'poorly', and not just with bodily sickness.[48]

Appendix I shows what the earliest surviving (July) version was like of the *Dejection* poem, which seems to have been the final outcome of the poem/letter to Wordsworth. The longer fragment which Coleridge sent the Wordsworths on 13 April could have been some version of lines 17–43 of the poem as it stood in July,[49] which would account for Wordsworth saying that this fragment had 'an admirable simplicity in the language'; the passage had ended

I see them all, so excellently fair!
I *see*, not *feel*, how beautiful they are!

That would have been exactly in tune with what he might have been hearing of the *Ode* during the previous two years. Furthermore, to judge by the fact that there was only one passage which Coleridge sent to both Sotheby and Southey, later in the summer, he may have sent Wordsworth some version of it.[50]

At some stage, however – perhaps on 4 April, perhaps well before 4 April, perhaps soon after – Coleridge found that he could address the material (or at least parts of it) as a kind of love letter to Sara Hutchinson. The more he thought about his depression and his marriage, the more it seemed to him that Sara was both the symptom and the answer and (in that way) an alternative focus for the poem. Whether this was true on 4 April we cannot be sure. The poetry sufficiently finished by the 12 April to be sent in the letter to Dorothy Wordsworth was clearly both impressive and depressing. More seems to have been finished by 20 April, when Coleridge came over to Grasmere and – on the 21st – 'repeated the verses he wrote to Sara'. Coleridge wrote other poems this spring which might be called 'verses . . . to Sara',[51] but Dorothy's wording confirms that the poetry she heard on the 21st was not a surprise to her. 'The verses' may have been the sections or fragments Coleridge had already sent in his letter, or extra sections of poetry which he had *not* included in his letter of the previous week. (Some lines addressed to Sara which he was drafting in his notebook between 16 and 21 April are clearly candidates for this development.[52])

It seems probable, however, that no one beside Mary Hutchinson and the Wordsworths would ever have been sent (or heard) that particular version. As a 'Letter to Sara', it was quite unpublishable: for her sake, and also for the sake of Sarah Coleridge. It is possible that Coleridge completed the *Dejection* version of the poem first (shorter versions of poems often precede longer versions), and then developed it into this private version, but more likely that the 'Work in Progress' developed in both forms over the summer, and – in one form – turned into a private poem to Sara, while – on the other hand – it became a very different kind of public poem, *Dejection*, in time for its appearance in the *Morning Post* in October, when there was no mention of Sara at all.

It was thus a poem (or perhaps we should better think of it as a pair of poems, sharing material) which at various times, for various reasons, in various forms, had been a letter to Poole, a letter to Wordsworth, a letter to Dorothy, a letter to Sara (some of it perhaps sent in January or February), a poem assembled in the letter sent to Sotheby, and a more carefully revised poem for the readers of the *Morning Post*. There was a constant transmission of poems in letters between Coleridge, the Wordsworths and the Hutchinsons; one of the three significant copies of this poem was actually made by Mary; another couple of fragments were sent to the Wordsworths at an early stage, and a full text given (or sent) to them later on, in the form of one of those hand-sewn booklets which made it easier to preserve and also to pass on to others. In each case, the poetry did its best to explain not just why Coleridge had been behaving as he had behaved recently. It was poetry, in all its forms, about depression and its paralysing effects; Coleridge wanted his friends to know about it and its intimate causes in his own case, as well as thinking it worthwhile for the general public to consider it (but not in the same depth).

IV

The same, of course, is true if we look at the way in which the *Letter* and *Dejection* may be (we have to be cautious) in some sense an engagement with the *Ode*, the poem of which Wordsworth had written something on the morning of 27 March, which Coleridge may already have known for a considerable time as work in progress, and the new (or perhaps simply updated) part of which Wordsworth probably recited to Coleridge during their visit to Greta Hall. The *Ode* in its new form, that is, may well have had something to do with that precise focus on 4 April which Coleridge clearly felt had contributed so profoundly to his own poetry that he made the date part of his title. If something of the material which ended up in the second half of the *Ode* had been recited to Coleridge on the Saturday or the Sunday – some version, say, of the lines stressing the 'higher sway' of the natural world,

190	And oh ye fountains, meadows, hills, and groves,
	Look not of any severing of our loves!
	Yet in my heart of hearts I feel your might
	I only have relinquished one delight
	Divine indeed of sense
195	A blessed influence
	To acknowledge under you a higher sway.[53]

– then Coleridge might well have felt like writing the lines which would appear in the July version of the poem, with their own diagnosis of where one might find something 'higher':

	O Wordsworth! we receive but what we give,
	And in our Life alone does Nature live:
	Our's is her Wedding-garment, our's her shroud!
55	And would we aught behold of higher Worth
	Than that inanimate cold World *allow'd*
	To the poor loveless ever-anxious Crowd,
	Ah! from the Soul itself must issue forth

A light, a Glory, a fair luminous Cloud

60   Enveloping the Earth![54]

On the other hand, the continued writing of the *Ode* during the summer
of 1802 allowed it to be a response to the *Letter* poetry as much as the other
way round: even the example just given would work just as easily as
Wordsworth responding to Coleridge. There is continual evidence of a two-
way transmission of ideas and language and response. Although it has become
habitual for us now to say that Wordsworth wrote the *Ode*, Coleridge wrote
the *Letter* in reply, and then Wordsworth replied again with 'The Leech-
gatherer', I suspect that the two poets would be astonished to find us so simply
marking out their agreements and disagreements, answers and responses.
Their writing was not so simple as the diagram has come to suggest; it was at
least as hard to disentangle as a friendship is. We know that copies of the
Letter and *Dejection* began to circulate, in one form or another, at some stage
that year; but Coleridge would have repeated parts of his own poem –
especially newly written parts which he could *not* recite to Sarah Coleridge –
when he met the Wordsworths over the spring and summer. We have no
evidence that any of the text of the *Ode* was sent out; it may have been. But
although Sara Hutchinson did not copy any part of it which we can now recognise, it would (like Coleridge's Work in Progress) have been quoted by its
author to the other man. Each poet was taking the chance of a peculiar
intimacy to reproduce the concerns of a group of friends talking together; it
would not really matter who first proposed an idea, or who rejected it: who
read it or who thought it first. As we have seen, this was certainly how
Coleridge and Wordsworth worked together.[55] What mattered was the conversation, the trust and inner belief of the people in the group. I suggest that we
might revive the term 'conversation poem' to describe what was happening
between the *Letter* poetry, the *Ode* and 'The Leech-gatherer' – and some of
Wordsworth's shorter poems of this period, too – even though we cannot be
wholly certain of the texts of the *Letter* and of the *Ode*.[56] The poetry participated in the lives of this group of people, and the people had a number of
opportunities to comment and participate. When Mary Hutchinson (or possibly Mary Wordsworth, after 4 October 1802) copied the *Letter* out, and
created the only copy which lacked both its title and its date, was she regarding such things as so well known, among the group, as not to need such anno-
tation (that depends partly on who the copy was for: the poet, the poet's friend,
the poet's beloved? And which beloved?) Or was she attempting to *disguise* the
nature of that utterance from eyes of outsiders to the group – eyes which might
have pried (those of her brothers, in particular?). Or – as the copy of the poem
she herself kept all her life, so that it ended up in her private papers after her
death – was it one made just for herself, out of her intense sympathy with its
author and with her sister's predicament: a copy which therefore needed no
introduction, no name in its title?

V

What were the poems about, that such a degree of interplay between them should occur?

Here we have to be very careful, as what the 1802 *Ode* was like we cannot be sure. But in the *Ode* as finished by 1804, Wordsworth was suggesting two, contradictory things, things split across the years it took to write the poem: on the one hand that (as an adult) he knew that the child saw more than the adult, felt more deeply, and that – as an adult – he was terribly conscious of loss. He had now for a long time been aware of things in the natural world which no longer affected him as they once had. But, on the other hand, at times like the spring of 1802 he also wanted to say that the loss was really not very important, because the adult saw in a different way, not just in a less compelling way, and that the child was only to be thought of as 'superior' in an odd, metaphorical way – because it was nearer its origin, nearer God, nearer nature, nearer 'home' (wherever or whatever home was):

	But trailing clouds of glory do we come
65	From God who is our home,
	Heaven lies about us in our infancy,
	Shades of the prison-house begin to close
	Upon the growing Boy
	But he beholds the light and whence it flows
70	He sees it in his joy.[57]

How conscious Wordsworth was that he was structuring the poem between two such contradictions need not detain us: we do not even know when this structure entered the poem's composition, though March 1802 looks as likely a time as any other. It was the same structure of opposition that he had used before, in 1798, in 'Tintern Abbey'. Now, however, he was doing so in a much more developed – and much more poignant – way. In 1798, he had seen the child's experience of the natural world as something almost frightening, certainly uncontrolled, certainly to be given up by the responsible adult, if with some regrets. It turned out, in that poem, that you are positively glad to have moved on from the child's state; that there are all kind of comforting adult things you can do now which the wild child you once were could not imagine doing.

In the period 1800–2, however, the child's experience was poignant because the adult would desperately like *not* to give it up: instead feels terribly nostalgic for what it was like to be a child, seeing the world in such a way, and feeling that capacity slipping away. By 1802, thinking about Hartley Coleridge had made this more complicated still. The child *may* be running into danger of sadness and distress very early indeed in its life, and cannot perhaps be relied on to have any direct vision of the world's realities, or even of reasons for simple optimism about the future. The narrator of the 1804 *Ode*, certainly, insists on the fact that – in spite of loss – he himself remains sensitive, emotional, tender:

> Thanks to the human heart by which we live
> Thanks to its tenderness its joys and fears
> To me the meanest flower that blows can give
> Thoughts that do often lie too deep for tears.[58]

But the trouble is that such an ending simply cannot engage with the awful bleakness and loss which has previously been expressed: the loss of what we might call the interior child.

> But there's a tree of many one
> A single field which I have look'd upon
> Both of them speak of something that is gone
> The pansy at my feet
> 55   Doth the same tale repeat
> Whither is fled the visionary gleam
> Where is it gone the glory and the dream[59]

And all the attempts at reassurance –

> O evil day if I were sullen
> While the earth herself is adorning
> This sweet May morning
> And the Children are pulling
> On every side
> In a thousand Vallies far and wide
> Fresh flowers: while the sun shines warm
> And the Babe leaps up in his Mother's arm
> I hear I hear with joy I hear –

cannot match the simple statements:

> It is not now as it has been of yore
> Turn wheresoe'er I may
> By night or day
> 50   The things which I have seen I see them now no more[60]

It is very hard to see how Coleridge's *Letter* (or *Dejection*) could have been any kind of an answer to any of *that*, except by way of saying that Wordsworth had located the cause of pain in the wrong place. The *Letter* and *Dejection* agree that, yes, the adult's pain and loss are real, and that as an adult you move around the world seeing things but *not* feeling them –

> Yon crescent Moon, as fix'd as if it grew
40 In it's own cloudless, starless Lake of Blue –
> A boat becalm'd! dear William's Sky Canoe!
> – I see them all, so excellently fair!
> I see, not feel, how beautiful they are![61]

This, however, is because you no longer respond to Joy in the way in which you should: and because your life has gone wrong in all kinds of ways. Restoration of the child's experience and insight as Wordsworth describes it in the *Ode* would, in the *Letter*, be of very little use:

> My genial Spirits fail –
45 And what can these avail
> To lift the smoth'ring Weight from off my Breast?
> It were a vain Endeavor,
> Tho' I should gaze for ever
> On that Green Light, which lingers in the West!
50 I may not hope from outward Forms to win
> The Passion & the Life, whose Fountains are within![62]

In Coleridge's poetry it is depression which is the real problem. Even Joy has become something you can only *talk* about: the whole point is that you do *not* feel it.

In lots of ways, then, the 1804 *Ode* looks more like a response to the *Letter* and *Dejection* than the other way round; as if Wordsworth were saying that all this unhappiness in the adult, this grief, which Coleridge writes about so very explicitly, is not because his marriage has gone wrong, or because the person he loves cannot respond, or because he is a depressive personality, but because – as an adult – he is handicapped in ways that if he looks at himself as a child he can understand. If your problem is not being able to feel, only to see, then – says the *Ode* – there is a reason for it: and it is not an absolute disaster, either.

The poems intermesh constantly, but without forming a simple structure of question and answer. What 'The Leech-gatherer' would say to the author of the *Letter* in particular, a couple of months later, would be that there are people so much worse off than you, that you should stop bothering about yourself and your fine feelings and the women you love and – instead – look around you: if you do, then you will find yourself a horrible object of your own contempt. Which, unfortunately, Coleridge knew all too well: that whenever he looked objectively at himself, he was aware of himself as a horrible object of his own contempt.

But what 'The Leech-gatherer' would also do, positively, as (itself) a kind of answer-in-progress to the *Ode*, is to say that the adult's unhappiness is *not* only because he is no longer a child. It comes because he has become the wrong sort of adult; and that, by recovering a way of looking as a child looks – which it is still possible to do, as an adult – then he can still see the world better and more comprehensively, in spite of everything: and he can start to realise the world as it really is, and has to be, for an adult, who is all the time going to come up against pain, and grief and loss. What the poet can do is clear the doors of perception, so that you can see as a child sees, after all: see the old man bent in half, and neither turn away thinking of your own problems, nor patronise him, nor bombard him with meaningless questions as if *he* were a prophet or a seer, possessed of all the answers. That in its own turn might have helped sharpen up the oppositions which were being built into (or might already have been built into) the *Ode*.

It is worth reminding ourselves that not a single datable text of the *Letter* or *Dejection* exists before 'The Leech-gatherer' was in Coleridge's hands; so we might also be looking for a response to 'The Leech-gatherer' in Coleridge's poetry, as much as the other way round. That would perhaps take the form of saying that, in spite of all your experiences with interesting (but admittedly boring) old men on moors who apparently have the answer to life's problems, the *real* problem is that you must find the answer to your problems within yourself; and the trouble with the admonition in the 'Leech-gatherer' to have a 'firm mind' was that *that* was really the problem, as Coleridge had experienced it: so that it obviously could not be the solution to the problem.

It should not surprise us that these poems should in such ways work together. It was the nature of the long and brotherly conversation which this book has been tracing that such poems are the audible fragments of conversations, the relics and common concerns of friendship, which went on in a number of different and – for the most part – now inaccessible ways. To 'The Leech-gatherer' as response to the *Letter* and *Dejection*, Coleridge's only answer would perhaps have been that unfortunately he loved Sara, but knew it would come to nothing, and that it hurt; and he published *Dejection* on Wordsworth's wedding day, as if to say 'this – unfortunately – is true for me, whatever else – luckily for you – may be true for *you* . . .'

But there were, too, many other small and detailed ways in which the conversation of the two men flourished. The next chapter will look at one fortnight's poetry writing, from late April, to see such conversation in progress: where we actually have written contemporary written evidence of it.

Chapter Seven

A Fortnight in Spring: 15 April to 1 May

Away from home in the spring of 1802, Wordsworth did not often write poetry; he preferred the everyday habits of contemplation and walking in the places to which he was used, in particular the orchard at Town End and the roads and hills around Grasmere. During the visit to the Coleridges which he and Dorothy paid between 28 March and 5 April, for example, he seems to have written nothing (though visits to Keswick were always so filled with talk – and this one with social events – that this cannot have been unexpected). It was Coleridge whom we can be sure was writing poetry. Wordsworth and Dorothy had then gone up to the Clarksons at Eusemere, and Wordsworth had ridden off to Bishop Middleham on his birthday, 7 April, to pay the visit to Mary which they had decided back in March he should make. He was there from the evening of the 8th until the evening of the 12th and – again – seems to have written nothing while there.

It would not, anyway, have been poetry which would have mattered during such a visit, although Mary would doubtless have been given – or have heard – what he had written recently; and in particular would almost certainly have been an audience for what was written of the *Ode*. But what Wordsworth must have needed to do, more than anything else, was to make right with her what had already been suggested by letter; that she approve the financial arrangements for Caroline, and the plan for her to become Annette's ward; and that they should only get married after he had been to France, which would obviously mean a later date for the wedding.

It is, however, too easy to assume that a few months more waiting, after all the years they had remained single, would not have mattered much to them. We know from two later recollections that the extra months *did* matter. Eight years later, in the summer of 1810, when Wordsworth had been away from home for three-and-a-half weeks on a series of visits accompanied by Dorothy, but with Mary staying behind in Grasmere – their son William had been born only six weeks earlier – he wrote to her about the state he was getting into. The separation

> really has left me nearly in the same state as I was when you were at Middleham and Gallow hill; with a thousand tender thoughts intermingled,

and consciousness of realized bliss and happiness, to render separation from you heavier and more uneasy. Our friends here[1] look forward to a repetition of this visit next year; but I cannot think of anything of the kind; nor will I ever, except from a principle of duty, part from you again, to stay any where more than one week. I cannot bear it. I feel the shortness and uncertainty of life; I feel that we must separate finally so soon, even if our lives be lengthened, that it seems criminal to me in a high degree, to part from you except from a strong call of unquestionable moral obligation. —[2]

And in another letter he remembered 'Middleham' as the place where he especially desired 'day and night to see you again'.[3] Only a 'strong call of unquestionable moral obligation' (such as would take him to France in August 1802) could come between them.

Why, then, did he not stay longer at Middleham on this particular journey? For one thing, the longer he 'realized' his happiness, the more it led to those feelings 'heavier and more uneasy'. For another, he was clearly caught between his feelings for Mary and his feelings for Dorothy, back in Eusemere awaiting his return. Dorothy appears to have taken separation and loss rather worse than Mary did; but that may only be because we *know* so much about her feelings, through her journal. The Wordsworths in general, however, all seem to have insisted that their feelings were paramount, and that they intended to respond to them, and demanded that others respect them. Wordsworth stayed in Middleham only four days.

But during the late afternoon of his return journey, on the 12th, riding through Raby Park near Staindrop in County Durham – and pretty well in the dark, too, by the time he finished, even if he had started in the twilight –

he began to write that poem of the Glow-worm not being able to ride[4] upon the long Trot – interrupted in going through the Town of Staindrop. Finished it about 2 miles & a half beyond Staindrop – he did not feel the jogging of the horse while he was writing but when he had done he felt the effect of it & his fingers were cold with his gloves.[5]

It was unusual for Wordsworth to compose while riding; but then riding was not something which he (not owning a horse) could afford to do very often;[6] and having to ride the horse at walking pace through the park obviously meant that he could turn his attention to other things, while the rhythm of the horse proved a sufficient substitute for his own usual pacing up and down. The distance he rode while working on the poem ('Among all lovely things my Love had been'), from the start of the park and missing out the town of Staindrop, is around five miles; so the poem took perhaps an hour-and-a-half to write. No wonder he had cold fingers, even with gloves on: there was snow on the ground and it was what Dorothy (over in Eusemere) called 'a sharp windy night'.[7]

The poem is one of his oddest and most characteristic: a 'Lucy' poem of the kind he had first written in Germany in the winter of 1798–9, in which the lover describes the events of his courtship, but transmuted into a 'Mary' or 'Emma' poem. In the manuscript sent to Coleridge four days later, the name of the woman the narrator loves would be 'Emma'; in the copy sent to Sara Hutchinson, the name would be 'Mary',[8] while the 1807 printed text would read 'Lucy'. It was clearly an 'Emma' poem in Grasmere and Keswick (Emma – like Emmeline – being one of the names reserved for Dorothy) but for obvious reasons it would be a 'Mary' poem over in Middleham and Gallow Hill. ('Lucy' would be an appropriate compromise for the eventual printed text.)

The poem describes how the narrator – riding at night – sees a glow-worm 'and at the sight' leaps off his horse. He puts the glow-worm on a leaf, and takes it 'through the stormy night / In my left hand' to Emma's (Mary's) house: for – although 'Among all lovely things my Love had been' – she has never seen one. He leaves it in her orchard,

15   . . . blessing it by name,
            Laid safely by itself beneath a tree.
            The whole next day I hoped & hoped with fear:
            – At night the Glow-worm shone beneath the tree:
            I led my Mary to the place, – 'Look here'
20   O joy it was for her and joy for me.[9]

It is one of those poems written directly about the feelings which to anyone not immediately captured by it probably seems absurd; and this in spite of Wordsworth's note – in the copy he sent to Coleridge – 'The incident of this poem took place about seven years ago between Dorothy and me'.[10] Wordsworth may have left Dorothy a glow-worm in the orchard at Racedown in the summer of 1796, but the horse-borne narrator in 1802 is a rather different kind of person. He behaves like a comic version of some medieval knight, leaping off his horse to rescue not a maiden but a glow-worm, and riding through the storm with his faintly shining glow-worm in his left hand, before laying it down as a kind of silent love token (it is hard *not* to think of a cat leaving its owner a thoughtfully-intended mouse). The glow-worm is obviously phallic too, grasped so determinedly (if gently) in the knight's left hand in a Blakean 'howling storm',[11] as a present to his lady who (strangely enough) has never seen one. He blesses it 'by name', as if christening it for its new vocation, and then – joy for her and joy for me! Parody is too easy. The poem works wonderfully well if one concentrates, undistracted, upon its emotional truths. As realism it is comic.

We may be surprised that Wordsworth should have been writing such a poem about his love Dorothy, on the way back from his love Mary: or (alternatively) that he should have written such a poem for his love Mary, out of material so closely associated with his love Dorothy. It is a poem containing a slightly self-conscious awareness of the oddity and complexity of being on such a journey from one love to another, with an ambiguity about which woman the precious (if only faintly shining) glow-worm was actually destined for. The action could easily be prefaced by the kind of comment which had got into an earlier 'Lucy' poem: 'What fond and wayward thoughts will slide / Into a Lover's head!'[12]

The ambiguity was not, however, for the recipients, and Dorothy was delighted with the poem (presumably in its Emma form), repeating it to herself during their journey back to Grasmere. Her brother must have taught it to her while they walked.[13] She it was who would write out and send a copy – Maryfied – to Sara, when they finally got home. She may even gracefully have offered to give up her rights to the poem when doing so, satisfied that she was its first recipient and originator.

From Eusemere, it took Wordsworth and Dorothy two days to walk home, stopping overnight once: not until Friday the 16th did they finally get to Grasmere. But the journey home was responsible for two more poems. Walking along beside Ullswater on the first afternoon in a 'furious' wind, they saw the daffodils which Dorothy described in her diary and which provoked the poem discussed above; they then stayed in Patterdale – 'a good supper and good beds, but they and the breakfast cost us seven shillings; too much!'[14] On the second day, after walking from Patterdale towards the Kirkstone pass during the morning – 'slow, with many rests' – they lingered at Brothers' Water, and Wordsworth wrote the other poem discussed above, 'The Cock is crowing'.[15] After pausing at the foot of the pass to have dinner (pies provided by the Clarksons' cook Ellen), and making another stop in Ambleside, they did not get home until nightfall. 'The garden looked pretty in the half moonlight half daylight':[16] it was the night of the full moon. Their way of making this journey is characteristic. They don't hurry at any time, although on both days (in particular on the second) they have a long walk ahead of them; 'We rested again & again'.[17] They stop and look at what interests them; and if poems come, poems have to be waited for too.

For poems were now coming regularly; as regularly as letters from Coleridge and from the Hutchinsons (a letter from Coleridge was waiting when they arrived, and another from him and one from Sara arrived the day after they got back). But it was of Coleridge they were thinking in particular. They had doubtless been discussing him on their walk, and Dorothy commented on him when she wrote to Mary (doubtless eager to know they had got safely back) the evening they returned. She is referring to the letter she had got on the '13th: he says he has been ailing for two or 3 days. This is sad news – poor fellow! I fear he has his own torments. He says if we wish to see him he will walk over next week, so perhaps he will be here before the week is over.'[18] Wordsworth also wrote to Coleridge that evening, telling him to come over 'as soon as ever you find an inclination to';[19] but he comments purely technically on the fragments of poetry Coleridge had sent ('admirable simplicity in the language . . . the fourth line wants mending sadly'). He is sorry for the pain, but he is not bursting with sympathy: any more than Dorothy is, with her acute comment on his having his own torments, 'poor fellow' (with the suggestion that he manufactured them, too); though, of course, writing to Mary, the last thing Dorothy would be was effusive about Coleridge's feelings for Sara.

How did Coleridge respond to this letter from Town End? He had sent a letter containing part of the most agonising poem of his adult life, and certainly one of his very best; and in return he got a poem about a glow-worm and 'The cock is crowing', an impromptu about birds and cows. He was also told to come over when he could. But Wordsworth was a notoriously reticent letter-writer, and Coleridge would not have expected advice or sympathy from his friend in a letter. The poems were a different matter. 'The cock is crowing' – looked at from the point of view of the man who found it in his mail a day or so later – would have seemed either banal beyond belief, or extraordinarily apposite. In its own tiny way it was as much a response to what Coleridge was doing in the *Letter* as the *Ode* or 'The Leech-gatherer' could be (as well as being its own response to the troubled moods of the *Ode*). It simply looked at the world, and forgot the troubled self while looking. It did not distinguish between what could be seen, and what could be felt; it did not look for beauty at all. It simply said 'this is marvellous: *look* at it, and (while looking) be aware of the simplicity of the language in which it can exist!' Coleridge, too, was very aware of the simple pleasures 'Of this sweet Primrose-month', and felt that he was '*vainly* woo'd' by them.[20] On the other hand, Wordsworth's simple statement 'There's joy in the mountains' might be at least momentarily disarming to a writer who had struggled so hard to say how impossible it was for the natural world to affect him:

> what can these avail
> To lift the smoth'ring Weight from off my Breast? . . .
> 50   I may not hope from outward Forms to win
> The Passion & the Life, whose Fountains are within![21]

Of course, if Coleridge had not yet written those lines, Wordsworth's poem would have been just the kind of thing to make him do so. We cannot know how extensive the fragments of the *Letter* were which Coleridge had sent; but even if this passage had not been among them, the simplicity of the poem Wordsworth now sent to Coleridge might be taken as its own commentary on the characteristic complexity of the other man's writing.

II

But Coleridge had also been out and about that brilliantly sunny Good Friday. Although he had been ill a couple of days earlier, he was not now. He would make a note in his pocket-book about the appearance of the moon (full that night) – the same moon by which the Wordsworths would view their garden in the evening, and which had figured so crucially as a new moon in the *Letter*: 'Great Mars making a circle under the Moon, on a white cloud. Good Friday – April 16, 1802.'[22] But Coleridge had been immensely active during the day. He had been up in the hills beside Derwent Water, probably on Castlerigg Fell, where he could look back to the mountains beyond Keswick, Skiddaw and Saddleback:

> From the summit above Walla Crag Skiddaw & Saddleback form one beautiful Ellipse – the vales of Threlkeld & Hutton [. . .] become one with Keswick – the islands in the Lake more dishy than ever – the mountains from Borrodale inclusive to Grysdale Pike more than any where a rude Jumble – After I had written this, I descended from the Man of Stones – & came all unawares on Walla Crag – tremendous indeed / there is nothing on Helvellin so terrible it is absolutely & strictly perpendicular on all Side – & in its outline forms an aweful Forehead & Aquiline Nose – on the saddle of the Nose a Tree & a [. . .] Bunch of *Juniper*, I believe – Come in a few yards to a noble ravine / one side rough & treeless rock – the other mossy, & shrubby green / in a 100 yards more to a grand slope, and one *leaning Tower* – on its Top a green shorn *Poll* or crown of Head / railed off with wooden rails – & above the ravine another small Precipice – and here too is one of the noblest Ravines ever seen / Rock on both sides, grey with white Lichens The long Bracken, unreapt, wet, & rotting, lying, strait dangling, from the mossy stone-hillocks like an unkempt red brown Hair – Good Friday –[23]

It is a typical Coleridge notebook entry: tremendously detailed, concerned to get as much actuality into its account as possible, occasionally slipping into metaphor: off-the-cuff nature journalism. It makes the Brothers' Water poem look thoroughly artificial. On the other hand, whereas Wordsworth's poem was sent to friends, and published, and brought pleasure to thousands, the notebook entry was only published in 1957, and is almost unknown. Without a map (or, better still, some actual experience of the place) it makes little sense: one wonders what exactly Coleridge was doing when he made it, for it is hard to see what use he could have made *of* it even in some kind of topographical book (or poem) about the region. Is it just an example of him talking to himself when there was no one there whose ear he could bend? Is it the journalist Coleridge seizing on a new topic, and making something of it (but what?) Is he making himself *see* the world as it is, as he had encouraged Dorothy to do in the winter of 1798? It may, of course, be all those things. In its own way, it also bypasses the question of 'what can these avail?' It simply says 'look at these!'

Coleridge's next notebook entry, however, was a four-line fragment of verse, almost certainly inscribed sometime between the 16th and the 21st (so immediately following the description of the Good Friday moon): but this was part of the work in progress, part of the evidence that the *Letter* took not a night but a period of weeks to write.

> Smile in the eye
> An Incarnation of the Soul in Light –
> A Light, a living Light, that is at once
> Language, & Thought, & Feeling –[24]

By sheer chance, these surviving lines are the missing partners of the fragment from early November 1801 which I used above to indicate some of the pre-history of the poem. Then, Coleridge had written a simple observation about a man: 'Health in his cheeks & the Light of honorable Thought in his Eyes –.'[25] The new fragment showed the final text of the *Letter* still clearly some way from being finished, but coming into place:

> Be happy, & I need thee not in sight.
> 145 Peace in thy Heart, & Quiet in thy Dwelling,
> Health in the Limbs, & in thine Eyes the Light
> Of Love, & Hope, & honorable Feeling –[26]

This little sequence of notebook entries ends with a simple insight taking us back to the life of this peculiarly extra-family gang: 'John that unperforming observer'.[27] Coleridge had spent quite a lot of time with John Wordsworth on the original journey to Grasmere in November 1799, and again in 1800, though we do not know what exactly brought him to mind now. But Coleridge would certainly have discussed him with Wordsworth, who between 1800 and 1804 wrote a poem ('When first I journey'd hither') describing John in ways that may have been his own first, or Coleridge's first: for Wordsworth stressed John's 'finer eye' and 'heart more wakeful' in discovering and then dwelling on a particular view ('a visionary scene') near Town End, and he also imagined that – as a sailor – John 'didst also become / A silent Poet!'[28] In so far as John *observed*, but did not *write*; looked, but kept his observations to himself; did not publish poetry, but loved poetry; did not write descriptions of nature, but loved nature – then Coleridge felt profound sympathy with him. There were times when Coleridge's own lack of performance deeply depressed him, and this spring was one of the times, in spite of the work in progress.

III

Over in Grasmere, after the return from Eusemere, life resumed its normal pattern. Dorothy gardened; Wordsworth dug the ground over; they walked in the moonlight on the evening of Saturday the 17th. And on the morning of Sunday the 18th, Wordsworth wrote another poem. He was still engaged with

extremely simple poems, drawn from the events (real and imaginary) of
everyday life, in the sequence he had started to write in March: and to that
extent, Coleridge's 'torments' (combined perhaps with what he was saying
about nature in *his* poetry) may have driven Wordsworth into a series of
responses. The morning after they had got back to Grasmere, Dorothy had seen
'a Robin chacing a scarlet Butterfly' in the garden; she may well have made the
journal entry on the Sunday, when Wordsworth actually wrote his poem
'The Redbreast chasing the Butterfly'.[29] It is one of the most easily parodied of
all his poems. It has been suggested that the poem is saved by its Miltonic
subtext of a post-lapsarian world in which Adam's crime has let loose
aggression among the animals.[30] It seems to me that the poem is interesting not
for a deeply buried subtext but for its oddly arch and self-conscious play with
rhyme and attitude; it is that rather interesting creation, a completely comic
poem by Wordsworth. But not, I think, funny enough: it exemplifies what
Jonathan Wordsworth calls the 'gaiety and feebleness' of Wordsworth's comic
writing:

> Art thou the bird whom Man loves best
> The pious bird with scarlet breast
>   Our little English Robin?
> The bird that comes about our doors!
> 5   When Autumn winds are sobbing?[31]

It turns out – how disgraceful! – that the little favourite chases butterflies!
Adam himself would be shocked –

> Could Father Adam open his eyes
> And see this sight beneath the skies,
>   He'd wish to close them again . . .

The rhymes and manner are playful if you enjoy them, ponderous if you do
not.

>   – In and out, he darts about –
> Robin! Robin!
> 20 His little heart is throbbing: –
> Can this be the Bird to man so good,
>   Our consecrated Robin!
> That after their bewildering,
> Did cover with leaves the little children
> 25   So painfully in the wood! –

The rhyme of 'bewildering' and 'children' is particularly striking.[32]
Wordsworth did have a comic vein to explore, but this was not a very good way

of doing so; the national love of the Robin is too slight a subject for a forty-line comic treatment, with a mock-serious final admonition:

40   If thou would be happy in thy nest,
             – O pious Bird whom man loves best
             Love him, or leave him alone!

It took Wordsworth until the evening of the 28th to finish the poem, and he may have got cold feet even before he finished; Dorothy's journal describes how, for once, a poem got shorter in revision: 'We sate up late. He met me with the conclusion of the poem of the Robin. I read it to him in bed. We left out some lines.'[33] There followed another morning's gardening: Wordsworth bringing himself down to earth.

Closer to the way he had been writing before going to Keswick and Middleham was the poem he wrote on 20 April – a reflection on, or (what Dorothy called it) 'a conclusion to' the Butterfly poem he had written at the end of March: 'I've watch'd you now a full half hour'. The difference now was that there really were butterflies in the garden, not just in memory, and the result was a different kind of poem: one which first watched the butterfly very closely –

             And little Butterfly! indeed
             I know not if you sleep or feed
5   How motionless! not frozen seas
             More motionless . . .

and then celebrated Grasmere, the place in which such peace and security were possible:

             Stop here whenever you are weary
             And feed as in a sanctuary
             Come often to us, fear no wrong
15   Sit near us on the bough
             We'll talk of sunshine and of song
             And summer days when we were young
             And childish summer days as long
             As twenty days are now.[34]

The nostalgia of the first poem is still there, but it is not operating as before; it is simply part of the warm, summery atmosphere of the poem. A literalist would point out that there cannot be much 'sanctuary' for butterflies in a garden where robins are marauding . . . but 'sanctuary' is not really a word for the butterfly. It is for the human beings in the poem, and it describes their feelings, not the butterfly's chances of safety. Their place is a kernel of safety and love, a centre: all lies before them, humans and garden creatures alike, as they are 'called forth' into experience:

> What joy awaits you when the breeze
> Shall find you out among the trees
> And call you forth again![35]

It was as much a poem about the 'us' as about the butterfly: it was a poem for Dorothy, a poem for Mary, a poem for Wordsworth himself, constantly return-ing to his garden, constantly found out and called forth again, in imagination and through poetry.

But this was not the only truth of the situation. Dorothy had not been well for a couple of days; she had not been able to 'rest when I got to bed' the pre-vious day.[36] Her experience on the day Wordsworth began to write his second 'Butterfly' poem starts to sound rather like that of the narrator of the *Letter*; her journal entry keeps reminding us of how beautiful the world is, in spite of (or even because of) the depression she feels: 'A beautiful morning the sun shone . . . I was quite out of spirits . . . it was a beautiful afternoon. The sun shone upon the Level fields & they grew greener beneath the eye – houses village all chearful, people at work.'[37] But she remains untouched by it: in the evening, too, 'I was in low spirits'. She may even have *learned* this experience from the *Ode* and the *Letter*, with whose author she was currently deeply in sympathy. Coleridge was feeling exactly the same, walking down to the Wordsworths at just that moment. He stopped on the way: 'April 20, 1802 Tuesday Evening, ½ after 7 / Cut out my name & Dorothy's over the S.H. at Sara's Rock –'[38] One can imagine why he added his own initials to Sara's, but the act was closely linked with the addition of Dorothy's. He must have worked at the names until it grew dusk, and then have walked on, to arrive in Grasmere not before half-past-nine at night: 'when we were sitting after Tea Coleridge came to the door. I startled Wm with my voice . . .' Presumably she screamed, as when she heard that William had got back to Eusemere on the 13th. Then, 'C came up palish but I afterwards found he looked well. William was not well & I was in low spirits.'[39] They had sat in the Orchard during the day '& repeated the Glow-worm and other poems': it sounds as if they both needed reassurance and com-forting. In this state, Coleridge was both good and bad for Dorothy; good in that he was a friend in need, whom she could take care of, and bad in that she sympathised deeply with him. To judge by what happened the following week, however, he does not seem to have told them what he had been doing at Sara's Rock.

The following day, Wednesday the 21st, when he eventually got up, Coleridge came up to the garden to them, to their look-out position in the orchard, '& repeated the verses he wrote to Sara –'[40] We can be reasonably certain that among those verses to Sara would have been some version of the lines which I quoted above and which his very recent notebook entry showed him contemplating. He did not need to *see* Sara to know that he loved her. His verses were very moving and disturbing to Dorothy, however: 'I was affected with them & was on the whole, not being well, in miserable spirits. The sunshine – the green fields & the fair sky made me sadder; even the little happy sporting lambs seemed but sorrowful to me.'[41] An even stranger thirty-line double poem which Wordsworth probably wrote in the second half of April needs looking at here, too. The next day, Thursday the 22nd, they all went out; Coleridge sounds restored to good form, as he 'talked of his plan of sowing Laburnum in the woods':[42] a wonderful fantasy, to turn the Lake District yellow, if rather more poisonous. The two men went off scrambling up the rocks by a stream, and – when they came back – she heard Wordsworth reciting: '"I have thoughts that are fed by the Sun". It had been called to mind by the dying away of the stunning of the Waterfall when he came behind a stone.'[43] It is one of his odder works, even though it used the language of the *Ode*, the *Letter* and 'To H. C.'. He never published it. The first half is an indoor poem which – in spite of its implicit reference to the fluttering fire in 'Frost at Midnight'[44] – might have struck even the author of the *Letter* as morbid:

> These chairs they have no words to utter
> No fire is in the grate to stir or flutter
> The ceiling and floor are mute as a stone
> My chamber is hush'd and still
> 5   And I am alone
>   Happy and alone
> Oh! who would be afraid of life?
>   The passion the sorrow and the strife
>   When he may lie
> 10   Shelter'd so easily
> May lie in peace on his bed
> Happy as those who are dead

Like so much of Wordsworth's poetry this spring, it took every imaginable risk in the course of setting out its discoveries: the first line sounds like the start of a piece of nonsense verse, although it also records exactly what is important to the narrator at such a moment: the way in which *things* feel more homely than people or language. Neither Wordsworth nor his sister had any problem with imagining death, either: they positively invited the thought. Exactly a week later, with her brother lying on the ground 'with his eyes shut', Dorothy

> lay in the trench under the fence . . . listening to the waterfalls & the Birds. There was no one waterfall above another – it was a sound of waters in the air – the voice of the air. William heard me breathing & rustling now & then but

we both lay still, & unseen by one another – he thought that it would be as sweet thus to lie so in the grave, to hear the *peaceful* sounds of the earth & just to know that ones dear friends were near.[45]

They were in effect enacting the poem. Coleridge's later criticisms in *Biographia Literaria* would get three lines from the *Ode* removed in editions from 1820 onwards which have a clear relationship with 'I have thoughts' and also with the imagination of lying in the grave: lines originally running

> To whom the grave
> Is but a lonely bed, without the sense or sight
> Of day, or the warm light
> A living place where we in waiting lie.[46]

Both the *Ode* and 'These chairs they have no words to utter' also hark back, however, to the 1800 poem 'The Mad Monk', where the explicitly Gothic context (its subtitle 'An Ode in Mrs. Ratcliff's Manner') had allowed the line 'Oh, let me lie in peace, and be for ever dead!' (in inverted commas, like the actual song of the hermit or monk) to pass relatively unnoticed.[47] This makes me wonder whether 'These chairs they have no words to utter' was not, like 'The Mad Monk', itself at one time part of the *Ode*'s work in progress. This may also have been why 'These chairs' was never independently published, though it did go to Sara Hutchinson for copying into her book; its stanza form, too, bears interesting relationships with those employed in the *Ode*.[48]

The poem – or poem fragment – divides in the middle and gives a precise time for its mirror-image second half:

> *Half an hour afterwards*
> I have thoughts that are fed by the sun
> 15   The things which I see
> Are welcome to me
> Welcome every one
> I do not wish to lie
> Dead, dead
> 20   Dead without any company
> Here alone on my bed
> With thoughts that are fed by the sun
> And hopes that are welcome every one
> Happy am I.
> 25   O life there is about thee
> A deep delicious peace
> I would not be without thee
> Stay Oh stay

Yet be thou ever as now
30   Sweetness & breath with the quiet of death
Peace, peace, peace.

Again, it seems quite likely that lines such as 'A deep delicious peace' and 'Sweetness & breath with the quiet of death' were part of the work in progress which became the *Ode*. Significant, too, is the habit of mind which is aware of the very opposite of its own deepest longings, and knows them also as its longings. The poem, said Dorothy, had been 'called to his mind by the dying away of the stunning of the Waterfall when he came behind a stone'. Jonathan Wordsworth has commented that this 'could presumably mean either that it had just been written in his head, or that it been *re*called'.[49] The latter seems more likely: it is too complex a poem to have sprung fully into his mind at a single moment, though it may only have existed *in* his head. But the shift in awareness caused by the sudden *absence* of the 'stunning' noise offered the poet a perfect image of a sensibility caught between two things, to both of which it was profoundly attracted. It was not simply a matter of peace and quiet being preferred to noise and fury, or of the stunning sound being preferred to peace and quiet. Both are realities in our world, and within us. 'Thoughts that are fed by the sun' (making the world and the self sound profoundly attractive, joyous and rewarding) appear to be the polar opposite of the quiet, potentially melancholy ideas of retreat in the first half of the poem: yet the 'deep delicious peace' made so attractive in the second half of the poem *also* sounds like death. Are the sensations of 'Sweetness and breath' simply those of life and joy, fed by the sun? No: they run immediately into the melancholy of 'the quiet of death'. In the midst of life we are in death, and vice versa: we live our life in a kind of dual longing, for loneliness *and* 'company', for joy *and* melancholy, for being happily fed by the sun *and* happily drawing in upon ourselves in stillness. It is fascinating that the sounds of life should themselves be described as 'dying away' in Dorothy's record, which must have depended on Wordsworth's own language as he reported the experience for her to write it down. It is significant, too, that Coleridge should have been the first apparent audience for this poem: it would have spoken to him very directly, both in its fascination with joy and melancholy, and in its faith in the unperforming and wordless.

Coleridge's visit meant however, as usual, a diminution in Wordsworth's writing of new poems, even though Dorothy's journal might later be used to re-animate those composed in his head like 'These chairs they have no thoughts to utter'. On Friday the 23rd, they all went out for the walk I described above, when they found their two bowers. The day ended in the kind of domestic happiness which they regularly achieved at Town End. Coleridge (of course) read; Wordsworth and Dorothy worked together in the garden; and a letter arrived from Sara.[50] To make up for the splendid sunshine of Friday, Saturday was 'very wet': but the stream which flowed down the hill beside the garden developed a waterfall which Wordsworth called Dorothy out to look at, and when they finally managed a walk in the evening, 'Coleridge & I lingered behind – C stopped up the little runner by the Road side to make a lake'.[51] In such moods he was an incomparable companion. It was only perhaps three weeks since he had reached his momentous realisation about his marriage, recorded in the *Letter*; but here he was, the old Coleridge back again: a very special visitor for the Wordsworths, as the nucleus of the gang enjoyed itself together. They walked, played, wrote, read and recited poems, and wrote letters to the others: and got letters from them too.

But Coleridge went back the following day, after they had all walked some of the way together towards Keswick (though not as far as Sara's Rock); and ordinary life at Town End resumed. The Wordsworths had visitors; they walked and read. The next day – Monday the 26th – Dorothy 'copied Wm's poems for Coleridge', almost certainly so as to give him a written record of what he had heard while with them; the total was mounting up since the last copying, which had probably been when they had got back from Eusemere ten days earlier. For his part, Coleridge did the same; 'a Letter & verses from Coleridge' came on Tuesday the 27th, possibly some more of the *Letter*, but as likely to have been the copy of 'The Full Moon in a Passion' which survives in Coleridge's hand on that large sheet of paper illustrated in Chapter One.[52] Perhaps the Coleridge poem had grown out of their talk and fantasy during the days in Grasmere: an exemplum of what a *really* comic poem would be like. At all events, it celebrated Wordsworth as the 'head of the Gang'.

IV

With Coleridge gone, Wordsworth began writing poetry again; another poem he never published, although he spent two days over it. He may have thought it too informal to join his serious poetry.[53] In 'The Tinker' he again indulged his capacity for comedy, but this time with perfect control. The resulting fifty-line poem is a ballad to carelessness, with all the cheerful rhymes of the genre – and, like everything else which belongs to this spring, it was part of yet another conversation with Coleridge. It too appears as an Illustration to Chapter One.[54]

In its first four lines, it disposes of Coleridge's two main problems: being married, and being too much of a philosopher.

> Who leads a happy life
> If it's not the merry Tinker
> Not too old to have a Wife;
> Not too much a thinker . . .

The tinker absolutely refuses to care: something extremely attractive to Wordsworth (this particular caring and responsible adult always envying the child's capacity for carelessness). The tinker just travels about, finding work and drinking: 'Batter, batter, batter' goes his hammer, in the first of the one-word-repeated lines (the poetry needs to be as easy and careless as the character it creates):

> He sings the sun to bed
> 20   And without making a pother
> Finds some place or other
> For his own careless head.

The tinker's role in ballad poetry for centuries had, of course, been that of sexual predator.

> What is this that's coming?
> Silly Maid as ever was
> 40   She thinks that she and all she has
> Will be the Tinker's booty

The tinker knows his reputation (though all he actually *does* is laugh):

> Not doubting of her dread
> 42a   Like a Bullfinch black & red
> The Tinker shakes his head
> Laughing, Laughing, laughing
> 45   As if he would laugh himself dead.[55]

Dead or alive, just as in the dual poem 'I have thoughts that are fed by the sun', it simply does not matter to him:

> And thus, with work or none
> The Tinker lives in fun
> With a light soul to cover him
> And sorrow & care to blow over him
> 50   Whether he's up or a bed.

This is not great poetry: but it *is* interesting that Wordsworth should have devoted himself to it as soon as Coleridge had gone home, and that Dorothy should have written it out on the sheet already containing 'The Full Moon in a Passion'. It reminds us of the lightness and cheerfulness of a good deal of Wordsworth's relationship with Coleridge: the way Coleridge made him laugh. Now Wordsworth not only writes poetry to make his friend laugh: he answers him.

A peculiar poem discovered by chance in 1964 and called 'The Barberry-Tree' was also probably a product of this spring; but Wordsworth – if he wrote it, as has generally been assumed – disowned (or forgot) it so completely that no copy survived in print or among his papers. It exemplifies all the faults of both his comic and his serious writing. The first half has an intrusive and exceptionally boring narrator, who – after explaining how deeply moved he is by the sight of a barberry-tree in blossom –

> No tree that grew in hill or vale
> 10　　　　Such blithesome blossoms e'er displayed
> They laugh'd and danc'd upon the gale;
> 　　　　They seem'd as they could never fade:
> As they could never fade they seem'd;[56]

– at enormous length considers what the *blossoms* might experience, as joy, as they dance in the wind: and he does so in a single sentence extending some twenty-eight lines, starting

> But whether it be thus or no;
> That while they danc'd upon the wind
> They felt a joy like humankind . . .

The narrator ends up saying that he actually has no idea whether the blossoms *are* 'alive and glad as we': but ignorance is (once again) something on which he spends an vast amount of time.

> If living sympathy be theirs
> 　　　　And leaves and airs,
> The piping breeze and dancing tree
> 40　　Are all alive and glad as we:
> Whether this be truth or no
> I cannot tell, I do not know;
> Nay – whether now I reason well,
> I do not know, I cannot tell.

Line 42, of course, is lifted from 'Anecdote for Fathers'.[57] All the narrator *can* do is conclude, in his maddeningly precise but also infuriatingly loquacious way:

> 45　　But this I know, and will declare,
> 　　　　Rightly and surely *this* I know;
> That never here, that never there,
> 　　　　Around me, aloft, or alow;
> Nor here nor there, nor anywhere
> 50　　Saw I a scene so very fair.

This time, it is 'We are Seven' ('Her eyes were fair, and very fair') which is plundered for the pointless conclusion.[58]

The poem also contains a rather different kind of set-piece humour in its second half: advice so banal that it must be a joke (a friend is admonished *not* to go and look at the wind-blown barberry tree by night, as it is 'possible the shrub so green / [And yel]low, may not well be seen': he is also advised not to go when the wind is not blowing . . .) But all the way through the poem shows extraordinary knowledge of Wordsworth's poetry. Besides the quotations already mentioned, 'The Pet Lamb' and 'Ruth' are both cited, and there is a good deal of resemblance between one passage and the *Ode*.[59] Extensive passages, in fact, read like a very intimate parody: a kind of insider's burlesque.

It is clearly another *jeu d'esprit*, and although by far the most likely person to have written its first half is Coleridge, the slightly different second half (which also contains the only poetry of any interest) reads a good deal more like Wordsworth.[60] It overwhelmingly suggests some game played between the two friends; it would be hard to imagine anyone except Coleridge who could (or would) have written its first half,[61] and only Coleridge was in possession of both an intimate knowledge of *Lyrical Ballads* and of unpublished poetry like the *Ode* which would have enabled him to make its language and its comedy so telling. Given the extensiveness of its discussion of 'joy' in the first half, too, the poem also reads like Coleridge saying to Wordsworth 'if *you* had written about JOY in the *Letter* in your usual way, thinking as you do about "Nature", this is the kind of thing you'd have come up with'. On the other hand, the poem is at moments (in its second half) also written in the crucial, serious language of the spring of 1802:

> . . . then like me
> Ev'n from the blossoms of the Barberry,
> Mayst thou a store of thought lay by
110 > For present time and long futurity . . .[62]

Such a poem is, once again, only really comprehensible as part of the conversation between Wordsworth and Coleridge. This poem is almost certainly a joint production; a burlesque first half from Coleridge inspiring Wordsworth to humour too, but also to reflection. Coleridge, later in 1802, would voice a complaint about his friend's capacity to risk 'a daring Humbleness of Language & Versification',[63] and poetry like 'The Tinker' would have been just the kind of thing which worried him (though it may also have been *meant* to worry him.) 'The Barberry-Tree' however shows how directly and dramatically Coleridge's criticisms of Wordsworth's humbleness were being driven home, in comedy and intimate parody, though it also shows how willingly his friend was prepared to listen to the criticism.

It is fascinating, too, that a poem like 'The Tinker', needing above all to exemplify ease and naturalness, should have required such very hard, concentrated and dutiful work. Having tried and failed to finish yet another poem on the afternoon of 28 April ('it kept him long off his dinner') – Wordsworth went straight back to 'The Tinker' after eating. Dorothy was tetchy: 'he is working at the Tinker, he promised me he would get his tea & do no more'.[64] One of her needs – even stronger than her desire to be loved – was to care for others. She was not, in the spring of 1802, forced to the measures to stop Wordsworth working which she had jokingly described in a letter to Coleridge a year earlier: 'Poor William! his stomach is in bad plight. We have put aside all the manuscript poems and it is agreed between us that I am not to give them up to him even if he asks for them.'[65] Such rules – and games – were part of the pattern of loving and caring which frequently operates between couples: as necessary for Dorothy as for Wordsworth. She was obviously aware of the spring turning into summer. It was the next day when they would lie side by side and wonder what death would be like. For Dorothy, it would be bearable 'just to know that ones dear friends were near':[66] William and John Wordsworth, Coleridge, Mary, Sara.

But they all came to mind in other ways too. In the middle of writing the slapstick comedy of 'The Tinker', Wordsworth wrote another poem, called by Dorothy 'Children gathering flowers', and apparently provoked by her remark 'that when I was a Child I would not have pulled a strawberry blossom'.[67] Wordsworth had regularly been reading poetry of the seventeenth century this winter and spring,[68] and it is at times like this that his reading becomes obvious; in 'Foresight' he manages something of the formal charm of what he had read.

> Violets do What they will
> 20   Wither'd on the ground must lie
> Daisies must be daisies still
> Daisies they must live & die[69]

Dorothy, perhaps in the next couple of days, once again copied the poem on to yet another blank space on the sheet containing Coleridge's 'Full Moon in a Passion' and 'The Tinker'.

V

The last days of April serve as a kind of apotheosis of all that Dorothy had felt, and Wordsworth had done, for months. They go into the orchard early on the 30th, and Wordsworth starts to write a new poem – 'The Celandine'. Dorothy writes a letter to Mary. The poem then demands that they walk up and down; so they do: Wordsworth 'repeated his poem to me – then he got to work again & would not give over – he had not finished his dinner till 5 o clock'. The usual loving complaint about work and mealtimes . . . It is not a warm day, but (of course) they go out, and poetry may still come. They take fur cloaks and find a new seat. Wordsworth has one of his daytime sleeps, tired from the concentration of writing; Dorothy sits looking 'at the prospect as in a vision almost I was so resigned to it'.[70] 'Resigned to' probably means 'happy with', but there is also a suspicion that there was a good deal to which Dorothy had to become resigned, this spring. On this particular day, they stay until the light starts to go; Dorothy observes the hills, describes the landscape, names the birds. Her journal writing continues while the poet sleeps: he has been having very bad nights recently. When at last they go indoors, at 8.00 p.m., they drink tea; Dorothy writes to Coleridge and half a letter to Mrs Clarkson. They go to their beds at 11.20 'with prayers that Wm might sleep well'.[71] Which he seems to do.

The following day, the pattern continues: garden, orchard. Wordsworth writes and this time finishes 'The Celandine'. Dinner: a walk. And a new poem – a second 'Celandine' poem – starts to manifest itself. They go home for tea and the poem is 'lost'. So (of course) they go out again: and by walking backwards and forwards recover the poem.

> The Landscape was fading, sheep & lambs quiet among the Rocks. We walked towards Kings & backwards & forwards. The sky was perfectly Cloudless N.B. is it often so? 3 solitary stars in the middle of the blue vault one or two on the points of the high hills. Wm wrote the Celandine 2nd part tonight. Heard the cuckow today this first of May.[72]

Two 'Celandine' poems thus got themselves written over these two days; the second part really a continuation of the first, in the same stanza form. If Wordsworth's subjects had been insignificant all month, these final poems went out of their way to concentrate on the thoroughly unimportant and over-looked. This allowed him to say that the work of the poet, just like that of the scientist or the astronomer, is to *see* what is not normally seen. Dorothy's journal had, three times already, described the flower, as a natural result of her developed habit of looking hard at things. The first occasion had been on the walk down from Eusemere, when she described it as if she had just seen it for the first time: 'that starry yellow flower which Mrs C calls pile wort'.[73] The next day, while Wordsworth was writing his poem at Brothers' Water, Dorothy had seen 'pile wort that shone like stars of gold in the Sun';[74] and back at home, there it had been in their own garden. She and Wordsworth had at least one flower book, and probably looked it up: Wordsworth's poems describe it under its more common name. It was a flower which, once you have seen it, you see it everywhere:

> Thou hast now, go where I may,
> Fifty greetings in a day.[75]

Dorothy saw it again while Coleridge was reading out his verses to Sara, and described it even more rapturously: 'The pile wort spread out on the grass a thousand shining stars'.[76]

The poems Wordsworth wrote at this juncture are polemics about seeing, about the commonplace and the ordinary; and they are as obsessive as any poems he wrote at any time of his life. Once he had worked his way into a subject, he wrote and wrote and wrote about it: the slightness of the poetry is no indication of his profound need to write it. But the Celandine poems are as much about writing poetry as they are descriptive: and they are explanations of what he had been doing the whole fortnight, as he thought back over it.

> Eyes of some men travel far
> 10   For the finding of a star;
> Up and down the heavens they go,
> Men that keep a mighty rout!
> I'm as great as they, I trow,
> Since the day I found thee out,
> 15   Little flower! – I'll make a stir,
> Like a great Astronomer.

For poets – wanting to be admired – are unfortunately prone to write poems about conventionally accepted things, and to love only the 'proper' subjects of poetry:

> Poets, vain men in their mood!
> Travel with the multitude;
> 35   Never heed them; I aver
> That they all are wanton Wooers;

That was probably a comment – and not even a guarded one – on Coleridge. The poem is yet another of these comic (but not really funny) productions in which Wordsworth was starting to specialise. Little yellow flowers get spurned by poets:

> Ill befal the yellow Flowers,
> 50   Children of the flaring hours!
> Buttercups, that will be seen,
> Whether we will see or no;
> Others, too, of lofty mien;

The comedy extends to politics. Shelley in the 'Mask of Anarchy' could hardly do better:

> Prophet of delight and mirth,
> Scorn'd and slighted upon earth!
> Herald of a mighty band,
> 60   Of a joyous train ensuing . . .[77]

Thus the poem looks forward to the day when the Common Pilewort will arise from obscurity and cover the earth: 'Ye are many, they are few!'

The second poem carries on in the same vein, whimsically insisting that those who have painted the sun, on inn sign boards for example, must have taken the lesser Celandine as their model. The poetry flows almost unstoppably (which is why there are two poems, not one) because – when you start to hymn the small and the overlooked – there is an awful lot to say. Yet the poem is also firmly tongue in cheek as it celebrates the glory of the insignificant, in what this time is a conscious recovery of seventeenth-century poetry:

> Thou art not beyond the moon,
> But a thing 'beneath our shoon;'
> Let, as old Magellen did,
> Others roam about the sea;
> Build who will a pyramid;
> Praise it is enough for me,
> If there be but three or four
> Who will love my little Flower.[78]

45

Joy takes many forms, as even 'The Barberry-Tree' had showed. This is pretty well as far from the capitalised 'JOY' of the *Letter* as it is possible to get; Wordsworth's language, as ever, is more modest, more realistic, and also in real danger of banality. His first daisy poem (written round about the same time) would define the sensation you could get from such flowers as 'An instinct, call it a blind sense, / A happy genial influence'. The poem 'To a Sky-Lark', probably written at some time in the same period, would also stress the way a narrator – under the influence of, but also very differently from the drunken, crazy joy of the bird – would go 'plodding on, / By myself, chearfully, till the day is done'.[79] But in their own way, such poems continued the conversation with Coleridge and added their own kind of commentary. Such poems concentrate on what is directly in front of us: the garden, the birds, the flowers. For as the daisy poem would also point out, the poet who 'some bright day of April sky / Imprison'd by the sun He lie' –

> He need but look about and there
> Thou art, a friend at hand to scare
> His melancholy.[80]

40

We can think of the platitudes of advice for the depressed: live one day at a time, enjoy the small pleasures of life. Coleridge would have been very aware of such advice, and we can find Dorothy actually offering it to a care-worn Mary on 16 April: 'Study the flowers, the birds and all the common things that are about you. O Mary, my dear Sister! be quiet and happy.' But now, at the start of May, although the spring continued wonderful – 'Again a heavenly morning' – a letter comes like a cloud over the sun: 'Letter from Coleridge'.[81]

VII

Wordsworth and Coleridge showed each other everything they wrote in this period, and this fortnight is a good example, with Dorothy rounding it off by sending a parcel of new poems up to Keswick. But, some three months later, we find Coleridge notably impatient with Wordsworth's writing. He told William Sotheby on 13 July, for example, that 'Poetry justifies, as *Poetry* independent of any other Passion, some new combinations of Language, & *commands* the omission of many others allowable in other compositions / Now Wordsworth . . . in his practice has too frequently sinned against the latter. –'[82] He means that Wordsworth has been allowing inappropriate kinds of language into his poetry. This judicious criticism was not just voiced for the sake of impressing Sotheby. He wrote at the end of July to Robert Southey:

> I am far from going all lengths with Wordsworth / He has written lately a number of Poems (32 in all) some of them of considerable Length / (the longest 160 lines) the greater number of these to my feelings very excellent Compositions / but here & there a daring Humbleness of Language & Versification, and a strict adherence to matter of fact, even to prolixity, that startled me . . .[83]

As I pointed out above, scholars and biographers have usually made too much of this, for the sake of suggesting a quarrel between Coleridge and Wordsworth which their combative individual approaches necessitate. In fact, as 'The Barberry-Tree' shows, the *jokes* obviously running between the two men about humbleness of language and versification are as striking as the criticism in this letter. Coleridge has also been presented as unwaveringly hostile to Wordsworth's 'publication of any small poems',[84] and distressed that he was not writing the great philosophical poem he *ought* to have been working on. Coleridge would, however, also tell Southey 'I need not say, that any diversity of opinion on the subject between . . . Wordsworth and myself, can only be small, taken in a *practical* point of view./'[85] That is, when it comes to actual writing, they agree. That is a significant modification of the critical position.

But what makes things particularly difficult in gauging the relationship between the two men is that we have relatively few of Coleridge's letters and very few of Wordsworth's from the spring and summer of 1802; we do not know very much of what they were actually saying to each other. But it is clear that Wordsworth continued to send Coleridge his shorter lyric poetry, with no sense of shame or embarrassment; two poems in his one surviving letter (of 16 April), and a whole parcel of them via Dorothy at the end of the month: while

Coleridge at times spread this poetry to a wider audience in his own letters, also without any kind of criticism (he sent, for example, copies of 'To a Butterfly' and 'The Sparrow's Nest' to Tom Poole on 7 May[86]). Coleridge also declared that he admired most of the poetry enormously: 'the greater number of those to my feelings very excellent compositions'.[87]

But, as time went by, Coleridge grew genuinely unhappy about the shorter poems. His numbering of them '(32 in all)' to Southey is nothing if not ironical, an attack both on their brevity and their facility. Deeply ironical too is the word 'daring' for the 'Humbleness of Language & Versification'. He is saying that some of Wordsworth's poetry is in danger of being commonplace, and – when not prolix – of being just terribly slight. Coleridge was an excellent critic, and this letter is really rather devastating about long poems describing the Common Pilewort.

By the spring of 1802, too, it was clear to Coleridge that, good poet though he had been – and still could be – writing poetry was not what he could do best, or with most reward to himself, or most acclaim from others. Poetry was a language he still shared with Wordsworth, but the poetic interchanges of the spring of 1802 were the last such conversations in that shared language which they would have. In the letters to Sotheby and Southey, what is really striking is the distressingly superior tone: as if Coleridge were addressing them as (unlike Wordsworth) people rather like himself – capable of superior understanding, and well above the intellectual level of such silly poems. It is a new and not very pleasant tone in Coleridge's correspondence: a kind of unhappy waspishness.

Urging Wordsworth on to the philosophic poem was also, to some extent, self regarding. Coleridge was genuinely unhappy that Wordsworth was not getting on with the long philosophic poem; but also felt that the philosophic poem was in a sense part of his *own* work. *The Recluse* was to be dependent upon him both for advice and for philosophical underpinning and was, to that extent, joint work. And as the years went by, and Wordsworth did not write it, the more Coleridge seems to have felt that this was a judgement not just upon Wordsworth but upon himself: one of *his* major works, planned and prepared for, was not getting written. He needed the poem as much as – perhaps more than – Wordsworth did. Although they were extraordinary friends, Coleridge knew that he was the better read and by far the more philosophically inclined of the two. After all, who had called his two first-born sons Hartley and Berkeley, and who would call his sons John and Tom? It was both odd and natural that Wordsworth had ended up saddled with the job of writing the poem; natural enough that (as the better poet) he should have to do it: and equally natural that he did not do it.[88] One should not, either, forget the simple irritation which may well have been caused by the constant arrival of poems ('32 in all') many of which were clearly not Wordsworth's best. What would it have been like to be the recipient of yet another handful of poems recommending the Daisy and the Common Pilewort as an inspiration to Joy and a cure for Melancholy? One might sum it up as an impatient 'I *know*, of course I *know*'.

Wordsworth had clearly got deeply involved with this kind of poetry, however. Poor fellow! He had *his* torments, too. The small poems about the small things had their own context, which we know about from the *Ode*: this said that things are not what they were; that you do *not* see the world as you used to; even the Common Pilewort speaks of something that is gone. The conversation between two poets was for Wordsworth also a conversation with the two sides of himself. And it is clear that when he had once started mining a particular poetic vein, he would go on doing so for an astonishing length of time. Only such resilience and concentration could ever have produced *The Prelude*; but it also meant that when he had once started writing short poems about flowers, he went on doing so for weeks; just as, when he had once started writing sonnets, he wrote little else for months. What brought this particular sequence to an end, we do not know; at the start of May, Dorothy was just finishing one journal notebook and starting another, and her records of a couple of days are lost. When she picks up the narrative of daily life again, Wordsworth is wrestling with a major poem, 'The Leech-gatherer'.

But one other thing needs to be said. Jonathan Wordsworth – scornful of poems like 'The Skylark' and 'To the Daisy' – has argued that the 'rare instances' of 'great poetry' from this spring only come when 'something occurs to take Wordsworth outside, or beyond, his too supportive roles and relationships'.[89] But any writer who managed between March and July to produce some of the *Ode* and the whole of 'The Leech-gatherer' can hardly be accused of writing only 'rare instances' of great poetry. What is more interesting is that Wordsworth should have written so much else which was so very different. What close examination of the record shows is that he needed, at some level, constantly to keep working through in poetry his feelings about the child and the adult, about shared childhood, about joy and melancholy, about care and carelessness, for particular people in his audience of readers, and for his own sake. I think it absurd to suggest that in some way it would have been better for posterity if Wordsworth in the spring of 1802 had ignored the feelings and needs of Coleridge, of Dorothy, of Mary and Sara, of Annette and Caroline, and just concentrated on the operations of his own mind and needs. One of the things biography can do (and literary criticism is very bad at) is to show how 'roles and relationships' are not optional, even to a great poet.

Dorothy Wordsworth very obviously felt herself deeply involved, this spring and summer, with Wordsworth's writing; nowhere else is her journal so full of descriptions of it. We must not ignore the fact that, this last spring together, Wordsworth also regularly concentrated on poems which *she* would enjoy, and in which she would be in some sense a participant (an observer, a recorder, sometimes a personage in the poem, always an audience). It does not matter how conscious he (or she) may have been of this. But some of the tension over the writing of short poetry which Coleridge felt at the time, and critics have been aware of ever since, may have been because Wordsworth was often writing to involve Dorothy (and sometimes Mary) more than he was to involve Coleridge. Wordsworth probably left Coleridge (by the middle of the summer) feeling a little neglected; and when he began to sound really revengeful, in July, Wordsworth was off on his journey to marry Mary. Carping criticisms were one of the very few ways in which Coleridge could deal with the profound admiration he felt for Wordsworth, with the growing sense of loss which he could feel in the coming change, *and* with the crevasses of despair about himself into which he was also regularly falling.

Chapter Eight

Dejection and its Cures: 2 May to 5 July

It has long been assumed that Wordsworth's next poem, 'Resolution and Independence', was directed at – one might say aimed at – Coleridge. It has been described as 'a strongly positive response' to Coleridge and his *Letter*, and a recent Wordsworth biographer has asserted that the poem reveals 'an attitude toward Coleridge's behaviour that was beginning to form, and harden, in the new household at Grasmere';[1] meaning that they were getting fed up with his addictions and depressions. The new household would not, of course, actually come into being until October: but there would be no sign, even then, that their feelings for Coleridge were anything other than totally sympathetic acceptance. (We can register the usual phenomenon of the Wordsworth biographer putting down Coleridge.) Paul Magnuson however argues that the poem is 'the sequel' to Coleridge's own poem, even though he also says that it 'turns as abruptly from its depression as other moments in the 1802 dialogue turn from their preceding moments',[2] thus exemplifying the attitude to his depression which Coleridge himself should be taking. 'The Leechgatherer', as I proposed, is not a criticism so much as another fragment of the conversation within the group: one which had been going on for a couple of years.[3]

The writing of the poem took place in circumstances which ensured that Coleridge would be the second person ever to hear it (Dorothy, as usual, being the first). Wordsworth started it during the evening of Sunday 2 May: exactly four weeks, to the evening, after the date inscribed in the title of Coleridge's *Letter*: it is hard to believe that he was unaware of the way he was following the *Letter* (and he also knew that he would be seeing Coleridge two days later). He went on with his poem in bed ('he wrote several stanzas') on the morning of Monday 3 May.[4] It was his second poem in three months to start with the words 'There was a ...': the other had of course been the *Ode*.[5] Letters from Coleridge seem recently to have been especially upsetting: three days earlier, on Thursday 29 April, a letter had arrived in the evening which had meant that Wordsworth was 'disturbed ... with reading C's letter which Fletcher had brought to the door';[6] he slept badly that night. On Sunday 2 May, they received another letter; and that evening Wordsworth began his poem.

On the Sunday night, Wordsworth had gone to bed 'nervous & jaded in the extreme'; a late eighteenth- or early nineteenth-century use of 'nervous' in its comparatively new sense implying some combination of 'irritable' and 'over-sensitive'.[7] The irritability was common when a difficult poem was under way; though we might also register the fact that Wordsworth was addressing the poem as much to himself as to Coleridge. On Tuesday the 4th, however, following a plan about which they must have corresponded over the previous few days, they set out to spend a day with Coleridge near Wythburn, on the road between Grasmere and Keswick. Dorothy spent the early part of the morning writing out 'The Leech-gatherer' as it then stood; and then, during the six-mile journey, they 'read and repeated the Leech gatherer'. It was extremely hot for early May, and climbing up Dunmail Raise meant that 'We were almost melted before we were at the top of the hill'.[8] They rested more than once; then dropped down the long slope to Wythburn, where they met up with Coleridge. They looked at the waterfall, scrambled up and down looking for shade, and finally ended up 'upon a moss covered Rock, rising out of the bed of the River. There we lay ate our dinner & stayed there till about 4 o clock or later – Wm & C repeated and read verses. I drank a little Brandy & water and was in Heaven.'[9] It was a day of extraordinary amity and happiness, not one in which Wordsworth would have recited a poem setting his friend right, or (indeed) one in which Coleridge much *needed* setting right. They all then went off for tea at a local farm house, and finally parted from Coleridge at the place which, up to now, they had called Sara's Rock. This was becoming an especially significant place.

The rock was by the roadside, about a mile beyond Wythburn Chapel going towards Keswick, about six miles from Town End and eight from Greta Hall: Wordsworth described it in 1806 as a 'smooth and dewy block', with a vertical side he called 'The surface of the upright rock . . .'[10] He wrote about it again in 1836:

> An upright block of mural stone
> Moist with pure water trickling down –
> A slender spring but kind to Man
> It is – a true samaritan
> Close to the highway pouring out
> It offering from a chink or spout
> Whence all howeer athirst, or drooping
> With toil may drink & without stooping.[11]

They had doubtless themselves often drunk there, and Wordsworth would celebrate it in 'Benjamin the Waggoner' as a spot to which the waggoner eagerly looks forward. Sara's initials had been carved on it during her long stay in Grasmere, 1800–1; she may even have cut them herself.

Coleridge, however, as they now saw, had been at work on the rock: 'after having looked at the Letters which C carved in the morning. I kissed them all. Wm deepened the **T** with C's penknife.'[12] Coleridge had actually cut his own initials and Dorothy's a fortnight earlier, but this was the first time the Wordsworths had seen them and apparently the first they knew about them. The rock was starting its transformation from 'Sara's Rock' into a celebration of the gang, its meetings, and its joy in the company of each other. A kind of stone (not concrete) poem, it was 'The Rock of Names' to both Coleridge and Wordsworth.[13] It would end up looking like this:

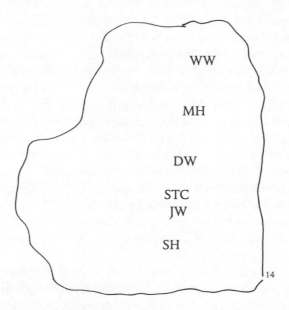

WW

MH

DW

STC
JW

SH

[14]

Coleridge had cut his own initials above Sara's original inscription, and had put Dorothy's a similar distance above that. The fact that Mary Hutchinson appears as 'M H' shows that her initials must have been cut on her behalf: she would not be making the journey either from Grasmere or from Keswick before her marriage on 4 October changed her to 'M W'. Wordsworth probably cut her initials for her, and may well have inscribed his own at the same time (his 'W's are distinctly different from the 'W' which Coleridge had cut); that would have been before he and Dorothy went away at the start of July. The 'J W' for John Wordsworth (not in Grasmere at all after 1800) must also have been added for him, and was probably cut by Coleridge. It is just possible that Coleridge had started work on the others on the morning of 4 May, but the fact that his own 'S T C' still needed work suggests that it suffered from having been done so fast in the dusk, back on the 20 April, and that 'S T C' and 'D W' were all that he had added. He and Wordsworth and Dorothy met at Wythburn again on 22 May, and the rest of the inscriptions might have been added then, or during any of the many subsequent journeys they would all make up and down the road.[15]

They worked hard at the cutting: many years later, Wordsworth recalled

> Their hands and mine, when side by side
> With kindred zeal and mutual pride,
> We worked until the Initials took
> Shapes that defied a scornful look. –

Time, of course, changed all that. The names, he wrote in lines published in 1836,

> were graven on thy smooth breast
> By hands of those my soul loved best;
> Meek women, men as true and brave
> As ever went to a hopeful grave:

John Wordsworth died in 1805, Coleridge in 1834, Sara Hutchinson in 1835. The rock ended up with 'monumental power', a symbol of what outlived the individuals whose initials were cut into it. In 1802, however, it was something less serious. The work had been started casually, and the rock's 'memorial-trust' had at first

> seemed only to express
> Love that was love in idleness;[16]

Wordsworth had not actually written a poem to the pansy or viola ('Love-in-Idleness') but cutting their names had at first seemed no more than a game for them: work of the 'staid heart but playful head'. But bringing them all together in this way also exemplified what Wordsworth later called 'kindness' – *kinship*. The fact that the rock was also a spring would not have escaped them; it was a symbol of the ever refreshing and the carelessly renewed ('not taking heed / Of its own bounty, or my need'). In 1806, thinking of Coleridge, Wordsworth would use the idea of the spring to describe love itself: 'this consecrated Fount / Of murmuring, sparkling, living love'.[17] In 1802, the carving and cutting became a way of bringing all the friends together symbolically as the gang they had become: a group on the edge of change, but delighting in marking the places where they met, and in remembering the absent.

II

Sometime during that long day together on 4 May, Wordsworth must have recited 'The Leech-gatherer' to Coleridge, in whatever form it then had;

Coleridge would also have been given the draft which Dorothy had written out that morning (it is hard to see why else she would have made it). Wordsworth would go back to work on the poem at the end of the week; there may well have been comments from Coleridge to think about, either given in person or coming by post later in the week. Rather than being a moral poem aimed at Coleridge, written so as to set him right, the poem – once again – was something growing naturally out of the conversation of people in the group. Their amity was unchanged, their love uninhibited: 'We sate afterwards on the wall, seeing the sun go down & the reflections in the still water. C looked well & parted from us chearfully, hopping up upon the Side stones.'[18]

Dorothy also recorded how, on their way home that evening, she and Wordsworth watched 'the Crescent moon with the "auld moon in her arms"'.[19] It was exactly a month since Coleridge had used that image at the start of the *Letter*, and Dorothy's reference confirms that the Wordsworths had, by now, heard or read its start. We still do not know where Coleridge had got to in it, but two entries in his notebook made between 20 April and 9 May give us some idea. The first one suggests the completion of some piece of work: 'Final correction / the last Touches, the ultima Basia, of your Muse –'. The reference to the *Basia* (*Kisses*) of Johannes Secundus[20] suggests Coleridge bringing to an end a piece of poetry of an especially loving kind, and the *Letter* is the obvious candidate. The next notebook entry offers a direct link both to the part of the *Letter* which described Coleridge's school-time, and to Wordsworth's remarks in the *Ode* about the child: 'N.B. The great importance of breeding up children *happy* to at least 15 or 16 illustrated in my always dreaming of Christ Hospital and when not quite well having all those uneasy feelings which I had at School / feelings of Easter Monday &c –'.[21]

'Easter Monday' is unlikely to be a reference to schooldays; it probably refers to the Easter Monday so recently past (19 April), the day before Coleridge walked down to the Wordsworths to read them 'the verses he wrote to Sara'.[22] It therefore seems at least possible that he had then been working on that part of the poem:

> Feebly! O feebly! – Yet
> (I will remember it)
> 60   In my first Dawn of Youth that Fancy stole
> With many secret Yearnings on my Soul.
> At eve, sky-gazing in 'ecstatic fit'
> (Alas! for cloister'd in a city School
> The Sky was all, I knew, of Beautiful)
> 65   At the barr'd window often did I sit,
> And oft upon the leaded School-roof lay . . .[23]

At some stage between 1800 and 1804 Wordsworth would write in the *Ode* about the way in which

1 & 2. Sara's Rock in the nineteenth century; its fragments today

3. Dorothy Wordsworth

4. Mary Hutchinson

5. Sara Hutchinson

8. William Wordsworth (life mask)

9. S. T. Coleridge (life mask)

13. The Wordsworths' rented cottage at Town End: £5 a year

14. The Coleridges' rented house ('Greta Hall') at Keswick: £40 a year

15. The Hutchinsons' farm house at Sockburn

Gallow Hill Farm House, where Wordsworth was married.

16. The Hutchinsons' farm at Gallow Hill

Sister & Friend of my devoutest choice!
Thou being innocent & full of Love,
And nested with the Darlings of thy Love,
And feeling in thy soul Heart, Lips & Arms
Even what the Conjugal & Mother Dove
That borrows genial warmth from these
Feels in her thrilled wings, blessedly outspread
Thou free'd awhile from Cares & human Dread
By the immenseness of the Good & Fair,
      Which thou see'st every where —
Thus, thus would'st thou rejoice,
To thee would all things live from pole to
Their Life the Eddying of thy living Soul.
O dear! O Innocent! O full of Love!
Sara! Thou Friend of my devoutest choice,
As dear as Light & Impulse from above!
So may'st thou ever, evermore rejoice!

If Thou wert here, these Tears were Tears of Light!
— But from as sweet a day-dream did I start
As ever made these eyes grow idly bright;
And tho' I weep, yet still about the heart
A dear & playful Tenderness doth linger
Touching my heart as with a Baby's finger.

2
My mouth half-open like a witless man,
I saw the couch, I saw the quiet Room,
The heaving Shadows & the fire-light gloom,
And on my lips, I know not what there ran,
On my unmoving lips a subtle Feeling
I know not what, but had the same been stealing

3
Upon a sleeping Mother's lips I guess
It would have made the loving Mother dream
That she was softly stooping down to kiss
Her Babe, that something more than Baby did seem
An obscure Mirror of its darling Father
And yet still its own sweet Baby self far rather

4
Across my chest there lived a weight so warm
As if some bird had taken shelter there
And lo! upon the couch a Woman's Form
Thine Sara! thine! O Joy, if thine it were!
I gazed with anxious hope, & feared to stir it

And now when I seemed sure my Love to see
Her very self in her own quiet Home
There came an elfish Laugh, & waken'd me
'Twas Hartley, who behind my chair had clomb
And with his bright Eyes at my face was peeping
I blessed him — try'd to laugh, & fell a weeping

17. Coleridge's support: Mary Hutchinson's copy of the *Letter* and 'The Day Dream'

18. Wordsworth's support: Dorothy Wordsworth's 1802 account of their arrival in Calais

These chairs they have no words to utter
No fire is in the grate to stir or flutter
The ceiling and floor are mute as a stone
My chamber is hush'd and still
    And I am alone
    Happy and alone

Oh! who would be afraid of life?
  The passion the sorrow and the strife
    When he may lie
    Shelter'd so easily
May lie in peace on his bed
Happy as they who are dead

——— ——— ———

Half an hour afterwards.
I have thoughts that are fed by the sun
  The things which I see
  Are welcome to me
  Welcome to ~~xxx~~ every one
  I do not wish to lie
    Dead dead
Dead without any company
  Here alone on my bed
With thoughts that are fed by the sun
And hopes that are welcome every one
    Happy am I.

O Life there is about thee
A deep delicious peace
I would not be without thee
    Stay oh stay
Yet be thou ever as now
Sweetness & breath with the quiet of death
    Peace peace, peace.

19. Wordsworth's support: Sarah Hutchinson's copy
of 'I have thoughts that are fed by the sun'

20. Man reading or dictating, woman writing: Wordsworths, Coleridges, Hutchinsons?

Shades of the prison-house begin to close
Upon the growing Boy . . .[24]

He did not *need* to know the Coleridge poem, of course, to write those lines,
now or at any time; he had his own school time to draw on, as well as
Coleridge's reminiscences of school in London. And yet the 'barr'd window'
and the 'prison-house' belong to an identical habit of mind; and, in Coleridge's
case, some connection between his reminiscences of school on 19 April,
and those lines of his poem, is likely. It also seems obvious that Coleridge's
own work-in-progress – if the *Letter* were still in progress – would also
have been recited during the long, hot 4 May, and perhaps a draft handed
over. At any rate, Wordsworth and Dorothy were both very conscious of the
moon as they came home that night, and probably also of the coincidence of
the date.

It may even have been because of that consciousness of Coleridge and
his predicaments that Wordsworth did not go on with 'The Leech-gatherer'
during most of Wednesday the 5th: it may simply have been a way of
not getting too worked-up. Writing poetry always distressed him. He 'kept
off work till near Bedtime when we returned from our walk – then he
began again & went to bed very nervous'. He had probably gone back to
'The Leech-gatherer': and the evening had been such as exactly to remind him
of the moon (and the sky canoe) in the Coleridge *Letter*. They had 'walked in
the twilight & walked till night came on – the moon had the old moon in her
arms but not so plain to be seen as the night before. When we went to bed it
was a Boat without the Circle'.[25] The fact that Dorothy was making such
references strongly suggests some very recent reading of Coleridge's *Letter*; she
was incorporating what she had read in the poem into the experiences of
every day.

The following day, Thursday 6 May, Wordsworth again seems not to have
worked on his poem; he and Dorothy were both busy in the garden, creating
their 'Bower', and Wordsworth also built a garden seat. But the subject at the
back of their minds could not escape them for long, any more than could their
awareness of the moon every evening. Coleridge's situation impressed itself
upon them in almost every postal delivery; and during every evening of clear
spring weather, the link with the *Letter* reasserted itself. After their evening
walk on the Thursday, for example, they came in to find 'a Magazine & Review
& a letter from Coleridge with verses to Hartley & Sara H. We read the Review
&c. The Moon was a perfect Boat a silver Boat when we were out in the
Evening.'[26] Wordsworth had first written about the moon as 'sky canoe' back
in 1798, in the first Prologue to 'Peter Bell', but Dorothy had actually copied
the passage out (recently revised) on 21 February; and then Coleridge had used
it in his *Dejection* poetry.[27] The links between the old poem, the new poem, the
friendly reference, the friendly recollection, and the new moon, were in all
their minds.

It is of course ambiguous whether they had been sent 'verses to Hartley and Sara' or 'verses to Hartley and verses to Sara'. If the latter, the verses to Sara were probably yet another instalment (or grouping) of the *Letter*. The verses to Hartley may well have been 'The Language of Birds: Lines spoken extempore, to a little child, in early spring' which Coleridge would print in the *Morning Post* in October, twelve days after the appearance of *Dejection: An Ode*. The poem as it existed in early May was probably in the form in which Sara Hutchinson entered it in her notebook, starting

> Do you ask what the Birds say? The Chaffinch, the Dove,
> The Blackbird the Thrush say 'I love & I love!' . . .

But the poem can also be seen as a coded way of writing about Sara Hutchinson; it ended

> But the lark is so brimful of gladness & Love,
> 10   The green Earth below him, the Blue Sky above,
> That he sings & he sings, & for ever sings he,
> I love my Love, and my Love loves me!
> No wonder that He's full of Joy to the brim
> When He loves his Love, & his Love loves him![28]

If those *were* the verses to Hartley which arrived in Grasmere on the 6 May, neither of the Wordsworths would have missed the point that his son offered Coleridge an opportunity to be both loving and fatherly, and also to be bitterly regretful that he was himself so unlike the Lark: so dejected, so lacking in 'Joy' (that crucial word in the *Letter*, the 1804 *Ode* and 'The Leech-gatherer'), so *un*loved. Sara, too, copying the poem into her notebook, would probably not have been allowed to miss the point Coleridge was making, or to miss the link he would later make between 'Singing and Loving' when he re-wrote his October 1799 notebook entries, and recalled the singing – and loving – round the fire at Sockburn.

However, it is possible that Dorothy meant 'verses to Hartley-&-Sara': which exactly describes Coleridge's poem 'The Day Dream'.[29] It too would appear in the *Morning Post* in October 1802, in that odd sequence of poems linked with Sara, Wordsworth, Mary and the wedding, but it then acquired a title (and modifications) which offered a poignant new reflection on it. It became 'The Day Dream, from an Emigrant to his absent Wife': a wife absent, of course, because (as Sara Hutchinson) she was irretrievable. A version sent to or acquired by Mary Hutchinson would however explicitly address Sara – 'And lo! upon the Couch a Woman's Form! / Thine, Sara! thine!' – and whereas the last stanza in the *Morning Post* would stress domestic tranquillity, with a child called 'Frederic', Mary's text addresses Sara as 'my Love', and introduces Hartley as himself:

25   And now when I seem'd <u>sure</u> my Love to see,
                Her very Self in her own quiet Home,
                There came an elfish Laugh, & waken'd me! –
                'Twas Hartley, who behind my Chair had clomb,
                And with his bright Eyes at my face was peeping –
30   I bless'd him – try'd to laugh – & fell a-weeping.[30]

A notebook entry Coleridge had made by the middle of February – 'a playful Tenderness; Touching the Heart, as with an infant's finger'[31] – coincides with a couplet in the *Morning Post* version ('A sweet and playful tenderness doth linger, / Touching my heart, as with an infant's finger'), suggesting when the poem might have been started. If this had been the poem sent to the Wordsworths in May,[32] they would have been very conscious how – like the *Letter* – it named Sara as the narrator's real love; and so marked a turning point in what Coleridge was prepared (to others in the gang) to express of his feelings for her. The Wordsworths and Mary Hutchinson were the only people to whom Coleridge could have sent such work; we do not know if Sara herself ever saw it.

Back in Grasmere – 'feeling himself strong' as he needed to be, to wrestle with his own poetry – on the Friday morning, 7 May, Wordsworth went back to 'The Leech-gatherer'. Here we regain the firm ground of Dorothy's dated entries in her journal. The poem still required a vast amount of work: on the 7th, 'he wrote hard at it till dinner time, then he gave over tired to death – he had finished the poem.'[33] But 'finishing' was only a stage in a process of composition which took another two months: and Dorothy does not record making a copy of the poem at this stage, as she usually did when Wordsworth actually finished work.[34] Although he started to think about yet another poem on the Friday evening, going to bed 'tired with thinking about a poem', and then spent the Saturday hard at work in the garden, on the Sunday morning he was back with 'The Leech-gatherer'. And this time he really finished it: and Dorothy copied it.

> William worked at the Leech gatherer almost incessantly from morning till tea-time. I copied the Leech-gatherer & other poems for Coleridge – I was oppressed & sick at heart for he wearied himself to death. After tea he wrote 2 stanzas in the manner of Thomsons Castle of Indolence – & was tired out. Bad news of Coleridge.[35]

Everything was centering on Coleridge at the moment; another letter had obviously come. Even those two stanzas in the manner of Thomson, which sound so innocuous, a mere poetical fancy, were (depending on where Wordsworth had started) either about Coleridge or about Wordsworth himself in comparison with Coleridge.[36] Of the eight stanzas which Wordsworth eventually wrote, the last four were about Coleridge and the others were a comic self-portrait. The Wordsworth character is always madly composing poetry while striding over 'the neighbouring height', either in the 'stormy night' or the midday sun, to the amazement of those who see (and hear) him:

> What ill was on him, what he had to do,
> A mighty wonder bred among our quiet crew.[37]

When he gets back, however, 'what he had to do' is irrelevant: he just sits around exhausted, not wanting to do anything except 'Look at the common grass from hour to hour' or go to sleep under the trees: just as Wordsworth had probably been doing this week, after working on 'The Leech-gatherer', in the final version of which a narrator would mercilessly cross-examine the old man: 'How is it that you live, and what is it you do?'[38] No one knows, either, what the Wordsworth figure does when he leaves the valley:

> Some thought he was a lover and did woo;
> Some thought far worse of him, and did him wrong;
> But Verse was what he had been wedded to;
> 35 And his own mind did, like a tempest strong,
> Come to him thus; and drove the weary Man along.[39]

Wordsworth had, of course, sometimes been seen going over to Middleham or Gallow Hill as a lover, doing his wooing, though he would have known that some people would have 'done him wrong' (especially when he went off with Dorothy). The point is that, in all situations, he is not so much dedicated to his craft as pursued and harried by it. Who *could* such a man marry, wedded to verse as he was?

The Coleridge figure, however, is really much happier, very cheerful and friendly and outgoing, to an extent that makes him seem almost half-witted. The only thing depressed about him is his lower-lip:

> Heavy his low-hung lip did oft appear,
> A face divine of heaven-born ideotcy!
> Profound his forehead was, though not severe . . .[40]

He is in fact so ingenious and so inventive that he never need get depressed at all: an interesting reflection upon what Coleridge was actually going through at that moment.

> 50 He lack'd not implement, device, or toy,
> To cheat away the hours that silent were:
> He would have taught you how you might employ
> Yourself; and many did to him repair,
> And, certes, not in vain; – he had inventions rare.

He is a wonderfully resourceful friend; his microscope, for example, opens up the natural world. But everything he does is compelling: 'He would entice that other man to hear / His music, & to view his imagery':

> And sooth, these two did love each other dear,
> As far as love in such a place could be:
> There did they lie from earthly labour free,
> Most happy livers as were ever seen![41]

Such writing is certainly engaged in a dialogue with the real Coleridge and with the fictional 'Leech-gatherer', which had described an equally untroubled narrator, before his disturbing plunge into melancholy:

> 30
> I heard the sky lark singing in the sky
> And I bethought me of the playful hare
> Ev'n such a happy Child of earth am I
> Even as these happy Creatures do I fare
> Far from the world I live & from all care[42]

That was something which both Wordsworth and Coleridge felt about themselves at times: that they were joyous, careless children. But they also explored the ways in which it was not true about them, either, because they were also caring, melancholy and anxious adults. The Thomson pastiche was, in that way, ironical about them both (*what* a carefree spring they were both having!) And both it and 'The Leech-gatherer' went straight to the heart of the problem of joy and melancholy, and showed them as part of a tension within Wordsworth as much as anything he could criticise in his friend. But the Thomson poem was also a good way of relaxing after the seriousness of the other poem: the Coleridge portrait and the self-portrait are comic, tender and acute. Because it took as its foundation the 'Castle' situation of the Thomson original, too, the poem constantly referred to the onlookers: the 'we' of the poem are, at different times, a 'gentle tribe', a 'quiet crew', living in a 'peaceful home' – 'our happy Castle'.[43] It sounds like an idealised mixture of Gallow Hill and Grasmere, with no allaying Greta Hall in it. And, most important of all, it insists that the activity of everyone – including the two central characters – keeps them happy. As a poem addressed to Coleridge, it says 'how *can* you be depressed: just look around you, as you yourself make others – like us, your friends – look around . . .'

Which is very largely what Wordsworth's lyric poems about nature had been saying during March and April. The Thomson poem was not especially serious, although it was certainly a way for Wordsworth to remind himself that Coleridge was a marvellous and wonderful person, not just a troubled one; and (just a little flatteringly: but a depressed person may need a little flattering) it would have served to remind Coleridge what extraordinary resources he commanded, and what an admiring audience of loving friends he possessed.

The Thomson verses – which Dorothy called 'the stanzas about C & himself' – took a couple of days to finish. On Monday 10 May, however, came 'an affecting letter from Mary H'.[44] Many things might have touched her, but if she had been sent Coleridge's *Letter* or 'The Day Dream', she would have had reason enough to be moved. Dorothy wrote a reply at once, and may well have enclosed a copy of 'The Leech-gatherer': one certainly reached Gallow Hill sometime in the next few days. On Monday 10 May, at any rate, Coleridge's own copy of 'The Leech-gatherer' (written out for him on Sunday the 9th, together with some other poems) was sent off. It had been posted to him because they did not expect to see him. However, on Wednesday the 12th, while they were sitting in their upstairs parlour in the evening as usual, Dorothy once more writing to Mary, there was a voice at the door downstairs: 'we were rouzed by Coleridge's voice below – he had walked, looked palish but was not much tired. We sate up till one o clock all together then William went to bed & I sate with C in the sitting room (where he slept) till 1/4 past 2 o clock.'[45] They were going to see a good deal of an extremely unhappy Coleridge over the next few days and weeks; and this in spite of the suggestion by one Coleridge biographer that 'the writing of "Dejection" was itself an act of release', and that May 1802 marked the start of a new and happier phase in the Coleridges' marriage: 'throughout the spring and summer he speaks no more of dejection'.[46] But this week he was obviously going through some kind of crisis. He had actually planned to go back the following morning, but the weather on Thursday the 13th was cold, and he did not set out until mid-afternoon. They went with him as far as Sara's Rock. Dorothy was thoroughly concerned: 'he did not look well when we parted from him'[47] – very different from the figure she had seen hopping over the stepping-stones when they had parted from him eight days earlier.

The attention Dorothy gave to Coleridge during May 1802 probably mattered rather more to him, too, than 'The Leech-gatherer' did, as a way of coping with melancholy. She had stayed up with him on the Wednesday night, talking for more than an hour longer than Wordsworth had; and she thought about him particularly on Friday the 14th, when she sat on the seat which the three of them had so often occupied the previous summer: 'William's unemployed beside me, & the space between where Coleridge has so often lain'.[48] Both she and Wordsworth wrote to Coleridge that Friday evening; and the following day (a miserable, cold and snowy one) 'had a melancholy letter from Coleridge just at Bed-time' – presumably written as soon as he had got back on the Thursday. 'It distressed me very much' wrote Dorothy in her journal, '& I resolved upon going to Keswick the next day'.[49]

What was Coleridge writing which made Dorothy feel she should go and see him at once? He does not seem to have been ill; he could obviously do the fourteen-mile walk without difficulty, and on 3 June he would note that his health was 'much better than it was'.[50] He may have been writing about his feelings for Sara Hutchinson; but the surviving fragment of a letter which he wrote to Sara in June is very striking for never getting anywhere near problematic subjects: it confines itself to descriptions of what Hartley and Derwent were saying and doing.[51] It is entirely possible, of course, that he had promised her to confine himself to such topics. It is even possible that he preferred to do so: his love was always as much for an ideal person as for an actual one.

However, it is more than likely that what Coleridge needed to talk to Dorothy about during May was the related (but not identical) problem of what he was to do as a married man who could no longer bear living with his wife. This too had been part of the *Letter*, and coming to the end of it may well have been a moment when Coleridge realised certain feelings very vividly ('Indifference or Strife') which had effectively been submerged or unspoken before. It seems certain, too, that at least some of the tension currently running very powerfully between Coleridge and his wife was over the extent of his friendship with the Wordsworths, and the fact that he was always going over to see them, and so neglecting *her* and the children. It would have made matters still worse that Sarah Coleridge was now pregnant, and ill. Dorothy may well have felt she ought to go to see Coleridge because he obviously needed to talk, but could not leave Keswick again just at the moment; and that can really only have been because of Sarah Coleridge. Sarah may also have preferred the idea of a visit from Dorothy at such a moment: Dorothy would not go off climbing Skiddaw with her husband, but would at least do some practical child care. (Dorothy had actually spent a lot of time between 7 and 12 May making 'frocks' for Derwent, which had been posted off on the 14th.[52])

It is also clear, however, that Coleridge was emotionally attaching himself to Dorothy. The last thing I am suggesting is that he wanted an affair with her, but with Sara Hutchinson the other side of England, and his wife either ill or antagonistic or both, he found Dorothy's sisterly company particularly important. It seems to me quite likely that, at some level, and at this juncture, he preferred Dorothy to any other woman. She was the sister he had always loved and wanted: his loss of his own sister Nancy in 1791 had touched him deeply.[53] On the other hand, the fact that Dorothy was also particularly disturbed at the moment – suffering her brother's decision to marry Mary Hutchinson, and contemplating the break-up of the Grasmere life which had been so important to her – made her more than usually vulnerable, and she may have been in love with him. The fact that, three weeks earlier, back on 20 April, Coleridge had carved her initials along with his on Sara's Rock would have been a sign to her of his special attachment. For her part, when she saw the initials, she kissed them rather than the person who cut them, but the person would probably have felt kissed. The fact that he asked *her* to go to Keswick with him, too, would have confirmed her sense of being vitally important to him . . . But exactly what they felt for each other we do not know.

I would simply hazard that she was more in love with him than he was with her.

Dorothy did not however go up to Keswick on the Sunday, after all. She may have wanted time to think, before rushing off like a love-struck girl; her brother was also at work all morning, and she may have felt that she shouldn't leave him while he was so busy. She went on thinking about them all, however, and – when writing her journal on the evening of Saturday the 15th – she sketched on the inserted blotting-paper page one of the inscriptions of all their names which shows how she, in her way, was perceiving the pattern of the group. It cannot have been an accident that she did this just three weeks after Coleridge's lettering on Sara's Rock had started to change it from a rock celebrating one person to a rock commemorating them all. Dorothy's blotting-paper inscription represents the way in which she herself might have ordered the names. She seems to have started by writing Coleridge's name, and then to have developed the rest:

                           S T Coleridge

        Dorothy Wordsworth   William Wordsworth
          Mary Hutchinson   –   Sara Hutchinson
                –   –
              William   Coleridge   Mary
                Dorothy   Sara
              - - - -   - - - -
                       15th May
                       1802

                   John Wordsworth[54]

Coleridge's position is a way of showing that he has, in effect, no balancing partner: so far as Dorothy is concerned, he is wife-less and childless. However, she equally clearly does *not* partner him with Sara Hutchinson, which it would have been very easy to do in such a pattern. She may have thought Coleridge's 'love' for Sara neither serious nor real enough for him to be linked to her in such a diagram: neither in the family names at the top nor in the interestingly organised familiar names lower down. One arrangement here seems to be elders followed by juniors, with Dorothy and Sara bringing up the rear. The other way is to see the four of them surrounding and in a sense cradling Coleridge. The extra name, slightly larger, and looking like a later addition – perhaps added, in sudden remorse, when the rest of the diagram was complete – was that of John Wordsworth; not in Grasmere for eighteen months now, but still one of the family and the gang, even if remembered tardily. Perhaps it was

Dorothy's adding him to her diagram which also led to his initials being cut on Sara's Rock: perhaps it was the other way round.

Dorothy did however go up to Keswick on Monday the 17th, Wordsworth coming with her as far as Wythburn. She turned out to be only one of several visitors at Greta Hall; some were there when she arrived, and others came the following day, while a letter from Mary Hutchinson coincided with her arrival. She managed to spend some time alone with Coleridge on her second evening there, however: 'C & I walked in the evening in the Garden'.[55] Her journal entries for these two days are again, however, remarkable for their failure to mention Sarah Coleridge. It is, once again, as if Sarah did not exist, any more than she had on Dorothy's diagram of the group and its partners. If Sarah Coleridge had imagined that Dorothy might be a more sympathetic and less distracting companion than Wordsworth, she could have had no idea of the way in which she was obliterated in the latter's record. Dorothy's concerns were only for Coleridge.

Dorothy walked back, accompanied by Coleridge for half the journey, on Wednesday the 19th, to be met by Wordsworth near Sara's Rock; and they probably arranged then that both the Wordsworths would go up for a proper visit in a day or two, probably on the Saturday. The following day, however, a letter came from Coleridge 'telling us that he wished us not to go to Keswick'. We can only assume that Sarah Coleridge was either feeling worse again, or had been difficult about visits from the Wordsworths. Instead, Coleridge asked them to meet him at Sara's Rock on Saturday the 22nd: a day with a blustery wind, this time a hot one, from which they all took shelter at different times. Coleridge 'was sitting under Sara's Rock when we reached him – he turned with us – we sate a long time under the Wall of a sheep-fold, had some interesting melancholy talk about his private affairs.'[56] That was one of the very few occasions in her journal when Dorothy bordered on the edge of indiscretion about what they had been discussing. It is striking how dissimilar her journal and her letters are, when one can compare them; the letters saying all kind of indiscreet things, living the life of the everyday in reminiscence, gossip, malice and love; the journal dedicated to recording nature, to recording Wordsworth's doings, to being a fairly sober record of event, weather and climate, and of anecdotes and language of the kind that Wordsworth might be able to use.[57] The only feelings about which Dorothy is regularly indiscreet in her journal are her own.

So we have no idea what that 'interesting melancholy talk about his private affairs' may have been about. But the fact that Coleridge then, after all, walked home with them tells its own story. A meeting arranged so that he could go home in the evening turned into a visit to Grasmere, during which he seems to have been with one or the other of them most of the time over the next two days. When they arrived, first both Wordsworth and Dorothy sat with him in the orchard; then Dorothy went in to prepare the meal; and then the two men came in to supper together. The following morning, Dorothy noted 'I sate with C in the orchard all the morning'. Coleridge then went down by himself to the rocky outcrops at the foot of Grasmere which they called Sara and Mary Points, before coming back to join them. He went home the next day; but that did not prevent Dorothy sending him a letter as soon as he had gone.[58] Her behaviour is, again, that of a woman in love; I am reminded of the previous November, when Coleridge had set off for London, and she and Wordsworth had seen him just before he went. On that occasion, 'every sight & every sound reminded me of him dear dear fellow – of his many walks to us by day & by night – of all dear things. I was melancholy & could not talk, but at last I eased my heart by weeping – nervous blubbering says William. It is not so – O how many, many reasons have I to be anxious for him.'[59] Her anxiety for him was certainly for him as the unhappy (and deeply depressed) husband of Sarah; but also, it seems to me, for him as a man she herself loved, even though she could hear and to some extent respond to the reproach in Wordsworth's tart phrase 'nervous blubbering'. At some level she was being a fool: she knew that. Whose melancholy were all these poems considering? They all had cause for it.

III

After the charged events of the middle of May, however, life seems to have become quieter; in part because Coleridge became less demanding, and partly because for the first time Dorothy and Wordsworth began seriously preparing for the radical change to their lives which his marriage to Mary would bring. I shall discuss these in Part III. They saw nothing of Coleridge for more than a fortnight, perhaps because – after running away from home on 22 May – he managed to work out a new relationship with Sarah Coleridge. This may well have been among the things Wordsworth and Dorothy had discussed with him. Coleridge told Southey, almost certainly about this period, that after a particularly savage row,

> Mrs Coleridge was made *serious* – . . . She promised to set about an alteration in her external manners & looks & language, & to fight against her inveterate habits of puny Thwarting & unintermitting Dyspathy – this immediately – and to do her best endeavors to cherish other *feelings*. I on my part promised to be more attentive to all her feelings of Pride, &c &c and to try to correct my habits of impetuous & bitter censure –.[60]

But although Coleridge insisted 'We have both kept our Promises' the relationship – even if it changed – did so only briefly. It is easy to promise not to criticise another person if that person promises not to do anything which might make you want to criticise them. The problems start when they *do* do something you don't like. It is also hard to see how anyone could promise to

fight against their own tendency to 'Dyspathy' – antipathy, dislike, the opposite of 'sympathy'. But there may well have been a lull in the hostilities until the
middle of June, and perhaps for longer; and not seeing the Wordsworths would
certainly have helped.

All this time, 'The Leech-gatherer' had of course been at a standstill;
Coleridge had had his copy since around 12 May (and probably Dorothy's
early draft as well). An entry made in his notebook sometime after 9 May picks
up an image which also appears in the poem, and thus points up beautifully the
impossibility of defining debt, authorship or ownership of the language, ideas
or observations which he and Wordsworth shared: 'The rocks and Stones
⟨seemed to live⟩ put on a vital semblance; and Life itself thereby seemed to
forego its restlessness, to anticipate in its own nature an infinite repose, and to
become, as it were, compatible with Immoveability. Kirkstone/'.[61]

The poem as it existed after June 1802 would describe how

<blockquote>

	As a huge Stone is sometimes seen to lie
65	Couch'd on the bald top of an eminence;
	Wonder to all who do the same espy
	By what means it could thither come and whence;
	So that it seems a thing endued with sense . . .[62]

</blockquote>

That stanza was not in the original draft of the poem,[63] but was almost certainly written early in July. The notebook entry may have been made before or
after Coleridge read the poem in its unrevised state; the poem may have been
revised before or after the notebook entry was made, though probably afterwards. Coleridge and Wordsworth were regularly in each other's company, but
never apparently when coming over the Kirkstone pass; Wordsworth had
however been that way on 14 February, and again with Dorothy on 16 April;
the liveliness of the streams, against the rocks, had caught his attention when
crossing it in snow in February, and he had pointed them out to Dorothy on 16
April: 'The Becks among the Rocks were all alive – Wm showed me the little
mossy streamlet which he had loved when he saw its bright green track in the
snow.'[64] Coleridge, so far as we can reconstruct his movements, does not seem
to have come over the Kirkstone pass at all during the winter, spring or summer
of 1801–2. But, as with the other parallels described above, seeking primary
authority is not wise; these are images which passed backwards and forwards
between them.

What happened to 'The Leech-gatherer' during June, however, confirms
how poetry mattered to the people in the group. All were sent copies; and comments from Mary and Sara had a significant effect on the poem. We should also
realise that quarrel, and disagreement and difference were characteristic of
them. They probably existed as a group, in part, because they were extremely
honest with each other, and said what they thought and meant. Egos got
bruised; poems got revised in consequence. I described above some of the ways

in which Coleridge may have responded to 'The Leech-gatherer'.[65] We do not know at which of their brothers' farms Mary and Sara currently were, but copies of the poem had been sent to them both if they were at different addresses. The rare chance survival of a letter from Wordsworth allows us to reconstruct a little of the way in which the sisters had both written critically about one of his poems; and since the poem at this stage of its development can also largely be reconstructed (see Appendix I) and Wordsworth's answers to their letters survive, we have a unique opportunity to gauge the nature of this particular exchange. So much of their involvement with the work of the two poets was confined (so far as the surviving record is concerned) to their dutiful copying of what lay before them, that an opportunity to observe what they actually thought about the work they copied is especially valuable. It is, of course, possible that this pattern of a poem sent, a response returned (critical or favourable), and some further comment sent, was one which actually recurred: it was unwise of Jonathan Wordsworth to refer to Sara's critical response in this present instance as 'unprecedented criticism',[66] as we have no idea how she normally wrote. To judge by her surviving correspondence, she never minced her words: but not a single letter she wrote to him in 1802 has survived. The only unprecedented thing about 'The Leech-gatherer' is that – because Wordsworth's response survives – we can intuit something of what she wrote.

Wordsworth addressed himself to Mary's criticisms first. She had commented on some particular words and phrases, and had criticised his use of the word 'view' meaning 'see' (apparently suggesting that he should indeed have used the word 'see'); and she also objected to the phrase 'a sickness had by him' because its English was unnatural. She would have preferred the phrase to run 'a sickness which he had'.

Both these criticisms Wordsworth brushed aside. 'The poem is throughout written in the language of men – "I suffered much by a sickness had by me long ago" is a phrase which anybody might use, as well as "a sickness which I had long ago".'[67] The brusqueness of the response is interesting; but he felt very much on top of this particular subject. On 31 May 'a complimentary & critical letter to W from John Wilson of Glasgow Post Paid'[68] had arrived, and Wordsworth and Dorothy had together worked hard to answer it, starting on Saturday 5 June and probably finishing the following day. Dorothy copied the letter they produced, which turned out to be a formidable statement of faith about the kind of poet Wordsworth wanted to be. The poet's job was not to fit in with the taste of his middle-class audience but to *lead* that audience to consider subjects (and language) which they would normally find unpleasant. It was – Wordsworth agreed – the poet's job to carry his reader with him, wherever possible, but 'He ought to travel before men occasionally as well as at their sides.'[69] What had particularly concerned Wilson was the exact nature of the language and experience of ordinary people, and a large part of Wordsworth's answer to him was devoted to what he did and did not mean by the phrase 'the language of men'.

The Hutchinsons' letters arriving at this juncture, therefore, made Wordsworth especially impatient. Here he was, using the language of ordinary people in an original and remarkable way – and here were they, suggesting that he should use a vocabulary which *they* would consider more 'natural' (that is, polite): while he knew (having just thought it all through) that such criticisms depended on how and where you defined the word 'natural', and what kind of person you were. Mary's small and slightly pedantic criticisms seemed to have been made at the price of ignoring the extraordinariness of a poem which had taken an unlikely figure, and had made him the centre of a poem designed to correct fine feelings of the very kind in which the narrator himself indulges. And here was his future wife suggesting that he should be taking a more sophisticated stance.

He made his sharp response . . . and then turned to a more attractive subject: his poem 'Coming for Mary', which she had already been sent a draft of, and which he wanted to improve. He enclosed a new stanza; and although in passing he assumed she would originally have misread the poem, as both Dorothy and Coleridge had (his letter was not very flattering about Mary's capacities as a reader), at least he acknowledged that in *that* poem 'my Idea was not as developed as it ought to have been'[70] – perhaps a way of apologising for his criticism of her comments on 'The Leech-gatherer'.

Sara's letter had, however, been rather more irritating. Both sisters had apparently insisted that there was nothing very much wrong with 'The Leech-gatherer', and that even the second half of the poem was 'very well', but Wordsworth insisted that if it were only 'very well' then he had failed. He refused to accept moderate praise. Either he was doing something revolutionary or he was not: there could be no two ways about it.

> I . . . describe him, whether ill or well is not for me to judge with perfect confidence, but this I can *confidently* affirm, that, though I believe God has given me a strong imagination, I cannot conceive a figure more impressive than that of an old Man like this, the survivor of a Wife and ten children, travelling alone among the mountains and all lonely places, carrying him with him his own fortitude, and the necessities which an unjust state of society has entailed upon him.[71]

He is laying it on the line. Either you agree that such a character is important for a poet not just to describe, but to make the moral centre of a poem about the weakness and childishness of a sophisticated narrator – or I cannot take you seriously.

Sara, too, had objected to certain words and phrases; but she had also come out and said that she sympathised with and understood the feelings in the first half of the poem – the exhilaration of the narrator, and the corresponding

depression – but then found the leech-gatherer himself really not very interesting. His employment did not much concern her, and his descriptions of his
own life she found positively 'tedious'. That must have been the word she used:
Wordsworth threw it back at her, while Dorothy also reprimanded her for
using it ('when you feel any poem of his to be tedious . . .').

As can be seen from the reconstruction of the poem in Appendix I, both the
speech and life-story of the leech-gatherer were a good deal more extensive in
the version of the poem sent to the Hutchinsons than they were later; if the
reconstruction is right, three whole stanzas were devoted to his reported
speech, and the poem had undoubtedly contained a long description of his way
of life, summer and winter:

> Feeble I am in health these hills to climb
> Yet I procure a Living of my own
> This is my summer work in winter time
> I go with godly Books from Town to Town
> Now I am seeking Leeches up & down
> From house to house I go from Barn to Barn
> All over Cartmell Fells & up to Blellan Tarn[72]

It was precisely this kind of detail which Sara found 'tedious'. Wordsworth
obviously took her criticisms seriously (he would remove this stanza during
the following month's revision), although he rejected her criticisms out of hand
in June. He wrote, 'My dear Sara, it is not a matter of indifference whether you
are pleased with this figure and his employment . . . it is of the utmost importance that you should have had pleasure from contemplating the fortitude,
independence, persevering spirit, and the general moral dignity of this old
man's character.'[73] What he insists on is *pleasure*; the poem should give it. We
have a lovely insight into just how far Wordsworth was prepared to go, in
trying his poetry out on non-literary people. At the very moment when
Dorothy was writing to the Hutchinson sisters on 14 June – either just before
or just after Wordsworth wrote his own fiercely defensive letters – she mentioned that 'We have our Haircutter below stairs, William is reading the Leech-
gatherer to him.'[74] On-the-spot research, doubtless. *Did* Mr Williamson get
pleasure from contemplating the moral dignity of the Leech-gatherer? *Was* its
language clear to him?

The Hutchinsons' response, too, had apparently assumed that Wordsworth
described such a man simply because he had once met him: the poem being
a piece of heightened realism of the kind a widely wandering poet would
produce who was always bumping up against odd people. Dorothy ticked
off Sara in language a good deal more offensive than her brother's: 'When
you happen to be displeased with what you suppose to be the tendency or
moral of any poem which William writes, ask yourself whether you have
hit upon the real tendency and true moral, and above all never think that he

writes for no reason but merely because a thing happened . . .'[75] She, of all people, knew exactly how far the poem was (and was not) simply a response to a real-life person. It had been back in September 1800 that she and Wordsworth had met

> an old man almost double, he had on a coat thrown over his shoulders above his waistcoat & coat. Under this he carried a bundle & had an apron on & a night cap. His face was interesting. He had Dark eyes & a long nose – John who afterwards met him at Wythburn took him for a Jew. He was of Scotch parents but had been born in the army. He had had a wife '& a good woman & it pleased God to bless us with ten children' – all these were dead but one of whom he had not heard for many years, a Sailor – his trade was to gather leeches but now leeches are scarce & he had not strength for it – he lived by begging & was making his way to Carlisle where he should buy a few godly books to sell. He said leeches were scarce partly owing to this dry season, but many years they have been scarce – he supposed it owing to their being much sought after, that they did not breed fast, & were of slow growth. Leeches were formerly 2/6 100; they are now 30/.[76]

The episode gives one an acute sense both of how careful Dorothy was to record in her journal details which might be useful, and of how good the Wordsworths must have been as cross-examiners; they learned a vast amount about the man. Wordsworth must have consulted the journal at some point, too; details like the 'godly books' were exactly transmitted.

It is striking that it was on just those particulars of the life of the real individual that Sara's criticisms should have fastened, and on which Wordsworth defended his poem; and it would be exactly these things which he subsequently cut. The discussion of the poem does seem to have worried him, as his asperity reveals. The following day, although a letter came from Mary '& one from Sara to C', and Wordsworth usually read his post at once, Dorothy comments that 'William did not read them'.[77]

He made, however, another link with the past when asked about the poem in 1843:

> Town-End. 1807. This Old Man I met a few hundred yards from my cottage at Town-End, Grasmere; & the account of him is taken from his own mouth. I was in the state of feeling described in the beginning of the poem, while crossing over Barton Fell from M[r]. Clarkson's at the foot of Ulswater, towards Askam. The image of the hare I then observed on a ridge of the Fell.[78]

The date of 1807, of course, is quite wrong.[79] But the last date before writing the poem on which Wordsworth had taken the route he remembered had been on his way to Middleham to see Mary Hutchinson on his thirty-second birthday, 7 April 1802.[80] The exhilaration of the narrator, then, in so far as it was

rooted in the real, was like that of the man on his horse, riding excitedly off to
see the woman he would soon be marrying (although probably also extremely
anxious about how they might manage financially), contrasted with the compelling image of the leech-gatherer, his wife dead and his children lost, broken
down physically, living in absolute poverty, and yet still firm-minded in spite
of all.

The comments from the Hutchinsons obviously preyed on Wordsworth; and
three things happened during the remainder of June which probably helped
him think the poem through more carefully. One was the extraordinary piece
of good fortune I described above: it suddenly seemed likely that the
Wordsworths would after all be paid the money owed to their father on his
death in 1783. The new owner of the Lowther estate, Sir William Lowther, had
announced his 'intention to pay all debts &c'.[81] The insecurity of the poet's
future had, after all, been stabilised: 'something' would indeed be 'given',
financially. It also meant that Wordsworth and Dorothy stayed longer in Town
End before going across to Yorkshire than they had probably originally
planned.[82] The second thing was that Coleridge came to stay, probably around
Sunday 27 June, and stayed until the 30th: and his arrival, as so often, seems to
have provoked Wordsworth to new imaginings. The image of the unmoving
stone perhaps came up between them during this visit, and so got into the
poem. And then a chance encounter on 30 June may well have done something to resolve further thoughts about how to present a poetic biography.
Wordsworth and Dorothy met a traveller whom, as usual, they persuaded to tell
his life story; a man of eighty-three, as tough-minded as anyone could hope.
Dorothy tried lifting his pack '& it was almost more than I could do'. She concluded the entry: 'A weight of Children a poor man's blessing'. Two days later,
Wordsworth was at work again on 'The Leech-gatherer'; Dorothy transcribed
alterations on the 2nd and Wordsworth finished the poem in its new form on
the 4th. The following day, Dorothy 'copied out the LG for Coleridge & for us.
Wrote to Annette Mrs Clarkson, MH & Coleridge.'[83] It was obviously important that Coleridge should get the poem as soon as it was finished; it was part
of a conversation with him. Three lines which he would single out for praise in
Biographia Literaria —[84]

> In my mind's eye I seem'd to see him pace
> About the weary moors continually,
> Wandering about alone and silently,[85]

– only came into the poem during this last revision, and Coleridge may well
have been involved in the writing of them. As always, deciding who was
responsible for what is impossible. It was a poem which – from Wordsworth's
point of view – belonged to them together: it had been addressed to the very
subjects closest to their hearts, their child-like joy and their adult anxiety
and melancholy. In that way it played its part in the long conversation of

this spring and summer; and we can be absolutely sure that Coleridge ended up extremely impressed by it. He paid it the compliment of copying it out to send it to the Beaumonts around 13 August 1803:[86] the copy once again proving the engagement of and interest of the copyist, not just his or her dutiful responsibility.

Part III
To the Wedding

Chapter Nine

Fallings from us, Vanishings: May to July

On Friday 9 July Dorothy and Wordsworth would be leaving house and garden at Town End for the journey which would take them to the Coleridges at Keswick, the Clarksons at Eusemere, and then across the Pennines to the Hutchinsons at Gallow Hill; down to London and Dover, to Calais to see Annette and Caroline, back to Dover and London to see the rest of the Wordsworth family; back to Gallow Hill for – at last – Wordsworth's marriage with Mary; and finally home, all three together, to Grasmere on 6 October.

Wordsworth and Dorothy had, of course, been preparing for this journey for months. It was somewhat delayed: they had originally hoped to get away by the last week of June. As early as 13 June, Dorothy had spent 'all day' writing out 'poems for our journey'[1] – probably drafts of the sonnets on which Wordsworth was currently working, and perhaps some part of the *Ode* in progress, so that Wordsworth could go on working while away. He would also be able to read aloud recent poems out to the people with whom they would be staying. But earlier still, on Saturday 29 May, Wordsworth had finished a draft of a poem which at that stage Dorothy (and perhaps he) referred to as 'Going for Mary'. This, as it turned out, would be his only poem explicitly about his forthcoming marriage: but it was not focused on his feelings about Mary, nor on hers for him. It was specifically about leaving the garden at Town End: it would mention 'the cottage' and a 'few things that lie about our door',[2] but addressed itself neither to her, nor to the house to which she was actually coming.[3]

The house itself Mary of course knew well; she had lived in it for six weeks in 1800, visited it on a number of occasions, and back in April Dorothy had reassured her 'No fireside is like this. Be chearful in the thought of coming to it.'[4] But there obviously had to be some changes before the marriage. Towards the end of June, Molly Fisher 'washed and glazed the curtains', while Dorothy herself whitewashed the ceilings, and they planned to colour-wash the walls (Dorothy got exhausted grinding paint on the 24th). We also know how carefully Molly Fisher would keep the newly painted house all summer, in preparation for their return.[5] Rather more significantly, changes were made in the sleeping arrangements. William moved downstairs to Dorothy's old wood-panelled and stone-floored room on the ground floor, next to the downstairs parlour. This would become his bedroom with Mary; Dorothy moved into the front room upstairs.[6] The house was small and noise carried easily; the new arrangement gave Wordsworth and Mary (and Dorothy) as much privacy as a small house could offer. They thus got the house into its new state, and themselves into their new quarters, well before the changes due to take place in the autumn. Part of making the house ready for Mary consisted in getting themselves ready, too.

The Town End garden, however, was something special. It had been a labour of love for two years. Dorothy and Wordsworth had made relatively few changes to the house, but they had actually created the garden: not only did it offer them one of their ways of living cheaply, but it was also full of memories of John Wordsworth (who had helped Dorothy make it in 1800), and it was now intimately connected with Wordsworth's life and work. As Dorothy's journal shows, he worked very hard in it not only as a poet, but also as a vegetable and fruit gardener. He worked there regularly, planted and cared for peas, flowers, runner beans and potatoes; he cut down the winter cherry, raked stones, chopped wood, spread dung, dug the garden and cleaned out the well.[7] He also planted out a 'Bower', built a seat, added a step and 'nailed up' the honeysuckle and the fruit trees.[8] We do not know how the 'shed' (meaning summerhouse) in the orchard got built in the spring of 1802, but he probably did that too, with Dorothy's help. They had gone together on 6 May to enquire about hurdles to build it, and although Wordsworth was probably better at 'hammering at a passage'[9] than building a summerhouse, and they failed to see any hurdles on the 6 May, at some stage during the next month he and Dorothy managed to erect an 'Indian shed', and felt as proud as amateurs always do about such things: 'Our own contrivance, building without peer',[10] he called it.

They were not what one might call deeply serious gardeners: you cannot go away for the first fortnight of April and then from 9 July to 6 October if you are. They also both thought poetry writing *in* the garden as important as keeping things tidy; on 4 July 1802, Dorothy would note tartly: 'The garden is overrun with weeds', though they went on caring for their garden produce.[11] But – probably to the surprise of their neighbours, whose plots would have been entirely functional vegetable and fruit gardens – they also made theirs something beautiful to look at. Dorothy was the chief flower gardener; Wordsworth had written, back in April, 'My trees they are, my sisters flowers'.[12] In particular she was interested in bringing wild flowers into garden cultivation: some taken from the edge of Grasmere, where on 14 May she noted 'Gowans are coming out – marsh marygolds in full glory'.[13] These became the 'gifts of tender thought' to the garden which Wordsworth wrote about in 'Farewell, thou little Nook' at the end of May 1802.

> Thou like the morning in thy saffron coat
> Bright Gowan, and marsh marygold farewell!

Whom from the borders of the Lake we brought,
And placed together near our rocky well.

Dorothy copied out a draft of the new poem on 29 May but Wordsworth then seems to have revised it.[14] When she copied it again two days later, she called it 'the poem on "Our Departure"':[15] a reference to her own sense of involvement in it. A copy went off very soon afterwards to the Hutchinsons, probably when Dorothy wrote to them on 1 June or on the 3rd.

But Wordsworth was still not finished; on 14 June he sent the Hutchinsons changes provoked by second thoughts. He was now shocked at the Spenserian language he had allowed into the penultimate stanza, with its rock 'clad in its primrose vest'[16] – but he was also disturbed by comments Dorothy and Coleridge had made about the poem (Coleridge had come over to stay on 10 June and had probably read it then). He thought they had misunderstood one stanza, so it needed more work. However, it may well also be true that he did not want to finish his poem too soon, thus symbolically and formally bringing to an end what it called 'this sweet spring, the best beloved and best'. On 17 June Dorothy found him 'attempting to alter a stanza in the poem on our going for Mary, which I convinced him did not need altering'.[17] He never gave the poem a title, which was unusual. It was a conversation between people who knew exactly what was meant by it, not a public statement needing a title. Nor did he publish it in 1807 along with nearly all of the other poems he had written this spring. It was clearly very close to his heart. When he finally put into print in 1815, he simply called it 'Composed in the Year 1802'.[18]

The poem is organised around a conceit: that Mary herself is one of those lake-side plants, lovingly brought in to the garden to become one of 'ours'. When her sister Sara copied the poem out, not only did she not insert a hyphen in 'marsh marygold',[19] she left the second word so open that it might be read as 'mary gold', emphasising the pun: that may well have been how Dorothy's manuscript had looked. The poem says that Mary, whose heart, appropriately, 'is lowly bred / Her pleasures are in wild fields gathered',[20] will find her natural place in the hearts (and the garden) at Town End: 'to you herself will wed'. Dorothy and Wordsworth are experts in bringing in the foreign, just as the garden is expert in absorbing new plants:

　　　　Bringing thee chosen plants and blossoms blown
35　　　Among the distant mountains, flower and weed
　　　　Which thou has taken to thee as thy own . . .

So they will bring Mary in; she will marry the flowers and the garden (and the gardeners); and they will live together happily. It is a very tender and caring poem, but also a very odd one to write to the person you are about to marry. The poem is absolutely confident that this spring *before* the beloved person comes is something which will never be repeated: it is 'the best belov'd and best'. It is the time when Wordsworth insists that he is writing poetry 'that will not die'.[21] Such a poem offers the beloved person no personal assurance at all: no love of any kind. Instead, it insists that Mary is coming to a place wholly right for her life, and for the lives of those already there.

Wordsworth had originally given the poem, as its last stanza:

O happy Garden! lov'd for hours of sleep
O quiet Garden! lov'd for waking hours
For soft half slumbers that did gently steep
Our spirits carrying with them dreams of flowers
Belov'd for days of rest in fruit-tree bowers!
And coming back with her who will be ours
Into thy bosom we again shall creep.

60

When he published the poem in 1815, he clearly thought the first two lines would give quite the wrong impression of him, and replaced them by something close to their exact opposite:

> O happy Garden! whose seclusion deep
> Hath been so friendly to industrious hours;[22]

But the 'sleep' really *is* the point. We know that Wordsworth constantly wrote in his garden: but he also slept in it. 'Farewell, thou little Nook' confirms how much he valued the garden for the rest it gave him during and after his work. In his Thomson parody, he had described the poet returning home to sleep in his orchard:

> Retired in that sunshiny shade he lay,
> And, like a naked Indian, slept himself away.[23]

Dorothy records Wordsworth lying on his back in their 'Indian shed' on 8 May, but she never mentions him actually asleep there, although the journal's regular 'Wm went after tea into the orchard' probably indicates some resting of the eyes.[24] But when they all come back together, once the summer is over, then the sharp distinctions between the 'she' whom the poem has previously addressed (Mary), the 'we' who have so far loved and cared for the garden (Dorothy and Wordsworth), and the 'ye' of the flowers, will all come to an end. Mary is already, complicatedly but precisely, 'she who will be ours', and the newly constituted 'we' ('her' and 'we' and 'ye') will creep together to sleep in this gentle, beloved, dreamy place. It is especially striking that a poem contemplating the greatest change of all – the fact that Wordsworth will be sleeping with Mary in that stone-flagged downstairs room – comes so very close to the idea, but then veers away from it. It turns the thought into an idea of them *all* symbolically at rest together: not in the house, but in the garden.

'Farewell, thou little Nook' was, however, a poem which needed to nego-tiate the desires and feelings of Dorothy (its immediate recipient and copyist) as well as those of Mary Hutchinson (to whom it was addressed and sent).[25] To that extent, it reveals a good deal about the complex dynamics of this last, best spring.

The simple metaphor of Mary as a wild flower is, for example, complicated by the nature of the garden to which she is being invited. It is not *simply* beau-tiful or dreamy; Wordsworth was too much of a realist to extend a conceit into fantasy. The garden he describes is – as gardens are – both 'most constant' and 'most fickle'. It goes its own way irresponsibly, 'easy-hearted', uncaring, as the natural world always is: happy to get rid of human beings altogether, and happiest of all to run to weeds, exactly as this beloved garden would do in July 1802:

> Who being lov'd in love no bounds dost know,
> 45   And say'st when we forsake thee 'Let them go!'[26]

This makes the greeting of Mary odder still: what kind of a *home* will such a place make? Bringing in a strange plant like Mary will not enhance the garden's human qualities, but will most certainly add to its wild ones.

But bringing in Mary will, too, assist the dominant 'we' and 'us' of the poem to do the hardest thing of all, which is to bring the new person not just into the *feeling* of the place but into actual possession of it. The 'we' already possess it, and are possessed by it. Mary – however much loved – is not yet in that situation. But the poem is very clear that it is not enough simply to expect Mary somehow to experience the 'Joy' of its previous possessors (that crucial word for the whole of this spring). Joy, this poem says bluntly, dies, just as a plant does: 'Joy will be gone in its mortality'. It is not to be relied on as something you can offer a bride, any more than a garden simply stays constant or unchanging. When you leave, the joy dies, just as the garden runs to weeds. Something else is necessary to help preserve the past and to pass it on to those whom we love: and that 'something' is both a place which will accept Mary as a garden accepts a new plant – and poetry.

> Help us to tell her tales of years gone by
> 50   And this sweet spring the best beloved & best . . .
> Something must stay to tell us of the rest[27]

What can 'stay' for Mary is, in one (very old and traditional) sense, poetry itself: the poetry of the marvellous, the beautiful, which can itself renew and recreate and actually pass on joy, not just vaguely hope that it might survive:

> Here with its primroses the steep rock's breast
> Glitter'd at evening like a starry sky;
55   And in this bush our sparrow built its nest,
> Of which I sung one song that will not die.[28]

The last line contains an interesting slip: 'The Sparrow's Nest' was not about the Grasmere garden at all, but about the Wordsworth family garden in Cockermouth:[29] and that poem, too, had focused upon Dorothy rather than on the sparrow. Wordsworth's relation with his own family cannot help infiltrating a poem trying to be about other things (being uncomplicatedly welcoming is never easy).

But the new poem does its best both to welcome the new person by taking her into the experience of recreated joy, *and* to be the poetry which will, after all, help her feel how joy can last: whilst never leaving the present gardeners out of account. Poetry recreates and preserves what, by itself, cannot last, any more than a flower can remain in bloom, or this garden stay unchanged. It is a poem which, very strangely but with extraordinary honesty and tact, stresses the distinction between the stranger and the garden. By not addressing itself at any point to Mary's new home, the sense of Mary's status as (literally) an *outsider* is maintained. To that extent, Dorothy's feelings as beloved partner are prioritised; the poem might be called 'Going with Dorothy' as much as 'Going for Mary'. But Mary is *in*vited; and Wordsworth writes poetry to her for the first time, even if the poetry stresses an existing partnership as much as it does the feelings of a man about to marry. If Dorothy had sent the early draft of the poem to Mary on 29 May, when she believed Wordsworth had finished it – a day when she also wrote to Mary – that might account for the fact that a 'very affecting letter came from MH' on 3 June. The poem was a small triumph in making Mary feel welcome at Town End, but Dorothy in no way excluded.[30] That was precisely the kind of negotiation which this group of people had to manage, as their lives changed this year.

The news of one major change had come on 27 May: the Wordsworth family's old enemy Sir James Lowther had died on the 24th, awakening the possibility that the family might be able to recover from his heir their massive debt from the Lowther estate. The news clearly provoked Wordsworth's decision to tell his brother Richard the news of his impending marriage to Mary: he was now able to represent himself as someone who had prudently delayed a desion to get married until his financial situation had improved.[31] The poem of the 29th was thus, for some of its readers, a kind of public announcement as much as it was a private communication.

But it was on the evening of the 29th, too, that Dorothy twice tried out the effects of certain names in her journal. She memorialised them exactly as Coleridge would have done, dated, timed and placed. Setting them out like this was her own way, perhaps, of confronting the new reality which her brother's poem had shown *him* confronting too. On the inner third of a page in her journal, the rest of the leaf torn off, she wrote:

Dorothy Wordsworth
William Wordsworth
Mary Wordsworth
May 29th 6 0 clock
Evening
Sitting at small table
by window. Grasmere 1802

Having done that, she seems to have turned to the front of her journal and tried it out again: this time with herself as the filling in the threesome.

Mary Wordsworth
Dorothy Wordsworth
William Wordsworth
Sat Eve: 20 past 6
May 29th[32]

Both are memorials, but they also look forward, quite un-self-pityingly, to the new household.

Preparing for Wordsworth's marriage involved a number of such strategies. Wordsworth seems to have conducted himself and his writing with a good deal more tact than some of his biographers, who refer unfeelingly to 'The coming joys'.[33] But there were problems even he could not solve. The main one was how Dorothy would survive financially.[34] She had no income or money of her own; she had lived in William's house and from the money which her brother John had ensured she be given while he was away at sea,[35] amounting to £20 a year; her brothers Richard and Christopher also gave her presents of money. William now suggested to Richard that, in the claim on the Lowther estate which the family were about to make – following the heir's announcement in June that those owed money by Sir James Lowther should apply for restitution – 'It would be proper to state the utter destitution of my Sister'.[36]

Richard, as eldest son in charge of the family's financial affairs, of course, enquired whether Dorothy was not still sure of a home with William and Mary. He may have been hoping for the answer that they would, of course, take care of her. But Dorothy was determined not to be a drain on William and Mary's finances. Their provision of a house was their contribution, and she told Richard 'I shall continue to live with my Brother William', and 'Mary Hutchinson is a most excellent woman – I have known her long, and I know her thoroughly; she has been a dear friend of mine, is deeply attached to William, and is disposed to feel kindly to all his family.'[37] But her real point was that William could not now afford to go on supporting her: 'Having nothing to spare nor being likely to have, at least for many years, I am obliged (I need not say how much he regrets this necessity) to set him aside, and I will consider myself as boarding through my whole life with an indifferent person.'[38] She therefore needed an income to be able to pay for her lodging with the newly married couple, and for all the other expenses of her life: 'Sixty pounds a year is the sum which would entirely gratify all my desires. With sixty pounds a year I should not fear any accidents or changes which might befall me. I cannot look forward to the time when, with my habits of frugality, I could not live comfortably on that sum.'[39] It has been pointed out that £60 a year was, too, 'the highest income free of the Income Tax imposed by Pitt in 1799 to pay for the French Wars'[40]; but it was also £20 times three, and a means of putting pressure on Richard to match what John and Christopher were already doing.

But it was not just an income Dorothy wanted. It was security. She needed (she told Richard) to be able to rely on an income 'independent of accidents of death or any other sort that may befal you or any of my Brothers, its principal object being to make me tranquil in my mind with respect to my future life'. She was sadly right; her brother John's death in 1805 would cost her any further income from him, and it would also put at risk the sums of money both she and William had invested in his commercial enterprises.

During 1802 Richard was unforthcoming. Perhaps he felt that the Lowther money would change everything, if they got it, so that there was no point in making interim arrangements. Meanwhile, Dorothy's brother Christopher promised her £20 a year. Dorothy eventually decided – given that the money from the Lowther estate *did* seem likely to materialise – that she would just go ahead and draw upon Richard too for £20 a year in the future; and this she seems to have done, with occasional requests for a little more.[41]

Money she could organise. Other things she had to leave to others. On the last day of May, the day she copied out 'Our Departure' for the second time, Dorothy recorded another loss and her simultaneous assurance of love in an entry at once sad, determined and touching: 'My Tooth broke today. They will soon be gone. Let that pass I shall be beloved – I want no more.'[42] Teeth, in an age before dentures, had to be taken seriously. The loss of a molar or incisor – and 'My tooth' sounds like one she relied on – would change the food she would be able to eat for the rest of her life. But Dorothy probably implied something else. The loss of her teeth meant that her face would be even thinner and (by contemporary standards) even less attractive. In 1810, Wordsworth would note that, after a period when she had been in better health than at any time since 1797, 'Her throat and neck are quite filled up; and if it were not for her teeth she would really look quite young'.[43] But as early as the summer of 1802 she was sure she would never get married; Mary Hutchinson would be getting married at the age of 32 in October, but Dorothy insisted that marriage 'would be absurd at my age (30 years) to talk of'.[44] She had obviously decided against it; she had, after all, found her way of life, and held fast to her determined priorities. Even the lost tooth does not really matter: let it pass. I shall be beloved, even with a beloved brother married. Mary and Sara are sisters, but dearer than before: Wordsworth continues as a brother; Coleridge continues as another and more exciting, if also far more troubling kind of brother. I shall be beloved.

II

There are a number of entries of this kind during her record of the remaining weeks at Town End. On Wednesday 2 June, she and Wordsworth went for a walk as usual: 'crawled up the little glen & planned a seat'.[45] It was important for them both, but especially for Dorothy, to feel that life would go on in just the same way after the great change of her brother's marriage. Seats must be planned and built, just as they had always been. Later in the evening they went out again, in a 'cold south wind portending Rain': but this time, 'After we came in we sate in deep silence at the window – I on a chair & William with his hand on my shoulder. We were deep in Silence & Love, a blessed hour. We drew to the fire before bed-time & ate some Broth for our suppers.'[46] The domestic detail of porridge for supper seems to have been as much a kind of reassurance for Dorothy – and perhaps for Wordsworth too – of the household continuing, and its inhabitants living mutually supportive and loving lives, as the special time of silence and love at the window. Other tiny details were probably written with a good deal more emotion than they now apparently possess. On Friday 4 June, for example, 'In the evening we walked on our favourite path. Then we came in & sate in the orchard'.[47] This 'favourite path' had only recently been discovered, and would be constantly traversed during the next few days: 'our path' on 5 June; 'first on our own path' on 12 June; 'first on our own path' and 'our favorite path' on 13 June; 'a long time in the Evening upon our favourite path' on 15 June; 'walked on our favorite path' on 17 June; 'walked upon our own path for a long time' on 20 June.[48] Paths were not only being discovered but being laid down as tracks, both literal and metaphorical, into the future.

On the 8th, too, had come one of those very special kinds of event for Dorothy: she herself was present at the making of a poem. Wordsworth had gone out

> & walked and wrote that poem,
>   'The sun has long been set' &c –
> . . . Afterwards he walked on our own path & wrote the lines, he called me into the orchard & there repeated them to me – he then stayed there till 11 o clock.[49]

He published the poem as a heavily revised 'Impromptu', telling Isabella Fenwick that it had been in the presence of Dorothy herself that 'the lines were thrown off'.[50] The original version survives in the form of the copy made by

Sara Hutchinson, which is near as we shall now get to what Wordsworth actually repeated out loud that evening in June 1802.

> The Sun has long been set
> That stars are out by twos and threes
> The little birds are piping yet
> Among the bushes and the trees.
> 5   – There's the Cuckoo and one or two Thrushes
> And a noise of wind that rushes
> With a noise of water that gushes:
> And the Cuckoo's sovereign cry
> Fills all the hollow of the sky.
> 10   Who would go parading
> In London, and masquerading,
> On such a night of June
> With that beautiful soft half moon;
> And all these innocent blisses,
> 15   On such a night as this is! –[51]

This summer, Wordsworth was giving Dorothy all he could of himself. But he was also giving her what he was cultivating to come naturally from himself: a simple rhyming lyric which expressed joy clearly and directly, even if the joy were (as she would have known) only the other side of the coin from melancholy.

III

In spite of the poem about the garden, and the changes in the house, another problem, however, was being forced on them by the Coleridges. Sarah Coleridge was pushing the idea of their moving up to Keswick. The Coleridges had a problem in that half of their house was falling vacant, and they very much wanted to ensure themselves compatible house-sharers. When Coleridge came over to them on 10 June, Dorothy was able to tell him in person what they felt, as she explained in a letter to Sara Hutchinson which presumably Mary would also have read: 'I talked with him about Mrs. C., told him of the letter I had written etc etc., and of our determination not to go to Greta Hall – he said something about going as lodgers for a short time; I said I could not see any good whatever to arise from this, and as I was so fully determined he pressed nothing upon me.'[52] It would probably have made Coleridge miserable to find that his marriage was preventing his best friends coming to live with him. He did not quite give up, all the same: 'He said he would look at Brow Top house and there we rested – it is evident he had much rather have us at Greta Hall than Brow Top – but I am *sure* that the former would do nothing but harm, and alas I have little hope from the latter, but we will talk of this when we meet.'[53] Brow Top house was on a hill about a quarter of a mile south-east of Keswick on the road to Ambleside, with a fine view of the head of Derwentwater. We do not know who lived there, nor whether it was even for rent. It is never mentioned again in the surviving record.

But it is striking how large a part Dorothy appears to be playing in a discussion of where she, her brother and Mary were going to live after the marriage. It would not be at Gallow Hill: that was her decision. Not at Greta Hall: that was her decision. She was the one who insisted on Grasmere, upon their house and their garden there. She also seems to have assumed that Sara and Mary had their minds as fully made up about Sarah Coleridge as she herself did, so that all she had to do was to generate the acid remarks they would have expected:

> Mrs. Coleridge is a most extraordinary character – she is the lightest weakest silliest woman! She sent some clean clothes on Thursday to meet C. (the first time she ever did such a thing in her life) from which I guess she is determined to be attentive to him – she wrote a note, saying not a word about my letter, and all in her very lightest style – that she was sorry the Wilkinsons were from home etc etc. . . . she concludes 'my love to the Ws—' Is not it a hopeless case? So insensible and so irritable she never can come to good and poor C.! but I said I would not enter on this subject, and I will not.[54]

So Dorothy has her cake and eats it: holds back from making rude remarks about Sarah – and makes them; records a sensible act (Coleridge being sent clean clothes) and renders it ridiculous; observes what must have been a letter to Coleridge (hence the 'love to the Ws—') and thinks it absurd for not replying to *her* letter; observes that the letter mentions one of the Coleridges' closest neighbours – and scoffs at it as mere social chit-chat; and finally laughs at Sarah for sending love to her and Wordsworth. Who, one might ask, is the hopeless case? So few of Dorothy's letters to Sara Hutchinson survive that it is impossible to judge how regular this kind of commentary may have been. It sounds habitual.

What would it have been like for Coleridge, to have Dorothy set fast in such an attitude? Only two complete letters survive of all those which Coleridge wrote between 24 February and the end of June 1802, while his notebook entries are also relatively sparse for the period: we know most about him from the mentions in Dorothy's journal, and from later reminiscences in later letters. We know surprisingly little about what he was thinking about the woman he called 'Rotha', though we saw above how close they had become during April and May 1802, and it is not inconceivable that it was *because* she felt like this about Sarah Coleridge that Coleridge knew he could say anything to her, make any confession.[55] And she was loyal to him, one hundred per cent. But it was her opposition, in particular, which ruled out the idea of the Wordsworths living in Keswick. And she clearly wanted to tell him in person what she thought.

She could not do this, however, until – after that sixteen-day gap – they saw Coleridge again on Thursday 10 June, when he walked over to them, and arrived to find Sarah's note and the clean clothes: Sarah now 'determined to be attentive to him'. He had gone via the Clarksons at Eusemere, and had come over the pass by Grisedale Tarn which Dorothy and Wordsworth had struggled over with such difficulty, in snow, rain and low cloud, back in February. His notebook gives a beautiful account of rainbows seen in the flying water of the beck, in the course of the journey. The notebook does *not*, however, contain a detail recorded in Dorothy's journal and her letter to the Hutchinsons: 'Coleridge came in with a sack-full of Books &c & a Branch of mountain ash he had been attacked by a Cow . . .'[56] The letter gives more details:

> he had had a furious wind to struggle with, and had been attacked by a vicious cow, luckily without horns, so he was no worse – he had been ill the day before – but he looked and *was* well – strong he must have been for he brought a load over those Fells that I would not have carried to Ambleside for five shillings.[57]

As usual, they all stayed up on his arrival: 'we went to bed latish. I slept in sitting room'. Coleridge seems to have been given her new room, whereas before he had often shared a room with Wordsworth.[58] But the latter was currently having problems sleeping, and probably wanted a room to himself: and there was only one bed, now, in his room. The story of the cow was doubtless a fine comic performance; but the previous day's illness which Dorothy records may well have links with his getting drunk the previous night, while staying overnight in Patterdale. He had written tipsily into his notebook: 'Half tipsy, all the Objects become more interfused by & diffused by Difference perceived & [?destroyed] at the same time –'.[59]

The drunken analysis sounds as muddled-headed as the evening had probably been. He was still suffering – or had been a week before, as he had told his brother George – from 'very frequent attacks in my Bowels. They are a seditious Crew; and I have need of the most scrupulous attention to my Diet to preserve them in any tolerable Order.'[60] His opium habit (hence probably the drunkenness on the road) was still damaging his digestion. He could, however, now mostly manage his health so as to keep some balance between withdrawal, opium intoxication, and actual drunkenness.

This visit to Town End was still not the last he would pay. He obviously held no grudge against the Wordsworths for refusing to move up to Keswick: he would, after all, increasingly feel that he did not want to live with Sarah Coleridge either. He came down again on the 23rd when Dorothy was on her own (Wordsworth had gone over to Eusemere, to the Clarksons). He and Dorothy stayed up late talking, 'till one o'clock', and she walked up Dunmail

Raise with him the following day. And he came down again a week later; on this occasion, a page torn out of the journal suggests that Dorothy may, just for once, have committed to it some indiscretions about Sarah Coleridge, or about the Coleridge marriage, of the kind she usually only put in her letters. It looks, too, as if he were taking his chance of spending all the time he could with the old household, and in particular with Dorothy.

One other thing is worth commenting on. On 15 June Dorothy recorded the arrival of a letter 'from Sara to C' and on 8 July another one.[61] It is possible that Sara was saving postage by putting notes for Coleridge in with the letters she and her sister sent to the Wordsworths, knowing that the Wordsworths could send them on to Keswick easily and cheaply (they would have taken the one which arrived on the 8th with them the following day). It is also possible that she was writing letters with extra information in them which she wanted the Wordsworths to see. On the other hand, it is possible that she was conducting a correspondence with Coleridge in a manner which would not bring it to the attention of Sarah Coleridge.[62] However, Dorothy added an odd detail to her note of the arrival of the letter from Sara to Coleridge (it had arrived together with a letter from Mary): 'William did not read them'.[63] This can only mean that they were *for* him to read; in which case Sara may have been sending letters via the Wordsworths precisely so that they *would* see what she was writing to Coleridge: would know that her correspondence with him was wholly 'honest' (to use Coleridge's word from the winter) and above board, even though his with her may not always have been. They would presumably have known, therefore, that she was not in love with him.

It may, then, simply have been a coincidence that the Coleridge marriage seemed to have been going through yet another of its crises in the first half of May 1802, but to be recovering in June. We can hardly be surprised that a writer who at some stage this spring or summer came up with the formulation 'my coarse domestic life', who described his marriage as 'Indifference or Strife', and who was extremely conscious of 'those habitual Ills'

> That wear out Life, where two unequal minds
> Meet in one House, and two discordant Wills —[64]

was finding his relationship with his wife difficult. The rare event of Sarah's sending of the clean linen to Grasmere may however even have been a sign that, as I suggested above, hostilities had been suspended: that Sarah was attempting 'to fight against her inveterate habits of puny Thwarting', that Coleridge was refraining from 'impetuous and bitter censure', and that Sarah had been 'made *serious* —'.[65] There are, however, no contemporary pieces of writing which actually allow us to say *anything* about the state of the Coleridge marriage at any particular date this summer, apart from a single reference to 'household Infelicity' which Coleridge made on 7 May.[66] The dated comments on the marriage which *may* at one stage have been lodged in Dorothy's journal were at some stage removed; and nearly all Coleridge's letters have likewise been lost. We do not even know exactly when he wrote those particular lines in the *Letter*. Attempts to turn his poetry dating from the summer of 1802 (in particular 'The Keepsake' and 'The Picture') into poems addressed to Sara Hutchinson tell us nothing: only 'The Day-Dream' (discussed above) is addressed to her. And even if they *had* all been poems to Sara, that would still tell us little about Coleridge's marriage, except that he was now in love with another woman: and that we would have been fairly sure of anyway. *If*, however, his poem 'The Happy Husband' belongs to 1802 – and *if* it has any autobiographical truth – then there is rather more evidence for attachment (if a rather deliberate, conscious attachment) to Sarah C. than there is for attachment to Sara H. In the case of each poem, however, Coleridge delighted in using realistic details – the married man in 'The Happy Husband', the woman named Sara and the child named Hartley in 'The Day-Dream', the woman in 'The Keepsake' having (like Sara) auburn hair – while nevertheless admitting no actual autobiographical revelations into any of them.[67]

It seems probable, too, that Wordsworth's impending marriage to Mary Hutchinson was more important to Coleridge's conflicted feelings for Sara Hutchinson than anything else. Putting it crudely, the closer Wordsworth came to Mary, and the closer they came to marriage, the more important Sara Hutchinson became to Coleridge. The fact that the Wordsworths at least sometimes bore the responsibility of transmitting Sara's letters suggests that they were party to Coleridge's feelings for her, and to her feelings about him (whatever they were); and this was most likely a role they had played from the very start.

IV

In some ways, in fact, Dorothy seems to have coped better with Wordsworth's impending marriage than Coleridge did; but that may be simply because we know more about what she did and felt. Her journal for the rest of June is marked by her special care for Wordsworth as he endured yet another of those bouts of sleeplessness which attacked him this summer. On the 14th – the day they had written those tetchy letters to Mary and Sara about 'The Leech-gatherer' – they went for a walk which looks very like an attempt to tire him out: 'we went to look at Rydale, walked a little in the fir grove, went again to the top of the hill & came home' – but Wordsworth stayed on outside, hoping to get sleepy: 'a mild & sweet night – Wm stayed behind me. I threw him the cloak out of the window the moon overcast, he.sate a few minutes in the orchard came in sleepy, & hurried to bed – I carried him his bread & butter.' But it didn't work: the next day's entry starts in the hushed tones of someone keeping her voice down, thinking that even the birds were quieter than usual: 'A sweet grey mild morning the birds sing soft & low – William has not slept

all night. It wants only 10 minutes of 10 & he is in bed yet.'[68] It sounds rather
as if she were writing in the downstairs parlour, in which case Wordsworth
would have been in bed only just the other side of the wood-panelled partition.
He would write three sonnets on sleep during this summer, and what he went
through in June must have contributed, especially to the second one, which
started by listing things which might help:

> A flock of sheep that leisurely pass by,
> One after one; the sound of rain, and bees
> Murmuring; the fall of rivers, winds and seas,
> Smooth fields, white sheets of water, and pure sky;

But none of them worked:

> I have thought of all by turns, and yet do lie
> Sleepless; and soon the small birds' melodies
> Must hear, first utter'd from my orchard trees;
> And the first Cuckow's melancholy cry.

All you can do is pray that things will change:

> Even thus last night, and two nights more, I lay,
> And could not win thee, Sleep! by any stealth:
> So do not let me wear tonight away:
> Without Thee what is all the morning's wealth?[69]

We should not, however, imagine Wordsworth, racked by sleeplessness, sitting
wearily up in bed and writing out such a poem in the early hours of a June
morning in 1802. Composition always required the greatest daytime concentration. Such a poem would, interestingly, have to be written when he was *not*
in the situation described by it. In its odd but constant reminiscence of Henry
V before Agincourt,[70] the poem may also suggest the size of the event for
which he was gearing himself up: something, anyway, was making him
particularly anxious. At the end of this week, on Friday the 18th, came the
news that '*just* debts' owed by the Lowther estate would be paid, and anxiety
about how the Wordsworth family should re-establish its claim seems to have
replaced all other anxieties. Wordsworth wrote at once to his brother Richard,
and went over to the Clarksons on Monday the 21st to get their advice on the
right strategy to adopt.

As well as worries about Wordsworth's insomnia, Dorothy developed
another anxiety in the saga of the swallows which were trying to build their
nest at the window of her own new room, now that the household had moved
around. To begin with she was 'afraid they will not have the courage for it'.[71]
But she wrote beautifully about them, seeing them as both bird-like and oddly

fish-like, the far side of the glass: 'They twitter & make a bustle & a little chearful song hanging against the panes of glass, with their soft white bellies close
to the glass, & their forked fish-like tails. They swim round & round & again
they come.'[72] By the 19th they were hard at work on the nest. Her new place;
their new place; a feeling of well-being, with the Lowther estate news being a
cause for great excitement and much fantasising (she and Wordsworth 'talked
sweetly together about the disposal of our riches' the following day.[73]) Six days
later, however, in the garden at the front of the house,

> I looked up at my Swallow's nest & it was gone. It had fallen down. Poor little
> creatures they could not themselves be more distressed than I was I went
> upstairs to look at the Ruins. They lay in a large heap upon the window ledge;
> these Swallows had been ten days employed in building this nest, & it seemed
> to be almost finished –

The attention she had given them takes us constantly into her own feelings
about the loss of security, about having one's own place, about companionship,
and about a beloved partner:

> I had watched them early in the morning, in the day many & many a time & in
> the evenings when it was almost dark I had seen them sitting together side by
> side in their unfinished nest both morning & night . . . they sate both mornings
> & evenings, but they did not pass the night there. I watched them one morning
> when William was at Eusemere, for more than an hour. Every now & then there
> was a feeling motion in their wings a sort of tremulousness & they sang a low
> song to one another.[74]

When Wordsworth came back from Eusemere on the 24th he was thoroughly
encouraged by what the Clarksons had said: 'It was a mild rainy Evening he
was cool & fresh, & smelt sweetly – his clothes were wet. We sate together
talking till the first dawning of Day – a happy time – he was well & not much
tired. He thought I looked well too.'[75] He and Dorothy sit as lovers, all night
together, side by side, singing their own 'low song to one another'; she is very
conscious of his body and how he smells; and he compliments her on her looks
too.

So the days pass away. The swallows – 'my swallows' – rebuild their nest, to
her great joy; she goes out in the garden to see them sitting side by side: 'I have
been out on purpose to see their faces.'[76] They had a last visit from Coleridge,
too, just at the end of June – but so many things were now the last: the last visit,
the last walk. 'The swallows have completed their beautiful nest. I baked bread
& pies', Dorothy writes on 6 July, now really getting ready for the journey. On
the 7th, 'Walked on the White Moss – glow-worms – well for them children
are in bed when they shine.' This observation led directly to what Wordsworth
would at some stage write for 'Benjamin the Waggoner':

Now that children are in their Beds
The little Glow-worm nothing dreads . . .

But he also wrote touchingly in that same poem about a sense of calm and stillness, in lines recording ending and closure:

In the sky and on the hill
Every thing is hush'd and still.[77]

On the evening of the 8th we find Wordsworth also doing last-minute things,
taking his coat to the tailor's and making arrangements for their horse for the
following day. But in spite of being busy, 'He came in to me at about ½ past
nine pressing me to go out; he had got letters which we were to read out of
doors.'[78] I cannot recall another such request in the whole of the journal: there
was something about going outside to read in the beloved garden, in the light
of the moon, this very last evening of all, which impelled him. 'I was rather
unwilling, fearing I could not see to read the letters, but I saw well enough'.
They read together; a letter from Richard (probably about money), one from
Mary ('a very tender affecting letter') and 'another from Sara to C' of the kind
discussed above. There was a letter from Coleridge, too, although they would
see him the following day; they write anyway, this group, this gang. It is also
characteristic that they should, on their last evening together, spend so much
time out of doors. The moon is still hidden behind the hill, so William hurries
his sister out along the road 'in hopes that I should see her', and they walk over
the hill to look down to Rydale: 'It was dark & dull but our own vale was very
solemn, the shape of helm crag was quite distinct, though black. We walked
backwards & forwards on the White Moss path there was a sky-like brightness
on the Lake.' The brightness would perhaps have reminded Dorothy of the
morning. But this final journal entry before leaving deserves to be given
without interruption; it shows a transition to the events of the final Friday
morning, as abrupt as if she had not slept at all. The writing is like the poetry
of Emily Dickinson in its terse, almost unemotional but intensely felt experience of loss.

The Wyke Cottage Light at the foot of Silver How. Glowworms out, but not so
numerous as last night – O beautiful place! – Dear Mary William – The horse is
come Friday morning – so I must give over. William is eating his Broth – I must
prepare to go – The Swallows I must leave them the well the garden the Roses
all – Dear creatures!! they sang last night after I was in bed – seemed to be
singing to one another, just before they settled to rest for the night. Well I must
go – Farewell. – – –[79]

The complexity of that ending lies (like other things in these lives) too deep for
tears. She says farewell to the swallows who sing each other to sleep (and there

are all kinds of memories there: of reading Wordsworth to sleep, of his falling asleep on her shoulder, of being very aware of him asleep, of being overjoyed when he starts sleeping again). She bids farewell to their way of life, to the brother whom this journal is so often for. And then, firm-minded as ever, she brings the journal up to date around 16 July with an entry as indomitable and prosaic as the first ending had been poetic: 'On Friday morning, July 9th William & I set forward to Keswick on our Road to Gallow Hill – we had a pleasant ride though the day was showery.'[80]

They would take seven days over this part of the journey. They took a horse for the journey up to Keswick, doubtless with one riding and one walking (they had more luggage than usual), and they stayed three nights. Coleridge lent Dorothy £20 'to pay off a Bill which I wished not to leave unpaid when I left home, and that I might bring something with me for other expences'.[81] It was going to be a long journey, and she was getting herself used to financial independence (the plan was for Coleridge to be paid back with the yearly £20 her brother John was giving her). On the morning of Monday the 12th they set off to Eusemere, Coleridge walking beside them as usual. But he 'was not well & we had a melancholy parting having sate together in silence by the Road-side'.[82] A record of Coleridge *in silence* is remarkable; the following day he would tell William Sotheby that he 'had but just recovered from a state of extreme dejection brought on in part by Ill-health, partly by other circum-stances . . .' He would however apologise to the Sothebys for being 'unpar-donably loquacious'[83] as a result. There is some evidence of his seizing on Sotheby as someone to be friends with, at this particular moment; he wrote Sotheby six tremendously exciting and intellectually stimulating letters between July and October, which suggest how he might have been preparing to map out his own future as a literary critic and commentator. The intel-lectually domineering friendship he struck up with Sotheby was perhaps his own best way of dealing with Wordsworth's forthcoming marriage. But with Wordsworth and Dorothy, beside the road, all he can manage is a melancholy silence. For him too, perhaps, it was a kind of final parting.

After Keswick and Eusemere, Wordsworth and Dorothy travelled during Wednesday the 14th across to Leeming Lane in Yorkshire, covering some sixty miles. On top of the coach, in the rain, 'we buttoned ourselves up, both together in the Guard's coat & we liked the hills & the Rain the better for bringing [us] so close to one another – I never rode more snugly.'[84] Buttoned up in the same coat, like the swallows in their nest together, brother and sister are as close as they have ever been: another little moment of marriage, ending when the rain becomes so heavy that Dorothy has to be sent into the coach. From Leeming Lane, where they stayed overnight, they took a coach to Thirsk, where they had their luggage forwarded; they could now walk most of the rest of the way across to Gallow Hill. They found themselves as a result 'despised' as 'foot-travellers' by the Thirsk landlady; middle-class people did not walk.[85] No matter, so far as Dorothy was concerned. It was an adventure for the two of them together. That day, very hot, they covered thirty-two miles in all, walking the last part across the hills to Rievaulx and (finally) to Helmsley, arriving after eight at night; they had ridden seventeen miles and walked fifteen.

They arrived at Gallow Hill on Friday 16 July, having covered the final twenty-two miles on foot; during that final day's walk they sat down 'upon the Turf by the roadside more than once'. They must have written ahead to tell the Hutchinsons when they would be arriving: Sara and Mary walked out to meet them, and they all met up seven miles from home, probably near Alleston. The four of them could thus make the last part of the journey together: 'Sheltered from the Rain beautiful glen, spoiled by the large house – sweet Church & Churchyard arrived at Gallow Hill at 7 o'clock.'[86] Four together: Wordsworth and the three women who made his life and work as a poet possible. A notebook entry Coleridge had inserted the previous August revealed his feeling of being left out of that particular group.[87] But it was not just Coleridge who might have felt left out as they passed the 'sweet Church' at Brompton where Wordsworth and Mary would shortly be getting married. Sara Hutchinson, too, was both part of the group, and now about to stop being part of it. In the charmed circle around Wordsworth: but not his sister, not his bride. Coleridge's beloved, but not his partner. Herself shrewd, entertaining, straightforward: doing now what she had begun to do in 1800 and went on doing all her life: 'I write Manuscripts for our Gentlemen most admirably, & have as much patience with it as anybody.'[88] Back in August 1801, she had actually written out the longest entry made in Coleridge's notebook for months (part of Aquinas' commentary on Aristotle).[89] In August 1802, she would again do a massive amount of copying for him. But, now in July 1802, having copied into her poetry book several new Wordsworth poems during April or early in May – for example 'Among all Lovely Things', 'The Cock is Crowing' and 'The Sparrow's Nest' – she seems to have brought her sequence of copying to an end. Sometime in the second half of May she had copied into her book the first version of 'The Leech-gatherer', 'To the Cuckow' and 'I grieved for Buonaparte'; the second of which had probably arrived at Gallow Hill several weeks, even a month, before. She was presumably doing some tidying up of poems sent earlier, and inserting those not yet copied. The same probably applies to her copies of 'To a Skylark' and 'The Tinker', which were copied after 'The Leech-gatherer' although composed long before it. The rest of the poems in Sara's collection may have been inscribed at any time over the summer. A number of them – again – may not have got into her book for quite a long time after their texts had arrived in Yorkshire. We know that the last poem she copied in 1802 had emendations made to its original text which cannot have arrived at Gallow Hill until 16 June; and as she incorporated all of them, her copy must also have been made after the middle of June.

And as that poem was 'Farewell, thou little Nook', Sara may also have regarded it as an appropriate conclusion to her twenty-four-poem sequence. For Wordsworth and Mary, the poem marked the anticipation of a new life. For

Dorothy, it heralded the opening of a new life as the third person in a marriage, though it also celebrated her role as keeper of the garden which welcomed Mary. For Sara, however, it would have marked the start of a life which left her more distant from her sister than for many years. What was it like for her to copy the poem which celebrated the expected marvellous harmony of three, at Town End, or to write out a line such as 'coming back with Her who will be ours', all too conscious that – when 'ours' – Mary would no longer be 'hers'? Within fifteen months, too, she would feel the 'distress' of losing her own home at Gallow Hill: 'she feels . . . that they have no certain abiding place, and in short that every thing is unstable in this world'.[90]

The life of the group was changing: the marriage extraordinarily disruptive of its previous patterns, as Coleridge and Sara would in particular have been aware. And once again, this may have contributed to Coleridge's sense that he and Sara were in some way marked out for each other.

Chapter Ten

A Month in Summer: August

One of the most enigmatic months in Wordsworth's entire adult life is August 1802. We know exactly where he was (in Calais, lodging with Dorothy 'opposite two Ladies in tolerably decent-sized rooms but badly furnished'[1]) – and we know something of why he was there (to see Annette Vallon and the nine-year-old Caroline, who were in rooms 'chez Madame Avril dans la Rue de la Tête d'or'). But we have really very little idea of what he and Dorothy did during the four weeks they spent in Calais, and no idea at all what it was like for Wordsworth to be with Annette and Caroline after such a very long time. He had not seen Annette for eight or nine years; he may never have seen Caroline at all.[2]

Having left Gallow Hill on Monday 26 July, he and Dorothy had journeyed southwards by coach via Beverley, Hull and Lincoln, arriving in London on Thursday the 29th, After various 'troubles & disasters' in London (William Sotheby helped them, perhaps with finding lodgings: they had arrived in the pouring rain[3]), they left for Dover early on Saturday the 31st and set sail for Calais the evening of the same day.[4] When they docked the following morning, after the twelve-hour voyage, 'Wm went for letters'; presumably to find a note from Annette saying where she and Caroline were lodging, and giving the address of the rooms she had found for them.

It seems certain that the Wordsworths had not originally intended to spend very long in France. A letter which Dorothy sent to Coleridge very soon after their arrival told him that they would be leaving Calais after ten days.[5] Why, or when, they changed their minds (it does not seem probable that Coleridge could have misunderstood), we do not know. It may simply have been that Annette had booked her own rooms (and theirs too) for a month; and that, after an initial hesitation, they had decided that it would be churlish not to stay four weeks as well.[6] It may have been because the arrangements for legally making Annette the guardian of her daughter took longer than they had imagined: or that there was some problem to do with transferring money from England. These had probably been the original reasons for the Wordsworths' agreement to meet up with Annette, and would explain why Dorothy had apparently given the impression that their visit would be quite short; just long enough to do what had to be done, see Annette and Caroline for a few days, and come back. Legal or financial complications of some kind would however have been a reason for a more extended visit.

But how Wordsworth and Dorothy actually spent their four weeks is a mystery. He certainly wrote (or at least drafted) five sonnets in Calais, and between six and eighteen other sonnets may have been worked on, or begun, there.[7] He and Dorothy of course both wrote letters (Coleridge had heard from them by the 9th), but not a single letter which they sent from France survives: nor do any which they themselves received. And Dorothy's journal, for once, does not include any details of letters received, though we can be certain of letters from Gallow Hill and from Keswick. They bought a supply of the small handy notebooks of the kind they subsequently regularly used for poems and journals (Dorothy would refer to one as 'a nice Calais Book'[8]) and at some point Wordsworth copied Andrew Marvell's 'Horatian Ode' into one of them, in his very best handwriting. The poem would in fact have been hard to acquire a copy of; it only existed in print in the 1776 edition of Marvell's work.[9] Not a single poem by Marvell had appeared, for example, in Anderson's famous *Complete Edition of the Poets of Great Britain*, which Wordsworth had been using in Grasmere ever since his brother John had left his thirteen-volume set there in 1800.[10] The title of Wordsworth's 1802 poem 'To H. C.' is however reminiscent of Marvell's poem 'The Picture of Little T. C.'; and Wordsworth's interest in Milton and in seventeenth-century English republicans and revolutionaries would have been sufficient to justify his interest in Marvell, whom he mentioned in another poem written this autumn.[11] Copying out the 'Horatian Ode' suggests that – whenever he did it – he had some considerable time on his hands. For that, no month in his life during these years would be so suitable as August 1802: and the notebook into which he copied it was itself certainly bought in Calais. This suggests that if indeed he *did* copy the Marvell while in Calais, then he had taken a borrowed volume of Marvell with him, and had transcribed a poem he could possess in no other way.

But we do not know what other books he and Dorothy may have taken with them, or what else he may have read. A manuscript copy of Dorothy's journal records that 'Two ladies lived in the house opposite to us, and we, in our idle moods, often amused ourselves with observing their still more idle way of spending their time – they seemed neither to have work nor books; but were mostly at the window.'[12] Even though she and Wordsworth also had 'idle moods', they at least had both 'work and books': obviously more than a single volume of Marvell. Presumably sewing (and copying) would have been at least some of the 'work', as would letter writing. But they also had time to observe the ladies at the window. This was a far cry from life in Town End, where the Ashburners in the cottage opposite would certainly not have spent time idly looking out of the window, and the Wordsworths would have had neither leisure nor inclination to watch them.

We know of one other detail of life in Calais, however. At some stage a plain gold wedding ring was bought. The ring which Wordsworth would put on to Mary Hutchinson's finger in October is marked with an erased horse's head on the outside, and in the early 1800s this was a Brussels mark (Belgium at the time being occupied as part of Napoleonic France).[13] Was this an impulse purchase – Wordsworth knowing that at some stage he would need a ring, seeing one in a window, and snapping it up with some francs left over at the end of the visit? Or should we read another kind of symbolism into the purchase – the ring for the new partner being bought in the presence of, or at least during this final time with, his previous partner? Wordsworth was someone who thought hard and conscientiously about how the times of one's life were 'bound' together; how the young man is both progenitor of the older man, and a self which (all the same) has to be outgrown and left behind. Buying the ring to solemnize the new life and new relationship would have been a significant moment for him. Choosing to do it in France would be a way both of confirming the occasion's links with the past, and also of leaving behind his younger self (and the person who had very nearly been his marriage partner), as he returned to England with a ring for the bride of his maturer choice. As careful an emotional thinker as Wordsworth could probably only have committed such a symbolic act deliberately. Parting with his child Caroline, he bought in France the ring for the English partner with whom he hoped to have children. For the time being, too, the ring was probably taken care of by Dorothy (she certainly had it during the evening of 3 October, and was very aware of its symbolic potential). It is hard to believe that the ring was either an impulse buy or simply an item on a shopping list ('Notebooks. Ink. Nb Ring!!!').

It was extremely hot: sometimes Wordsworth and Dorothy walked down to the beach during the day, and presumably tried to find some shade. Dorothy did not bathe at first, as she had a cold, but presumably she did later; she may have been inhibited by the fact that there would have been only Annette as female companion for her. (Wordsworth's bathing is, incidentally, omitted from a manuscript copy of the journal made for perusal by others; his nakedness is not to be thought of.[14]) For the rest of the day, they may well have stayed indoors a good deal, occupying those 'tolerably decent-sized rooms', reading, sewing and writing, even if not especially comfortable on the poor furniture. One did not escape the facts of Calais simply because one was indoors, however: Dorothy recalled the 'large store of bad smells & dirt in the yard, & all about'.[15] Wordsworth and perhaps Dorothy too certainly went for extensive walks outside Calais; within a few days of arriving, Wordsworth had retraced the road towards Ardres which he had followed with his Cambridge friend Robert Jones in July 1790 at the start of their walking tour of the continent.[16] And he had become sharply aware of the massive difference from twelve years earlier. Then,

> this Way,
> Where I am walking now, was like the May
> With festivals of new-born Liberty . . .

It had been the first anniversary of the fall of the Bastille, and he and Jones, abroad for the first time, had shared in the celebration. In 1802, however,

> . . . sole register that these things were,
> Two solitary greetings have I heard,
> '*Good morrow, Citizen!*' a hollow word,
> As if a dead Man spoke it![17]

The hollowness, of course, was in the ear of the auditor. But it is striking how conscious of tyranny Wordsworth found himself to be, now that he was back. France had once been synonymous with his highest aspirations for liberty; but the word 'citizen' seemed the only survival of those heady days. As recently as May, he had been writing about Napoleon as a tyrant who had risen to power entirely because of his military skill, without any understanding of people or society: 'What knowledge could *He* gain?' Napoleon, in that poem, had never ascended the 'degrees' of understanding and learning which to Wordsworth were the only proper foundations of power. Now in August, ironically observing people streaming across the channel 'to bend the knee / In France, before the new-born Majesty' – Napoleon was declared Consul for life on 4 August 1802, and 16,000 English people were reported to be in Paris for the celebrations[18] – Wordsworth was aware only of loss. In Calais he was observing a distinctly unrevolutionary France at first-hand, while being once again with Annette, who had been a supporter of the royalists throughout, and who had suffered for it. However distant from his own political views she had been, and still was (he remained republican), Annette would doubtless have told him a great deal he had not previously known about events in France during the past decade. She would, for example, have made him sharply aware of the celebration, half way through their time in Calais, of Napoleon's birthday. Wordsworth still thought of Napoleon as 'young Buonaparte' though the French ruler was actually eight months older than himself. On the 15th, the birthday was celebrated – or, to be exact, should have been celebrated:

> Heav'n grant that other cities may be gay!
> Calais is not; and I have bent my way
> To this sea coast, noting that each man frames
> His business as he likes . . .[19]

The day (a Sunday) was clearly going on just as usual: also as usual, Wordsworth was out walking. Again, it was the difference from 1790 which struck him:

> Another time
> That was, when I was here twelve years ago:
> The senselessness of joy was then sublime![20]

Now even a national holiday celebrating its ruler's birthday seemed ordinary, even dull.

Dorothy may have gone with him; but she makes it clear how she particularly enjoyed the walks with Wordsworth when it grew cool in the evening. The evening sounds the time when life (for her) really started again, after the heat indoors, the reading and sewing and writing, the shade and smells of the day: 'We walked by the sea-shore almost every Evening with Annette & Caroline or Wm & I alone . . .'[21]

II

The thinking which Wordsworth did during these weeks in France, as evidenced by the sonnets he drafted and may have written while there, was, interestingly, almost entirely political, and may have extended to sonnets such as those 'On the Extinction of the Venetian Republic', 'The King of Sweden' and 'To Toussaint L'Ouverture' (all published in the *Morning Post* in January 1803). When he himself published these three sonnets in 1807, Wordsworth would enclose them within a frame of those undoubtedly provoked by his visit to France and return to England: they may well have been linked in his mind with what he had seen and felt during the visit.[22]

Biographers sigh at these political sonnets: 'now he wrote not about Annette but about the public events which so deeply moved him': 'One longs for more evidence on which to speculate about Wordsworth's feelings about Annette . . . A series of sonnets on political themes is no substitute'.[23] But Moorman is surely right to remark that Wordsworth 'was, as a poet, capable of a remarkable detachment from his immediate circumstances'. I would suggest that writing about politics was a sure way of encouraging and developing that detachment. Whether he still found Annette 'horribly attractive, actually',[24] or whether he found her unrecognisable as someone who could ever have attracted him, either way he would have been determined to have no feelings whatsoever about her: that was what duty demanded. Sonnets, and sonnets about France and England, were a good way of keeping off forbidden ground. Of the relation which either of them formed with Annette, therefore, we know absolutely nothing. Of the relationship with Caroline, practically nothing. Of the relationship Annette may have formed with Dorothy, almost nothing. Of the relationship they had during the month with Coleridge, or with Mary, or with Sara, again we know nothing directly. They must at some early stage have written to Gallow Hill to explain that they would be staying a good deal longer than originally planned. The fact that Coleridge's next journalism for the *Morning Post* was a series of essays on France, concentrating upon tyranny, suggests too that some of Wordsworth's disillusion was communicated to his friend.[25] We know that Dorothy looked at and thought a good deal about England, and that her brother did so as well. Their habits of sharing observation and the language of description would not have changed: '. . . we had

delightful walks after the heat of the day was passed away – seeing far off in
the west the Coast of England like a cloud crested with Dover Castle, which
was but like the summit of the cloud – the Evening star & the glory of the
sky.'[26] One of the sonnets Wordsworth wrote either in Calais or very soon
afterwards records his feelings of being particularly close to England, looking
across to it from a country which was not just abroad but which had been, until
so recently, a hated enemy, and (to Wordsworth) was still a monstrous tyranny.
He writes impressively not about his feelings for mother or child, but about
England at war; these are home thoughts from abroad with a vengeance. It is
England as military power and enemy of France that he sees: he has 'many a
fear / For my dear Country, many heartfelt sighs'. The evening star is not only
shining *over* England: it is appropriated *for* England.

> Thou, I think,
> Should'st be my Country's emblem; and should'st wink,
> Bright Star! with laughter on her banners, drest
> In thy fresh beauty. There! that dusky spot
> Beneath thee, it is England; there it lies.
> Blessings be on you both! one hope, one lot,
> One life, one glory!

Abroad, he is 'Among Men who do not love her'; which makes him feel that 'I
. . . linger here.'[27] He was thinking politically rather than personally: he was
actually surrounded by women, even in the rooms opposite, and both Annette
and Dorothy had very particular reasons to love Englishmen, if not England.
But lingering was what the time in Calais felt like. Apart from the sonnets
he drafted and worked on, the unexpected time on his hands – and the proxi-
mity of Annette – probably meant that he was obliged to go over the past one
more time, to taste and feel and remember his younger self, in a process that
may well have left him thoroughly reconciled to giving it up. It seems quite
likely that he and Dorothy were both a little bored, their only profound desires
and longings going out to the country to which they would shortly return:
England in itself, and England for the people (and the future) it contained. As
time went by, seeing Annette and Caroline may well have felt increasingly like
a duty.

III

Dorothy's journal entries are beautifully written, and (there is no denying)
thoroughly frustrating for the reader: exactly perhaps as they were intended to
be. She would have composed her journal for it to be read by Mary, after all,
and even though she apparently made notes in Calais, these were probably
only written up after Wordsworth's marriage, and after they got back to Gras-

mere on 6 October.[28] But there is also evidence that she was writing this part of the journal for a wider audience than usual. A manuscript copy of the Calais part of the journal dates from the period and was made (Pamela Woof speculates) 'for friends such as Mrs Clarkson'[29]: it may also have gone to Coleridge. Anyone looking into the journal or into the copy for thoughts about Annette, then, will be (and probably actually was) disappointed. In the copy, Annette only appears under an initial, and the single reference to Caroline disappears completely. It is possible that Dorothy's letters from Calais were rather more gossipy (as they always tended to be, in comparison with her journal), though she would have been extremely discreet when writing to the Hutchinsons, in particular. But we know that a letter to Coleridge surprised him by its lack of reference to the subject of Annette and Caroline, so Dorothy may have been discreet to everyone.

The last thing she would have done, of course, is to fill either her letters or the pages of her journal with descriptions of Annette's beauty, or other attractions, or even of her oddity or fadedness; or of anything Wordsworth might have said or thought about her, or anything which Annette might have said about the past. Dorothy was impulsive but also deeply loyal. She would have been in no doubt that Wordsworth's other partner had to be seen, and his daughter seen, while the chance of a visit to France could be taken: she would certainly have been determined to do her best to create as good a relationship as could be made, and she would have been thoroughly supportive of the idea of Caroline becoming Annette's ward. But she would not interfere with her brother's feelings: they were not her business.

The journal, in one manifestation for public consumption, for Sara and Mary and probably for her brothers, as well as for Coleridge, is accordingly almost entirely about what Dorothy herself saw and experienced; looking back to England, observing the patterns of the lights, enjoying the coolness of the evening. It does not intrude on what Wordsworth himself would (or might) have told Mary when he got back; nor upon whatever existed, or now no longer existed, between Annette and Wordsworth. This might have been easier because Dorothy would have had problems with spoken French, and Annette and Caroline spoke no English. Dorothy may well not even have known exactly what was being said until Wordsworth paraphrased it to her afterwards. Her tactfulness and loyalty may thus have been imposed upon her as well as deliberate.

The long journal entries she made about Calais are, instead, devoted – perhaps a little self-consciously – to the beauties of the water and the evening light: 'The Reflections in the water were more beautiful than the sky itself, purple waves brighter than precious stones for ever melting away upon the sands.'[30] There is not a single word of description of Annette or of Caroline in the journal, though we are told exactly what the Fort at the entrance to Calais harbour looked like: 'its shape which was far more distinct than in perfect daylight, seemed to be reared upon pillars of Ebony, between which pillars the sea was seen in the most beautiful colours that can be conceived. Nothing in Romance was ever half so beautiful.'[31] Dorothy means 'nothing in literary romance', of course; but it is still a finely ambiguous remark. Dorothy wishes to tell Mary nothing that Wordsworth himself would not tell her directly; but she is also saying that there is nothing to tell. Nothing has been stirred up from the past, no nostalgic longings liberated. The fort is the most beautiful and glamorous object around. Wordsworth's poems about the incredible and never-to-be-repeated situation of 12 years ago tell the same story as could be told of the never-to-be-repeated relationship of 10 years ago. Nothing is left of those heady days; nothing but surprise that so little should remain.

Dorothy's own prose is loyal in another way too. It says, by its very omissions, that Wordsworth's relations with Annette were Mary's affair, not hers. She is, at least once in the long journal entry, brought to a pitch of feeling, but not by the relationships which were going on (or were probably *not* going on) around her. What she cannot forget, as always, is her companionship with Wordsworth; and when she thinks about that, his past, Annette and Caroline all pale into insignificance.

> One night, though, I shall never forget, the day had been very hot, & William & I walked alone together upon the pier – the sea was gloomy for there was a blackness over all the sky except when it was overspread with lightning which often revealed to us a distant vessel. Near us the waves roared & broke against the pier, & as they broke & as they travelled towards us, they were interfused with greenish fiery light. The more distant sea always black & gloomy.[32]

The 'we' who perceive that 'distant vessel' are brought into stark and lonely definition by the light and dark. Together they experience, find language for, and weather the storm. The one mention in the journal of Caroline's feelings comes at the end of a description of another kind of night altogether, one hot and placid: 'It was, also beautiful on the calm hot nights to see the little Boats row out of harbour with wings of fire & the sail boats with the fiery track which they cut as they went along & which closed up after them with a hundred thousand sparkles balls shootings, & streams of glowworm light. Caroline was delighted.'[33] Dorothy's heart is more deeply in the drama and the play of light and darkness which she shares with Wordsworth, on both the stormy night and the placid one, than it is in the reference to Caroline. The word 'delighted' falls with sad inadequacy after the vividness of her own description.

Wordsworth's own mention of his daughter is far more famous. It comes in the ninth line of the sonnet 'It is a beauteous Evening, calm and free' which was part of his commemoration of the encounter and which he later claimed was actually 'composed on the beach near Calais';[34] it comes after language which makes evening holy, virginal, nun-like. This was an especially interesting context to create for a child so memorably the issue of sexual desire. The other context which the sonnet offers is that of creation itself. In spite of the intense quiet of the evening,

> Listen! the mighty Being is awake
> And doth with his eternal motion make
> A sound like thunder – everlastingly.

So the evening is both 'quiet as a Nun' *and* filled with a 'sound like thunder'. It is at such a moment that we realise that both responses are constructs; neither is a simple description. It all depends upon what you attend to. Both silence and sound reflect on the girl to whom the narrator finally turns his attention.

> Dear Child! dear Girl! that walkest with me here . . .[35]

First as a child, then as a girl, as Wordsworth would have realised her existence in those months in 1792 before leaving France, and for long afterwards. Now they walk. Is it a solemn moment of shared communion, of parent and child? No. She is a child, wild and careless. But

> If thou appear'st untouch'd by solemn thought,
> Thy nature is not therefore less divine . . .

The appearance of quiet, the actuality of thunder, are paralleled by the appearance of frivolity in the child, and the actuality of divinity. The child is utterly safe in her childishness; she lies 'in Abraham's bosom all the year' and God is with her 'when we know it not'.[36] The thunder continues to rumble through her, so to speak, even while she is turning cartwheels on the beach. The *Ode* is not far away; but it never was, during the summer of 1802, as experience after experience made Wordsworth think again over what it was like to be a child, and what it felt like to be the adult no longer a child. The references in the *Ode* to seeing, in the mind's eye, 'the children sport upon the shore, / And hear the mighty waters rolling evermore',[37] may well go back to August in Calais, and the sense he had there of both the unthinking gaiety of the child, and the rumble of the eternal in the ear of the adult. The passage may first have been conceived, even written, there.

It was after almost exactly four weeks in France that Dorothy and Wordsworth finally embarked for home at noon on Sunday 29 August. The journey back took thirteen hours, and they arrived in Dover at one in the morning. One thing they remembered was their encounter with the Negro woman about whom Wordsworth wrote shortly afterwards in the sonnet which the *Morning Post* published under the title 'THE BANISHED NEGROES': she had been expelled from France because of her race and colour, but did not protest.[38] (Her refusal to complain seems to have angered Wordsworth as much as the injustice of her banishment.) The other thing which stood out was that poor Dorothy 'was sick all the way', exactly as she had been on the journey to Hamburg with Coleridge in 1798. Things constantly conspired to remind them of their previous partnership. On that occasion, too, Dorothy stayed below the whole voyage: as a result her experience of the harbour on arrival was especially vivid. 'It was very pleasant to me when we were in harbour at Dover to breathe the fresh air, & to look up and see the stars among the Ropes of the vessel.'[39] They presumably found somewhere to sleep (or had already arranged lodgings). The next day was 'very hot': 'We both bathed & sate upon the Dover Cliffs & looked upon France with many a melancholy & tender thought. We could see the shores almost as plain as if it were but an English Lake.'[40] They would not see Annette and Caroline again until 1820, by which time the girl who had sported on those shores across the channel had herself married (in 1816) and had her own daughter (christened Louise Dorothée). By then, too, Wordsworth would have two surviving sons and a daughter from the five children Mary had borne (his eldest son John would have been seventeen in 1820). Caroline, ward of Annette though she now probably was, remained oddly English, in at least part of herself; she 'had been christened, was married, and would finally be buried under the name Wordsworth'.[41] She was the careless Wordsworth child whose carelessness, at least for those moments on the Calais beach, he loved. She was the child he had never really had but to whom he had been able to communicate 'fatherly' thoughts.[42] Walking on the beach at Calais, and thinking solemnly about the gentleness of heaven and the eternal motion of the sea, he was happy to find that

> Thou dost not seem to heed these things one jot
> I see it, nor is this a grief of mine . . .[43]

The child he wanted her to be was, quite rightly, uncaring of adult solemnity. And he could not grieve for the loss of her, either: she was the embodied past, while he was about to move decisively away from his own youth and take on the role of father which he had never really been for Caroline. If leaving her was like leaving behind his own past, that would not have been simply a grief, either. As he would write in the *Ode*,

> We will not grieve, but rather find
> Strength in what remains behind[44]

What remained 'behind' for him was England, Mary and marriage.

IV

The Wordsworths' passive month in Calais is even more striking when we compare it with Coleridge's month in the Lake District. After all the illnesses and depressions of the spring, Coleridge felt remarkably well again during the summer of 1802; we can assume that a regular but controlled opium intake (such as we have details of from November) was preventing the outbreak of withdrawal symptoms.[45] He had also implied to Southey at the end of July that – after the agonies of the early summer – his marriage was again functioning happily, and the Wordsworths' absence certainly meant that he was not always irritating Sarah by walking off to Grasmere; while she in turn was not angering him with slighting references to them and his visits. July was remarkable, too, for the lengthy letters he managed to write, and for the fact that he also got his poem to Sara into publishable shape.[46]

But the weather had been bad, making him feel penned up in Greta Hall at just the time when 'Mrs Coleridge is but poorly'.[47] Three months into her pregnancy, she was suffering. Having spent July dutifully at home, Coleridge now wanted something more exciting. He made extensive and meticulous plans for an excursion into the mountains at the start of August, hoping that the weather would change.

What he actually managed to accomplish during the first nine days of August was quite extraordinary: a burst of disciplined and muscular activity so utterly different from the Wordsworths' sensitive passivity in Calais, and from Sarah Coleridge's enforced placidity and ill-health, that it might suggest a man flying from what he feared as much as one seeking what he loved. But it was not just a desire for strenuous activity which motivated him: he was demonstrating, at every point, a deep desire to write it down, and to preserve it.

His excursion had originally been no more than a plan for a scholarly visit to St Bees, on the west coast of Cumberland: 'I wait only for a truly fine Day to walk off'. A guidebook had told him of an 'excellent library presented to the school by Sr. James Lowther';[48] he needed to take every chance he could get of accessing rare books, and the same applied to his brother-in-law Southey (currently planning his own move to Keswick). Coleridge decided to get to the library over the hills rather than going the long way round by road; having worked in the library, he would come back by a different route. He drew a map in his notebook of the circular route he intended to take; the return journey would involve a good deal of fell-walking, so he would combine a scholarly trip with a walking holiday. What was also remarkable was that he recorded what he was doing in such great detail. The contrast with Dorothy Wordsworth's travel journal could not be more marked. In Calais, the flood of Dorothy's journal becomes a mere trickle; but Coleridge's notebook shows a good deal of pre-planning, in the course of which he consulted William Hutchinson's book *The History of the County of Cumberland* and drew himself a map (from Hutchinson). He also made notes about questions he would ask people in the various places he came to. When actually on the road, he continued to fill his notebook with details; he asked what things were called, recorded topographical features, drew sketches, inserted lists of names, noted down striking effects of sun and shadow. He made it in fact possible for us to follow him exactly, and to experience something of what he experienced.

He was also going, perhaps significantly, to cover some of the same ground he had walked with Wordsworth back in November 1799, on his very first visit to the Lakes: that tour had been so comprehensive that he was almost bound to retrace some of it. But he was also going to look at things there had been no time to explore properly before. It seems likely, in fact, that this was his *first* piece of real exploring of the region, on his own, since that original expedition in the company of his friend. Just as the Wordsworths travelled across to France, so he set off into the wilds of England.

V

He did not leave until 12.30 on Sunday the 1st, 'after morning church'. This may have been because he got up late, as usual, and he was certainly engaged in some last-minute arrangements. He wanted a stick for walking and commandeered a broom handle, 'in spite of Mrs C. & Mary, who both raised their voices against it, especially as I left the Besom scattered on the Kitchen Floor'. In his knapsack he had 'a Shirt, cravat, 2 pair of Stockings, a little paper & half a dozen Pens, a German Book (Voss's Poems) & a little Tea & Sugar, with my Night Cap, packed up in my natty green oil-skin, neatly squared, and put into my *net* Knapsack . . .'[49] Fit thus for walking in rain and sleeping in draughts, with a change of clothing, reading matter, materials for writing and the luxury of tea and sugar. He did not record the notebook in his pocket which went with him at all times; he also had a portable inkhorn and wafers (small adhesive slips for sealing up letters), as well as money, a pencil and a pocket knife.

The first afternoon gave him eight miles of walking along rough roads to Buttermere. (In 1799, he and Wordsworth had also gone to Buttermere from Keswick, but they had taken the long way round, up the valley of the Cocker.) At Buttermere he 'drank Tea at the little Inn, & read the greater part of the Revelations'. The Bible (or Testament) was presumably the property of the Inn: it was typical of Coleridge to make the best use of what he came across, just as Wordsworth had in the Patterdale inn, back in April. Then up over the next hills, a further eight miles to Ennerdale, where he would be staying with John Ponsonby, a friend of William Jackson; he recorded the sun setting as he walked, and cannot have reached his destination until dark was falling. This was part of the route he had followed with Wordsworth in 1799: but this time he constantly stopped and made entries in his notebook – the notebook as audience for his perpetual interior monologue.

His host took him out walking on the Monday, and told him the names of the mountains around ('Monsters of the Country, bare bleak Heads'), which he wrote down; after tea he followed the valley of the Ehen first down to Egremont and then on to St Bees, hoping to start work on the Tuesday morning. But here his problems started. He had planned to stay in Egremont, but the man with whom he had planned to stay was away for the night. He pressed on to St Bees, but there could only find 'an apology' for a bed in a pot-house; he got no dinner apart from gin-and-water and was obliged to sleep ('or rather dozed') in his clothes. The following morning, the famous library proved a complete waste of time: 'some 30 odd volumes of commentaries on the Scripture', serviceable, he thought, only 'for fire-lighting'. It was raining; the landscape dull. The only good thing was that he had spent very little indeed: his gin-and-water nightcap, bed and breakfast had cost 11 pence in all.[50] Disappointed by the whole experience of St Bees, Coleridge went back to Egremont, where at least he got a decent bed for the night (probably with the man who had been away on the Monday). The Wednesday morning, however, proved fine and sunny: he went via Calder Abbey up to Wastdale, and there, sitting in the shade of a sycamore tree 'at an Alehouse without a Sign', he drank tea, before walking on to Kirk Fell, where he stayed at 'Thomas Tyson's House where W & I slept Novr. will be 3 years'. He was remembering the night of 11 November 1799: once again, Wordsworth was not far away, just as when (in April) Wordsworth had stayed overnight at Barnard Castle, and had thought of Coleridge: he had wished he had stayed at the inn 'where we were together' back in 1799.[51]

Because of the uselessness of the St Bees library, Coleridge was now considerably ahead of schedule (he had allowed for at least two days there); hence what looks like a major change to his route, compared with the map he had drawn at home the previous week. On that map he had inserted Scafell, but only as a feature to look out for while skirting southwards; he and Wordsworth must also have looked at Scafell when they were at Thomas Tyson's house in November 1799, but put off any attempt to climb it until a better time of year. Now Coleridge was able to devote a whole day to an excursion, and – following his previous ascents of Skiddaw and Helvellyn – determined to do the other major climb of the Lakes. He set off on the Thursday morning, the 5th, presumably having received some good advice from Thomas Tyson about how best to tackle the mountain. Good advice, too: he went up 'by the side of a torrent, and climbed & rested, rested & climbed', until he 'gained the very summit of Sca' Fell – believed by the Shepherds here to be higher than either Helvellyn or Skiddaw'.[52]

He wanted to go on and climb what he believed to be Bow Fell (he was doing the whole journey without a map apart from the one he had drawn into his notebook), but what he could see, to the north-east, was in fact the even higher Scafell Pike. He also thought he could see how to get across to it; but this was a serious mistake. As A. P. Rossiter confirmed, 'from Scafell (proper) it does look as if you can walk (= scramble) down to the 'hyphen' which joins the two – i.e. Mickledore ridge. You can't; and that is how you get 'cragfast', unless you are prepared to "drop".'[53] Coleridge soon found himself 'cragfast', so started to drop down vertical faces on to narrow ledges, on what is today called Broad Stand: Rossiter described it as 'the only possible way in which – with some risks – an ordinary man can get down on that side undamaged'. But Coleridge eventually found himself on the edge of what was, to him, an impossible drop, and no way of going back up: 'cragfast', indeed.[54] A dead sheep on one of the ledges reminded him of what his own fate could easily be:

> My Limbs were all in a tremble – I lay upon my Back to rest myself, & was beginning according to my Custom to laugh at myself for a Madman, when the sight of the Crags above me on each side, & the impetuous Clouds just over them, posting so luridly & so rapidly northward, overawed me / I lay in a state of almost prophetic Trance & Delight . . .[55]

He felt 'calm & fearless & confident', and observed quietly how, if this had been a dream, 'what agonies had I suffered! what screams! –' As it was, he used his wits. The rock beside him 'was rent from top to bottom'. What a sheep could not imagine, a man could; he invented in that moment the climbing manoeuvre called chimneying, slung his knapsack round to his side and managed to descend the crack. At the bottom, he found his chest covered in great red heat-bumps. Rossiter dryly commented that 'he exaggerated the drops, both in height and number; but people who have narrow escapes always do this'.[56]

The storm heralded by the rushing clouds was now coming up, and – after his escape – he wisely decided not even to try to get on to the supposed Bow Fell, but down into Eskdale. This he managed to do, and to find a bit of shelter from the storm and the rain among some sheepfolds, in a place where the thunder crashed and echoed. When the rain stopped, he tried the echo himself, and sent the names of Wordsworth, Dorothy, Sara and Mary – followed by Hartley and Derwent, and finally Joanna – echoing down the valley. That night, he spent at the house of John Vicars Towers, pronounced Toe-ers: Coleridge delighted in thinking of this man living precisely on the Toes of the mountain.[57]

Scafell was undoubtedly the highlight of his journey. The next day (Saturday) he got up late, spent the middle part of the day talking rather than walking, and set out only after dinner; he then found his way down to Ulpha Kirk via Devoke Water. It was in the middle of the afternoon that he made a significant resolution, which followed up something he had thought of while on Scafell: 'Here it was seated on this Mount, on Saturday, August 7, that I resolved to write under the name of The Soother of Absence, the topographical poem which I had long mummel'd about in my mind, & the day before thought of under the name of the Bards of Helvellin or the Stone Hovels . . .'[58] That night he spent at a 'public House at Ulpha a very nice one /

& the Landlord, a very intelligent man'. He obviously spent some time talking with him.[59]

The next day he spent walking across to Coniston, up to Borrowdale, and to Old Brathay, where he slept at the house of his friends the Lloyds. He got back to Keswick on the evening of Monday the 9th, where he found seven letters waiting for him.[60]

VI

'The Soother of Absence' is a work which haunts Coleridge's notebooks between 1802 and 1808, but which he never actually managed to write.[61] Sara and Wordsworth were to be included in it, to be sure; in 1804, Coleridge noted,

> In some part of the Soother of Absence introduce a passionate address summo Poetae, optimo maximo Amico, W. W. – to receive, avow, support, sustain me, si quidem Asaharae animum divine audacem amor dedisset. – [to the greatest poet, the best and dearest Friend, W. W.... if only love had given Asahara a supremely daring spirit][62]

A good reason for not writing 'The Soother of Absence' in 1804, however, might well have been because it would have become the *Letter* all over again, full of regrets about Sara. This later manifestation, however, still retains some links with what we know of the 'topographical' 1802 original. For one thing, place and setting continued to play a large part in it:[63] in an entry which takes us directly back to 1802, but was inserted in his notebook sometime late in 1806, Coleridge wrote: 'The Rock of Names – indignant answer to Australis [Southey] – / the view of the lake from Sunset – / the lines of Foam / 'I have it down in my pocket-book' – / all the answer to be introduced in the Soother of Absence.'[64] Like so much of Coleridge's poetry after 1800, this poem seems to have been planned to embrace the interlocked subjects of place and friendship, and to have grown – again like the *Letter* – out of Coleridge's experience of the family group in its own special context.[65] In particular, the 'Rock of Names', the very embodied manifestation of the group, would answer the scepticism of Southey, and go into the poem. In such ways, Coleridge was attempting to vivify and perpetuate the idea of the gang in his poetry.

The fact that he had first thought of calling it 'The Bards of Helvellin or the Stone Hovels' is also significant. It immediately links the poem with Wordsworth. An ascent of Helvellyn had been one of the great features of his very first experience of the Lake District with Wordsworth in 1799; he surveyed from Helvellyn's summit the country which he would take as his own home in the summer of 1800, and his constant naming of it on that very first occasion represented a kind of symbolic taking possession of it. Wordsworth must have been supplying the names which on that occasion Coleridge was scribbling into his notebook: Coleridge produced a kind of tape-recording of Wordsworth's Cumberland pronunciation of 'Coniston', his short 'u'd 'Ullswater', and his special old-fashioned version of 'Windermere':

> On the top of Helvellin First the Lake of Grasmere like a sullen Tarn / then the black ridge of mountain – then as upborne among the other mountains the luminous Cunneston Lake – & far away in the Distance & far to the Lake the glooming Shadow, Wynandermere with its Island – Pass on – the Tairn – & view of the gloomy Ulswater & mountains behind, one black, one blue, & the last one dun . . .[66]

He had only been in Keswick five weeks when, in an extraordinary day's walking, on Sunday 31 August 1800, he had first climbed the 2,381-foot-high White Pike, south of Threlkeld, the mountain nearest to Keswick in the sequence which runs above Thirlmere in ridges along to Helvellyn. He had then spent the entire day walking south from summit to summit, ending up on Helvellyn itself. At every point he entered details in his notebook, including all the names, then adding his own kinds of perception. On the evening of that day, he found himself

> now at the Top of Helvellin – a pyramid of stones – Ulswater. Thirlemere. Bassenthwaite. Wyndermere, a Tarn in Patterdale On my right Two tarns, that near Grasmere a most beautiful one, in a flat meadow – travelling along the ridge I came to the other side of those precipices and down below me on my left – no – no! no words can convey any idea of this prodigious wildness/that precipice fine on this side was but its ridge, sharp as a ⟨jagged⟩ knife, level so long, and then ascending so boldly – what a frightful bulgy precipice I stand on and to my right how the Crag which corresponds to the other, how it plunges down, like a waterfall, reaches a level steepness, and again plunges! –

He only got off Helvellyn in the half dark, helped by moonlight, sliding across loose screes of stones down to the road near Dunmail Raise.[67] He then had to find his way down to Grasmere, arriving at Town End at 11 at night. Dorothy, walking in the garden in the moonlight, noted, rather undramatically, 'he came over Helvellyn',[68] as if she had not quite realised what he had accomplished. But Wordsworth (who had gone to bed) got up, put on his dressing gown, and they then stayed up until half past three in the morning, while Coleridge read them part of 'Christabel'. (It is slightly reassuring to find that, after such an exhausting day and night, the following day Coleridge was obliged to go to bed after tea, though he later had a mutton chop which Dorothy cooked for him, and which he ate sitting up in bed.) They walked again all day on the Tuesday, and that evening – 'It was a lovely moonlight night' – Coleridge, Dorothy, John and William 'talked much about a house on Helvellyn',[69] obviously a development of what Coleridge had seen and felt. It would be a house with fantastic views in all directions of the 'prodigious wildness'; a house they could afford to build, and where they could (obviously) all live together: a sure precursor of the 1802 *Letter*'s 'One Home the sure *Abiding* Home of All!'[70] (It may have replaced Coleridge's early fantasy subject for a romance – 'finding out a desert city & dwelling there' – which the Wordsworths knew all about; in December 1801, on the road to Eusemere, they would look back towards Skiddaw and think of 'dear Coleridge's desert home'.[71]) The following day, probably in search of an actual location for the fantasy, Coleridge climbed Helvellyn again, with William, John and a neighbour, on his way home to his real house in Keswick: this time he saw 'The whole prospect in one huge sunny mist / Wednesday, Sept. 3 – 1800 – on the top of Helvellin'.[72] For his part, Wordsworth had always had a special fondness for Helvellyn, which is probably why he had taken Coleridge up it in 1799. He went up it with Sir Walter Scott in 1805 and climbed it for the last time in August 1840, following his 70th birthday. Benjamin Haydon's 1842 painting of him showed him (presumably with Wordsworth's consent and probably according to his instructions) on the mountain in a pose of deep contemplation.

All this incidentally starts at last to make sense of that otherwise enigmatic entry in Coleridge's notebook dating from February 1802: 'Poem on this night on Helvellin / William & Dorothy & Mary / – Sara & I –'[73] Coleridge's 'Soother of Absence' poem may well have been conceived in February, and looks as if it had planned to centre on the proper place for poets to live, while also naming their ideal partners. It is more than likely that the *Letter* took over some of this poem's potential material, but Coleridge's thoughts about the poem in August suggest not only that the *Letter* was by now safely stowed, but that the new poem would have a new direction too. It would be 'topographical'.

Coleridge had written remarkably little poetry about the landscape of the Lakes: a few lines about Skiddaw in 'A Stranger Minstrel', a line and a half (and a note about the word 'Tairn') in the *Letter*. Wordsworth had done so constantly, of course; Coleridge was probably present when his friend had invented the section 'Poems on the Naming of Places' for the two-volume *Lyrical Ballads*. But his new poem would draw on that sense of *place*, and the identity of place, which Coleridge had been storing away so constantly in his notebooks since his first visit to the Lakes in November 1799. The projected poem would even survive his discovery, on 7 August, that Scafell 'caps Helvellin hollow': it may even have been encouraged by it. The point was that, unlike Scafell, Helvellyn was *not* simply 'terrible' – Coleridge's word for Walla Crag, by Skiddaw: 'there is nothing on Helvellin so terrible'.[74] A house on Helvellyn was a theoretical possibility. It could be inhabited, just as the poem could be populated; and such

a poem could describe how people could live in this landscape, and draw
strength from it: and in particular how it could also soothe their absence from
it, just as Wordsworth had described in 'Tintern Abbey'.

> Though absent long,
> These forms of beauty have not been to me,
> As is a landscape to a blind man's eye:
> But oft, in lonely rooms, and mid the din
> Of towns and cities, I have owed to them
> In hours of weariness, sensations sweet,
> Felt in the blood, and felt along the heart;
> And passing even into my purer mind
> With tranquil restoration: —[75]

Coleridge's projected poem would, like his notebooks, name places; it would
root itself in a landscape.[76]

The difference between what Coleridge planned to write about the topography of the mountains, and the poetry he actually *did* write, is however
brought very sharply into focus by the poem he produced in the late summer
of 1802 and which, on 10 September, he claimed was a direct consequence of
climbing Scafell. He told William Sotheby how, on Scafell,

> I involuntarily poured forth a Hymn in the manner of the *Psalms*, tho' afterwards
> I thought the Ideas &c disproportionate to our humble mountains – and acci-
> dentally lighting on a short Note in some swiss Poems, concerning the Vale of
> Chamouny, & it's Mountains, I transferred myself thither, in the Spirit, &
> adapted my former feelings to these grander external objects. You will soon see
> it in the Morning Post . . .[77]

According to the theory spelled out in the letter to Sotheby, such a transfer of
feelings and ideas from Scafell to Mont Blanc was perfectly natural. His was
not (he insisted) the poetry of 'Fancy . . . the aggregating Faculty of the mind',
which put things *together* into their 'true' form, but the poetry of '*Imagination*, or
the *modifying*, and *co-adunating* Faculty', which made new wholes, exactly as he
hoped 'The Soother of Absence' would: 'Mix up Truth & Imagination, so that
the Imag. may spread its own indefiniteness over that which really happened,
& Reality its sense of substance & distinctness to Imagination / For the Soother
of Absence —'[78] In those terms, the poem which he produced between late
August and early September might even be the first fruits of 'The Soother of
Absence'.

There is however evidence of Coleridge once again rather desperately
poem-making this August and September; the *Morning Post* was about to
publish an extended sequence of his work, for which he was being paid a
guinea a week. He had no problem producing prose, but his shortage of poetry

seems to have led not only to the publication of some rag-bag poems which he never bothered to reprint or collect, but also to his speedy adaptation of a poem about Mont Blanc by Friederike Brun to create his own (much longer) poem about the mountain: 'Chamouny: the Hour Before Sunrise A Hymn'. The remark to Sotheby that this poem began as something 'involuntarily' poured forth on Scafell has been treated with contempt by scholars ('the involuntary hymn story was an estecian myth, an imposition on the guileless Sotheby'[79]), and there can be no doubt that, without acknowledgement, Coleridge *did* use Brun's notes and poem as a springboard for his own work. It would not have been the first time he had drawn on outside assistance to help him meet a dead-line for the *Morning Post*. However, when Coleridge sent a copy of the poem to the Beaumonts in September 1803 he continued to stress its origins on Scafell when there was absolutely no reason to mention them – he commented 'I had written a much finer Line when Sca'Fell was in my Thoughts – viz – O blacker than the Darkness all the Night, And visited &c –'[80] The only deception to Sotheby, perhaps, was how much of the poem he had 'involuntarily' poured forth, and how much he worked up afterwards, using the hints he found in Brun.

For modern readers there is, however, an astonishing difference between the spontaneous overflow of response to the actual mountains, recorded in his notebooks, and the poetic effusiveness of his poem. A sample:

> Ye living flowers that skirt the eternal frost!
> 65   Ye wild goats sporting round the eagle's nest!
> Ye eagles, play-mates of the mountain-storm!
> Ye lightnings, the dread arrows of the clouds!
> Ye signs and wonders of the element!
> Utter forth God, and fill the hills with praise![81]

The switch to Mont Blanc destroys any possibility of using the 'topography' of the Lake District, of course; but Wordsworth at some stage 'condemned the Hymn in toto . . . as a specimen of the Mock Sublime'. Coleridge chose to defend it as 'the image and utterance of Thoughts and Emotions in which there was no Mockery', because it resulted from 'the Author's address-ing himself to *individual* Objects actually present to his Senses'.[82] Scafell had been present to his senses in a variety of painful and unforgettable ways, but whether poetic theory about the imagination successfully transferred them into an experience of Mont Blanc is another matter. There can be no doubt, however, that the Mont Blanc poem is today a dead exercise in what Wordsworth said it was, the mock sublime, while the writing which Coleridge actually produced about Scafell continues to startle and excite its readers.

For, in the course of the August 1802 trip, he not only made some of the longest entries in his early notebooks, but produced another kind of writing as well: a series of journal-letters, of which copies of the first two survive (the third was probably never completed). He had started the first under the shady sycamore tree while having his tea on the afternoon of Wednesday the 4th, and wrote up the first three and a half days of his travels. Having got to the top of Scafell the following day, he took great pleasure in taking out the incomplete letter, his inkhorn, and the wafers used to seal a letter, and finishing the first journal-letter on 'a nice Stone Table' – 'surely the first Letter ever written from the top of Sca' Fell!' – though he could not yet post it. He finished a second letter (very largely about his experiences coming down Scafell) on the following day, the Friday, while staying with the Towers family in Eskdale, breaking off because dinner was ready. He was able to post both letters when he reached Ambleside on the Sunday evening.

The journal-letters survive only in the copies Sara made of them, and it has been assumed that they were letters to her. And yet Coleridge is writing for a wider audience than a single person.[83] The addressees become clear, in the last paragraph of the second letter, when Coleridge describes how, in a 'little Village of Sheep-folds / there were five together', 'After the Thunder-storm I shouted out all your names in the Sheep-fold – when Echo came upon Echo / and then Hartley & Derwent & then I laughed & shouted Joanna . . .'[84] He was shouting Wordsworth's poem 'To Joanna': but 'all your names' shows how the letter-journal was being signed off to 'all' of them: possibly 'all' the Hutchinsons (male and female) at Gallow Hill, but far more likely to Sara and Mary, Dorothy and William: the five (excluding Sarah) together.[85] He was taking his role as one of the Bards of Helvellin seriously, and flexing his poetical mind through prose; and he was writing for that family group of five people whom, back in February, he had envisaged at the centre of his Helvellin poem.

Again, when setting out from Buttermere, Coleridge describes how he had, on his right, the hill Melbreak, but adds – quite unnecessarily for topographical accuracy – '(the Mountain on the right of Crummock, as you ascend the Lake)'.[86] Only one other person would immediately have registered that view: Wordsworth, with whom on 8 November 1799, walking from Keswick to Buttermere, Coleridge had come up the valley towards Buttermere, around Crummock water, so that Melbreak was on their right. Again, Coleridge suddenly remarks: 'of all things a ruined Sheepfold in a desolate place is the dearest to me, and fills me most with Dreams & Visions & tender thoughts of those I love best –'[87] The Wordsworth circle would immediately appreciate the reference to 'Michael': but only the other four of them would have been able instantly to identify themselves as 'those I love best', or to pick up the implicit reference to the *Letter* ('When thou, and with thee those, whom thou lov'sd best'[88]). There is a passing reference in the first journal-letter to 'Thomas Tyson's House where W & I slept Novr. will be 3 years',[89] showing (incidentally) that the letter is not simply to Wordsworth; but the reference is one which probably only Wordsworth and Dorothy would be much interested by. The fact that the absurd apology for a library at St Bees had been given by Sir James Lowther would also have produced a grim smile from Wordsworth and Dorothy: another trick played by the old enemy of their family.

It is clear that, just as Dorothy Wordsworth's journal of the French visit was written for perusal by a wider audience than usual, so were Coleridge's journal-letters. He normally kept his notebooks to himself, but now we find him using the entries to create another kind of writing. He may well have thought of them as travel letters which he could turn into something publishable. Back in 1799, he and Wordsworth had written a journal-letter of their first visit to the Lakes together, which Mary Wordsworth transcribed,[90] and Coleridge wrote something (or more likely planned to write something) which would 'in a pecuniary way have made the Trip answer to me':[91] this would probably have been a developed version of the journal-letter. Following his German travels of 1798–9 he had developed the plan of writing Letters about his experiences for which he actually found a publisher (Thomas Longman);[92] and in 1801, planning to go and live in the Azores for the winter, he was sure that 'Even in a pecuniary Light it will be a good plan / for my Letters will bring me at least a hundred Pound.'[93]

Now he wrote at least two journal-letters: in the first instance, letters posted to Sara Hutchinson (the 1799 tour journal-letters had been sent to Dorothy Wordsworth at Sockburn, again for the extended Hutchinson–Wordsworth family). The fact that Sara made copies of them is, of course, a confirmation that she actually handed or sent the originals to someone else. Coleridge himself may have wanted the letters back, but he may simply have wanted Sara to make and keep copies, while the originals continued to travel around the group.[94] He knew, of course, that Sara was an excellent copyist: knew that she had been copying his poems into her notebook (she was also one of the few people he permitted to enter things into his own notebooks[95]); the fact that she would be passing the letters on to other recipients is implicit in a comment such as 'you shall call this letter when it passes before you the Sca'Fell Letter /'.[96] The letter would necessarily 'pass before you' because it is going on to someone else. When Coleridge first posted the journal-letters, he believed that the Wordsworths would be back in England shortly, on their way to Gallow Hill. It seems in fact quite possible that, having learned that they would be staying in Calais for the month (and guessing that they might be short of reading matter), Sara copied the letters out and sent on the originals to Calais. But she would have known from the start that the journal-letters were not (in the strictest sense) letters *to* her at all. She was acting as a kind of postal delivery system, not as the intimate addressee of a letter. The coincidence, however, of Coleridge's journal-letters starting on Sunday 1 August, and being planned to cover a ten day journey, and of the Wordsworths' French travels (and Dorothy's journal) also starting on 1 August, and being originally planned to run for ten days, is very striking. A possible conclusion is that the journal-letters were not just by accident written to be read by both the Hutchinsons and by the Wordsworths too, but that both were planned for the people in the group, just as Coleridge's projected 'Bards of Helvellin' had been a poem *for* the group.

VII

We also know a little of the conflicting emotions Coleridge went through this summer, without Wordsworth and Dorothy. It was his longest absence from them for two years, but interestingly he compared it with the much more distressing time in Germany, in the winter of 1798–9, when – after travelling to Hamburg together – they had separated, and the Wordsworths had gone to Goslar in the depths of winter. Now, on 10 August 1802, writing to Sara Hutchinson in the aftermath of the great walk, Coleridge articulated his feelings for the Wordsworths very powerfully: 'I seem, I know not why, to be beating off all Reference to Dorothy & William, & their Letters – I heard from Sotheby of their meeting . . . I wish, I wish, they were back! – When I think of them in Lodgings at Calais, Goslar comes back upon me; & of Goslar I never think but with dejection. –'.[97] He still retained an awful feeling of having abandoned them in 1798, which is especially interesting at such a moment. Back in 1798, they had been marooned in the cold of the German winter because *he* had wanted to go to Germany, and out of loyalty they had gone with him – only to end up hundreds of miles away from him, but still loyal, supportive, uncritical. That supportive role was something he would now like them to play from *their* position of strength, for *his* corresponding isolation. But he also cannot bear the thought of their being cut off, in the exercise of duty in Calais, while *he* does what he wants: they make him feel bad, and their letters (the plural shows that he already has more than Dorothy's first letter, of 1 August) depress him. More than anything else, he says, he simply wants them back. That, however, was not as simple as it sounds. When 'they' came back to Grasmere, it would (he knew) be as a different kind of 'they' altogether: a threesome. He was actually losing them, in the course of this summer.

It has been suggested that 'Coleridge was disturbed by the visit to Annette',[98] but this seems another instance where evidence which disturbs the biographer is assumed to disturb the biographical subject. What is odd is the fact that, on 11 October 1802, in the *Morning Post*, Coleridge would publish a poem entitled 'Spots in the Sun'. It is worth reproducing as it has not been included in any edition of Coleridge's poetry for the last ninety years:

> My father confessor is strict and holy,
> *Mi Fili*, still he cries, *peccare noli*.

> And yet how oft I find the pious man
> At Annette's door, the lovely courtesan!
> 5   Her soul's deformity the good man wins
> And not her charms! he comes to hear her sins!
> Good father! I would fain not do thee wrong;
> But ah! I fear that they who oft and long
> Stand gazing at the sun, to count each spot,
> 10   *Must* sometimes find the sun itself too hot.[99]

Those who go to 'Annette', whatever their motives, and however strong their determination to be moral, *must* find themselves inflamed by the encounter (or at least find Annette inflaming) – that seems to be the point. Coleridge would doubtless have declared the poem a perfectly stupid joke: and, as if to confirm its insignificance, he never reprinted it. It seems doubtful if any of the Wordsworths could have read it quite so casually; it seems quite a destructive little missile to hurl into the life of a newly married couple, with Mary terribly aware that she was not Wordsworth's first sexual partner. But Gill is surely insensitive in his own way when he describes it as 'A vicious squib ... which ... can only be read as convicting Wordsworth of sanctimoniousness and hypocrisy.'[100] There are many possible ways of reading it, and that is perhaps the least likely. No one is convicted by such a poem. Coleridge's sense of humour regularly took his friends by surprise; in 1797 his relationship with Charles Lloyd had been permanently damaged by his publication of a poem parodying Lloyd's poetic style. 'Spots in the Sun' was not the only joke he concocted for the Wordsworth wedding. On 9 October a spoof wedding announcement appeared in the *Morning Post* for which only Coleridge can have been responsible, and which I shall discuss in the next chapter.

But Coleridge may well have had a worrying sense of Wordsworth moving calmly and steadily into this crucial new relationship, while he seemed only to be stuck in the old ones; he would also have had a strong sense of how he himself had rushed enthusiastically and joyfully and unthinkingly into marriage in 1796, whereas Wordsworth would carefully and intelligently and in the most adult – and irritating – way get married when he knew what he was doing. A contrast between his own great, exciting walk through the Lakes, and the Wordsworths' calm contemplation in Calais during the month of August showed rather the same. And the wife Wordsworth was marrying was, of all people, Mary Hutchinson, leaving Wordsworth doubly bolstered and supported. Coleridge may well have felt that such a *very* prudent and sensible marriage needed a touch of fun injected into its proceedings. It is actually his own sense of loss, and his rather desperate attempts to keep this alternative family group together, which are more significant than his attempts at jokes. He would regularly insert names into the corners of his notebook pages: his Malta notebooks dating from July and August 1805 show the layout of his universe of enopentas (i.e. the five in one) which he could have drawn at any time after 4 October 1802:

ΣAPA	Coleridge	W + M + D = W	Coleridge
William	Dorothy	William	Mary

[101]

Coleridge is thus substantially outweighed (in his support systems of assisting women) by Wordsworth. Against the simple 'Coleridge' is the 'W + M + D = W' sum of lucky William; and even where Coleridge ideally has a ΣAPA to comfort and support him (not that she did much of that), William has a Dorothy *and* a Mary. Wordsworth's marriage in October 1802 was clearly a very double-edged event from the point of view of an STC. Although on the one hand it would formalise part of the group in exactly the way Coleridge liked to think of it (a letter Coleridge wrote his friend at the end of July 1803 would end 'God love you all W. D. M + dearest John'), it would within a year set Coleridge's teeth on edge that Wordsworth should be 'living wholly among *Devotees*'.[102] The marriage would have left Coleridge profoundly aware of his own isolation.

VIII

At the end of his walking tour in August, Coleridge had found himself coming back towards Keswick on the road which led through Grasmere, and in need of a bed for the night: but he stopped at the Lloyds' house at Brathay, in spite of the fact that the Wordsworths would have been more than happy for him to have spent the night in Town End (they must have mentioned the idea to him before leaving in July: and later in the summer the Lambs and the Clarksons would sleep in the house). But Coleridge noted how 'I slept at Bratha on Sunday Night – & did not go on to Grasmere, tho' I had time enough, and was not over-fatigued; but tho' I have no objection to sleep in a lonely House, I did not like to sleep in *their* lonely House.'[103] It would have brought them back to mind too vividly: and himself there with them, as one of them, as he had so often been. All he did was go into the garden on his way past, the following day, where he helped himself to some of the peas perhaps nourished by the dung delivered that sunny morning back in March: 'pulled some Peas, & shelled & drest them, & eat them for my dinner with one rasher of Bacon boiled – but I did not go up stairs, nor indeed any where but the Kitchen. Partly I was very wet & my boots very dirty – & Molly had set the Pride of her Heart upon it's niceness – & still more – I had small desire to go up!'[104] The idea of sleeping there overnight, without Wordsworth and Dorothy, was bad enough; but even the upstairs parlour was too painful to be ventured into: it would have brought back the past too vividly. He feels extraordinarily tenderly towards them both, as in his memory of the time at Goslar. Only with the peas in the garden – relic of their spring plans, now left ungathered because of their absence – is he completely happy. And it is important that he could write these things to Sara: one within the charmed circle of the group of those who loved and needed each other, but one who was also losing her sister and companion in the imminent marriage, just as Coleridge would have felt he was losing a sister *and* a brother.

Chapter Eleven

Wedding Nature to Us: 4 October

4. W. Wordsworth, esq. of Grasmere, to
Miss Hutchinson, of Wykeham, Scarboro'.[1]

When they got back to England on Monday 30 August, Dorothy and Wordsworth had been away from Town End for seven weeks, almost as long as they had originally planned (both had predicted a 'two months' absence[2]). However, they set out neither for Grasmere nor for Gallow Hill. Instead, having lingered in Calais, and having returned to London only on Tuesday 31 August, they intended to linger another ten days but – because their brother John unexpectedly turned up, and Dorothy fell ill – the ten days became three weeks.

The date of the wedding in Yorkshire may possibly have been arranged all along for the start of October; the Coleridges' wedding anniversary was the 4th, which perhaps mattered to Wordsworth. But the fact that at some stage Wordsworth and Mary had acquired a marriage licence is evidence that they did not want to fix a particular date in advance.[3] The Wordsworths had probably originally expected to get back from France around 13 August, see Richard and other friends in London for ten days or so, and then go to Yorkshire, celebrate the wedding either at the end of August or early in September, and so return to Grasmere with Mary in the first ten days of September (within the expected 'two months').[4] The extra weeks in France had put paid to that; any plans previously made now had to change. They stayed in London, this time fortunately being able to stay cheaply in the rooms of Basil Montagu (currently away in Cambridge) until around the middle of September. As late as Sunday the 12th, Dorothy was still not absolutely sure when they would be leaving. No one seems to have been the least put out by this delay; indeed, Wordsworth and Dorothy were able to make good use of their time in London by helping Tom Hutchinson with some business connected with the purchase of a gig (a small carriage).[5] The delay also had the advantage for Wordsworth of ensuring that his wedding would, after all, coincide with the Coleridges' wedding day.

A visit to London in late summer was also a good chance for Wordsworth and Dorothy to see their family and friends. They had just spent four weeks in France on a trip which Wordsworth's brother Richard (in fact most of his relations and friends) would probably have assumed was just a holiday. Both family and friends would rightly have felt irritated if, having at last got back to London after such a visit, Wordsworth and Dorothy had chosen to leave again after just a couple of days, for the second time that summer.

And the timing of their London visit could not, as it turned out, have been luckier. They could spend time with Richard: something Wordsworth would have been keen to do, as the negotiations with the Lowther Estate were coming to a head. And during the first week of their time in London, Charles and Mary Lamb returned from the Lake district, where they had been with Coleridge, and had climbed Helvellyn: they had lodged in the house at Town End, too, and would have news of friends and neighbours. In London, the Wordsworths' lodgings were only just around the corner from the Lambs', and – Lamb commented – they 'past much time with us';[6] they all went to Bartholomew Fair in West Smithfield on the 7th, for example. Then Christopher Wordsworth came up from Cambridge with the unexpected news that their brother John's ship had arrived off the Kent coast but was detained by adverse tides. While waiting for him to come up the Thames, Christopher, William and Dorothy went out to Windsor to see their uncle Canon William Cookson (a chaplain to George III, who had also tutored some of the royal children), their aunt and the four children. This was truly a summer of reconciliation. After Calais, here they were paying a visit to the couple with whom Dorothy had lived for six years, from the age of 16 to 22, all of whose children she had helped bring up, but who had thoroughly disapproved of Wordsworth: and whom she had left so as to go and live with him. (They had not met since, though Dorothy had continued to correspond with her aunt.) Going with their eminently respectable brother Christopher (himself a clergyman) was a sensible idea, and they spent two days in Windsor 'very pleasantly', Wordsworth doubtless keeping his republican views to himself. They then got the news they really wanted to hear: John's ship had moored in the Thames on Friday 10 September. Christopher stayed on in Windsor, but Wordsworth and Dorothy went back to London immediately:

> We hastened towards our own Lodgings, and just as we entered the Temple Court we met Richard and John who were walking backwards and forwards by the light of the moon and the lamps. I could just see enough of John to know that he looked uncommonly well, and when we got him into Paper Buildings and had lighted the Candles I saw that he was grown fat and looked very handsome.[7]

As their brother Christopher then came back from Windsor, for the first time in many years all five Wordsworths were together: 'the set' itself, a most significant group.[8] Dorothy had naturally sent the news to Gallow Hill the previous week, but now wrote: 'We shall certainly leave London before the end of the week [i.e. by the 17th], but as we can see a good deal of John . . .

we cannot find in our hearts to leave him till we have been a few days together'.[9] She also wrote to Coleridge with the news: he too would naturally be part of the rejoicing concern.[10] The happiness of the occasion was diminished only by the fact that Dorothy was ill again, this time having caught 'a violent cold . . . by riding from Windsor in a long–bodied coach with 12 passengers', on their journey back to see John. (It was an illness bad enough for Coleridge to be informed about it by Montagu; but it was only the most recent of a succession of disabling colds and illnesses which Dorothy suffered that summer.[11]) Again they had to linger; but Wordsworth would have had time to talk to his brothers, about the Lowther Estate obviously, but also about the (now) rather troubled state of John's fortunes. His recent voyage had not been a success, and as Richard, Christopher, William and Dorothy all had money invested in his enterprise, they would have wanted to hear his plans for the future. Wordsworth would also have had time to work on his sonnets, including the new ones started in England on their return.[12] It was not until 22 September that he and Dorothy set off for Yorkshire.

II

One other matter connected with the London visit needs to be looked at. John Wordsworth had known Mary Hutchinson almost as long as William; and in the spring of 1800 both Mary and John had spent a month and a half in the Town End house with William and Dorothy. William and John had then gone over together to see Mary in May 1800. Kenneth Johnston has argued that William and John had then been rivals for Mary's hand between 1800 and 1802: they 'had taken their turns, and their chances, wooing Mary over the past two years. William had won out . . .'[13] Johnston has, however, not a single piece of evidence for John's wooing Mary between 1800 and 1802. His case has to be based on the words of the touching brief note which John added to his sister Dorothy's letter to Mary on 12 September 1802:

> I have been reading your Letter over
> & over again   My dearest Mary
> till tears have come into my eyes & I known
> not how to express myself – Thou ar't kind
> - - - - - - - - - - - - - - - - - -
> & dear creature   but whtat ever fate
> Befal me I shall love to the Last
> And bear thyy memory with me to t grave
> > Thine aff'ly –
> John Wordsworth[14]

A message from Mary must have been delivered to him on his arrival in London, by Wordsworth, Dorothy or Richard (Mary would not otherwise have known where to address him). Johnston, however, does his best to prevent his reader realising that this apparently independent love letter was actually only a postscript at the bottom of Dorothy's answer to Mary. He prints John's reply as if it were a separate letter starting 'My dearest Mary' (those words are actually deleted at its start); he says that 'John sent a letter to Mary', which is simply untrue; and he inserts 'thee' after 'I shall love' to make it more directly emotional. Johnston also assumes that the 'letter from Mary' would have contained 'her explanation to him of her reasons for marrying William', a thoroughly twenty-first-century activity (what could such 'reasons' be?)[15] But not only are we ignorant of what was in Mary's message to John, we cannot even be sure that she wrote him a letter. She may simply have included a special message for him in her letter to Dorothy, just as he sent his reply back in a letter from Dorothy.

There is no other evidence of any kind that John Wordsworth had the slightest interest in marrying Mary Hutchinson, or that Mary had ever thought of him except as a future brother-in-law. There was, however, one extremely good reason why she should have wanted to address John at this particular moment. She would have wanted to say that, whenever he returned to England (as he just had), he must continue to think of their home as *his* home. That was something which certainly needed saying to an extraordinarily shy unmarried man of no fixed address: back in 1800 he had had problems even lifting the latch at the house occupied by William and Dorothy, and had turned away 'without the courage to enter'.[16] An offer of a home now would have been enough to touch sensitive John's feelings profoundly: and it is confirmed by his reply. He responded by adapting, from his brother William's poem 'Michael', the lines in which Michael promises to his son Luke that he will always love him, in spite of the impending change in their lives; Michael, thinking constantly of the time 'when thou return'st', promises to build a sheepfold which will be 'a covenant . . . between us' while Luke is away. It seems likely that Mary would have stressed that she and William and Dorothy would always love John, and that their home would always be his, whether he was in England or whether he was away.[17]

Johnston, however, insists on love and passion (failed), and the wrong man married: Juliet Barker, too, is certain that John was deeply in love with Mary, entirely on the strength of this single postscript. In Chapter Two I described the carriage journey home taken by Dorothy, William and Mary after the wedding. According to Johnston, a fourth person was also present – in Mary's recollection: 'William and Dorothy kept their thoughts to themselves . . . or read them silently in each other's eyes . . . But Mary also had thoughts of her own to nurse, musing on John's letter.'[18] I think it more than likely, however, that this drama of passion, loss and regret has been manufactured entirely by biographers.

III

From London, Wordsworth and Dorothy took the same three-day journey up to Gallow Hill which Coleridge had taken back in February. They arrived on Friday 24 September to stay with the Hutchinsons for the nine days before the wedding. 'Mary first met us in the avenue. She looked so fat & well that we were made very happy by the sight of her . . .' Wordsworth could remember, nearly ten years later, exactly how Mary looked

> when thou came down the Lane to meet at Gallow Hill on my return with D –
> from france. Never shall I forget thy rich & flourishing and genial mien &
> appearance. Nature had dressed thee out as if expressly that I might receive thee
> to my arms in the full blow of health and happiness.

Mary was never fat in the modern sense (in 1812, for example, she weighed '7 stone 13' – 111 lbs.). But Dorothy, who had been ill constantly this summer (first in Calais, then in London, now at Gallow Hill) and who was 'very thin', had observed wistfully how healthy – that is, 'fat' and full-faced – first John and now Mary had looked.[19]

The reception party seems carefully planned. Mary had met them first, of course: 'then came Sara, & last of all Joanna. Tom was forking corn standing upon the corn cart.' The harvest was still in progress, and the late flowers were out in the fields and hedgerows; Dorothy 'looked at everything with tranquillity & happiness but I was ill both on Saturday [25 September] & Sunday & continued to be poorly most of the time of our stay.'[20] It had been a long journey, and she had been constantly ill this summer, but other instincts beside tiredness and illness were working in her. For her brother's sake she was very happy. For herself – as the woman who had had his care and trust and affection for six years – it was the final week when she would come first in his affections. At some point on this visit (or perhaps back in July) she scribbled a sketch map of the situation of Gallow Hill on to the back cover of her notebook: it very distinctly marks the farm track down to the main road, and the direction 'Brompton' to the right, where the church was.

The family assembled fully during the following week: the dates and names in Dorothy's diary fall like inscriptions on tombstones. 'Jack & George came on Friday Evening 1st October.' These were Mary's eldest brother Jack and her youngest brother George, by now sometimes regarded as the black sheep of the family. Jack was farming and prospering; George farming but not prospering. Mary's other elder brother Henry, a sailor (like Wordsworth's brother John), could not come. None of Wordsworth's own brothers came, but he and Dorothy had seen them all in London only a fortnight earlier; one imagines they had done something together to celebrate William's impending marriage.

The newly combined families gave themselves a trip out on Saturday 2 October, Tom leaving the farm to itself for the day: 'On Saturday 2nd we rode to Hackness, William Jack George & Sara single, I behind Tom.' Mary and Joanna appear not to have come. Dorothy presumably rode behind Tom on his own – large – farm horse. Hackness was at the end of a long, beautiful ride up through Scarwell Wood; there was a small lake there, a church, the local Hall. We do not know why it was chosen, except for its beauty.

Dorothy's careful, memorial diary entries continued. 'On Sunday 3rd Mary & Sara were busy packing.' Mary had lived in Yorkshire and County Durham, on her family's farms, since 1793; but it was a bride's trousseau which was now being packed. The Hutchinsons' mother Mary had been dead for nineteen years; the girls were used to supporting and helping each other. 'On Monday 4th October 1802, my Brother William was married to Mary Hutchinson . . .'[21] Dorothy wrote her account of the wedding in a long continuous narrative of the summer and autumn which (perhaps from notes[22]) she composed between 7 and 9 October 1802, after she, Mary and Wordsworth had finally reached Grasmere. Hers is – as so often – the only account we have of these events, and her journal had always played a special role in her life with her brother. It was now the place where she could ensure that she and Wordsworth would continue to the very end the special kind of 'marriage' in which they had so long existed. Before the ceremony which formally separated them on the Monday, the journal records how they put themselves through two tiny, intimate ceremonies which meant that her brother's immediately following marriage to Mary Hutchinson constituted a kind of bigamy.

In the first place, Dorothy slept the night of the 3rd wearing the wedding ring which Wordsworth would give Mary Hutchinson the following morning. They had bought the ring in Calais, and it would have been in character for Dorothy to have made herself its custodian between its purchase and its use. The fact that at this point she mentioned sleeping with it on her finger suggests, however, that this was a special, not a regular, ritual. It would have been interesting if Wordsworth had put it on her finger himself before she went to bed, though this we cannot know. It would, at any rate, be her one night of marriage to him.

She said what we can only see as goodbye to him the following morning, upstairs: 'I gave him the wedding ring – with how deep a blessing! I took it from my forefinger where I had worn it the whole of the night before – he slipped it again onto my finger and blessed me fervently.' And so for a second time the marriage ring was on her hand; this time put there by Wordsworth himself, half an hour or so before he would put it on Mary Hutchinson's finger in church.[23] More to the point than Wordsworth choosing Dorothy as his bride, however, is the fact that their heads would have been together, their faces very close, as the action said 'no, not only her: you too'. It was an act of the sheerest love and intimacy. It has been suggested that this matter of the rings was a proof to Dorothy that she would not be excluded from the marriage.[24] It seems to me to go a good deal further than that: it was a better proof than any words could be that she, too, was still chosen by her brother – not sexually, but emotionally; she was as much in the marriage as Mary was. Someone – perhaps Dorothy, perhaps Mary, perhaps an editor – later erased these two sentences in her journal, but they remain readable.

She stayed upstairs after 'William had parted from me': yet another in the sequence of partings, as they had parted from Grasmere in July, as he had parted from Annette and Caroline in August. She stayed by the window: 'at a little after 8 o clock I saw them go down the avenue towards the Church.' Gallow Hill lies 200 yards from the road between Ruston (to the east) and Brompton in the west; Brompton church is three-quarters of a mile along the road. While the rest of the family party was out, Sara took charge of arrangements for the breakfast: 'my dear little Sara' Dorothy called her. Dorothy was losing a brother, but Sara was losing a sister: she would stay housekeeping for her brother Tom.

Dorothy herself did not go the wedding ceremony; just as Wordsworth did not go to his own beloved daughter Dora's wedding in 1834. It has been asserted that she was too distraught to attend, but there is no evidence of that. Neither Coleridge nor Sarah Coleridge were there, but even William's three brothers stayed in London; it seems to have been conceived as a Hutchinson family event, for which the entire immediate family came to Gallow Hill. Sara Hutchinson did not go to the church, but she was in charge of the wedding breakfast: it may also have been felt that Dorothy should not be left at home by herself. Nonetheless, the formal bonding of Wordsworth and Mary clearly stood outside the informal family group in which the five had recently existed; the marriage in fact marked a kind of ending for the Gang, in spite of all their attempts to continue in an identical relationship with each other.

It would have taken the wedding party – consisting of Wordsworth, Mary, her brothers Tom and Jack (and almost certainly George) and her sister Joanna[25] – fifteen minutes or so to walk to Brompton church: a brief excursion between the autumn fields. One can imagine the farmers Tom, George and Jack commenting on how other farmers were getting on with the harvest, Joanna taking care of her sister, Wordsworth perhaps on his own, perhaps talking to the farmers. The wedding service – to be conducted by the vicar, the Revd John Ellis – was probably arranged for 8.15 or 8.30, and could not have taken more than fifteen minutes. On the marriage certificate, Wordsworth appeared as 'William Wordsworth of Grasmere in Westmoreland – Gentleman': Joanna, Tom and Jack were the witnesses. The party would have got home shortly before 9.00, two of the Hutchinson brothers arriving first, according to Dorothy's account. She had obviously gone back to the window of her room: 'I kept myself as quiet as I could, but when I saw the two men running up the walk, coming to tell us it was over, I could stand it no longer & threw myself on the bed where I lay in stillness, neither hearing or seeing any thing . . .'.[26] Dorothy's phrase 'it was over' sums up the event for her. The second part of her life was at an end. She can 'stand it no longer' – literally and figuratively – and throws herself down on the bed, not feeling sad, or happy, or anything at all. It can only have been for a few moments, and Sara, as always, comes to the rescue: 'Sara came upstairs to me & said "They are coming"' – meaning, presumably, not the men running ahead, but the bride and groom. She described how 'This forced me from the bed where I lay & I moved I knew not how straight forward, faster than my strength could carry me till I met my beloved William & fell upon his bosom. He & John Hutchinson led me to the house & there I stayed to welcome my dear Mary.'[27] She managed, that is, to get up, out of the door, along the passage, down the stairs, and out of the front door, all in that headlong run 'faster than my strength could carry me': it was a manic possession, a violent rush triggered by Sara's single phrase, and quite unstoppable. She found Wordsworth (but not Mary) and was then taken indoors; decorum follows.

Wedding presents there were none: many years later, Mary wondered 'Whether . . . it was in consequence of our friends' thinking us an improvident pair, I do not know – but it is a fact'. She herself, however, received a new gown from John Wordsworth, who commented 'I am glad and rejoiced to hear that my *sister* Mary likes the *choice* of my new gown'.[28] One of the Ferguson cousins just leaving for America sent Dorothy a set of six silver spoons.[29] Not getting married, she was naturally regarded as her brother's future housekeeper.

The Grasmere party – Dorothy, William and Mary – drove away soon after the wedding breakfast; they were going to travel fifty-six miles that day, the three of them in the carriage – and in the marriage – together. Nothing had changed.

IV

Except that people do change, move on, find themselves in new situations. I shall spend the rest of this chapter suggesting how that was true for each of the people concerned with this marriage.

I discussed above Dorothy's response to the marriage in her journal entries about the journey across to Grasmere, and the way in which those entries both correspond to, and diverge from, her brother's poem about the journey. Those entries are, of course, all that we know of her response. I commented:

The journal entry is, perhaps appropriately for Dorothy recording this day, also rather more ominous, with its 'Ruins among groves, a great, spreading wood, rocks, & single trees'. Dorothy is seeing things which will not be seen again: 'But there's a Tree, of many, one, / A single Field which I have looked upon, / Both of them speak of something that is gone'. There is also a hint of the grimmest of the 'Lucy' poems of 1799: Lucy dead and rolled around with 'rocks and stones and trees'. The married man's poem, however, shows that westward, look, the land is bright.[30]

All that is true. Such an account of the journal, however, creates a symbolic significance of difference (gloom for Dorothy, joy for Wordsworth) which is only one way of reading it. Another way could just as easily note how extraordinarily cheerful and detached are Dorothy's entries about the journey. She sympathetically records her new sister-in-law's agitation when 'she parted from her Brothers & Sisters & her home' (Dorothy knows *very* well what that would have meant). But she follows it with the sentences 'Nothing particular occurred till we reached Kirby. We had sunshine & showers, pleasant talk, love & chearfulness.'[31] Stoical? Through gritted teeth? Or (even) genuinely cheerful? But, again, we read such passages differently when we recognise that they are written to be read by the other two occupants of the carriage, with whom Dorothy is on terms of the deepest intimacy. She is memorialising the happy start of a marriage, and her journal is hardly going to be a reliable source of 'genuine' information. The journal is, however, all that we have. Sunshine & showers, indeed.

At Helmsley, during a pause, Dorothy persuades Wordsworth to come exploring the castle ruins while they leave Mary sitting by the fire in the Inn. We can read what we like into that, as we can into Dorothy's note that, 'Every foot of the Road was, of itself interesting to us, for we had travelled along it on foot Wm & I when we went to fetch our dear Mary, & had sate upon the Turf by the roadside more than once.'[32] Of more interest to Wordsworth and to Dorothy, one would have thought, than to Mary, in spite of the sentence being careful to include her. But, over and over again, the journal account is palpably the construct of a woman determined to be satisfied with her lot. As a result, for the first time since 1798 Dorothy's writing becomes almost opaque. Only in reminiscence does she allow herself to feel: not just in memories of her journey with Wordsworth in July, of which there are several, but of her original journey with her brother to take up residence at Town End ('our Road to Grasmere 2 years & ¾ ago'). At Sedbergh, for example, while the horses are changed, she finds herself 'in the same Room where we had spent the Evening together in our road to Grasmere'. When they reach Wensley, 'my heart was melted away with dear recollections, the Bridge, the little water-spout the steep hill the Church – They are among the most vivid of my own inner visions, for they were the first objects that I saw after we were left to ourselves, & had turned our whole hearts to Grasmere as a home in which we were to rest.'[33] And when they get to Stavely, her memories of journeys shared with her brother reach even further back: she remembers it as 'the first mountain village that I came to with Wm when we first began our pilgrimage together'.[34] She is thinking of April 1794, and her language suggests that the pilgrimage is continuing.

On the other hand, in spite of her intense nostalgia for the time when 'we were left to ourselves', we can also see her *making* a threesome, carefully and rather beautifully, just as she makes her unrevealing journal out of their new life together. 'Mary & I got tea, & William had a partridge & mutton chops & tarts for his supper. Mary sate down with him.' 'Mary was much pleased with Garsdale. It was a dear place to William & me.'[35] She has to work out this new relationship; and in the most intelligent and work-woman-like way she does so.

The second day they ride thirty-one miles; on the third day, another forty-four miles, and get to Town End at six in the evening. They immediately go into the garden 'by candle light' and are 'astonished at the growth of the Brooms, Portugal Laurels, &c &c & –'. So 'our' Mary is welcomed into the garden: 'for my part I cannot describe what I felt, & our dear Mary's feelings would I dare say not be easy to speak of'.[36]

The ending of the Grasmere journal is quite different from that of the Alfoxden journal. Dorothy kept up her journal conscientiously once they had got back to Grasmere, albeit with short entries, for a fortnight. She was in effect saying 'this is normal, this new life'. The diary's discipline, back at home, was a way of asserting normality, just as its attempts at fair-minded opacity (with flashes of haunted memory) had been on the journey back from Gallow Hill.

Then Wordsworth went away, on 23 October: and immediately Dorothy's journal stopped for a week. Her life at home with Mary was not something she was concerned to document. She started to write it again on the 30th, when her brother got back. The following day, she and Mary both took a rest after dinner: 'Mary slept. I *could* not for I was thinking of so many things'.[37] And then suddenly, on 9 November, there is no entry. And thereafter no more until Christmas, when there is a long reminiscent entry (including an account of the arrival of Coleridge from Somerset to hear that his daughter Sara had been born) and a tiny note about her own birthday: 'It is today Christmas-day Saturday 25th December 1802. I am 31 years of age. – It is a dull frosty day.'[38]

She then fails to write anything for another fortnight – reproaches herself – writes up what she can remember on 11 January – and resolves to 'write regularly &, if I can legibly'.[39] She does make a tiny entry for Wednesday the 12th: and then another on Sunday the 16th, about going out in the cold to get gingerbread for Wordsworth because he suddenly wanted some. And then, just 'Monda' – and the journal has ended.

It has been suggested that she stopped making entries because, with Mary three months pregnant, there was simply too much to do for Dorothy to keep a journal.[40] It is possible: she had abandoned her journal for a month in the summer of 1800 when the three Coleridges (Sarah six months pregnant) had come to stay.[41] But that is not how the existing journal fragments of January 1803 read, nor how she herself seems to have thought. Again, it has been suggested that she now no longer needed to keep a journal: she had a companion in Mary with whom she could share her thoughts.[42] But her resolution to keep her journal does not quite square with that. The real point seems to have been that there was nothing to keep it *for*, now the old Home at Grasmere had come to an end. She was not, as in 1798, writing her observations for poets to consider; she was not, as in 1800 or in the spring of 1802, writing about the world which she and Wordsworth were making in Grasmere, as a kind of confirmation of their love for each other.

We should not see Dorothy as a tragic figure. She was only thirty-one: she had many fulfilling years ahead of her; she would spend her life caring for others and would (incidentally) enjoy the Wordsworth children enormously: she would write hundreds of letters on behalf of them all. But in the winter of 1802–3 her journal writing, the creation of her self as the one who saw, and helped others see, and so – uniquely – worked alongside Coleridge and Wordsworth, came to an end. Instead, three of the group were now together, soon to be joined by Sara as the fourth. Dorothy's writing would continue in her copying and in her letters to other people, and in that way largely disappears underground again, so far as we are concerned. It vanishes, in fact, into the group.

V

Coleridge's extraordinary series of publications (poems and prose) in the *Morning Post* between 6 September and 11 October 1802 in many ways showed him, too, marking out his sense of the new situation. Even his four essays on France under Napoleon probably drew on what he had heard from Wordsworth and Dorothy.[43] But it cannot have been an accident that on the day of the wedding itself (of all days) *Dejection* (of all poems) should have appeared: an act typical of the life within this extra-family group: life and literary comment always overlapping.

The whole sequence of poems may indeed have started so that he could have *Dejection* published on the appropriate day; the delay in the Wordsworths' marriage meaning that he had to extend his sequence for some weeks. But a surprising number of the poems related in one way or another to people in the group. 'The Picture' appeared first, on 6 September (one of the poems Sara Hutchinson had copied into her manuscript book). On 11 September, the Chamouny poem was published, with its links to the ascent of Scafell; on 17 September appeared 'The Keepsake', which was probably the earliest of his poems to Sara Hutchinson (and another poem she had copied into her manuscript book). That was *his* betrothal (but not his marriage) poem. On 24 September, he published his 'Inscription for a Fountain on a Heath', about a tiny spring which – when he discovered it – had immediately made him think of the group.[44] That, too, had been copied into her book by Sara Hutchinson. On

16 October appeared 'The Language of Birds' (also sent to Sara and copied by her) and, on 19 October, that quintessential group poem 'The Day-Dream', previously copied by Mary Hutchinson along with a text of the *Letter*. All these poems, Mary and Sara, Dorothy and William would have known, and would have recognised in them not just the part they had played in Coleridge's own life but in the intimacies they had all shared.

But other, less explicit poems, in the context which the October wedding brought to them, took on meanings which only the others in the group would have appreciated. The day before the 'Inscription' was published, an epigram – 'The Good, Great Man' – had appeared. It asked,

> If any man obtains what he merits
> Or any merit that which he obtains.

A question which – in this context – related directly, of course, to Wordsworth, Mary, Sara and Coleridge himself. The 'Reply to the Above', which accompanied 'The Good, Great Man' in the newspaper, suggested that 'LOVE, and LIGHT, / And CALM THOUGHTS' were the proper rewards of the 'good great man': rewards which Coleridge may have assumed Wordsworth would indeed be blessed with on 4 October, but which were exactly the inheritance into which he himself had *not* come.

It is, of course, perfectly possible that Coleridge would have denied any such meanings: would have declared that the *Morning Post* poems had been written months if not years before, and might have insisted that none of them had had *any* particular reference to 4 October: he was just clearing out his bottom drawer. That is what he told Tom Wedgwood: 'The Poetry, which I have sent, has been merely the emptying out of my Desk. The Epigrams are wretched indeed; but they answered Stuart's purpose better than better things – /. I ought not to have given any signature to them whatsoever / I never dreamt of acknowledging them . . . .'.[45]

This was true of one or two fragments. The 'Westphalian Song' of 27 September, for example, was at least three years old (if not older) and unmemorable, to say the least. Some of the epigrams on 11 September were also long in the tooth and short in the memory.

Yet there would only have been one way for the gang to read the bulk of the work; only they would have known what was afoot. Three days after *Dejection*, there appeared 'An Ode to the Rain', a poem written on 2 October 1801, celebrating the intimacy and joy of life which Coleridge felt with Dorothy and Wordsworth at Town End, and a heartfelt desire that visitors and strangers who interfered with such perfect, intimate happiness would simply leave – another extraordinary commentary on the marriage. (Coleridge mentioned it explicitly to Wedgwood as another poem he had never dreamt of acknowledging: but this time, perhaps, because it was too personal, not too silly.) On the 11th the paper printed the body of epigrams, one of them 'Spots in the Sun', referring very precisely to the Wordsworths' recent visit to Calais, and discussed above. And in between, on the 9th, appeared a spoof wedding announcement:

> Monday last, w. WORDSWORTH, Esq. was married to Miss HUTCHINSON, of Wykeham, near Scarborough, and proceeded immediately, with his wife and his sister, for his charming cottage in the little Paradise – vale of Grasmere. His neighbour, Mr. COLERIDGE, resides in the Vale of Keswick, 13 miles from Grasmere. His house (situated on a low hill at the foot of Skiddaw, with the Derwent Lake in front, and the romantic River Greta windidg [sic] round the hill) commands, perhaps, the most various and interesting prospects of any house in the island. It is a perfect *panorama* of that wonderful vale, with its two lakes, and its complete circle, or rather ellipse, of mountains.[46]

The entry may have been a joke by Stuart, Coleridge and Lamb,[47] but crucial information in it must have come from Coleridge (only he would have known about the carriage journey of Wordsworth, Mary and Dorothy back to Grasmere), and it seems possible that it was entirely his own work, with Stuart's connivance. He did not however confess to it; three years later, Dorothy was still fulminating about Stuart ('Upon my Brother's marriage he inserted in the Morning Post the most ridiculous paragraph that ever was penned'[48]). A recent biographer finds the paragraph 'strange', yet 'perhaps . . . normal' for a rejected lover like Coleridge.[49] But a rejected lover has got nothing to do with writing like this. It is a very knowing composition in a style which Coleridge had come across quite recently: Richard Warner's *A Tour through Northern Counties of England, and the Borders of Scotland* (1802) had described 'The animated, enthusiastic, & accomplished COLERIDGE, whose residence at Keswick gives additional charm to it's impressive scenery', and added a passing reference to 'a kindred Intellect, his Friend & Neighbour at Grasmere, WORDSWORTH'.[50] Coleridge had told Sara Hutchinson about the book, and it is hard to imagine that he had not told Wordsworth too. If he had, the paragraph in the *Morning Post* might have made Wordsworth smile, if grimly. Dorothy was thoroughly offended, however, and told John about it, only to find him also responding with the wintry smile of someone despairing of being able to make someone else see a joke: 'It is not quite so bad as I thought it would have been from what you said.'[51] The fact that Coleridge actually came to stay with them in Town End between 11 and 13 October shows how close the relationships they shared actually remained. Nothing had changed.

And everything had changed. Even more significant than such publications was the fact that Coleridge would publish no poetry for almost a year after his poems in the *Morning Post*. It had indeed been an 'emptying out'. The Wordsworth–Hutchinson marriage struck him very hard indeed; not simply because he was jealous of Wordsworth, nor even because their marriage offered him such a bitter contrast with his own marriage (though it probably did), but because he was losing a sister in Dorothy *and* a brother: a man and a woman who were, crucially, *family* to him. This autumn things went still further down-hill for him and Sarah, but it may not even have been the fantasy of a new part-nership which drove him deeper and deeper into his idealising of Sara Hutchinson. It was, just as much, a desire to make her his loving sister: a replacement for Wordsworth and Dorothy. A series of dreams which he recorded from 3 October, the eve of the wedding, may give some clue about what was happening to him.

> I dreamt of Dorothy, William & Mary – & that Dorothy was altered in every feature, a fat, thick-limbed & rather red-haired – in short, no resemblance to her at all – and I said, if I did not <u>know</u> you to be Dorothy, I never should <u>suppose</u> it / ⟨Now⟩ Why, says she – I have not a feature the same / & yet I was not sur-prized – I was followed up & down by a frightful pale woman who, I thought, wanted to kiss me, & had the property of giving a shameful Disease by breath-ing in the face / & again I dreamt that a figure of a woman of a gigantic Height dim & indefinite & smokelike appeared – & that I was forced to run up toward it – & then it changed to a stool – & then appeared again in another place – & again I went up in great fright – & it changed to some other common thing – yet I felt no surprize.[52]

His point is that, in dreams, one feels no surprise. But the thought of women *changing*, in every feature, is compelling. Dorothy becomes unrecognisable – looking like one of the torturing boys Coleridge associated with Christ's Hospital – and she herself agrees that she is different. She is still there: yet you lose her. The other woman who can infect you (presumably with some form of sexual disease) by breathing in your face, with all the terror of an untouching intimacy of breath, is succeeded by the woman constantly shape-changing. She turns to 'a stool' (either a turd or a three-legged seat), but you are forced to run after her. Guilt about desiring women who are not your wife is mixed with fear of losing those you love, and anxiety about the frightening power of women.

VI

Most commentators regard *Dejection* as a perfectly natural thing for Coleridge to have published. Those who wish to make something of it find themselves, however, handicapped as to what exactly *can* be made of it. It has, for example, been suggested that the poem was 'C's wedding gift'[53] to Wordsworth and Mary; but – if so – it was a rather odd one. For one thing, they had both seen it before. A public statement (even one in a newspaper they would not see for a couple of days) was of course something else; but as a wedding present it was decidedly second-hand.

Holmes suggests that 'Coleridge must have considered [it] as a kind of epithalamium in its specially edited version'.[54] If an odd wedding present, it would
have been an even odder epithalamium [a poem written to celebrate a mar-
riage]. It did not mention marriage at all, but concentrated for its first three
stanzas on a description of 'A grief without a pang', a 'stifled, drowsy, unim-
passion'd grief', in which the narrator concludes 'My genial spirits fail'.[55]
Reading that in the context of a wedding, one conclusion would be that the
narrator was complaining that *he* was being abandoned by the man (or woman:
or both) who were getting married. It is a poem of abiding melancholy,
after all.

Knowing however, as Mary and William Wordsworth did, that the poem
had in different ways also been 'to Wordsworth' and 'to Sara', and that the
addressee 'Edmund' in the *Morning Post* was a loving reminiscence of a name by
which Coleridge had once addressed Wordsworth, would at least have meant
that a certain tender intimacy was being shown towards the man who was
getting married. On the other hand, the poem declared its faith – 'we receive
but what we give' – in the very things in which Wordsworth had equally pas-
sionately stated he did not believe. Did these things make up for the fact that
in its declaration of faith in 'joy' – 'Joy, EDMUND! is the spirit and the pow'r,
/ Which wedding Nature to us gives in dow'r' – its language was appropriately
celebratory? It was, after all, still as much a tribute to the sister who was *not*
getting married as to the one who was: Edmund is 'friend of my devoutest
choice', 'Brother and friend of my devoutest choice'.[56] That is why he is dear:
not just for his own sake. Most strikingly of all, Edmund's own new wife, the
one to whom he is now getting married, at no point enters the poem. This –
again – may be thought exceptionally dubious in a wedding present (or an
epithalamium) for a new couple, especially one published on 4 October, the
writer's own wedding day.

Was it tasteless of the Wordsworths to have chosen 4 October for their
licensed wedding, given what they knew of the Coleridge marriage? No: the
marriage had lasted, and had been fortunate in producing children;
where Coleridge and Sarah had previously gone, Wordsworth and Mary
(in this the junior partners) would now go. But marrying Mary Hutchinson,
on that day of all days, corresponded exactly to what was said so often in
the poem's unspoken (and unpublished) other text: that a Hutchinson sister was
the woman of a lifetime, and that she could change your life if you were partnered with her. To publish *Dejection* on that day, of all days, made it – if not a
poem to Mary Hutchinson – at least a poem of love to the unnamed
Sara Hutchinson, published in the only way such love could publicly be
demonstrated.

It is hard to escape the fact that *Dejection* is a sad and self-mocking self-
tribute rather than a present. It was less a genuine gift to the man and the
woman getting married than a deeply ironical, self-regarding gift to a man
already married, and unable to marry again. It was a kind of un-wedding

present. But only five people in England could have read it like that: Dorothy, Wordsworth, perhaps their brother John, Mary and Sara herself. Only they could have known the battlegrounds it hinted at, the ongoing energies it recalled, the stasis it represented. Its publication on 4 October was, truly, for this gang: only they would have known how to read it.

Epilogue

There is really very little that can be said about Wordsworth and Mary, once they were married. Just one deleted phrase in a letter Mary wrote in 1810 reveals how her marriage affected her. She was writing (in response to an extremely tender letter from Wordsworth) about the 'underconsciousness' which marriage had brought to her 'that I had my *all in all* about me'; and she started to describe '*that* feeling which I have never wanted since I slept with . . .', but then obviously hesitated, deleted 'I slept with' and replaced it with 'the solitary night did not separate us'.[1] But even the replacement phrase is touching. Their garden may have been 'lov'd for hours of sleep', and Town End 'a home in which we were to rest', but there were now no more solitary nights for either of them.

Yet apart from Wordsworth's poem (yet another sonnet) commemorating the journey home after the wedding,[2] almost nothing that he wrote during the next few months in any way related to *his* sense of his new situation. He seems to have confined himself to writing and revising sonnets (there were some new ones by December[3]), and to working on translations from the Italian; that, at least, is all we know about. However, one neglected poem survives, which may say just a little about the Wordsworth marriage: a version of one of Milton's Italian sonnets, the translation allowing Wordsworth to make one of those restrained public declarations so characteristic of him. As it would be published in the *Morning Post*, of all papers, on (of all dates) 5 October 1803, in spite of being written probably eight months earlier, it looks very much like a first anniversary present:

> A plain Youth, Lady! and a simple lover,
> Since of myself a last leave I must take,
> To you devoutly of my heart I make
> An humble gift, and doing this I proffer
> A heart that is intrepid, slow to waver,
> Gracious in thought, discreet, good, prompt, awake;
> If the great earth should to her centre shake
> Arm'd in itself, and adamant all over;
> Not more secure from envy, chance, desire,
> And vulgar hopes and fears that vex the earth,
> Than wedded to high valour, wit, and worth,
> To the sweet Muses, and the sounding lyre:

Weak only will you find it in that part
Where Love incurably hath fixed his dart.[4]

The translation allows Wordsworth discreetly to take 'a last leave' of his own old self, his youth, without being confessional about it; but he is also able publicly to state both his devotion to Mary, and his dedication to his poetry, again without apparently doing so. Those at Greta Hall and Gallow Hill, however, would have known exactly what they were reading; Wordsworth actually visited the Coleridges on 9 October 1803 and would doubtless have shown them the poem if they had not already read it in the paper.

But it would be published, too, in a rather different climate from that in which it had been written. While Coleridge would certainly have appreciated the fact of the date, one small related fact is significant. The translation ends with the same cliché – 'Where Love incurably hath fixed his dart' – which Coleridge would employ in the rewritten version of what he reckoned had been his crucial experience in November 1799 of falling in love with Sara: 'tunc temporis, tunc primum, amor me levi spiculo, venenato, eheu! & insanabili . . .'[5] This would have been the merest of coincidences if Coleridge had not actually inserted his rewritten version into his notebook sometime during the fortnight after the publication of Wordsworth's Milton sonnet, at some date between 12 and 19 October 1803. He thus seems to have appropriated, for Sara, the phrase appearing in Wordsworth's poem on 5 October, addressed (as it would naturally seem, on such a day) to Mary. Coleridge thus insisted that *he* was the one in love; the one horribly (and wonderfully) pierced: the one whose hurt was incurable. He jealously confirmed the intimate parallel he so often drew between Wordsworth's feelings for Mary and his own love for Sara: he started, in fact, to insist upon his own love for Sara as the *real*, passionate attraction.

It cannot have been a coincidence that it was at exactly this time, on 14 October 1803, that Coleridge would also voice his first savage criticisms of Wordsworth. He was writing to Tom Poole: and there was, doubtless, a good deal of self-pity and wisdom after the event in the complaints he would now make. But the old easy and mutually supportive contact between him and the Wordsworths had clearly broken down:

I now see very little of Wordsworth: my own Health makes it inconvenient & unfit for me to go thither one third as often, as I used to do – and Wordsworth's Indolence, &c keeps him at home.[6] Indeed, were I an irritable man, and an unthinking one, I should probably have considered myself as having been very unkindly used by him in this respect – for I was at one time confined for two months, & he never came in to see me / me, who had ever payed such unremitting attentions to him.[7]

Wordsworth's absence from Keswick during April and May (when Coleridge had been ill) can fairly simply be attributed to the fact that, with Mary heavily pregnant, he was far more reluctant to leave home than he had been during 1802: baby John would be born on 18 June 1803. But it was clearly the whole household at Grasmere from which, by October, Coleridge felt excluded, as his criticisms of Wordsworth show: 'I saw him more & more benetted in hypochondriacal Fancies, living wholly among *Devotees* – having every the minutest Thing, almost his very Eating & Drinking, done for him by his Sister, or Wife – & I trembled, lest a Film should rise, and thicken on his moral Eye. –'. The regret is not only for a beloved brother unmanned by the women caring for him. It is also a criticism of a man gone soft, incapable of seeing the world truly or writing about it well. Coleridge would complain in October about the appearance in the *Morning Post* of yet another (and very minor) sonnet by Wordsworth, 'I find it written of Simonides'.[8] The badness of yet another short poem proved to Coleridge the decline of both the poet and the friend. But it is, finally, a criticism of the regime at Town End that he is making; the friend fussed over, the women stupidly devoted, Coleridge excluded: dedicated (now) to the love for Sara/Asra which he had decided was the only thing that really mattered in his life.

This attack on the very idea of the group was something new. It seems, however, to have resulted less from Wordsworth's marriage than from differences which had been growing over the year. For one thing, Coleridge himself had been away from Keswick and Grasmere between 4 November and 24 December 1802, and then again from 20 January to 8 April 1803[9]; he had then been 'confined' during April and May. And something very destructive would happen in Scotland in August. But as late as June 1803 Coleridge was still prepared to rejoice over the new Wordsworth family member, baby John: he had gone down from Keswick almost at once to see him, and journeyed down again a month later, on 17 July, to be one of the child's two godfathers, accepting the role in spite of his quarrel with baptism. For a sister and a brother, he would become a child's godfather; while a surviving letter from late July, shortly before the tour, shows him as warm and friendly as ever to his 'Dearest, dearest, dearest Friends – I will have 3 dearests, that there may be one for each': the same letter ends 'God love you all W. D. M. + dearest John'.[10]

The tour of Scotland on which Coleridge, Wordsworth and Dorothy set out on 15 August 1803, and which may even have been planned to bring the three of them closer together again, had ended with the party splitting up on 29 August. Coleridge had made a number of irritated entries in his notebook about, for example, 'Dorothy's Raptures' and his own lonely and dejected state before the break,[11] but his (literal) turning away from Wordsworth and Dorothy was something else. He was certainly intensely irritable, suffering from the weather in the open 'jaunting car', but it is also clear that he was trying to do without opium at the time ('I have abandoned all Opiates except Ether be one'), and the opium withdrawal was doing awful things to his health, his ability to sleep and his general state of mind.[12] His subsequent comments about Wordsworth do, however, suggest that the latter had been severe or moralistic about something: and that can hardly have been simply about opium, as has been suggested, as Coleridge was so very obviously trying to give it up (he would, however, have been very touchy about the subject). There may well have been some quarrel over Coleridge's feelings for Sara Hutchinson; it was during this tour that he first seems to have used his special name 'Asra' for her.[13] Either Wordsworth or Dorothy may finally have told him to stop being ridiculous (they would have been very aware of Sara's awkward position); or they may just have been unsympathetic. Wordsworth was now a man with a wife and a young child, and would have been touched by the particular callousness implicit in Coleridge's turning away from his own wife and his own recently born child to a woman to whom he was not married. Coleridge ended up, at any rate, terribly conscious of what he thought was the thickening of a film on his friend's moral eye: Wordsworth getting blindly moralistic, losing his clear-sightedness. Some unsympathetic comment from his friend on Coleridge's love for Sara would have been reason enough for that, coming as it would have done while Coleridge was so intensely miserable for other reasons.

II

But six months earlier, back in the winter of 1802–3, such touchiness was a world away. It would be quite wrong to conclude that nothing except rifts in the relationship were showing. We know for example how those in the Town End house had continued caring for Coleridge, and worrying about him, during October and November 1802. And he, of course, had been the Wordsworths' very first visitor when they returned to Grasmere in October 1802. He had walked down to them on 11 October, the very day 'Spots in the Sun' was published. Dorothy commented: 'he was well but did not look so'.[14] He stayed a couple of nights; the three of them (as we must now think of the Wordsworth household) then walked all the way back up to Keswick with him and stayed there another three nights, taking the chance of 'Mrs C not being at home'. And when Dorothy and Mary walked home on the 16th, Wordsworth stayed on an extra night with Coleridge alone: his first night away from Mary since their marriage. When he himself got back the next day, he was 'much oppressed',[15] probably with Coleridge's state of health, certainly with Coleridge's state of mind. He went back to Keswick within the fortnight. (That was precisely the kind of attentiveness which Coleridge would be mourning, twelve months later.)

Coleridge had then gone down to London in mid-November in order to travel with Tom Wedgwood, but also to get away from Greta Hall. He saw Sara Hutchinson at Penrith on his way, as she travelled over to Keswick to stay with Sarah Coleridge, now nearly eight months pregnant:[16] Sara was clearly continuing to play for the Coleridge children the role she had played for the children of her brother Jack, and would subsequently play for the Wordsworth children. Sara then went on to Grasmere to be with the Wordsworths for the rest of November and December. Coleridge only came back up to the Lake District on Christmas Eve – and it was the Wordsworths who would tell him, when he called at Town End on his way up to Keswick, about the birth of his own daughter Sara the previous morning.[17] At New Year it was Dorothy who went up to Keswick for three days. Coleridge, however, although obviously glad she was there, could not help thinking about Grasmere, as his notebook entry shows: 'Jan. 1. 1803 – at Grasmere William, Mary, Sara; but not dear Dorothy. William Wordsworth Mary Wordsworth Sara Hutchinson Dorothy Wordsworth no'.[18] Dorothy then came back with Coleridge, being met first by William on horseback and then by Mary and Sara on foot: and so the group reassembled itself.

While Coleridge was actually back in the region, therefore, all their lives had continued to overlap to an extraordinary degree. It would take another eight months of increased emotional isolation for Coleridge, and whatever happened in Scotland in August, to change the dynamics of the relationships so profoundly that Coleridge would feel excluded: to make his fears of loss apparently come true.

III

On Tuesday 11 January 1803, in one of the very last entries in Dorothy's journal (containing her modest confession 'here ends this imperfect summary') we find an almost perfect final image of them together: literally, in memory and in longing.[19] It really is a final image: the journal stops a couple of days later, and we know relatively little subsequently about the details of the lives this biography has been about.

On 11 January, however, although fourteen miles distant, Coleridge was as much a presence in the Town End house as he had ever been, and by late afternoon the house was in typical literary activity. A letter from Keswick had arrived earlier in the day, and Dorothy's response was characteristic: 'C poorly, in bad spirits – Canaries'.[20] It was another letter of 'complainingness'.[21] But there were particular reasons for Coleridge being in a bad way. He had got soaked to the skin struggling over the Kirkstone pass to Town End the previous Thursday afternoon: 'The rain-drops were pelted, or rather *slung*, against my face, by the Gusts, just like splinters of Flint'. He had made the journey (he told Southey) because he had 'something of importance to talk to Wordsworth about', but another reason was that he had promised to escort Sara Hutchinson back up to Keswick. This he had done the following day, Friday the 7th, but on getting home had 'felt unwell all over' and had gone down with 'another sad bowel-attack' and the usual swelling of joints. The symptoms suggest that he may have resorted to opium to relieve the discomfort he had suffered, though to Tom Wedgwood he denied it.[22] What doubtless made matters still worse for him was being ill at Greta Hall, anguished and alone in his study, with Sarah absorbed in breast-feeding the new baby, and Sara Hutchinson busy looking after the other children, once again nested with her darlings: a comforting sister at least, though regularly plunged by Coleridge into the role of the ideal love.

Coleridge had written a surviving letter to Tom Wedgwood about his situation on Sunday 9 January, thus allowing us to guess something of the contents of the letter to the Wordsworths which he probably wrote 'in bad spirits' the same day, and which they got on the 11th. He had told Wedgwood that he was again baffled by his health, and was determined to try something new. He was now seriously considering whether he should go to the Canaries: would it be suitable for a sick man in winter? If, however, Wedgwood were intending to go to Italy or Sicily, then Coleridge would go with him: and when there he would 'look about for two houses – Wordsworth & his family would take the one, & I the other'.[23] So – on the one hand – Coleridge was experimenting with a new idea of solitude: a Canaries visit alone, the Wordsworths remaining in Grasmere, Sarah Coleridge staying in Keswick. This makes him sound already more detached from all his family groupings than he had been a year before. On the other hand, very little seems to have changed when it came to potential companions: his first thought took him back to the Wordsworths as his natural family.

In the morning, when they get their letters, and before Wordsworth has got up, Mary reads Chaucer aloud to Dorothy; Mary then probably does something domestic, and Dorothy sits for two hours reading Chaucer to herself, 'with exquisite pleasure', in the upstairs parlour by the fire. Wordsworth's habits are obviously unchanged by his marriage, though he also seems to have been ill with a cold and cough: he gets up even later than usual ('Wm promised me he would rise as soon as I had carried him his Breakfast but he lay in bed till between 12 & one'). But he can be forgiven: the day is 'very cold', following a day Dorothy called 'furiously cold'. Unusually, it is too cold for even the Wordsworths to venture out, although they have probably been waiting for William to get up and dressed ('the blackness of the Cold made us slow to put forward'). But eventually they have tea, and settle to household business. Mary works downstairs, probably in the parlour by the fire, or possibly by the stove in the kitchen (but not in the normally unheated bedroom). She is 'copying out Italian poems for Stuart' – including, probably, Wordsworth's translation of the Milton sonnet, for publication in October as their own anniversary present and celebration. Another copyist is now at work in the house . . . Dorothy, in the parlour upstairs, has given up reading and has probably been writing letters, but by late afternoon she is writing her journal and resolving to keep it properly again, after many lapses. She is actually writing on the very last of the usable pages in the leather-bound notebook she had been using since the spring (it had been started the day they set off with the first draft of

'The Leech-gatherer' to meet Coleridge at Wythburn): a whole volume of their life since May is drawing to a close. Dorothy is writing while sitting next to her brother, who is up and functioning at last: he is 'working on his poem to C', which we now know as *The Prelude*. In spite of the trials of friendship, this poem is being written as one of the great tributes to Coleridge. The journal, too, one of the elements of their common life, must be sustained: and Dorothy's resolution is dated and timed, exactly as Coleridge would have done it, 'I will take a nice Calais Book & <u>will</u> for the future write regularly &, if I can legibly, so much for this my resolution on Tuesday night, January 11th 1803.' They are remembering Sara Hutchinson (Dorothy had noted her letter of the previous day in the journal she is now writing), as well as Coleridge and his plans; while the special 'Calais Book' Dorothy promises herself for starting the next volume of her journal would also have reminded her of Annette and Caroline. A letter from Annette had actually come the previous day: too late to congratulate on the wedding, too early to congratulate on the expected child, though both events would have been intensely interesting to her.

But then Dorothy returns home in her thoughts, to the three of them; what will they have for supper? Molly Fisher is probably also in the house, in the kitchen, preparing supper for them. 'Now I am going to take Tapioca for my supper, & Mary an Egg, William some cold mutton – his poor Chest is tired.' *The Prelude* may be under way, but Dorothy's journal has always been as much concerned with the domestic as with the literary. And her brother has been coughing, so he gets the cold meat.

IV

Wordsworth had dreamed, in the spring of 1800, of the perfect household, the one which would make him feel rich: though the riches would (as ever) not be monetary, but the people of the significant group. For

> Such is our wealth: O Vale of Peace we are
> And must be, with Gods will, a happy band[24]

The reality had turned out, as always, stronger and stranger than the dream. Happy they may have been, but in their own peculiar way: up in Keswick, Coleridge loving Sara Hutchinson, Sara Hutchinson loving his children, Sarah Coleridge loving her children and her husband, Coleridge planning to go away on his own as soon as he could. In Town End, Dorothy loving Wordsworth, Mary loving Wordsworth, Wordsworth loving all of them, including those at Keswick.

Band, gang or group, they are thus projected into the stillness for us by Dorothy's journal: reading, writing, copying, thinking, complaining, planning: frozen for us into a final image of relationship, that cold, cold winter's day.

Appendix I

Wordsworth's 'The Leech-gatherer' in May 1802

The loss of the first full version of 'Resolution and Independence' – 'The Leech-Gatherer' of 1802 – is a major blow to Wordsworth scholarship; the poem is one of those which we know changed massively between its original conception and its final state. Wordsworth drafted the poem at the start of May, but nothing at all survives of the original draft, which we should still, however, call version one. He completed the second version a week later, and this text is peculiarly important for having been subject to criticism by SH, MH and STC to which WW responded in revision. It would be useful for the reader to have as complete a text as possible of this second version of the poem.

Fortunately, there exists a partial manuscript of the poem which SH transcribed into her notebook *Sarah Hutchinson's Poets* (DC MS 41) some time in the early summer of 1802. This manuscript has been published in facsimile in *P2V* and also edited by Jared Curtis in *Wordsworth's Experiments with Tradition* (Ithaca, 1971), pp. 186–94. This transcription represents the text which SH and MH had been sent in the middle of May. WW revised the poem extensively early in July 1802, to create what we can think of as version three (a copy of the revised poem sent to STC on 5 July 1802 was itself copied in STC's letter to the Beaumonts of 13 August 1803, and best represents this intermediate version). Eventually, after still more revision, the poem reached print in 1807 in what we can think of as version four.

The problem in attempting to recover version two, however, is that a whole leaf (11ʳ and 11ᵛ) has been torn from the notebook (DC MS 41) in which SH made her transcription of it, depriving us of nine-twentieths of the poem. Version two of the poem originally had twenty stanzas, of seven lines each; the first eight and a half survive intact in MS 41, the destruction of the leaf has deprived us of the next eight (along with two half stanzas), and we still possess the final two and a half stanzas.

All, however, is not lost. On the surviving stub of leaf in the notebook, recording where the page was torn out, twenty-seven line openings out of sixty-three (all on 11ʳ) and four closures (of especially long lines, all on 11ᵛ) survive. Closures – though few – are especially useful, as they allow us to reconstruct the rhyme scheme of a regularly rhyming seven-line stanza; while the extremely neat handwriting of SH's transcription allows us to tell exactly how many lines and stanzas were originally on the recto and verso of the now missing leaf.

In one or two cases, as Curtis showed in 1971, it has proved possible to restore almost everything which has been lost through the loss of the leaf. For example, a stanza surviving only in the form of its seven opening letters and words on the leaf stub proves to be identical (in those openings) with a stanza from version three of the poem, as copied in STC's August 1803 letter to the Beaumonts, and can safely be restored as representing something probably very close indeed to what existed in version two (see lines 71–7).

In other cases, several consecutive line openings have proved identical with those existing in version three at similar moments in the poem, and it has proved possible to reinstall lines which almost certainly existed in that (or a very similar) form in versions three (see e.g. lines 64–70 and 78–84).

Given the existence of this material, and the desirability of getting as close as we can to version two of the poem, I have endeavoured to do a conservative reconstruction of the poem, using MS 41 as my base text. In two instances, WW's letters to MH and SH of 14 June 1802 allow us to recover still further lines or words of version two (see lines 61 and 63). I have then used the text of the poem which survived into version three to reconstruct appropriate consecutive passages to fill the missing lines and stanzas: stanza 16, for example, simply imports its lines 106–9 and 111–12 from version three of the poem (lines 120–3, 139–40). In a small number of cases (especially around lines 61–4 (stanza 9), lines 89–91 (stanza 13) and lines 99–105 (stanza 15), I have endeavoured to fill in the partly surviving rhyme scheme with the kind of text which we know existed in the poem, describing the old man's life and his wife and family.

This reconstructed part is, of course, highly tendentious. There are two unanswerable questions: (i) whether the old man was further described by the narrator between lines 99 and 124, or whether he spoke (he is certainly speaking at lines 125–6 and had probably spoken throughout that stanza); (ii) whether the old man's description of his way of life extended all the way from line 99 down to line 126, or whether at some point in the missing part of the text he was interrupted by the narrator (as in version three). It seems to me likely that the description which had certainly extended from lines 56 to 98 was at an end, and that lines 99–124 were either continual speech, or speech with an interruption. I have opted for an interruption, and have used lines 120–3 and 139–40 from version three to construct it. It would of course have been possible to reconstruct the poem differently, so that lines 99–117 were all speech (either reported or direct); or with an interruption at a different point. The tiny mark of closure which appears either at line 111 or 112 – probably 111 – 'd' – may be a clue to a word such as 'renew'd' or 'pursu'd', and I have taken it as such.

The reconstructed passages – when made up of non-Wordsworthian text – are clearly marked in the text to ensure that they are not mistaken for a recov-

ery of Wordsworth's own writing, to which they are the sheerest approxima-
tion. The lines are also the weakest poetry in the poem, and draw attention to
themselves for that reason, if no other. I believe them, however, more useful
than blank spaces would have been; they are an exercise which I invite the
reader to improve upon.

In the text which follows, therefore, roman text in bold represents what SH
copied and is certainly version two: italic text in bold represents Wordsworthian text derived either word for word from version three or from the letter of
14 June 1802: italic text not in bold type (and in a smaller typeface) represents
what I have supplied myself. As SH did not in general transcribe punctuation
(if indeed any existed in WW's second version) I have removed all but the
lightest and simplest marks of punctuation from those parts of the text supplied
from version three.

The Leech-gatherer (May to June 1802)

1	**There was a roaring in the wind all night**
2	**The rain came heavily and fell in floods**
3	**But now the sun is rising calm and bright**
4	**The Birds are singing in the distant wood**
5	**Over his own sweet voice the stock-dove broods**
6	**The Jay makes answer as the Magpie chatters**
7	**And all the air is fill'd with pleasant noise of waters.**
8	**All things that love the sun are out of doors**
9	**The sky rejoices in the morning's birth**
10	**The grass is bright with rain-drops: on the moor**
11	**The Hare is running races in her mirth**
12	**And with her feet she from the plashy earth**
13	**Raises a mist which glittering in the sun**
14	**Runs with her all the way wherever she doth run.**
15	**I was a Traveller upon the moor**
16	**I saw the hare that rac'd about with joy**
17	**I heard the woods and distant waters roar**
18	**Or heard them not, as happy as a Boy**
19	**The pleasant season did my heart employ:**
20	**My old remembrances went from me wholly**
21	**And all the ways of men, so vain and melancholly.**
22	**But as it sometimes chanceth from the might**
23	**Of joy in minds that can no further go**
24	**As high as we have mounted in delight**
25	**In our dejection do we sink as low**

26   To me that morning did it happen so
27   And fears and fancies thick upon me came;
28   Dim sadness & blind thoughts I knew not nor
          could name.

29   I heard the sky lark singing in the sky
30   And I bethought me of the playful hare
31   Ev'n such a happy Child of earth am I
32   Even as these happy Creatures do I fare
33   Far from the world I live & from all care
34   But there may come another day to me
35   Solitude pain of heart distress & poverty.

36   My whole life I have liv'd in pleasant thought
37   As if life's business were a summer mood:
38   Who will not wade to seek a bridge or boat
39   How can he ever hope to cross the flood?
40   How can he e'er expect that others should
41   Build for him, sow for him, and at his call
42   Love him who for himself will take no heed at all?

43   I thought of Chatterton the marvellous Boy
44   The sleepless soul who perish'd in his pride;
45   Of Him who walk'd in glory & in joy
46   Behind his Plough upon the mountain's side
47   By our own spirits we are deified
48   We Poets in our youth begin in gladness;
49   But thereof comes in the end despondering madness.

50   Now whether it was by peculiar grace
51   A leading from above, a something given
52   Yet it befel that in that lonely place
53   When up & down my fancy thus was driven
54   And I with these untoward thoughts had striven
55   I to a lonely place, a Pond did come
56   By which an old man was, far from all house or home

57   He seem'd like one who little saw or heard
58   For chimney-nook, or bed, or coffin meet
59   A stick was in his hand wherewith he stirr'd
60   The waters of the pond beneath his feet
61   Him *did I view before I could him greet*
62   But *seeing his a plight for ever to be ruing*
63   *How came he here thought I or what can he be doing?*

64   He *seemed a Man not all alive or dead*
65   **Proud** *still in his extreme old age*
66   **But** *bent his body was, feet and head*
67   **Coming** *together in their pilgrimage*
68   **As** *from some dire constraint of pain, or rage*
69   **Of** *sickness had by him in times long past*
70   **Wh**ich *more than human weight upon his age had cast.*

71   He *wore a Cloak the same as women wear*
72   **As** *one whose blood did needful comfort lack*
73   His *face look'd pale as if it had grown fair*
74   **And** *furthermore he had upon his back*
75   **Ben**eath *his Cloak a round & bulky Pack,*
76   **A l**oad *of wool or raiment as might seem*
77   **But** *on his shoulders lay as if it clave to him.*

78   **The**n *himself unsettling, he the Pond*
79   **B**efore *me stirred and fixedly did look*
80   **Up**on *the muddy water which he conn'd*
81   **As** *if he had been reading in a book*
82   **W**ith *him such freedom as I could I took*
83   *And, drawing to his side, to him did say*
84   'T*his morning gives us promise of a glorious day.'*

85   **A** *gentle answer did the Old Man make*
86   **I**n *courteous speech which forth he slowly drew*
87   *And him with further words I thus bespake*
88   "W*hat kind of work is that which you pursue?*
89   *This is a lonesome place for one like you."*
90   *He answer'd me with pleasure and surprize*
91   *And there was while he spake a fire about his eyes.*

92   *His words came feeble, from a feeb* le *chest*
93   *Yet each in solemn order follow'd each*
94   *With something of a pompous utterance drest*
95   *Choice word and measured phrase beyond the reach*
96   *Of ordinary men; a stately speech*
97   *Such as grave Livers do in Scotland use*
98   *Religious Men who give to God and Man their* **dues.**

99   *He answered then 'I to the Pond have* **come**
100 *To gather leeches, being old and poor*
102 *That is my calling, better far than some,*
103 *Though I have many hardships to endure:*

103   *From Pond to Pond I roam from moor to moor*
104   *Housing with Gods good help as it doth come*
105   *But still preparing for my own* **last home.**'

106   *My former thoughts return'd: the fear that kills*
107   *The hope that is unwilling to be fed*
108   *Cold, pain, and labour, and all fleshly ills*
109   *And mighty Poets in their misery dead*
110   *And now, not knowing what the old Man said*
111   *While I these thoughts within myself pursu'd*
112   *My question eagerly I then renew'd.*

113   *The man was courteous, standing* **by my side**
114   *But now* **his** *voice to me was like a stream*
115   *Scarce heard, nor word from word could I divide*
116   *And the whole body of the Man did seem*
117   *Like one whom I had met with in a dream*
118   *Or like a man from some far region sent*
119   *To give me human strength, & strong admonishment.*

120   *But he, then smiling, did his words repeat*
121   *And said* '*Wheresoe'er they may be spied*
122   *I gather Leeches, stirring at my feet*
123   *The waters in the Ponds where they abide*
124   *Once I could meet with them on every side*
125   I yet can gain my bread tho' in times gone
126   I twenty could have found where now I can find one

127   Feeble I am in health these hills to climb
128   Yet I procure a Living of my own
129   This is my summer work in winter time
130   I go with godly Books from Town to Town
131   Now I am seeking Leeches up & down
132   From house to house I go from Barn to Barn
133   All over Cartmell Fells & up to Blellan Tarn.'

134   With this the Old Man other matter blended
135   Which he deliver'd with demeanour kind
136   Yet stately in the main & when he ended
137   I could have laugh'd myself to scorn to find
138   In that decrepit Man so firm a mind
139   God said I be my help & stay secure
140   I'll think of the Leech-gatherer on the lonely Moor.

Appendix II

Coleridge's 'First Dejection': 'Letter written Sunday Evening, April 4.'

The text I have presumed to call Coleridge's 'First *Dejection*' reproduces the poem which Coleridge included in his letter to William Sotheby of 19 July 1802. He quoted some 138 lines composed in what – six days earlier – he had described to Sotheby as 'a state of extreme dejection brought on in part by ill health, partly by other circumstances' (STCCL ii. 809). On the 19th itself he would describe it as 'a poem written during that dejection to Wordsworth' (STCCL ii. 814). The line numbers in the first column of the text given below are those of the Cornell MS of the *Letter*; those in the second column the line numbers of *Dejection* in the *Morning Post* text of 4 October 1802. The right hand column gives the line numbers of this particular poem.

In his letter to Sotheby, Coleridge first quoted two extracts – separated by two lines of dashes – which I have marked in the text below S^{1a} and S^{1b} respectively (lines 80–91 and 92–8). After saying that he had 'nothing better to fill the blank space of this sheet with', he then quoted two extracts from what he called 'the introduction of that Poem' (STCCL ii. 815), which I have marked S^2 and S^3 (lines 1–79 and 131–8 below). The latter extract was certainly not the Introduction but actually a version of the ending. After explaining that he was only selecting extracts from the poem, he then quoted 'as a *fragment*' (STCCL ii. 818), the part I have marked S^4 (lines 99–130 below).

It is clear from all the available evidence (and this Sotheby letter is the most convincing piece) that by 19 July a good deal – possibly all – had been written of the poem which Coleridge would give a title commemorating the date of 4 April 1802. At latest by 19 July, and perhaps provoked by the opportunity which this letter to Sotheby presented, Coleridge did what he could do to prepare a publishable text. The references to his wife and family and to Sara Hutchinson in the full-length poem (or drafts) made any more complete text not only inappropriate for Sotheby but also unpublishable. On the other hand, a man who had Coleridge's problems with actually *finishing* work may, for once, have been confronted with a different and more soluble kind of problem. Cutting down, revising and modifying a number of long drafts for a poem, to create a publishable version, was a very different matter from (say) completing *Christabel*. The letter to Sotheby shows Coleridge making what may well have been a first attempt at a public version of his poem.

One straightforward task was to ensure that there was no reference to 'Sara' in this text. Coleridge decided to use Wordsworth as the person to whom this draft of the poem was addressed (Sotheby fortunately knew Wordsworth slightly, having met him in Coleridge's company at the end of June: see STCCL ii. 813). An addressee whose name may have appeared in the drafts of the poem was Thomas Poole, but although thinking about Poole may well have played some useful part in the earlier stages of composition, Wordsworth was (for several reasons) now more appropriate as an addressee. For one thing, the addressee in all the surviving drafts needs to be more than monosyllabic: e.g. 'Sara', 'William', 'Wordsworth'. ('Poole' would not have been appropriate, though 'Thomas' would.) For another thing, Wordsworth *was* his closest friend, and many of the things which he might have said to Sara he could equally well say to Wordsworth: and (of course) vice versa; lines addressed to Poole, or Wordsworth, might also be addressed to Sara. And, of course, Sotheby – knowing Coleridge's relationship with Wordsworth – would not be surprised to find him figuring so crucially in the poem.

The address to Wordsworth instead of Poole, or Sara, actually involved making relatively few changes, but (for example) the phrase describing the moon and quoting Wordsworth's own poetry – 'Dear William's Sky-Canoe' (l. 41) – thoroughly appropriate in the drafts of a poem addressed to Sara Hutchinson recording the lives and works of the group – had to be altered. It would appear as 'a lovely sky-canoe!' in the *Morning Post* in October (l. 37), as there would be no reason why 'Edmund' (not necessarily a poet) should be linked with the line. But to Sotheby, reading a poem addressed to the poet Wordsworth, the phrase became the convincing 'thy own sweet Sky-Canoe!' (l. 41). There would, however, be problems in particular with the ending, where it would be impossible simply to adapt as an address to Wordsworth lines such as 'O dear! O innocent! O full of love!' and 'As dear as Light and Impulse from above!' (Cornell ll. 336, 338), which may have been in existence by July. I shall return to the problem of the ending in a moment.

Other tasks were more complex. Coleridge had found no way of solving the problem of how to carry the poem forwards after the passage culminating in the line 'My shaping spirit of imagination' (l. 91 below). There was some writing following that part of the poem, at least in the drafts, which he would obviously have liked to keep, in any version of it, but he had made the point to Sotheby that the poem was 'the greater part of a private nature' (STCCL ii. 815), and a good deal of this section was especially personal (in the *Letter* it described his marriage and his feelings for Sara). All he found he could do was leave a gap after l. 91 before going on to the next passage which he could use: two lines of dashes appear at this point in the letter to Sotheby. Ten days later, he had no better solution to the problem in the letter he was writing to Robert Southey in which he wanted to quote the same two passages; all he could do was insert, in the gap between them, '(Here follow a dozen Lines that would give you no pleasure & then what follows –)' (STCCL ii. 831). As Coleridge's brother-in-law, Southey would have been especially concerned by anything suggesting problems with Coleridge's marriage: and there were lines probably already written and belonging to this part of the work which described how 'two unequal minds / Meet in one House, and two discordant Wills' (Cornell ll. 243–4).

In July, however, Coleridge was still including, in his letters to Sotheby and Southey, the seven line fragment (S^{1b}) starting 'For not to think of what I needs must feel' which was clearly of considerable importance to him, but which for some reason he decided not to include in *Dejection*. Although it made no reference to Sara Hutchinson or to Sarah Coleridge, it was extremely personal to Coleridge himself.

Coleridge had done nothing else to solve the problem by October either, and after 'My shaping Spirit of Imagination!' in the *Morning Post* text he simply relied on the device he had come up with in July, of leaving a gap. In October he inserted three lines of asterisks, together with the explanation '[The sixth and seventh Stanzas omitted.]' to cover the obvious lacuna in his text. When he produced his final version of the poem, in the text of *Dejection* published in *Sibylline Leaves* in 1817, he partly solved the problem by putting back the seven-line fragment S^{1b}, being obviously happy to include what he had always thought a particularly good piece of writing. Its omission in October 1802 may well have prompted the declaration that not just one stanza but two had been removed from the text in the *Morning Post*.

II

The closeness of this version of the poem to the *Morning Post* text has not been sufficiently attended to. Of the 139 lines which would make up *Dejection* in October, 122 had previously appeared in the 138-line text of the Sotheby letter, very nearly all of them in the order in which they would appear in the *Morning Post* text, and also in a state of text remarkably close to their state in October. In all, only sixteen lines in the Sotheby text would not reappear in the poem printed in the *Morning Post*; while there would be seventeen extra lines in the *Morning Post* version of the poem which had not appeared in the Sotheby letter.

The differences mostly occurred in four particular passages.

(1) The seven lines starting 'For not to think of what I needs must feel' (92–8) in the Sotheby letter would not appear in the *Morning Post* text, for the reasons explained.

(2) A section of nine lines early in the Sotheby letter (also appearing in the manuscripts of the *Letter*) – lines 21–9 below – would be almost completely cut in the *Morning Post* (just one line survived).

(3) Four new lines would appear for the first time at the end of the first stanza of the *Morning Post* text, following l. 16 of the text in the Sotheby letter; none of these appeared in the text of the *Letter* either.

(4) Eight of the seventeen new lines of *Dejection* would appear in the ninth and last stanza in the *Morning Post*, together with another six lines also used in the *Letter* which had not appeared in the Sotheby letter. It may be that these had been written by July, but that Coleridge had not transcribed them; we should also consider the possibility that they were written after 19 July. The stanza representing the ending in the Sotheby letter (144–51) is made up of only eight lines, all but one of which would appear in some form in the *Morning Post*, but in a different order and also revised.

It thus seems fairly clear that the ending of the poem was the section of the text on which Coleridge worked between July and October, in order to prepare a text of *Dejection* for the *Morning Post*. It seems likely that the new lines were written, the extra lines added, and the slight re-ordering engineered, together with a few small cuts made, in the period between July and October.

III

The first 119 lines out of the 139 lines of *Dejection*, then, seem to have reached some state of textual stability by July, although Coleridge had made no final decision about exactly what was to follow 'My shaping Spirit of Imagination'. Far from the Sotheby letter being a random selection of bits and pieces of a long verse-letter, therefore, and the *Morning Post* text being a poem carefully reshaped and constructed out of that same verse letter, the same principle of organisation which would make *Dejection* such a good poem had also very largely constructed the poem's text in the Sotheby letter. The October printing appears to be simply a further refinement of the July text; and this has considerable consequences for how we think about the making of the whole poem, both in its form as *Dejection* and in its form as the *Letter*.

I do not believe that one question has previously been asked about the nature of the text in the Sotheby letter. Were there constraints on space in the Sotheby letter which might explain why the ending sent to Sotheby was so much briefer and less satisfactory than what would appear in the *Morning Post*, given that so much of the rest of the *Morning Post* text was clearly in position by 19 July? If there were few or no such constraints, then it is a reasonable assumption that Coleridge gave Sotheby pretty well all of the poem as he had developed it.

IV

The Sotheby letter presents two sheets of paper very nearly completely filled on both sides, partly with a letter and partly with the text of the poem. The fact that there were two sheets at all is the first significant point. At a date when the recipient paid the postage – and it was usual to employ every square inch of sheets which cost 1 shilling each to receive – Coleridge had apparently no compunction in doubling the cost of the letter to Sotheby by adding a second sheet. We can also be sure that, as early as half way down the first side of his first sheet, he had made the decision to run on to a second sheet. He failed to leave the small blank space in the middle of the right hand side of side 1 which would be needed to take the letter's seal, if it had been planned as a letter consisting of a single folded sheet of paper. He knew at that stage, therefore, that he would be using a second sheet. He may have made it sound as if the poetry were an unpremeditated addition – having 'nothing better to fill the blank space of this Sheet with' – but if he had wished to send a letter without poetry, he could easily have got the complete text of his letter on to the two sides of the first sheet, even allowing for the space necessary for address and postmark on side two. The letter would not have *needed* a second sheet if he had not previously decided to include a good deal of poetry.

The sequence of writing was as follows. He filled sheet 1, side one with the first part of his letter. He had two-thirds filled side two of sheet 1 with the continuation of his letter before starting to inscribe poetry. At this point he inscribed the S^{1a} passage (lines 80–91), then inserted his two lines of dashes, and then inserted line 105, the start of the S^{1b} passage, before going over on to the second sheet of paper for the rest of the S^{1b} passage (lines 106–11).

Up to this point he had been writing the poem into the letter without apparently taking any care over the fact that the lines of poetry by no means ran from margin to margin; they only occupied about two thirds of the space available. But as he had known from the start that he had a second sheet ahead of him, that probably did not strike him as a problem.

Having gone on to sheet 2, however, to complete the transcription of S^{1b}, he continued to write fairly sprawlingly across the page – and having inscribed line 111, he then went on with his letter for another seven lines, in the course of which he announced that – as he had 'nothing better to fill the blank space of this Sheet with' (he was only about a quarter of the way down) – he would 'transcribe the introduction of that Poem to you'.

When he re-started his transcription of the poem, however, it was in a very different style. He now made a real effort to use the space as economically as possible, and started to write in two columns. He was obviously planning to get a good deal of the poem into the letter – a great deal more than if he had continued to write sprawlingly across the sheet. On the third side of his paper, therefore, beneath ll. 106–11 and the seven lines of letter, he managed to inscribe the title ('Letter written Sunday Evening, April 4') and then lines 1–79 – thus taking himself all the way down to the passage he had originally started by transcribing, at l. 80. After a great deal of compressed writing in the left hand column, and at the top of the right hand column, there are signs of visible relaxation in the writing further down the right hand column, as if he were now sure that he would comfortably get to line 79 in the space available, thus linking up with what he had already transcribed. This he managed to do even while leaving the space necessary for the letter's seal, a space which protruded some way into the right hand column of poetry.

He had thus written out the first two thirds of the poem pretty well as it would appear in the October *Morning Post* and which I am suggesting represented its first organised version. The problem was what to do next, on the fourth side of the letter.

The fourth side of the letter would be a very different matter from the first three. It would serve as the page for the address and the postmark, and something like half of it would have to be used for that purpose. Only a strip at the top and a strip at the bottom would be available – with perhaps a little space on the extreme right hand side of the middle of the sheet, a long, narrow space which could be used for prose but would be difficult for lineated poetry.

Although knowing the limitations of the space now available, Coleridge seems to have started by not bothering about how much space he used up. At the top of the fourth side, sheet 2, he first wrote out the eight-line stanza which represented an ending for his poem – lines which would appear revised, re-ordered and supplemented as the poem's ending in the *Morning Post* – and he inscribed them in long sprawling lines similar to those he had used on side two and at the start of side three. The fact that one of the very few major corrections of the text in the entire manuscript appears in line four of this stanza – 'must' being replaced by 'dost' – perhaps confirms that this part of the poem was still textually less secure than the rest of it: that it was still being worked on.

Most significant of all, however, is the fact that there would have been a perfectly adequate amount of space at this point for him to have included not only the six lines beginning "Tis midnight, and small thoughts have I of sleep' which make such an excellent start for the last stanza of the *Morning Post* text (lines also used in the *Letter*, though not in this position, at the end of the poem), but a good deal more besides. The fact that he did not include the crucial six lines in the Sotheby letter suggests not only that the idea of adapting them for the ending had not yet occurred to Coleridge; it also raises the possibility that they were not yet even written. The fact that the stanza he actually inscribed was only eight lines long is a very strong indication that he still only had a vague idea of how he was going to finish the poem in this cut-down form, and that the twenty-line-long last stanza which would appear in the *Morning Post* – some of it already drafted in the Sotheby letter, some of it perhaps existing in the *Letter*, some of it brand new – was not yet in existence.

He had apparently decided that – as he had at least transcribed an ending – he would not worry about how much space he was now taking up. But – just as before – he then started to write out some more lines using the economical two-column format he had used on side three; this time, inserting a complete stanza (which he called 'a fragment' but which would retain that exact shape in all versions of the poem: he must have realised that it was in fact a self-contained unit) which he had probably estimated would comfortably fit into the remaining space. He used the scrap of paper to the top right of the sheet – which would not have been wide enough to write poetry into – to explain what it was he was now doing:

> I have selected from the Poem
> which was a very long one,
> & truly written only for 'the solace
> of sweet Song', all that could be
> interesting or even pleasing to
> you – except indeed, perhaps,
> I may annex as a *fragment*
> a few Lines on the Eolian lute,
> it having been introduced in
> its 'Dronings in the 1ˢᵗ Stanza.
> I have used 'Yule' for Christmas.

The stanza he had thus at the last minute decided to transcribe took up the remaining part of the upper third of the paper, and was finished in one and a quarter columns in the bottom third. His decision to include it, however, out of all the material in the *Letter* which in theory he could have used, shows how the shape of the *Dejection* poem had become clear to him; with the inclusion of this section of text, *Dejection* effectively came into being.

All the space he had now left for poetry transcription was a space which would have accommodated nine or ten lines, in the bottom right hand corner of the page. If there had been more poetry of a sufficiently compact kind, which did not take him into the 'private areas' which he was obviously not including, then he could certainly have found room for it. He could, for example, have included the ten-line stanza 19 of the *Letter* – 'With no unthankful Spirit I confess' – if he had wished to: or if it had actually existed on 19 July. But I suspect he now realised that in effect he had a poem, complete. Instead of poetry, Coleridge filled the space with prose, and finished his letter in the long narrow slip of paper in the centre of the sheet.

For all its extremely fragmentary appearance, he had (except for the last stanza) completed a version of the poem *Dejection*, and had transcribed it into his letter. There was no more he wanted to add, although there would have been space to have done so.

He was giving Sotheby the impression that he was simply giving him fragments of a much longer poem: and in one sense that was true. But he did not tell him that he was in effect making a poem out of the drafts. The exercise of making the cuts for Sotheby, however, seems to have helped Coleridge realise how he could use material from the drafts successfully; and he would shortly come up with the inspired decision either to take – or to create – the lines which formed lines 216–22 of the *Letter* and use them as the beginning of the final stanza. With that, and a few detailed revisions, the poem would be complete.

This reconstruction, therefore, offers Coleridge's first version of *Dejection* as he created it in mid-July 1802.

Coleridge's 'First *Dejection*': 'Letter written Sunday Evening, April 4.'

Cornell Nos.	*Morning Post*	Sotheby Letter		This Text
1	1	S²	Well! if the Bard was weather-wise who made	1
2	2	S²	The dear old Ballad of Sir Patrick Spence,	2
3	3	S²	This Night, so tranquil now, will not go hence	3
4	4	S²	Unrous'd by Winds, that ply a busier Trade	4
5	5	S²	Than that, which moulds yon Clouds in lazy Flakes,	5
6	6	S²	Or the dull sobbing Draft, that drones and rakes	6
7	7	S²	Upon the Strings of this Eolian Lute,	7
8	8	S²	Which better far were mute.	8
9	9	S²	For lo! the New-Moon, winter-bright:	9
10	10	S²	And overspread with phantom Light;	10
11	11	S²	(With swimming phantom light o'erspread,	11
12	12	S²	But rimm'd and circled with a silver Thread;)	12
13	13	S²	I see the old Moon in her Lap, foretelling	13
14	14	S²	The coming on of Rain & squally Blast!	14
15	15	S²	And O! that even now the Gust were swelling,	15
16	16	S²	And the slant Night-shower driving loud & fast!	16
17	21	S²	A Grief without a Pang, void, dark & drear!	17
18	22	S²	A stifling, drowsy, unimpassioned Grief,	18
19	23	S²	That finds no natural Outlet, no Relief	19
20	24	S²	In word, or Sigh, or Tear!	20
21		S²	This, William! well thou know'st,	21
22		S²	Is that sore Evil which I dread the most,	22
23		S²	And oft'nest suffer. In this heartless Mood,	23
24	26	S²	To other Thoughts by yonder Throstle woo'd	24
25		S²	That pipes within the Larch-tree, not unseen –	25
26		S²	(The Larch, that pushes out in Tassels green	26
27		S²	It's bundled Leafits) woo'd to mild Delights	27
28		S²	By all the tender Sounds & gentle Sights	28
29		S²	Of this sweet Primrose-month – & vainly woo'd!	29
30	25	S²	O dearest Poet, in this heartless Mood	30
31	27	S²	All this long Eve so balmy & serene	31

32	28	S²	Have I been gazing on the western Sky	32
33	29	S²	And it's peculiar Tint of Yellow-green –	33
34	30	S²	And still I gaze – & with how blank an eye!	34
35	31	S²	And those thin Clouds above, in flakes & Bars,	35
36	32	S²	That give away their Motion to the Stars;	36
37	33	S²	Those Stars, that glide behind them or between,	37
38	34	S²	Now sparkling, now bedimm'd, but always seen;	38
39	35	S²	Yon Crescent Moon, as fix'd as if it grew	39
40	36	S²	In it's own cloudless starless Lake of Blue –	40
41	37	S²	A Boat becalm'd! thy own sweet Sky-Canoe!	41
42	38	S²	I see them all, so excellently fair!	42
43	39	S²	I *see*, not *feel*, how beautiful they are!	43

44	40	S²	My genial Spirits fail	44
45	41	S²	And what can these avail	45
46	42	S²	To lift the smoth'ring Weight from off my Breast?	46
47	43	S²	It were a vain endeavour,	47
48	44	S²	Though I should gaze for ever	48
49	45	S²	On that green Light, that lingers in the West.	49
50	46	S²	I may not hope from outward Forms to win	50
51	47	S²	The Passion & the Life, whose Fountains are within.	51

295	48	S²	O Wordsworth! we receive but what we give,	52
296	49	S²	And in our Life alone does Nature live:	53
297	50	S²	Our's is her Wedding-garment, our's her shroud!	54
298	51	S²	And would we aught behold of higher Worth	55
299	52	S²	Than that inanimate cold World *allow'd*	56
300	53	S²	To the poor loveless ever-anxious Crowd,	57
301	54	S²	Ah! from the Soul itself must issue forth	58
302	55	S²	A light, a Glory, a fair luminous Cloud	59
303	56	S²	Enveloping the Earth!	60
304	57	S²	And from the Soul itself must there be sent	61
305	58	S²	A sweet and pow'rful Voice, of it's own Birth,	62
306	59	S²	Of all sweet Sounds the Life and Element!	63
307	60	S²	O pure of Heart! thou need'st not ask of me	64
308	61	S²	*What* this strong Music in the Soul may be –	65
309	62	S²	What and wherein it doth exist,	66
310	63	S²	This Light, this Glory, this fair luminous Mist,	67

311	64	S^2	This beautiful and beauty-making Power!	68
312	65	S^2	JOY, blameless Poet! JOY, that ne'er was given	69
313	66	S^2	Save to the Pure, and in their purest Hour,	70
314	67	S^2	Joy, William! is the Spirit & the Power	71
315	68	S^2	That wedding Nature to us gives in Dower	72
316	69	S^2	A new Earth and new Heaven	73
317	70	S^2	Undreamt of by the Sensual and the Proud!	74
318	71	S^2	JOY is that sweet Voice, Joy that luminous cloud –	75
319	72	S^2	We, we ourselves rejoice!	76
320	73	S^2	And thence comes all that charms or ear or sight,	77
321	74	S^2	All melodies an Echo of that Voice,	78
322	75	S^2	All colors a suffusion from that Light!	79

230a	76	S^{1a}	—Yes, dearest Poet, yes!	80
231	77	S^{1a}	There was a time when tho' my Path was rough,	81
232	78	S^{1a}	The Joy within me dallied with Distress,	82
233	79	S^{1a}	And all Misfortunes were but as the Stuff	83
234	80	S^{1a}	Whence Fancy made me Dreams of Happiness:	84
235	81	S^{1a}	For Hope grew round me, like the climbing Vine,	85
236	82	S^{1a}	And Fruit and Foliage, not my own, seem'd mine,	86
237	83	S^{1a}	But now Afflictions bow me down to Earth –	87
238	84	S^{1a}	Nor car'd I, that they rob me of my mirth	88
239	85	S^{1a}	But O! each Visitation	89
240	86	S^{1a}	Suspends what Nature gave me at my Birth,	90
241	87	S^{1a}	My shaping Spirit of Imagination!	91

264		S^{1b}	For not to think of what I needs must feel,	92
265		S^{1b}	But to be still & patient all I can;	93
266		S^{1b}	And haply by abstruse research to steal	94
267		S^{1b}	From my own Nature all the natural Man;	95
268		S^{1b}	This was my sole Resource, my wisest Plan –	96
269		S^{1b}	And that which suits a part infects the whole,	97
270		S^{1b}	And now is almost grown the Temper of my Soul!	98

184	88	S^4	—Nay, wherefore did I let it haunt my mind	99
185	89	S^4	This dark distressful Dream?	100

186	90	S⁴	I turn from it, & listen to the Wind	101
187	91	S⁴	Which long has rav'd unnotic'd! What a Scream	102
188	92	S⁴	Of Agony by Torture lengthen'd out	103
189	93	S⁴	That Lute sent forth! O thou wild Storm without,	104
190	94	S⁴	Bare Crag, or mountain Tairn, or blasted Tree	105
191	95	S⁴	Or Pine-grove, whither Woodman never clomb	106
192	96	S⁴	Or lonely House long held the Witches' Home,	107
193	97	S⁴	Methinks, were fitter Instruments for Thee,	108
194	98	S⁴	Mad Lutanist! that in this month of Showers,	109
195	99	S⁴	Of dark-brown Gardens & of peeping Flowers	110
196	100	S⁴	Mak'st Devil's Yule, with worse than wintry Song	111
197	101	S⁴	The Blossoms, Buds, & timorous Leaves among!	112
198	102	S⁴	Thou Actor, perfect in all tragic Sounds!	113
199	103	S⁴	Thou mighty Poet, even to Frenzy bold!	114
200	104	S⁴	What tell'st thou now about?	115
201	105	S⁴	Tis of the rushing of an Host in Rout	116
202	106	S⁴	With many Groans from men with smarting Wounds –	117
203	107	S⁴	At once they groan with Pain, & shudder with the Cold!	118
204	108	S⁴	But hush! there is a Pause of deepest Silence!	119
205	109	S⁴	Again! – but all that Noise, as of a rushing crowd,	120
206	110	S⁴	With Groans, & tremulous Shudderings, all is over;	121
207	111	S⁴	And it has other Sounds, less fearful and less loud.	122
208	112	S⁴	A tale of less affright	123
209	113	S⁴	And temper'd with delight,	124
210	114	S⁴	As thou thyself had'st fram'd the tender Lay –	125
211	115	S⁴	'Tis of a little Child	126
212	116	S⁴	Upon a heathy Wild	127
213	117	S⁴	Not far from home – but she has lost her way;	128
214	118	S⁴	And now moans low in utter Grief & Fear,	129
215	119	S⁴	And now screams loud & hopes to make her Mother hear. –	130

———

	136	S³	Calm stedfast Spirit, guided from above,	131
323	129	S³	O Wordsworth friend of my devoutest Choice	132

Acknowledgements

I owe a vast amount to previous biographers and scholars of the Wordsworths and Coleridge; in particular to the work of Kathleen Coburn, Stephen Gill, Earl Leslie Griggs, Richard Holmes, Kenneth Johnston, Mary Moorman and George Whalley. Though I have often disagreed with them, I have never failed to learn from their serious application to the job in hand. I owe a special debt to Pamela Woof, without whose meticulous work on Dorothy Wordsworth's journals I would often have been left helpless; and to Stephen Parrish, whose edition of the earliest manuscripts and printings of Coleridge's *Dejection* has been a constant source of inspiration. Parts of Chapter Four appeared in the *Cambridge Quarterly*, and I am grateful for permission to reprint them here. The University of Nottingham awarded me a semester of sabbatical leave 1997–8 and generously supplemented it with a semester of a Senior Research Fellowship; I am very grateful for these two awards.

Robert Woof and Jeff Cowton were generous with time and assistance at the Wordsworth Library in Grasmere, while Sam Lett, Tanya Flower and Michelle Kelly inexhaustibly found materials for me. I gratefully quote unpublished and original materials by permission of the Wordsworth Trust, with whom copyright and publication rights remain. Alex Black and Simon Collins both produced superb photographs for me. Lindeth Vasey and D. G. Worthen read the first draft and made helpful comments; Sam Dawson made me re-think some crucial things. David Ellis was characteristically shrewd about a draft Introduction. Peter Preston gave me his two volumes of Mary Moorman's biography of Wordsworth. John Turner and Susan Gagg listened patiently to my innocent forays into a field they know far better than I ever shall, while Carl Turner was an inspiration. Jill Farringdon was exceptionally helpful with Qsum analysis. Sue Wilson heard more of the book over her breakfast than anyone should ever be obliged to; Paul Heapy and Jane Gibson offered me wonderful, unusable titles. Claude Rawson effortlessly solved a problem. Linda Bree commented incisively on an early version and worked to find me a publisher; Andrew Brown listened to the book's story under the stars in New Mexico, and *did* help find me one. Seamus Perry gave me the best advice I have ever had from a publisher's reader; the index was compiled to her usual high standard by Christine Shuttleworth. John Nicoll was wonderfully patient and Adam Freudenheim asked searching questions, all of which badly needed answering. I am very grateful to them both. The book was written in sun, wind, snow, hail, rain, heat, dust and much anxiety, all of which my wife Cornelia Rumpf-Worthen helped me to overcome.

John Worthen
Budapest 1997–2000

Notes

Preface

1 S. Schoenbaum, *William Shakespeare: Records and Images* (Scolar Press, 1981); e.g. *Mozart: Dokumente seines Lebens*, ed. Otto Erich Deutsch and Joseph Heinz Eibl, revised edn. (Kassel, 1981).

2 Mark L. Reed, *Wordsworth: The Chronology of the Early Years, 1770–1799* (Cambridge, MA, 1967), and *Wordsworth: The Chronology of the Middle Years, 1800–1815* (Cambridge, MA, 1975).

3 S. Schoenbaum, *William Shakespeare: A Documentary Life* (Oxford, 1975).

4 Jorge Luis Borges, *Collected Fictions*, tr. Andrew Hurley (London, 1999), p. 135.

5 *Collected Fictions*, tr. Hurley, p. [325].

6 Ibid., p. [325].

7 Borges, 'The Library of Babel', *Collected Fictions*, tr. Hurley, p. 115.

8 *Journals of Dorothy Wordsworth*, ed. William Knight, 2 vols (London, 1898), pp. vii–viii. His examples of trivia do not appear in the surviving journals of Dorothy Wordsworth (hereafter DW); he was either showing his contempt for trivialities, or indicating things he had cut. We can see the kinds of cuts he made in his edition of the Grasmere journal, where the notebooks survive. He stated that 'In all cases, however, in which, a sentence or paragraph . . . are left out, the omission is indicated by mean of asterisks' (*Journals of Dorothy Wordsworth*, ed. Knight, i. viii); he did not however signal shorter cuts, of a phrase or a few words. Two pages of DW's journal were also excised after her death; the page covering STC's return to Grasmere on 6 October, down to his return to Keswick on the 9th, was removed at some date after 1851 (see DWJ 37, 183): probably because DW revealed something of STC's feelings about SC. Some passages in her surviving journals were also inked over at some stage: see e.g. DWJ 249–50. See too *Journals of Dorothy Wordsworth*, ed. Mary Moorman, Oxford, 1971, p. viii).

9 *Journals of Dorothy Wordsworth*, ed. Knight, i. 104.

10 Dorothy Wordsworth, *The Grasmere Journals*, ed. Pamela Woof (Oxford, 1991) [hereafter DWJ], p. 106.

11 DWJ 87. William Wordsworth (hereafter WW) dug in potatoes on 14 May (DWJ 100) while the peas and beans flourished up to the cold and rain at the start of July, when DW recorded 'The peas are beaten down. The Scarlet Beans want sticking' (DWJ 117). They had grown peas before, and had given them to their friends as well as eaten them themselves (see below, note 15). At least some of the 1802 peas were eatable: Coleridge (hereafter STC) made a meal out of them on 9 August (see p. 249): perhaps the final fruits of the dung.

12 See Richard Holmes, *Coleridge: Early Visions* (London, 1989) [hereafter Holmes i.], pp. 162–8.

13 DWJ 79, 82. The Olives were leaving; their daughter Sarah had died in March: see Jane West, *Delighted with Grasmere* (Upton-upon-Severn, 1993), p. 56.

14 DWJ 88.

15 See DWJ 16, 94, 97, 102, 103, 111, 117; 9; 2, 4, 7, 9, 11, 15, 16, 17. 117; 11; 11; 100; 2; 9; 2; 4; 108; 22, 96; 22, 96.

16 *Poems, in Two Volumes, and Other Poems, 1800–1807*, ed. Jared Curtis (Ithaca, 1983) [hereafter *P2V*], p. 393 (l. 181).

17 DWJ 83.

18 I shall refer to Sara(h) Coleridge (née
    Fricker) as 'Sarah' [hereafter SC], and to
    Sara(h) Hutchinson as 'Sara' [hereafter
    SH]. STC delighted in their names, but
    preferred the spelling 'Sara' for both.
    See his comment to his old friend (and
    his wife's brother-in-law) Robert
    Southey of 29 July 1802: 'why, dear
    Southey! will you write it always, Sara*h*?
    – Sara, methinks, is associated with
    times that you & I cannot & do not wish
    ever to forget' (*The Collected Letters of
    Samuel Taylor Coleridge*, ed. Earl Leslie
    Griggs, Oxford, 1956–71, 6 vols. [here-
    after STCCL], ii. 830). As he wrote a
    poem to 'Asra' – SH – it seems sensible
    to retain that spelling for her.

19 See *Coleridge's Dejection*, ed. Stephen
    Maxfield Parrish (Cornell, 1988) [here-
    after *Dejection*] (ll. 271, 243–4, 41, 210,
    323, 157–8, 100, 104–5, 323, 337, 254);
    DWJ 89.

20 *Samuel Taylor Coleridge, The Complete
    Poems*, ed. William Keach (Penguin
    Books, 1997) [hereafter STCCP], p. 138;
    'The Nightingale' was 'A Conversa-
    tional Poem' in its 1798 subtitle and 'A
    Conversation Poem' in 1817 (STCCP
    244).

21 STC knew that it would be the wedding
    day at least four days before the event
    (STCCL ii. 874), and probably earlier. In
    all, twenty-five poems, epigrams and
    verse scraps by STC were published in
    the *Morning Post* between 6 September
    and 19 October, and five substantial
    pieces of prose; the publication of *Dejec-
    tion* (by far the most substantial of the
    poems) on the 4th must have been the
    result of a particular request.

22 STCCL i. 355; STC repeated the date to
    James Gillman (*The Life of Samuel Taylor
    Coleridge*, 1838, p. 11). His father had
    actually died on 6 October (see Norman
    Fruman, *Coleridge, The Damaged
    Archangel*, New York, 1971 [hereafter
    Fruman], p. 567).

23 He used it as the title for his third
    chapter of *Romanticism and the Forms
    of Ruin* (Princeton, 1981) [hereafter
    McFarland].

24 See George Eliot, *Middlemarch* (1872),
    chap. xix.

25 There have of course been group
    biographies; a recent one which lies
    close to my area of concern is Kathleen
    Jones's *A Passionate Sisterhood* (London,
    1997) [hereafter Jones]. The book
    draws, however, almost exclusively
    upon secondary sources, contains many
    inaccuracies (e.g. a letter misdated by
    two years), and is unreliable on many
    key issues.

26 For a WW biographer on e.g. STC's
    Dejection, see Mary Moorman, *William
    Wordsworth A Biography* (Oxford, 1957)
    [hereafter Moorman], i. 528–9; for an
    STC biographer, see Holmes i. 316–20.
    Stephen Gill pursues his usual policy of
    showing up STC's failures as well as
    WW's: see *William Wordsworth: A Life*
    (Oxford, 1989) [hereafter Gill], pp.
    205–6. For Fruman, see e.g. chap. 19,
    'The Annus Mirabilis Begins'.

27 Cf. Gene W. Ruoff: 'the
    Wordsworth/Coleridge industry . . .
    has increasingly devoted more attention
    to questions of mutual influence than to
    biography' (*Wordsworth and Coleridge:
    The Making of the Major Lyrics
    1802–1804* (New Brunswick, 1989)
    [hereafter Ruoff], p. 13). E.g. Juliet
    Barker's generally excellent biography
    Wordsworth: A Life (London, 2000)
    [hereafter Barker] is extremely unsym-
    pathetic to STC; she denounces his
    'incredible lack of sensitivity' (284) and
    'incomparable insensitivity' (296), and
    assumes that he was 'drawn inexorably'
    by an 'almost pathological desire for
    self-destruction' (279). In his dealings
    with WW she constantly sees 'jealousy'
    (287, 296) and she even blames STC for
    making DW so miserable in October
    1801 'that she too had resorted to lau-
    danum' (281), where there is no evi-
    dence of DW suffering anything more
    than a pain which she treated in her
    usual way (see e.g. DWJ 33, 35, 101).

28 Holmes i. 283, 295.

29 McFarland 101.

30 Molly Lefebure, *The Bondage of Love: A
    Life of Mrs Samuel Taylor Coleridge*
    (London, 1986) [hereafter *BL*], p. 132.

31 Gill also believes the 'Christabel'
    affair in October 1800 'unquestionably

marked a severance' (Gill 187), while Paul Magnuson identifies the autumn of 1800 as the time when 'Literary disagreements . . . proliferated' and STC's 'friendship with Wordsworth cooled' (*Coleridge and Wordsworth: A Lyrical Dialogue*, Princeton, 1988 [hereafter Magnuson]); he calls the chapter in which he describes these things 'A Farewell to Coleridge', although his own reading of the poetry shows how deeply the relationship of the texts continued. But part of his evidence for the 'Farewell' – 'In the fall of 1800 Coleridge's visits to Dove Cottage became less and less frequent' – is not true: see DWJ 28–35. From December 1800 we know less about STC's visits simply because the journal DW kept between 23 December 1800 and 10 October 1801 is missing, and – anyway – as Magnuson himself points out, STC was ill (Magnuson 228–9, 262).

32 STCCL i. 592 n. By STC's own admission, part II of 'Christabel' was only half finished.

33 McFarland 101.

34 Holmes i. 283–6; *BL* 132; McFarland 101 n. 146.

35 DWJ 24–5.

36 Holmes i. 284.

37 Holmes i. 285–6.

38 STC and WW planned a joint edition of 'Christabel' and *The Pedlar* (a poem by WW also omitted from the 1800 *Lyrical Ballads*): the decision to omit 'Christabel' on 6 October immediately followed a reading of *The Pedlar*, and may well have been linked with the question of what to do with both poems. Nothing came of the plan, but it is wrong to decry the possibility of other forms of publication as Holmes does ('The only substitute scheme that emerged was that "Christabel" should be printed the following year in a luxury edition with "The Pedlar"; but this was never done' – Holmes i. 284). Less than two years before, Joseph Johnson – 'perhaps the greatest radical publisher of his day' (Holmes i. 201) – had published an edition of three of STC's poems ('Fears in Solitude', 'France: an Ode' and 'Frost

at Midnight') in London as a quarto pamphlet, whereas none of WW's poems had ever been published in such a way. If STC could have finished 'Christabel', he might have been able to publish it; he had better London contacts than WW, although by 1800 they may have been becoming disillusioned over his failures to produce promised work (see Holmes i. 286). In March 1801, at any rate, he decided to print 'Christabel' 'by itself', and himself approached a publisher (STCCL ii. 707, 716).

39 *The Notebooks of Samuel Taylor Coleridge*, ed. Kathleen Coburn et al. (1957–) [hereafter STCNB], 834 4.117: the full entry runs: 'He knew not what to do – something, he felt, must be done – he rose, drew his writing-desk suddenly before him – sate down, took the pen – & found that he knew not what to do.'

40 STCCL i. 642–6. Only two essays materialised, one printed on 3 October and one (dated 8 October) on 14 October.

41 STCCL i. 643.

42 See STCCL i. 592–3.

43 Lefebure comments that STC 'had a strong streak of masochism in his make-up' and was 'increasingly prepared to dedicate himself to the establishment of Wordsworth's reputation at the cost of irreparably damaging his own' (*BL* 132); Griggs also testifies to 'Coleridge's utter disregard of anything but Wordsworth's reputation' (STCCL i. 592).

44 What began as George Whalley's reading of the episode in *Coleridge and Sara Hutchinson and the Asra Poems* (Toronto, 1955) [hereafter Whalley] – 'Wordsworth decided not to print it' (p. 39) – has become the standard account; see e.g. Ted Hughes's introduction to *A Choice of Coleridge's Verse* (London, 1996), p. 59n.

45 Moorman i. 489–90.

46 Moorman i. 490.

47 Gill 187.

48 Moorman i. 570–1; see Robert Woof, 'Wordsworth and Stuart's Newspapers:

1797–1803', *Studies in Bibliography*, xv (1962), 149–89.

49 See pp. 138–41.

50 DWJ 24; STCCL i. 628–9.

51 *The Letters of William and Dorothy Wordsworth, The Early Years, 1787–1805*, ed. Chester L. Shaver (Oxford, 1967), [hereafter LWDW i.], p. 305.

52 LWDW i. 305–6.

53 *William Wordsworth: The Poems*, ed. John O. Hayden, 2 vols (Harmondsworth, 1977) [hereafter WWTP], i. 472.

54 DWJ 26–7.

55 DWJ 27.

56 DWJ 28.

57 See my essay 'The Necessary Ignorance of the Biographer', in *The Art of Literary Biography*, ed. John Batchelor (Oxford, 1995), pp. 227–44.

58 No single body of texts exists within which one can follow a constant (or interweaving) connection. No matter where one starts, other texts – preceding or subsequent – might always be considered. Most accounts of the spring of 1802, for example, play down WW's *The Pedlar*; Magnuson suggests that STC 'must have been disappointed' (277) with it; as he himself finds it 'relatively unimpressive' (276) he assumes that STC would also have done so. Yet WW worked extremely hard on it between December 1801 and March 1802 and did some more work in July 1802 (see DWJ 49–50, 76, 118).

59 E.g. the autobiographical letters STC wrote at Nether Stowey 1797–98 (see STCCL i. 302–3, 310–12, 346–8, 352–5, 387–9); while WW's own accounts of the importance of his childhood occupy a good deal of *The Prelude*.

60 I am not going to distinguish the 'great' writing of Wordsworth and Coleridge from the less great. As late as 1970, William Heath wrote a very good book about the same people with whom I am concerned, but – at that date – had to make his focus the great poems which the two men wrote and the 'literary relations' between them. There could be no other focus for the University Press which was publishing him. See *Wordsworth and Coleridge: A Study of their Literary Relations in 1801–1802* (Oxford, 1970) [hereafter Heath].

61 Just as the 'constant light' in the cottage in his poem 'Michael' – 'so regular / And so far seen' – shines out (WWTP i. 458).

62 'Prospectus', MS I (ll. 58–71): ll. 1029–42 of *Home at Grasmere*, ed. Beth Darlington (Ithaca, 1977) [hereafter *HaG*] p. 261: text slightly adjusted to what I judge WW left as his final reading text, ready for copying or printing.

63 See, however, George Dekker, *Coleridge and the Literature of Sensibility* (London, 1978) [hereafter Dekker], p. 43.

64 As a result of their affair in Blois, Annette Vallon had given birth to a baby girl in December 1792, but WW had either never seen his daughter or can only have seen her very briefly, in October 1793. Kenneth R. Johnston argues that he got to Paris in 1793, but not to Blois (*The Hidden Wordsworth: Poet, Lover, Rebel, Spy*, New York, 1998 [hereafter Johnston], pp. 358–400). At all events, he would effectively meet her for the first time in August 1802.

65 LWDW i. 359.

66 The Wordsworth establishment as WW and DW had organised it since 1794 was founded on that very common basis of the unmarried daughter taking care of the house of her unmarried brother, in return for his financial support: exactly as the Hutchinson family had organised itself. For STC's loss of the sister who might have done the same for him see Chapter Three note 16.

67 DWJ 126.

68 OED2 I.1.c.; cf. 'A Man's a Man' ('Man to Man, the world o'er, / Shall brothers be for a' that').

69 *HaG* 381–3 (ll. 864–71).

70 STCNB 1065 21.190.

71 STCCL i. 818: see Appendix II.

72 *Dejection* 129, 131 (ll. 322, 337).

73 LWDW i. 350. With this number of sisters and brothers all simultaneously aware of each other, we might recall the narrator of 'We are Seven' trying to

keep count: 'Sisters and brothers, little maid, / How many may you be?' (*LB* 66, ll. 13–14).

74 STCNB 2537 17.95.

75 'W + D + M = W + STC + SH = Εηορεητασδ' (STCNB 2623 18.1) WW is made up of WW, DW and MW: see too Chapter Four note 109, Chapter Ten note 101 and p. 248; *HaG* 373, 377 (ll. 820, 823); LWDW i. 571.

76 Gill 127.

77 'A Soliloquy of the full Moon', STCCP 311 (l. 27).

78 See OED2, II 10b for this 17th century meaning.

Chapter One

1 Cf. WW for an account of going up Dunmail Raise:

> though tough
> The road we travel, steep and rough.
> Though Rydal heights and
>   Dunmail-raise,
> And all their fellow Banks and Braes,
> Full often make you stretch and strain,
> And halt for breath, and halt again . . .

(*Benjamin the Waggoner*, ed. Paul F. Betz, Ithaca 1981, p. 55, 1819 text, ll. 138–43.)

2 See DWJ 37 for a seven-hour journey on 10 October 1801. In spring and summer they could do it in a long afternoon – on 19 April 1801, e.g., 'We left home at one o'clock on Sunday – and reached Keswick at about six' (LWDW i. 330). On a mild spring evening with a full moon, however, they could set off from Keswick at half-past five, take many breaks along the way and still get home by midnight (LWDW i. 331). About a mile and a half up from Town End was the Simpsons' house at High Broadrain, where WW and DW sometimes paused on the way home before tackling the final stretch down to Town End.

3 In one way of arguing – superlatively well expressed in the *Letter* and *Dejection* – Nature is defined by human beings: it is something humans themselves effectively make, so that one finds 'Nature' operating in the lives of people,

not in some way outside them, or upon them. It is in our lives alone that 'Nature' lives: we define it, not the other way around. WW's *Ode* of 1804 directly opposes this point of view: Nature is an extraordinary power, and ordinary things such as streams and fields impress us with their glory and splendour: they radiate, in fact, 'celestial light' and give us an impression of supernatural forces, rather than simply being natural things. WW mourned the fact that such a visionary awareness of the world (the word he uses three times for our experience is 'glory') does not last. The child experiences it; at some stage, adults lose it, though they retain a crucial memory of it, which goes on affecting them. WW's own poem says that he has lost it. Part of the stimulus for his *Ode* was the fact that STC had been thinking, and finding ways of believing, something so different from what he himself (perhaps under pressure from STC) found he believed. But it is also important that the version of the poem which we have was written after the birth of WW's own first child.

4 Ll. 6–8, 20–4 of MS B, *HaG* 273, 277.

5 DWJ 132, 156n, 60.

6 Dove Cottage [hereafter DC] MS 38, 15r, final readings; the spring 1802 version of 'There is a little unpretending Rill' (*P2V* 647). See DWJ 91 for the stream turning into a waterfall after heavy rain.

7 'Its last surviving licence was issued in 1793' (DWJ 148); it had apparently been empty for some years when WW and DW rented it at the end of 1799.

8 WW and STC stayed in Grasmere 3–5 November 1799 with JW; when JW had to leave, they stayed on 5–8 by themselves, again at Robert Newton's inn. They then went to Keswick over Dunmail Raise; some of the patterns of the next three years thus being established.

9 STC would himself think of Mary Hutchinson [hereafter MH and after 4 × 1802 MW], SH, WW and DW as living happily together and also used the word 'abiding':

When thou, and with thee those,
  whom tho lov'sd best
Shall dwell together in one quiet
  Home
One home the sure *Abiding* Home
  of All.   (*Dejection* 27 (ll. 133–5)

10   Ll. 165–70 of MS B, *HaG* 293.
11   SC to Mrs George Coleridge, 10 Sep-
     tember 1800, HRHRC (UT).
12   LWDW i. 661; Stopford Brooke gave it
     the name in 1890 (DWJ 140).
13   Ll. 165–70 of MS B, *HaG* 293.
14   STCCL ii. 1026. The house in 1799
     comprised three downstairs rooms: a
     back kitchen (10 ft. × 12 ft.), with a small
     buttery opening off it (where the inn's
     beer would have been kept: a stream
     under the floor kept the room cool
     summer and winter), and the two wood-
     panelled, stone-flagged public rooms of
     the *Dove and Olive Branch*. They made
     the larger (rather dark, 15 ft. × 11.5 ft.),
     into which the house door opened,
     the downstairs parlour, often used for
     women's work of sewing and copying;
     the other (11 ft. × 11.5 ft.) became DW's
     'lodging room'. In the summer of 1802
     this became WW's bedroom, and in
     October 1802 MW and WW's bedroom.
     There were four rooms upstairs: the
     upstairs parlour, light and airy (15 ft. ×
     12 ft.), where WW worked and into
     which guests would be invited, a front
     'lodging room' with two beds (11.5 ft. ×
     11.5 ft.), which male guests could share
     (until 1802) with WW, and which
     became DW's bedroom in the summer
     of 1802, a 'sort of lumber room' at the
     back (10 ft. × 11 ft.) which also eventu-
     ally became a lodging-room, and a low
     'unceiled' room (9 ft. × 7.5 ft.) in the
     'outjutting' (LWDW i. 622) over the
     buttery, which DW lined with news-
     paper and which they called the news-
     paper room; they put a new window
     into this in June 1800 (DWJ 158), clearly
     visible in the *c.* 1806 picture of Town
     End by Amos Green (Illustration 13),
     and it could be used as an extra
     bedroom when the house was filled
     (they were expecting STC, SC and the
     children in the summer of 1800).

15   Gill 166.
16   Ll. 873–4 of MS B, *HaG* 383.
17   *HaG* ll. 722–3, 807–8, 818–20;
     Wordsworth: Play and Politics (London,
     1986), p. 199.
18   STCNB 579. 5. 74.
19   See e.g. STCNB 1208 2.4 and 1209 2.5,
     and STCCL ii. 836–7.
20   Susan Levin assumes that the naming of
     places – as recorded in DW's journal –
     represents DW's 'need to control . . .
     nature's autonomous process' (*Dorothy
     Wordsworth & Romanticism*, New
     Brunswick, 1987 [hereafter Levin], p.
     15); an example of what goes wrong
     when the psychology of the individual
     is the biographical starting point, rather
     than the habits of a group.
21   LWDW i. 560.
22   See DWJ 15, 16 and 101. Mary Point
     was a 'heath-clad Rock' in Bainriggs
     Wood at the foot of Grasmere; the
     'eminence' nearby was named after SH.
     See 'Forth from a Jutting Ridge' and
     DWJ 161; 'while thence they gazed /
     The blooming heath their couch, gazed,
     side by side, / In speechless admiration.
     I, a witness / And frequent sharer of their
     calm delight / With thankful heart, to
     either Eminence / Gave the baptismal
     name each Sister bore' (WWTP ii.
     895–6). They were 'Up-led with mutual
     help', says WW: they helped each other
     and yet somehow ended up on different
     peaks. It looks rather as if – one peak
     having been named after one sister – the
     other peak had to be named too.
23   DWJ 26.
24   See DWJ 37, 41, 74, 104. Almost imme-
     diately after they heard of JW's death in
     1805, WW wrote to Southey: 'We see
     nothing here that does not remind us
     of our dear brother; there is nothing
     about us (save the children, whom he
     had not seen) that he has not know
     n or loved' (LWDW i. 542). Two of the
     three poems he wrote on JW's death
     ('Sweet Flower! belike one day to have',
     'I only look'd for pain and grief')
     focused upon Grasmere itself ('Our
     home and his, his heart's delight') and
     Grisedale Tarn, where they saw him for
     the very last time ('The precious spot is

all my own . . .'). They thought for a
while, in the spring of 1805, of leaving
Grasmere because of these associations:
DW wrote to Mrs John Marshall: 'when
I am walking out in this Vale once so
full of joy . . . I can turn to no object
that does not remind me of our loss. I
see nothing that he would not have
loved with me and enjoyed had he been
by my side . . . he loved our cottage, he
helped us to furnish it, and to make the
gardens – trees are growing now which
he planted' (LWDW i. 559–60). In the
garden at Town End was for example
'John's Rose tree' (DWJ 104).

25 LWDW i. 332: in the part of Lady Wood
above the Wishing Gate, on the road
leading south from Town End, near the
eastern shore of Grasmere lake. See
WW's poem 'When first I journey'd
hither, to a home' for a description of
how JW had made the Grove his own.

26 DWJ 39.

27 LWDW i. 332–3.

28 *HaG* 724.

29 See p. 182.

30 See WWTP i. 445–7 and DWJ 84. Not
only people's names were given:
another rock was christened 'Glow-
worm Rock' (DWJ 91); 'We have been in
the habit of calling it Glow-worm rock
from the number of glow-worms we
have often seen hanging on it' (see DWJ
217n, 219n, 221n): WW's poem on
the 'Glow-worm' ('Among All Lovely
Things') was written on 12 April 1802.
They referred to Easedale, the north-
western arm of the Grasmere valley, as
'the Black Quarter' (DWJ 4, 149). On
the other hand, they apparently had no
name for their house at Town End: see
above, note 12.

31 DWJ 61, 199.

32 DWJ 182n, 76.

33 Ll. 84–6.

34 LWDW i. 304–6; WWTP i. 472.

35 DWJ 90. Cf. WW's poem 'The Waterfall
and the Eglantine' in *Lyrical Ballads*, ed.
R. L. Brett and A. R. Jones (London,
1991) [hereafter *LB*], pp. 155–6.

36 DWJ 90–1. STC recorded it purely
botanically: 'Friday, April 23rd 1802,
discovered the Double-bower among

Rydale Rocks – Ivy, Oak, Hawthorn,
Mountain Ash, Common ash – Holly,
Yews – / Fern & Wild Sage, Juniper, &c.
Carpet of Moss – & Rocks /' (STCNB
1164).

37 Cf. the same pattern in a letter DW
wrote in 1793 to her friend Jane Pollard:

The evening is a lovely one, and I
have strolled into a neighbouring
meadow . . . But oh how imperfect is
my pleasure! I am *alone*; why are not
you seated with me? and my dear
William why is not he here also? I
could almost fancy that I see you
both near me. I have chosen a bank
where I have room to spare for a
resting-place for each of you. I hear
you point out a spot where, if we
could erect a little cottage and call it
our own we should be the happiest of
human beings. (LWDW i. 97)

38 *HaG* ll. 155–8.

39 DWJ 74: his preparations for the
journey and concern to 'settle the dress'
also suggest a social event.

40 STCCL ii. 830.

41 STCCL ii. 778.

42 STCCL ii. 875.

43 STCCL ii. 888.

44 STCCL ii. 876.

45 STCCL ii. 787.

46 STCCL ii. 813 (see 808 n. 2); 829–30.

47 STCCL 829–30 n. 5.

48 STCCL ii. 782.

49 STCCL ii. 776.

50 Notebook entries 1070–1 suggest a vast
range of reading but are in fact the
result of a close reading of Cave's Bibli-
ographies, although – as Kathleen
Coburn points out – 'He is reading
closely, for the facts he gathers in this
entry are well embedded in Cave's
work' (STCNB 1071 21.196n).

51 STCCL ii. 783.

52 STCCL i. 172.

53 STCCL ii. 832.

54 STCCL ii. 783.

55 STCCL i. 629.

56 STCCL ii. 784.

57 STCCL iii. 630.

58 His eventual hatred for them may

be gauged from the extraordinary entry of 3 November 1810, concluding – in one of many self-pitying conclusions – that 'what many circumstances ought to have let me see long ago, the events of the last year, and emphatically of the last month, have now forced me to perceive – No one on earth has ever LOVED me.' (STCNB 4006 M 17)

59 'I griev'd for Buonaparte' (*P2V* 146–7, 157–8), *Morning Post*, 16 September 1802. 'If grief dismiss me', 'Dear Child of Nature' and 'Calm is all nature as a resting wheel' (WWTP i. 89, *P2V* 231, 146–7) had all appeared in the *Morning Post* (2, 12 and 13 February 1802), but anonymously.

60 STCCL ii. 913: i.e. 'confined to a particular sect'.

61 See pp. 6–10.

62 Holmes i. 194n.

63 WWTP ii. 801.

64 *P2V* 125, l. 43.

65 See Dekker 58–100.

66 *P2V* 582, l. 47.

67 LWDW i. 189.

68 *LB* 214, l. 10.

69 *P2V* 583 (ll. 59–61).

70 See e.g. STCCP 498–9.

71 STCCL ii. 830.

72 STCCL ii. 812.

73 'Dulce est inter amicos rarissimâ Dissensione condiri plurimas consensiones' (STCCL ii. 812).

74 STCCL ii. 830–1.

75 Holmes i. 325.

76 See pp. 248–9.

77 LWDW i. 343.

78 Cf. WW's 'We are Seven' and the early WW poems which STC published in the *Morning Post* in 1798: 'Beauty and Moonlight' became STC's 'Lewti'. See Holmes i. 43n, McFarland 95, WWTP i. 947n and 46, STCP 458 and 253.

79 DC MS 40: with chain lines, watermarked with a fleur-de-lys, measuring 27.3 × 43.9 cm. See Robert Woof, 'A Coleridge-Wordsworth Manuscript and "Sara Hutchinson's Poets"', *Studies in Bibliography*, xix (1966), 226–31.

80 The poem was not that enclosed in his letter to DW which arrived on 13

April, and which WW referred to in his letter of 16 April as having a 'first fragment' and 'the 2nd' (LWDW i. 347): 'The Full Moon in a Passion' is complete.

81 See *P2V* 589.

82 DC MS 40. The STC poem was not printed until 1955.

83 'To a Butterfly', *P2V* 203 (ll. 4, 6).

84 The others are 'There is a little unpretending rill' in DC MS 14, and her copies of the poem written by Brothers Water in the letters to STC and MH of 16 April (LWDW i. 348–9, 352).

85 DWJ 15, 35 (31 July 1800, 17 October 1801).

86 DWJ 82, 91 (26 March, 26 April).

87 LWDW i. 338; DWJ 65.

88 DWJ 65, 66, 67, 70, 71, 74, 75, 76, 78.

89 See *The Ruined Cottage* and *The Pedlar*, ed. Butler, pp. 24–6.

90 DC G Papers; the other letter is of 16 April (LWDW i. 349–52).

91 SH had at some point made a copy of the poem ('Stay near me – do not take thy flight') in its two-stanza form on the page she numbered '6' in DC MS 41. There would not have been room for the third stanza to have been added after the insertion at the bottom of that page of 'Extempore', written on 26 March. This shows that 'Extempore' was sent before the sheet with 'To a Cuckow' and the third stanza of the Butterfly poem. SH inserted 'To a Cuckow' on p. 22 of DC MS 41.

92 The sheet was probably originally 30–2 cm. high × 19.3 cm. wide; the surviving fragment is 7.2 cm × 19.3 cm., and thus probably represents a little less than the bottom quarter of the original sheet. There is no watermark visible.

93 DWJ 88. This was what we now know as the second 'To a Butterfly' poem, starting 'I've watched you now a full half hour'.

94 The idea DW and WW developed of staying at Gallow Hill on their way to France may have originated during the visit to MH which WW paid 7–12 April.

95 DWJ 121. The letter of 14 June 1802 from DW and WW to MH and SH (LWDW i. 361–8) is addressed simply to 'Miss Hutchinson' (i.e. Mary, the elder sister) but is to them both: it starts 'My beloved Friends . . .'

96 See p. 116.

97 By October 1803, WW's new friends the Beaumonts were also helping; a letter filled with DW's copies of his poetry ended 'If you think either you or Lady Beaumont that these two last Sonnets [patriotic calls to action: 'To the Men of Kent' and 'Anticipation'] are worth publication, would you have the goodness to circulate them in any way you like?' (LWDW i. 411).

98 DC MS 41. A recent editor referred to MS 41 as 'a MS notebook or keepsake of Sara Hutchinson' (STCCP 557), but a keepsake is 'a gift that evokes memories of a person with which it is associated'. There is no reason for making that assumption about SH and STC: and the notebook contains even more work by WW than by STC.

99 Whalley 3–4.

100 In DC MS 41 then follow 'The Language of Birds', 'Tranquillity – an Ode', 'Ode after Bathing', 'Inscription on a jutting Stone, over a Spring', 'The Picture', 'Song from Lessing', 'Psyche', 'Hope and Time' and 'The Keepsake'. The eleventh poem is 'The Devil's Thoughts' by Southey and STC together.

101 DC MS 40; Jonathan Wordsworth, *William Wordsworth: The Borders of Vision* (Oxford, 1982) [hereafter *BV*], p. 171.

102 She copied an intermediate state of the text, when it had the two opening stanzas appearing in the *Morning Post* in December 1801 (but not in subsequent texts) but lacking the final ten lines; the text probably dates some time before December 1801.

103 See p. 186; l. 36 (see above p. 24).

104 He wrote about it as an image of creative life and freshness beneath a placid surface, constant pulsing change miraculously covered by absolute stillness: a 'spring with the little tiny cone of loose sand ever rising & sinking at the bottom, but its surface without a wrinkle.—W.W. M.H. D.W. S.H.' (STCNB 980 21.132).

105 Poems seven to nine of those by STC (two short poems and an unpublished fragment) have nothing to do with SH. The tenth poem, 'The Keepsake', has the date of its publication in the *Morning Post* added (17 September 1802), but its text does not derive from the *Morning Post*; SH may have entered it in her notebook at any time between 1802 and 1810. It was the one most obviously addressed to her. Its inclusion, however, after the fragment poems – and with the publication noted – suggests that it was not one of the same sequence of poems. The eleventh poem was probably added by STC either in 1804, or 1806–7, or at Allan Bank, 1808–10.

106 She copied it on to the same sheet.

107 The last poem – WW's 'Praised be the Art' – was written in 1811 and presumably transcribed into the old notebook around then. The WW poems she transcribed in 1802 were: 'Alice Fell', 'The Emigrant Mother', 'To a Butterfly' ['Stay near'], 'Extempore' ['My heart leaps up'], 'The Sailor's Mother', 'Redbreast and Butterfly', 'Beggars', 'To a Butterfly' ['I've watched'], 'Repentance', 'Among all lovely things', 'The Cock is crowing', 'The Sparrow's Nest', 'The Leech-gatherer', 'To a Cuckow', 'I griev'd for Buonaparte, 'The Tinker', 'To a Skylark', 'Stanzas written in . . . Thomson's Castle of Indolence', 'That is work which I am ruing', 'Travelling', 'The sun has long been set', 'These chairs they have no words', 'I have thoughts that are fed by the sun', 'A Farewell'. For WW's copy of Anderson see DWJ 187; see too Chapter Five note 15.

108 Curtis has suggested that SH was operating some principle of selection in her choice of pieces for her book: 'The common element in most of the Wordsworth poems . . . is their source in familial or familiar occasions that were shared by or known to the

Hutchinsons' (*P2V* 4). Whalley's effort to determine 'the reason for the selection' of STC's poems by SH concluded 'At first reading, the Coleridge poems in *Sarah Hutchinson's Poets* seem to be a random selection: when we reflect more closely upon them, we discern a compact and intricate coherence which arises not from the way the selection was made but from the informing impulse of the poems themselves' (Whalley 97–8). But it is probable that there was *no* principle of selection beyond the preservation of poetry collected from the manuscripts WW and STC had sent.

109 DWJ 68.
110 DC MS 40.
111 The most astonishing home-made booklet of all would be DC MS 44, the collection of almost the complete corpus of WW's unpublished poems which DW and MW compiled between 6 and 18 March 1804, for STC to take to Malta.
112 *The Letters of John Wordsworth*, ed. Carl H. Ketcham (Ithaca, 1969), p. 116.
113 DWJ 89; see Illustration 18.
114 LWDW i. 298: STC had noted in July 1800 how WW 'meditates more than his side permits him even to attempt' (STCCL i. 613).
115 LWDW i. 407.
116 STC i. 659 n.
117 *The Letters of John Wordsworth*, ed. Ketcham, p. 105.
118 LWDW i. 402.
119 STCCL i. 403–5.
120 LWDW i. 367.

Chapter Two

1 *The Letters of Sarah Hutchinson from 1800 to 1835*, ed. Kathleen Coburn (London, 1954) [hereafter LSH], p. 3. SH and MH seem to have exchanged housekeeping duties regularly; e.g. at the end of July 1801 SH had been housekeeping at Bishop Middleham.
2 *HaG* 385 (l. 905).
3 See e.g. DWJ 59.
4 Cf. STC's outburst to William Godwin of April 1801: 'I feel the utmost aversion at writing an unnecessary Letter since

the increase of the postage, that brutal Tax upon the affections & understanding! You need not be half as poor as I am; & yet look *blank* & fretful on any *idle* Letter, that has taken a shilling from your pocket' (STCCL ii. 724).

5 DWJ 73.
6 DWJ 114, 8, 81.
7 DWJ 111, 84; letter from Jessie Harden (1804) quoted in Daphne Foskett, *John Harden of Brathay Hall 1772–1847* (Kendal, 1974), p. 20.
8 Hardwicke Drummond Rawnsley, *Reminiscences of Wordsworth among the peasantry of Westmoreland* (1968) [hereafter Rawnsley], pp. 13, 22, 17.
9 DWJ 57.
10 LWDW i. 336, 342 and n. 3; DWJ 61–2, 68; LWDW i. 337, 385.
11 Gill 169.
12 Rawnsley 27.
13 *P2V* 283 (ll. 1–4).
14 DWJ 79.
15 *Journals of Dorothy Wordsworth*, ed. Mary Moorman (Oxford, 1971), p. 96 n. 3.
16 DWJ 68; James Butler suggests that a fair-copy manuscript 'was accidentally destroyed or misplaced' (*The Ruined Cottage* and *The Pedlar*, ed. James Butler (Ithaca: Cornell University Press, 1979), p. 28), though in a house as compact as the Wordsworths', something would probably only finally be 'misplaced' because it *had* been destroyed.
17 DWJ 31.
18 Rawnsley 37.
19 STCCL i. 459.
20 Gill 127; Robert Gittings and Jo Manton, *Dorothy Wordsworth* (Oxford, 1985) [hereafter Gittings and Manton], pp. 105–6.
21 DWJ 70.
22 F. W. Bateson argued for incestuous feelings between them in *Wordsworth: A Re-Interpretation* (London, 1954), and in rather vaguer terms many critics and biographers have followed him. Gill states that the relationship between DW and WW was not only 'exceptionally intense' but 'unquestionably, profoundly sexual' (Gill 203): he does not explain what that means. John Mahoney, in *William Wordsworth: A Poetic Life* (New

York, 1997), says that there is 'no existing evidence of a sexual relationship', thus ingeniously implying that the evidence has been destroyed; but he also states that the couple were 'unquestionably, some might say excessively, close as brother and sister' (pp. 50–1). Again, he leaves it to the reader's imagination to decide what 'excessively' might actually mean. The word 'unquestionably' employed by both Mahoney and Gill is a way of leaving the questions they raise wide (and intriguingly) open. Johnston suggests that lying on the ground and thinking about death (see DWJ 92) 'seems to have been a form of therapy for subduing their strong erotic attraction to each other' (779), which sounds bizarre; but although critics have shown what they thought was DW's erotic attraction to WW, from her journal, I know of no evidence purporting to show his to her: 'to each other' is a biographer's invention. Other critics are cruder: Richard Matlak remarks that WW 'treated his sister very dearly, and . . . had a sexual relationship in France with Annette Vallon who seems to have been a woman very much like Dorothy' (Matlak 17); obviously incest displaced.

23 DWJ 61, 74, 69, 79. The fact that at some stage the words in bold in the following sentence were crossed out in DW's journal shows some extraordinary over-sensitivity: 'We went to bed pretty soon **and we slept better than we expected & had no bad dreams**' (DWJ 70, 206).

24 There was an old man from Up Lyme
 Who married three wives at a time.
  When asked 'why the third?'
  He replied 'One's absurd:
 And bigamy, sir, is a crime.'

25 STCCL i. no. 195; l. 45.
26 See DWJ 64–5. Mrs Olivia Lloyd, wife of Charles Lloyd, had (with her husband), moved to Ambleside in the autumn of 1800 because of their friendship with STC. For a while during 1801 she had been on friendly terms with the Wordsworths too but 'a coolness developed' (DWJ 151); when the Lloyds called, one day in June 1802, DW noted cheerfully 'luckily we did not see them' (LWDW i. 362). They were obliged to remain sociable, however; Charles Lloyd's sister Priscilla had married WW's and DW's brother Christopher. If Mrs Lloyd shared her husband's opinion of WW ('not a man after my own heart – I always feel myself depressed in his society') she probably did not stay long on 1 March either.

27 Cf. eight weeks later: 'The copses green*ish*, hawthorn green' (DWJ 93).
28 Levin 4.
29 Hunter Davies reported that, in the late 1970s, her journals sold more than any other book in the Dove Cottage bookshop (Davies, *William Wordsworth*, London, 1980 [hereafter Davies], p. 133).
30 See e.g. Levin's account (Levin 12–15).
31 Gittings and Manton 146.
32 *Journals of Dorothy Wordsworth*, ed. Moorman, p. 1.
33 Gittings and Manton 76; Gill 128.
34 STCCL i. 330. Holmes usefully describes an electrometer – 'a tiny piece of exquisite gold foil in a glass vacuum, responding to minute fluctuations of an external electrical charge' (Holmes i. 154) – but does not make the crucial point that the electrometer does not just respond, but *measures* a current of electricity. Sir Humphry Davy's electrometer, described in 1812, 'consists of two gold leaves attached to a metal plate' (*Chemical Philosophy*, 128). STC told Thomas Wedgwood in October 1802 that – in matters of 'the sentiment, the imagery, the flow of a Poem' – he, too, was 'a perfect electrometer' (STCCL ii. 876–7): he registered, measured and judged these things to perfection. STC's use is unique and characteristic in using a scientific implement (the word dating from 1749) figuratively.
35 STCNB 13 G.5, 14 G.6.
36 STCNB 202 G.198; 179 G.174.
37 STCNB 213 G.209, 217 G.213. In perhaps the most interesting of this cluster of entries – though not one

which actually contains much description of nature –

> Hartley fell down & hurt himself – I caught him up crying & screaming – & ran out of doors with him – The moon caught his eye – he ceased crying immediately – & his eyes & the tears in them, how they glittered in the Moonlight! (STCNB 219 G.215).

38 Gill 126. Probably in the sense of OED2 5: 'fig. Glowing with passion, animated by keen desire; intensely eager, zealous, fervent, fervid'. But the word also suggested fierceness and rage on the edge of madness: both Pope and Dryden used the phrase 'ardent eyes' thus (see OED2).

39 *Journals of Dorothy Wordsworth*, p. 4 n. 4.

40 *P2V* 273 (l. 66).

41 *Journals of Dorothy Wordsworth*, p. 9; STCCP 189 (ll. 48–52).

42 Levin 14. How criticism and biography see this relationship depends on their period. Mary Moorman, writing in the mid-1950s, assumed that (except in one instance) the debt *must* have been DW's, and STC the originator: she expressed surprise that 'Some have even surmised' the contrary (Moorman i. 343). When confronting compelling evidence to the contrary (STC was away from Nether Stowey when DW made her entries for 25, 27 and 31 January) she remarked 'we are therefore faced with the probability that . . . Coleridge was actually drawing on Dorothy's journal' (Moorman i. 357). Being 'faced with' such a probability was clearly something for which she needed to brace herself. By the 1980s, the boot was on the other foot; scholars naturally assumed that DW's journal came first and the men's poems afterwards: see, e.g. Levin's statement 'The words that compose the Alfoxden journal also compose William's and Coleridge's poems' (13). Although Levin admits the 'mutual development of a vocabulary' between DW and WW she also declares that 'Often Dorothy works with words

or subjects well before William' (14). A 'mutual' vocabulary and the uncertain evidence of the chronology of the poetry preclude such certainty: the only evidence she gives is of WW copying out the first sentences of the journal into his own notebook, and STC using the image of the leaf in 'Christabel'. It seems important not to prioritise either men or women because of the obvious superiority of their gender.

43 STCCP 153 (ll. 202, 204).

44 STCCP 152 (l. 176).

45 *Journals of Dorothy Wordsworth*, p. 2; WWTP i. 262; *Journals of Dorothy Wordsworth*, p. 3; STCCP 187 (ll. 18–19); STCNB 216 G.212.

46 DWJ 24; STCNB 769 5½.25.

47 Gittings and Manton 80.

48 DWJ 1.

49 DWJ 2–3.

50 DWJ 3.

51 E. de Selincourt, *Dorothy Wordsworth* (London, 1933), p. 78.

52 DWJ 145 (cf. entry for 12 September 1800). See too Gittings and Manton 77.

53 See p. 199.

54 DWJ 85.

55 In the 1802 revision of the Preface, 'kindred': the use of his own 'kin's' journal would have made the pun particularly appropriate.

56 *LB* 266.

57 I owe it to Hunter Davies that I understand the phrase not as one describing a theoretical process but as one describing the work of a writer; though I do not entirely agree with his account (Davies 126–7).

58 *P2V* 207 (ll. 1–18).

59 *BV* 149, 152; though see too pp. 170–1.

60 See DWJ 145n, 198n.

61 The story described how a turtle dove adopted a mouse as its partner. WW and DW had only returned on 25 January from a period away, during which they spent time with Thomas Wilkinson (DWJ 56); if Barbara had been a relation of his (e.g. an unmarried sister), he might have been the source of the anecdote. Alternatively, they had been to tea with the Oliffs on the 28th and 'talked a

while'; the story may have been told there.

62 DWJ 9.

63 Pamela Woof demonstrates DW's care with this entry:

> she inserted 'before me' to define where precisely she saw the two boys; replaced the pronoun 'her' with 'the woman who had called at the door'; crossed out 'at Ambleside' where the boys 'sauntered so long' and replaced it with the phrase 'in their road'; and inserted the phrases 'through Ambleside' and 'in the street' to define precisely where she met the mother on her return. (DWJ 157n)

64 DWJ 77.

65 DWJ 77.

66 DWJ 78.

67 DWJ 87.

68 WW to STC, 16 iv 1802 (DC MS), LWDW i. 348–9: *P2V* 206–7 (ll. 1–20).

69 DWJ 86.

70 N.b. the characteristic title 'Written while resting on the Bridge near the foot of Brother's Water, between one and two o'clock at Noon April ⟨15⟩16th. 1802' (WW to STC, DC MS). It was published as 'Written in March, While resting on the Bridge at the Foot of Brother's Water.' Although written in April, to a reader it was more convincingly March.

71 Pamela Woof makes this claim ('D's account owes something to W's prior composition'); see DWJ 217n.

72 See Epilogue note 2.

73 *P2V* 138–9, 459–60 (ll. 5–10: variants from DC MS 44).

74 DWJ 128. WW's 1827 revision recovered another word ('groves') from the journal entry, as well as inserting 'citadels' (cf. 'Castles'): but other features of the journal's language were lost ('the western sky', 'Minaret', 'distinct'):

> Yet did the glowing west with
>   marvellous power
> Salute us; there stood Indian citadel,

> Temple of Greece, and minster with
>   its tower
> Substantially expressed – a place
>   for bell
> Or clock to toll from! Many a
>   tempting isle,
> With groves that never were
>   imagined, lay
> 'Mid seas how stedfast! (WWTP
>   580–1)

75 WWTP 997n.

76 Arthur Hugh Clough, 'Say not the struggle nought availeth' (1849), l. 16.

77 DWJ 82.

78 DWJ 82.

79 STCCP 231, ll. 13–16.

80 See too Chapter Seven section IV.

81 LWDW i. 401, 353.

82 See DWJ 53; they paid £1–11 odd, suggesting thirty-plus letters, to people other than STC (the carter Fletcher would have been paid for carrying their letters to him). See too DWJ 39.

83 LWDW i. 362.

84 Robert Matlak lists 'letters of biographical interest; about 170 printed pages of journals of natural description and daily life; an occasional poem; and a few children's stories' (p. 3). He is using the Moorman edition of the Alfoxden and Grasmere journals (166 pages in all) and so forgets her other journals (the 1820 Continental journal by itself made a book of 336 pages). She also wrote at least thirty poems: see Levin 175–237.

85 In the letter to MH composed on the evening of the 16th, DW wrote 'I went into the garden and I think things have come on nicely, but there was not much daylight to see by, and the moon had not reached it' (LWDW i. 352); in her journal she remarked 'The Garden looked pretty in the half moonlight half daylight' (DWJ 87). If the moonlight had really reached the garden, that sentence was written later; but it also reads far more like a careful construction, as on the 16th itself there clearly *was* no 'half moonlight half daylight'.

86 The Ashburners lived across the road

in Town End: Thomas and Peggy Ashburner had five daughters, four of whom (Aggy, Jane, Molly and Sally) at different times worked for WW and DW. Molly Fisher (1741–1808) was their regular servant, however: for 2s. a week she cleaned, lit the fires, washed dishes, prepared vegetables and helped with the washing.

87 See LSH and *The Letters of Mary Wordsworth 1800–1855*, ed. Mary E. Burton (Oxford, 1958). Fifty-one letters from John Wordsworth survive, but only five from 1802; see *The Letters of John Wordsworth*, ed. Carl H. Ketcham (Ithaca, 1969), pp. 125–35.

88 Levin points to a sentence from May 1802 – 'He completely finished his poems I finished Derwent's frocks' (DWJ 123) – as evidence that DW does not find her household role 'a situation she can accept easily . . . neither Dorothy nor the reader can be totally convinced that sewing and writing are equal' (Levin 24–5). The construction of the sentence, on the contrary, demonstrates that she *does* find them parallel, and that equality has nothing to do with it. DW has work to do, and she does it.

89 STCCL ii. 788.

90 LSH xxvii.

91 DWJ 73.

92 STCCL ii. 779, 786.

93 DWJ 72.

Chapter Three

1 On 19 February he had told SC that he would be leaving London on 5 March and getting back to Keswick on the 7th (STCCL ii. 786); a few days later he told her about WW's marriage, and announced that he would now be travelling back via Derby and staying there a few days too, on the road to York, thus buying himself still a few more days unqueried absence (STCCL ii. 789).

2 *Dejection* 27, l. 128.

3 STCNB 1912 9.33.

4 LWDW i. 189.

5 WW was also a parent, but inaccessibly and (for the most part) theoretically: see Preface note 63.

6 STCCL ii. 740.

7 LWDW i. 339.

8 STCCL i. 562, 571.

9 See Preface note 8.

10 See pp. 27–8.

11 STCCL ii. 776.

12 STCCL ii. 762.

13 STCCL ii. 767.

14 *Dejection* 31 (ll. 242–6).

15 STCCL ii. 875.

16 He also had three half-sisters (all married before he was born), but Nancy was his only sister to survive childhood: 'she loved me dearly and I doted on her!' (Holmes i. 15) STC had written about her illness in 1789 (see 'Life', STCCP 10) and her death in 1791 (see 'On Receiving an Account that his only sister's death was inevitable' and 'On seeing a Youth affectionately welcomed by a sister' (STCCP 24–5).

17 STCCL ii. 876. Holmes says 'There was a recurrence of domestic rows' in the autumn of 1802 (Holmes i. 336), but the letter to Wedgwood shows that these 'screams of passion' belonged to the end of 1801 and the spring and summer of 1802.

18 STCNB 979 21.131.

19 STCNB 979 21.131. There were two brothers Le Grice at Christ's Hospital with STC, the elder Charles Valentine, and Samuel (who joined the army and died in the West Indies), but Charles Lamb's reference to Samuel as 'ill capable of enduring the slights poor Sizars are sometimes subject to in our seats of learning' and as 'sanguine' and 'volatile' ('Christ's Hospital, Five and Thirty Years Ago', *Essays of Elia*) suggests he was in STC's mind.

20 STCCL ii. 747. For the humour, see STC's notebook for December 1800: 'Sara sent twice for the measure of George's Neck – he wondered, Sara should be such a fool, she might have measured William's or Coleridge's, as all poets' Thropples were of one Size' (STCNB 873 1.27).

21 STCNB 979 21.131.

22 Holmes i. 306.

23 STCCL ii. 894.

24 E.g. *BL* 95, 139.

25   LWDW i. 117, 300.
26   STC in 1807 described SC's objections
     to separation: 'that it will not look
     respectable for her, is the sum into which
     all her objections resolve themselves'
     (STCCL iii. 7–8).
27   Davies 287.
28   Rawnsley 14.
29   Thomas de Quincey, *Works*, ii. 64–5.
     DW was probably De Quincey's
     original source.
30   LWDW i. 368, 364.
31   Thomas de Quincey, *Works*, ii. 64–5.
32   The rent became £8 when WW got
     married; but they also paid 6s. window
     tax a year (DWJ 148).
33   STCCL ii. 789 and i. 303.
34   STCCL ii. 881.
35   STCCL ii. 908.
36   STCCL ii. 788.
37   DWJ 82.
38   *BL* 127. Lefebure puts the move down
     entirely to pressure from DW and WW:
     she refers to 'a species of tug-of-war . . .
     with Coleridge as the prize' (*BL* 126)
     taking place between the Wordsworths
     and Thomas Poole.
39   LWDW i. 298.
40   LWDW i. 381; DW's is also probably the
     glee of one living in an ex-inn thinking
     of SC in 'Greta Hall'.
41   LWDW i. 336.
42   *BL* 127 (Harry Ransom Humanities
     Research Centre, University of Texas).
     Cf. STCCL i. 562: 'Sara being Sara, and
     I being I, we must live in a town or else
     close to one, so that she may have
     neighbours and acquaintances'.
43   STCCL i. 644.
44   DWJ 46.
45   As can still be seen in one unpainted
     and preserved patch in the kitchen.
46   DWJ 37. William Jackson (the
     Coleridges' landlord) lived in the other
     half of Greta Hall.
47   LWDW i. 330.
48   A fiddle-faddler is 'a foolish trifler', and
     to fiddle-faddle is 'to be busy about
     petty trifles'; but to faddle is also 'to
     make much of a child; pet, caress'
     (OED2). So – while faddling – Sarah
     fiddle-faddles.
49   DW would be thoroughly critical of

MW's insistence on breast-feeding,
and commented in 1806, after the birth
of Thomas (MW's third child): 'I am
very sure that she is not fit to suckle her
child many months; and that if we
were to suffer her to go on after her
own inclinations she would in a very
few years be worn out . . . William has
made up his mind. Well or ill, she is to
wean the child at six months' (LWDW
ii. 50).
50   *BL* 152.
51   In 1807, STC would tell his brother
     George that 'The few friends, who have
     been Witnesses of my domestic Life,
     have long advised separation, as the
     necessary condition of every thing
     desirable for me' (STCCL iii. 7). He
     probably means the Wordsworths in
     1806. Whether they did so in 1802 is
     more doubtful.
52   LWDW i. 351.
53   DWJ 83, 46.
54   LWDW i. 166. She explained further:
     'We teach him nothing at present but
     what he learns from the evidence of his
     senses. He has an insatiable curiosity
     which we are always careful to satisfy to
     the best of our ability . . . He knows his
     letters, but we have not attempted any
     further step in the path of *book learning*.
     Our grand study has been to make him
     happy in which we not been altogether
     disappointed . . .' (LWDW i. 180)
55   LWDW i. 396; *BL* 192.
56   STCCL ii. 782.
57   STCCL iii. 489–90.
58   STCNB 3304.23.8.
59   WW knew this pattern: if, in the
     summer of 1801, STC entered on some
     engagement with a bookseller to
     produce a book, the worry about it
     would prevent him writing the book: it
     would be 'an engagement which it is
     ten to one he would be unable to fulfil
     and what is far worse, the engagement
     while useless in itself would prevent him
     from doing any thing else.' (LWDW
     i. 340).
60   STCCL ii. 875.
61   See *BL* 144–5.
62   See Bate's *Coleridge* (1968) [hereafter
     Bate], pp. 101–6. Griggs' *Collected Letters*

contains a useful footnote (STCCL 731 n. 1). Lefebure was professionally understanding and (to a surprising degree) judgmental about it in 1974 and 1986. Richard Holmes's early STC is addicted and suffers nightmares, but withdrawal symptoms do not play a very large part in his account. The overdosing STC of the later years is marvellously depicted in his second volume.

63 Bate 102.

64 Holmes i. 297: see STCCL ii. 661, 663, 665.

65 LWDW i. 338–9; STCCL ii. 719.

66 STC made a note for a recipe for 'the gutta Asiatica or black Drop' late in 1807 (STCNB 3161 12.22). See too Lefebure, *Samuel Taylor Coleridge: A Bondage of Opium* (London, 1974) [hereafter *BO*], pp. 493–5, and STCCL ii. 1019.

67 STCCL ii. 731–2.

68 STCCL ii. 1019.

69 STCCL iii. 496; iv. 627.

70 Holmes i. 297.

71 STCCL ii. 721.

72 STCCL iii. 490.

73 'In 1825 Kendal Black Drop sold at eleven shillings for a phial of four ounces . . . and would seem to have been much the same price from the commencement of its manufacture in the late eighteenth century' (*BL* 134).

74 STCCL ii. 722.

75 STCNB 1577 21.297; STCCL vi. 894.

76 LWDW i. 330.

77 LWDW i. 362; STCCL iv. 630.

78 STCCL ii. 740.

79 STCCL iii. 310.

80 *Dejection* 32 (ll. 277–82).

81 'But they pluck out the wing-feathers from the mind——' (STCCL ii. 1173).

82 Fruman says 'his love for his children in an unhappy marriage' was responsible (p. 360): it was not his love for them but the demands he felt they made on him.

83 See e.g. STCCL ii. 917 ('playing . . . rompingly with Hartley & Derwent'). In 1808, SH described how she could hear STC 'making racket enough for twenty with Sissy [Dora Wordsworth, aged 4] below – he does tieze her in such a way

for she cannot be too naughty for his taste; he calls her "beautiful Cat of the Mountain" & she is more like a cat with him than any thing else . . . ' (LSH 12). Making his children rowdy was yet another way of asserting his commitment to a lack of restraint in upbringing which SC's child-care inhibited.

84 STCCL i. 572.

85 STCCL ii. 799; he may mean 'disapproved of', but may be using the word in its older and stronger meaning of 'prayed against as an evil'.

86 STCCL ii. 828.

87 *Dejection* 29 (ll. 179–82).

Chapter Four

1 Holmes i. 316.

2 See pp. 20–1.

3 Whalley 36. Holmes describes how SH 'then twenty-four, looked on with sunny, sceptical amusement' and how STC 'did not disappoint.' (Holmes i. 246).

4 STCCL i. 545; STCNB 1587 21.310.

5 STCNB 576 5.71, 577 5.72, 578 5.73.

6 STCNB 1575 21.296(a). Holmes translates the Latin elegantly:

> and I held Sara's hand for a long time behind my back, and then for the first time, Love pierced me with its dart, envenomed, and alas! incurable. (Holmes i. 250)

Whether he held her hand behind his back or behind her back, or whether just secretly, is however unclear. 'Pierced' is also more dramatic (and significant) than 'pricked'; while Coleridge does *not* say 'envenomed, and alas! incurable'; he says 'envenomed, alas! and incurable'. See too p. 268.

7 The phrase 'train of thoughts', which STC makes not just an image of mental process but a picture of the convolutions of the living brain, was initiated by Thomas Hobbes: 'By . . . Trayne of Thoughts, I understand that succession of one Thought to another, which is called (to distinguish it from Discourse in words) Mental Discourse' (*Leviathan*, i. iii. 8).

8   STCCP 318, l. 36.

9   STCNB 3472 62.4.

10 His 1808–10 'Definition of Love' supplies a highly significant definition of what, by that date, had become his idea of love:

> whether my love has not been <u>love</u> –
> I <u>love</u> <u>you</u> <u>as</u> <u>a</u> <u>man</u> <u>loves</u> <u>a</u> <u>w</u> it is true,
> but yet <u>I</u> <u>love</u> <u>you</u> – that is, <u>I</u> wish <u>to</u>
> <u>be</u> <u>made</u> <u>happy</u> by <u>you</u>, and only <u>by</u>
> <u>you</u> can have the <u>happiness</u> <u>I</u> <u>wish</u>
> . . . (STCNB 3472 62.4)

STC's experiences in 1799 must be understood through the events and language of 1799, and not from those of a later period.

11 STCCL i. 546 n.; Holmes i. 250.

12 STCCP 331 (ll. 13–16). It appeared in the *Morning Post* on 21 December 1799 and found its way into the 1800 *Lyrical Ballads (LB* 119–23).

13 STCCP 334, between ll. 80 and 81.

14 Cf. 'the first of many poems Coleridge was to write to or about Sara' (Whalley 38).

15 In 1929, T. M. Raysor counted fifteen 'Asra' poems (with eight fragments) but in 1955 Whalley added another thirty 'which can now be identified as referring to or inspired by Sara Hutchinson' (p. 151); he included some 'simply because they combine the theme of hope or love with an acute sense of loss' (p. 152), adding e.g. 'The Happy Husband' (resolutely in favour of the married state) as an 'Asra Poem'. See next note for a briefer list. Holmes is misled by Whalley into dating 'The Keepsake' to 1800 and describing it as 'the first of the "Asra" poems – poems secretly dedicated to Sara Hutchinson' (Holmes i. 250). There was no secrecy (the poem was published in the *Morning Post* on 17 September 1802) but also no dedication. 'The Keepsake', mentioning as it does the auburn hair which is one of the few physical attributes we can be certain that SH possessed, is a better candidate than most for a poem to her. And yet it is a poem STC was perfectly prepared to publish, whereas the publi-

cation of a poem such as 'To Asra' would have been deeply embarrassing to STC, SH and SC. It is the *idea* of the beloved's name being worked on silk in her own 'auburn hair', along with the flowers she knows her lover likes best, which matters more than anything else. The poem develops a sentimental idea: it does not describe anything which actually happened. And the description of 'Emmeline' –

> In the cool morning's Twilight
>   early wak'd
> By her full bosom's joyous
>   Restlessness
> Leaving the soft Bed to her
>   sleeping Sister
> Lightly she rose . . .
> There in that Bower, where first
>   she own'd her Love,
> And let me kiss my own warm Tears
>   of Joy
> From off her glowing [. . .]

is a poetic creation rather than a description. Are women really woken up by the restlessness of their full bosoms? Sara Hutchinson was solid and small, not Junoesque: it is hard to see her being woken up like that. When she copied the poem into *Sarah Hutchinson's Poets*, she omitted the last word completely (the published versions have 'cheek'). She may have been censoring the word, believing that even poetical fancy should have its limits ('cheek' being right in the sense it would, unfortunately, only acquire in the 1850s).

16 See Whalley 154. The only STC poems possibly addressed to SH are 'To Asra' (STCCP 315), 'A Day Dream' (STCCP 313–14), 'The Day-Dream' (STCCP 314–15), the *Letter* and 'The Keepsake' (STCCP 317–18). No other candidates do more than suggest the problems or satisfactions of love, and cannot be directly linked to SH. It is striking that although he wrote 'To Asahara' in a dedication to her in December 1800, he did not use the 'Asra' form of the name in his notebooks until August and

October 1803 (STCNB 1451 7.4 and 1577 21.297). It is an interesting but unprovable possibility that STC only started to use it himself around then, and that the poem 'To Asra' (variously dated between 1799 and 1804, but first appearing pasted into a copy of 'Christabel' which STC gave to SH in 1804) therefore belongs to 1803 or 1804. The name also appears in the poem 'A Day Dream' which in its original form dates from 27 March 1802, but we have no text of the poem before its appearance in the *Bijou* in 1828; it seems probable that the 'Asra' form of the name was a revision. Biographers and critics use the name indiscriminately, however: see e.g. Whalley passim and Holmes i. 295, 299.

17 STCNB 718 5½.1.
18 Lefebure invents a visit paid by STC to SH, for her to give it to him, for which there is no evidence (*BL* 142). Holmes postulates either a flying visit, or Mary Hutchinson bringing 'this teasing memento from Sockburn' (Holmes i. 270).
19 Holmes omits 'Mr Coleridge' from his record of the entry (Holmes i. 270), which allows him to develop the 'keepsake' theory.
20 E.g. Johnston's passing reference to Earl Henry, in Coleridge's play *The Triumph of Loyalty* (written in the summer of 1800), feeling 'an impossible love for his queen, doubtless reflecting some of Coleridge's passion for Sara Hutchinson' (Johnston 720).
21 *The Prelude 1799, 1805, 1850*, ed. Jonathan Wordsworth, M. H. Abrams and Stephen Gill (New York, 1979), p. 432 (XI 317); Moorman, i. 78.
22 Gill 37.
23 Moorman i. 78.
24 See Chapter One note 78; see too Moorman i. 77.
25 LLWMW 61–2.
26 Gill 117.
27 Elizabeth Monkhouse (1750–1828).
28 See STCNB 999 21.151 and DWJ 183; DW commented 'expecting Mary' on 25 October (DWJ 36) but the fact that

they had the Clarksons as visitors from 28 October to 5 November may have prevented an invitation to another visitor.

29 DWJ 37, 183, 32. A letter which DW sent while SH was there was headed 'Miss Hutchinson or Mr Coleridge' (LWDW i. 319).
30 STCCW xii. 1. 227. Holmes's version of the episode – for which the only evidence is the inscription STC made in the copy of the book he gave to SH on 19 December 1801 – turns it into 'a winter afternoon at Grasmere spent reading Bartram's *Travels* with Asra': the *whole* afternoon is thus employed, and the intimacy involved in 'reading . . . with' contradicts the actual evidence of 'read to you parts of the "Introduction"' (xii. l. 227). As the book only arrived in January 1801, the episode must have been in the period February–April 1801.
31 See pp. 23–4.
32 STCCL ii. 762 n. 1, Dekker 44.
33 Whalley 35–9, 44, Ruoff 83.
34 Holmes i. 294.
35 *BL* 143. The quotation she gives – STCCL iii. 814 – belongs to a letter of 1810 and does not refer to SH.
36 Parrish 9.
37 LWDW i. 330.
38 *BL* 133–8; STCCL ii. 726.
39 STCCL ii. 726.
40 LWDW i. 339.
41 See pp. 86–9; LWDW i. 330.
42 STCCL nos. 429, 441, 442, 448 and 453.
43 *Dejection* 34, l. 325.
44 STCCL ii. 747.
45 Southey would not have minded confidences about SC (cf. STCCL ii. 767, 774–5), but declarations of love for SH would have been a different matter.
46 STCCL ii. 761.
47 Holmes i. 305.
48 Holmes i. 307, Whalley 40–1, STCCL ii. 753–5, STCNB 973A 22.1. The books were returned to the library on 24 August.
49 STCCL ii. 753.
50 STCCL ii. 767.
51 See p. 74. Barker, however, declares this

the moment when his 'interest' in SH 'had turned to obsession' (280): see note 53.

52   STCCL ii. 774–5.

53   DWJ 37. His visit to Grasmere of 6–9 November 1801 was recorded on one of the two pages torn out of the journal: see Preface note 8. See DWJ 37 and 183. Barker comments 'one can only presume it included the revelation of Coleridge's love for Sara' (281); it was rather more likely to have contained indiscretions about SC. For the word 'nervous' see Chapter Eight note 6.

54   STCNB 986 21.138, 1032 6.39.

55   STCCL ii. 760.

56   The fact that STC's surviving letters to SH were so often mutilated suggested to Griggs – when taken with the notebook entry (STCNB 1601 21.361) – 'the intimate nature of their letters' (STCCL ii. 780). But it only suggests the intimate nature of STC's letters. It says nothing about SH's letters. The passages missing from STC's letters were more likely to have been removed not because of the state of SH's feelings revealed in them but because of the potentially adulterous nature of *his*.

57   Holmes i. 307; Whalley suggests that 'To Asra' was a product of the visit and that 'The first consistent use of the "Asra" anagram belongs to this summer' (Whalley 41).

58   Holmes i. 307, Whalley 125n.

59   Lefebure insists that 'The Day-Dream' is 1798 work, addressed to SC, and that in 'A Day Dream' STC was using poetry originally addressed to one Sara(h) to flatter another. John Beer dates 'A Day Dream' 27 March 1802, following advice from the Bollingen editor J. C. C. Mays (see S. T. Coleridge, *Poems*, ed. John Beer, rev. ed., Everyman's Library, 1993); a version of ll. 5–6 of 'The Day-Dream' appears in STCNB 1105 6.59 and dates from January–February 1802.

60   STCNB 985 21.137. Holmes cuts out the central section and thus changes its meaning, which is about seeing a face in the darkness ('twas all spectral'). His

version emphasises the face and the bed, and runs:

> Prest to my bosom & felt there – it was quite dark. I looked intensely towards her face – & sometimes I *saw it* – so vivid was the spectrum … sopha / Lazy Bed – Green – the fits of Light & Dark from the Candle going out in the Socket – Power of association – that last Image how lovely to me now. (Holmes i. 307–8)

61   Rosemary Ashton describes STC's notebook as 'full of references to the "dearly beloved Darling"' and cites this entry (Ashton 198). There is in fact only one reference to her, made in Keswick in the autumn of 1801 (STCNB 984 21.136).

62   Holmes i. 307.

63   'The Day-Dream', Cornell MS, *Dejection* 141, 142 (ll. 7–9, 19–22).

64   See note 16.

65   STCCP 314 (ll. 20–30).

66   Magnuson 294.

67   STCCP 313, l. 12.

68   STCNB 1156 6.147.

69   *Dejection* 26 (ll. 99–107).

70   STCNB 3708 18.21.

71   STCCP 313.

72   STCNB 3304.23.7.

73   Whalley 42, *BL* 149, Jones 139, Holmes i. 316.

74   *BL* 153, repeated by Jones 129. The speculation is based upon the fact that – writing to SC on 24 February 1802, and spinning her fantasies about his flirtation with various London ladies of fashion – STC remarked 'I won't tell you her name / you might perhaps take it into your head to write an Anonymous Letter to her' (STCCL ii. 789).

75   Holmes i. 337. This fabrication (which has given a huge boost to the importance of SH in STC's life late in 1802) originates in the standard edition of STC's letters edited by Griggs. The surviving fragments of letters between STC and SC in the winter of 1802–3 are prefaced by a note to no. 466:

Undoubtedly the missing passages in this letter included an account of the time Coleridge spent in the company of Sara Hutchinson at Penrith on his way to London. The letters immediately following show that Mrs. Coleridge, cognizant of her husband's intimacy with Sara Hutchinson and thoroughly angered by it, wrote in high dudgeon of this visit. Thus Coleridge was led to berate his wife for her jealousy . . . (STCCL ii. 879–80)

On 4 November 1802, SH was in Penrith, travelling westward via her aunt towards Keswick (DWJ 134) and Grasmere (DWJ 135); STC was waiting for a mail coach to London ('went to Penrith, could not get a place in the Mail – passed the day with Sara at Miss Monkhouse's' – STCNB 1261 8.10). The meeting exactly corresponded to the one on 14 November 1801 when STC – en route to London – saw SH for the day in Penrith; the 1801 meeting proved by the fact that SH made a number of entries in STC's notebook (STCNB 1007 21.159 to 1010 21.162). STC and SH probably met fortuitously in 1802; STC's plan to travel had been made only the previous day (STCCL ii. 878–9). SH went to Keswick on the 8th, to stay (as obviously arranged before) with SC for one or two weeks: a useful extra pair of hands for a woman seven months pregnant.

STC makes only one subsequent reference to SC's 'Feelings concerning Penrith', in which he describes those feelings as 'merely a little tiny Fretfulness' (STCCL ii. 886). If SC had really been 'thoroughly angered' by a meeting between STC and SH in Penrith, and by STC's account of it in his letter, such a dismissal of her anger would have been extremely provocative; and by the date he wrote those words (23 November) STC – realising that the long and extremely critical letter about her character he had written on 13 November (no. 467) was probably the wrong thing to send her, particularly now that she

was eight months pregnant – was doing his best to build bridges. The quarrel – over after one letter from each partner – arose not from SC's 'Feelings concerning Penrith' but from a sentence in SC's letter about STC's relationships with and his love for his friends. It may well have been SC's response to a phrase actually extant in the surviving fragment of STC's original letter: 'try to *love* & be *kind* to, those whom I love' (STCCL ii. 881). Presumably SC responded with something to the effect of 'if you loved me with one scrap of the love you show your worthless friends, life would be a good deal easier'. In return STC sent SC a lengthy analysis of the defects in her own character: 'the Eye & the Ear are your great organs, and you depend upon the eyes & ears of others for a great part of your pleasures. . . .' (STCCL ii. 882). In the course of this letter, he also told her that she paid far too much attention to 'rank & consequence'. STC is addressing himself to SC's desire to move in a different social circle of friends from that of the Wordsworths. The fact that SH was actually at Keswick throughout the exchange of angry letters, and the fact that less than a month later STC was strongly recommending SH to SC to go on caring for her and the children in the last stages of her pregnancy, confirm that the quarrel was not about SH. His letter of 4 January 1803 confirms that SC's real objection was to WW and DW.

The 'little tiny Fretfulness' connected with Penrith was probably about money. Having failed to get the mail coach in Penrith on Thursday 4 November because 'all the Places . . . are engaged' (STCCL ii. 879), STC spent freely in Penrith, so that the journey 'cost me two pound, perhaps, more than it would have done, if I could have taken my place in the Mail' (STCCL ii. 880); he felt that he had to defend his expenditure to SC but probably got seriously criticised for it (the whole journey would cost him £8.11.6 – STCCL ii. 880). If he spent money on accommodation, as seems likely, then obviously he was not being accommodated at Miss Monkhouse's; but 'two pound' was a lot to spend in a day.

Lefebure takes it for granted that the quarrel was about SH: 'Unfortunately he visited Sara Hutchinson during his stop at Penrith and this brought some complaint in a letter from his wife'. She assumes that the crucial sentence by SC was 'probably highly critical of him' (*BL* 156). Jones makes the identical assumption, arguing that STC 'managed to organise his journey so that he could spend the day in Penrith with Sara Hutchinson . . . this clandestine meeting seriously upset Sarah Coleridge who sent her husband a letter of rebuke' (Jones 148). Holmes agrees that SH was the cause of the dispute, but also says that the argument 'precipitated a long and angry exchange of letters between Coleridge and Sara, which continued throughout November and December' (Holmes i. 337). SC sent her critical letter around 11 November, STC sent his angry reply on 13 November, and the hostilities were over. Holmes and Whalley assume that STC's 'lack of marital tact had become quite formidable' (Holmes i. 337) in suggesting that SH would be the right person to come in to help SC in December (Whalley 45); they forget that SH was actually at Greta Hall in November, staying with SC.

76 DWJ 45.
77 STCCW xii. 1. 226–7; he had given her some corrected proof sheets the previous year (see Whalley 39 n. 1).
78 STCNB 1065 21.190; see p. 144.
79 DWJ 45, 59.
80 LWDW i. 17.
81 STCNB 1120 6.74.
82 STCNB 1133 8.2; DWJ 45, 48.
83 DWJ 45.
84 *Dejection* 27 (ll. 123, 115–18, 128).
85 STCNB 1912 9.33.
86 STCNB 1141 6.79.
87 Holmes i. 316.
88 Holmes i. 312.
89 He takes the fragment from STCCL ii. 780.

90 The text of the whole entry runs:

> Some painful Feeling, bodily or of the mind / some form or feeling has recalled a past misery to the Feeling & not to the conscious memory – I brood over what has befallen of evil / what is the worst that could befall me? What is that Blessing which is most present & perpetual to my Fancy & Yearnings? Sara! Sara! – The Loss then of this first bodies itself out to me / – & if I have not heard from you very recently, & if the last letter had not happened to be full of explicit Love & Feeling, then I conjure up Shadows into Substances – & am miserable / Misery conjures up other Forms, & binds them into Tales & Events – activity is always Pleasure – the Tale grows pleasanter – & at length you come to me / you are by my bed side, in some lonely Inn, where I lie deserted – there you have found me – there you are weeping over me! – Dear, dear, Woman! (STCNB 1601 21.361)

91 Ll. 324–9.
92 Holmes i. 316.
93 Holmes i. 316.
94 STC remarked in 1801 that he had lived since 1796 as 'a very Christian Liver' (STCCL ii. 734), meaning only having sexual relations with his wife; and he stated in 1814 that 'since my twenty second year' (i.e. 1794) he had 'never had any illicit connection' (STCCL iii. 515).
95 DWJ 76.
96 STCNB 1140 6.78.
97 SH had access to some supply of clothes; a parcel had arrived in Grasmere on 5 February 1802 with 'waistcoats, shoes and gloves from Sara' (DWJ 63): probably cast-offs from one of her brothers.
98 STCNB 1144 6.82.
99 See e.g. Holmes i. 9–10; and cf. a notebook entry from 1801: 'Laudanum, Friday, Septem. 18. 1801. Poem, dream from Dor. – both dead – feelings after

death – seeking the children.' (STCNB 990 21.142.)

100 STCNB 1150 6.141.

101 Kathleen Coburn suggests that it may be 'Related to Lamb's stammer ... or to calling out names to hear an echo, or to Coleridge's preference for *Sara* spelled without a final "h"?' (STCNB 1150n.) In December 1800 STC had called her 'Asahara, the Moorish Maid' (Whalley 39 n. 1).

102 STCNB 1151 6.142.

103 Holmes i. 317.

104 STCNB 3304 23.8.

105 DWJ 77, 78.

106 A journey which started with three consecutive days travelling by chaise and mail coach to London also required forty-eight hours rest in London before he went on to Somerset (STCCL ii. 878).

107 See DWJ 81.

108 STCNB 3304 323.8. Kathleen Coburn's note states that 'The night-long conversation with WW ... took place at Keswick, 3 April 1802' and adds that a 'consequence of the night's talk was *Dejection: An Ode*, written the next day'. But no evidence allows us to date the night-long talk to 3 April 1802, or to link it with the writing of *Dejection*: and the dating ignores the fact that WW had taken his decision to get married by February 1802 (STCCL ii. 788). Jonathan Wordsworth agrees that the decision to marry 'seems to have been taken at the end of 1801' (*BV* 431).

109 See e.g. an 1804–5 note written on the fly-leaf of STC's copy of Tetens' *Philosophische Versuche* (Leipzig, 1777):

> Sarah Hutchinson
> S. T. Coleridge
> Dorothy + Mary Wordsworth
> William Wordsworth
> Malta

He also inserted over and over again a scheme into the corners of his notebook pages in Malta which showed all of them together (see p. 248 and Chapter Ten note 101): see too Preface note 75.

110 Holmes i. 312; see STCNB 3304 23.7.

111 WW b. 7 April 1770; MW b. 16 August 1770; DWJ 38.

112 LWDW i. 341.

113 See e.g. LWDW i. 644 for WW and MW's income in November 1805.

114 DWJ 69.

115 DWJ 208, 72; see Preface note 63.

Chapter Five

1 DWJ 78.

2 DWJ 10; *P2V* 114 (ll. 21–2).

3 DWJ 76, 118.

4 *P2V* 203–4 (ll. 1–18; variants from DC MS 41).

5 DWJ 59.

6 See *The Ruined Cottage and The Pedlar*, ed. James Butler (Ithaca, 1979), pp. 327–9; the Introductory part had either not been there or had replaced what had been there in the 1799 version.

7 See p. 40.

8 DWJ 78.

9 'The Leech-Gatherer', Appendix II, l. 27; DWJ 78.

10 *P2V* 423.

11 See Preface note 63.

12 Ll. 16–17; DWJ 79.

13 DWJ 80. Mr and Mrs John Olive (nb DW's pronunciation) lived in 'the new house, a "trim box" D called it ... later known as The Hollins (until recently a hotel). It is half way between DC and the Swan' (DWJ 152n); the houses are about 600 yards apart. It is not clear whether they are walking on the road or over the fields between the two houses.

14 DWJ 81.

15 DWJ 76; 'An Elegy', *A Complete Edition of the Poets of Great Britain, Volume the Fourth*, ed. R. Anderson (London, 1793), p. 577 (see DWJ 187).

16 Ruoff suggests 'My Picture Left in Scotland' because of the parallels it offers with the stanza form of the *Ode* (Ruoff 48), but Jonson's 'mountain belly' and 'rocky face' would probably have denied the poem DW's adjective 'beautiful'.

17 See e.g. p. 267.

18 LWDW i. 335.

19 DWJ 81; see Moorman ii. 578; STCCW, xii. 1. 42. Derwent was baptized when

very ill in September 1800 (STCCL i.
626 n. 3); Sara would be baptized
within six weeks of her birth, Hartley
not until 8 November 1803. See also
p. 269.

20 DWJ 82.

21 DWJ 50.

22 DW recorded the arrival of seven letters
between November 1801 and July 1802
(on 21 December, 15 February, 22
February, 21 March, 7 June, 12 June, 3
July – DWJ 50, 69, 71, 82, 106, 108,
117), which – given the slightly greater
likelihood of her recording the arrival
of such letters – suggests a correspondence of at least one or two letters each
way each month. Moorman assumes
that because there is no record of WW
writing to Annette before 26 January
(DWJ 58), the December letter 'naturally gave rise to many anxious consid-
erations, which may account for the
delay in answering it' (Moorman, i.
554). But DW never kept a record of
every letter's arrival and reply and
abandoned her day-to-day account of
events between 4 and 22 January,
replacing it with a retrospective account
probably written on the 23rd. Between
the 4th and the 14th, there is no
record of any kind; and no record of
a single letter written by DW or WW
between the 4th and the 23rd. WW
or DW probably wrote at least once in
the first half of January, and that
they heard once or twice more from
Annette.

23 DWJ 82.

24 Gill 205.

25 Moorman i. 155. Did, in fact, either JW
or RW know about Annette and
Caroline? The former probably did;
but some covering of tracks suggests
that RW was still being kept in the dark:
the long journey to Gallow Hill,
London and France which WW and
DW had planned was, in a letter to him
of June 1802, foreshortened to 'we are
going into Yorkshire to Mr Hutchinson's to spend a couple of months
before William is married' (LWDW
i. 360). Others too were certainly kept
in ignorance; some friends naturally

believed it was the Lowther Estate
which caused WW and DW to be 'in
London upon that business' (LWDW
i. 378 n3).

26 STCCL ii. 849. Barker sensibly suggests
that 'Annette would have wanted some
sort of security for Caroline' (285) but
does not say what that might have been,
and ignores the matter completely in
her account of the August visit to Calais.

27 *P2V* 106, 305 (ll. 25–32).

28 WW knew what it was like to be in a
country with which his nation was at
war; his journey to France in October
1793 (see Preface note 63) had put him
in exactly that position.

29 DWJ 82.

30 LWDW i. 377; in 1801 his harvest had
been complete by 16 October, when he
arrived in Grasmere (DWJ 35).

31 DWJ 82.

32 *P2V* 212–13 (ll. 5–10, 11–14, 16–20;
variants from DC MS 41).

33 *P2V* 215 (ll. 16–23; variants from DC MS
41).

34 *P2V* 215 (ll. 25–8; variants from DC MS
41).

35 DWJ 82.

36 STCCL ii. 789.

37 STCNB 1001 21.153.

38 STCCL ii. 774–5; the letter ('Monday
Night') was written shortly after arriving back home (STC, DW, WW and
MH had walked to Keswick that
day).

39 STCCL ii. 776: I am grateful to the
Victoria University Library, Toronto,
for supplying me with a photocopy of
this manuscript. Griggs fills the gap
after 'my' with '[children]' and inserts
'[I saw]' after 'dreamt'.

40 STCCL ii. 780.

41 STCNB 1092 6.126, 1094 6.128. In
March, STC – thinking about school
again – would record schoolboy slang at
Christ's Hospital:

Crug – Jack – Piggin / Spadges of
Butter / Spadging Skulk – Faz – Pun
/ Flux – Pazzy – Ditto Wig – Tub-
boy / Jack-boy – Grecian / Deputy
Grecian / Little & Great Erasmus,
First & second Merchants & 8 first /

Monitors & Markers / Jolly first
order / (STCNB 1103 6.57)

42 STCNB 1105 6.59.
43 See p. 108; STCNB 1144 6.82.
44 STCCL ii. 804. Hartley's 'motto' may
    itself be an allusion to Wordsworth's
    Ode: 'To me alone there came a thought
    of grief . . .' (*P2V* 272, l. 22).
45 STCCL ii. 740.
46 STCCL ii. 804.
47 STCCP 141.
48 See Chapter Three note 83.
49 STCCL ii. 827.
50 STCCL ii. 827–8.
51 Hartley had been born on 20 September
    1796; he had made his poetic debut in
    his cradle in STC's 'Frost at Midnight'
    early in 1797.
52 LWDW i. 298.
53 Holmes i. 304.
54 LWDW i. 334.
55 LWDW i. 335.
56 STCCL ii. 828.
57 See *P2V* 100. A later title for the poem
    linked it with Hartley being 'six years
    old' and he would only be six on 20
    September 1802. It may well have been
    revised later: the link with Marvell (see
    p. 226 and Chapter Ten notes 9 and 11)
    suggests September 1802. STC quoted
    'exquisitely wild' in a letter of 14
    October 1803 (STCCL ii. 1014).
58 *P2V* 100 (ll. 1–14; variants from DC
    MS 44).
59 *P2V* 101 (ll. 15–18, 21–33; variants from
    DC MS 44).
60 At this stage, the graves of SH (d. 1835),
    and the two children of WW and MW
    (Catherine and Thomas) who had died
    in 1812. See Gill 422.
61 Cf. the story 'England, My England' by
    D. H. Lawrence, written in 1915, drawn
    from a man (Percy Lucas) whom
    Lawrence believed could not cope with
    his life. The story showed the character
    getting killed, and was written twelve
    months before the real-life original was,
    indeed, killed. Lawrence felt guilty: 'It
    upsets me very much to hear of Percy
    Lucas. I did not know he was dead. I
    wish that story at the bottom of the sea,
    before ever it had been printed'. But in

a postscript, he changed his mind: 'No, I
dont wish I had never written that story.
It should do good, at the long run' (*The
Letters of D. H. Lawrence*, vol. 2, ed. James
T. Boulton and Andrew Robertson
(Cambridge, 1981), 635–6.

62 DW says 'he had been trying without
    success to alter a passage, in Silver How
    poem – he had written a conclusion just
    before he went out' (DWJ 82). It is
    possible that the reference is to some
    part of *Home at Grasmere*; the previous
    week, DW had quoted in her journal a
    version ('That needs must be a holy
    place') of two lines in the poem about
    'this favoured Vale' ('They who are
    dwellers in this holy place / Must needs
    themselves be hallowed' – ll. 366–7)
    See *HaG* 60.
63 Cf. the way 'Beggars' stalled at night,
    was left unfinished, and WW went tired
    to bed, but – the following morning –
    finished it before he got up (DWJ 77–8);
    or how the first writing of 'The Leech-
    gatherer' had sent WW to bed 'nervous
    and jaded in the extreme', but he then
    wrote several stanzas in bed the follow-
    ing morning (DWJ 94); see pp. 180–1
    and Chapter Eight note 7.
64 DWJ 82.
65 DWJ 100.
66 *P2V* 206 (ll. 1–9; variants from DC
    MS 41).
67 In editions of his poetry from 1809
    onwards WW had them printed in
    italics.
68 *P2V* 206.
69 STCCL ii. 800.
70 Possibly from a later copy; it was
    already slightly but significantly altered
    from the text sent to SH ('Dorothy' had
    become 'Emmeline' and 'Thou Bible of
    my infancy' was now 'Historian of my
    Infancy').
71 See pp. 176–8.

Chapter Six
1 Holmes i. 321; *BV* 160.
2 Ruoff 173; *BV* 154–5.
3 Kerns 146; Ruoff 24; see too e.g. Ashton
   203.
4 Johnston 777.
5 Mary Moorman sums the matter up for

most biographers and critics when she says that 'on April 4th, a Sunday . . . Coleridge wrote, between sunset and midnight, the "Letter" in verse to Sara Hutchinson . . .' (Moorman, i. 528). The distinguished scholar Kathleen Coburn reiterated the idea in her notes to Coleridge's *Notebooks*, stating that the poem was written '"between sunset and midnight", 4 April 1802' (see note on STCNB 3304 23.8). See too Ashton 201.

6   'Every line has been produced by me with labor-pangs' he wrote on 17 September 1800 – and even by early October 1802 he had still not managed to finish it. See STCCL i. 623 and STCCP 505–7, 510.

7   See Dekker 223. 'Religious Musings' was not finally finished until April 1796; the first publication of 'Ode to the Departing Year' was dated 27 December 1796, the next year's publication claimed that it was 'written on the 24th, 25th and 26th days of December, 1796'; one manuscript has the date '23 December' on it, the 1817 edition claimed 'the last day of the year'. A sub-title to one manuscript of 'To William Wordsworth' reads 'Lines Composed, for the Greater Part, on the Night, On Which He finished the Recitation of His Poem . . .' (STCCP 573). Fruman makes the point about the claims for spontaneity (6–7, 511–12), but regards them as lies.

8   DWJ 83.

9   'The Voice from the Side of Etna; or the Mad Monk: An Ode in Mrs. Ratcliff's Manner', *Morning Post* (13 October 1800), ll. 9–16 (signed *Cassiani junior*).

10 P2V 271, 517 (ll. 1–9: non-verbal variants Commonplace book).

11 It was republished in 1804 as STC's, though he never included it in any of his collections of poetry. It appears in one edition of WW's poems (WWTP i. 421–2) and in most editions of STC's (e.g. STCCP 546). Computer analysis using the Qsum technique – taking for comparison material from STC's *Dejection* and WW's 'The Leech-gatherer' –

shows the whole poem clearly by STC apart form one brief passage; and that one passage (which is the single stanza quoted above) fits the pattern of WW's writing almost exactly (report from Jill Farringdon, 11 August 2000). See too Chapter 7 note 60.

12 See pp. 10–11.

13 See S. M. Parrish and D. V. Erdman, 'Who Wrote *The Mad Monk*? A Debate', *Bulletin of the New York Public Library*, lxiv (1960), 209–37.

14 See pp. 11–12.

15 All that is known from external sources of the date of the writing of the *Ode* fits the period 1800–3 as well as the accepted period of 1802–4. There survive four small pieces of evidence: a date WW supplied in 1836, some notes he dictated to Isabella Fenwick in 1843, the 1804 manuscript, and the entry in Dorothy's journal already quoted (DWJ 106). The last is obviously capable of several kinds of interpretation; it does not tell us whether what he wrote was the start or the conclusion or even part of the middle of an ode. But the fact that by the time she came to write up her journal DW knew – and WW knew – that it was an Ode (the first he had ever written) suggests a certain certainty, at least by evening, of the nature of what he was writing. It may only have been started that morning; but it may not. The second relevant piece of information about the writing of the *Ode* is the date '1803–06' which WW gave the poem in his 1836 *Poetical Works*. He supplemented this seven years later in a note he dictated to Isabella Fenwick: 'This was composed during my residence at Town-End, Grasmere, two years at least passed between the writing of the first four stanzas & the remaining part.' (*The Fenwick Notes of William Wordsworth*, ed. Jared Curtis, Bristol, 1993 [hereafter FN], p. 61). WW's dates, however, are (as has always been recognised) unreliable; he was recalling things which had happened forty years back, and he had only an ordinary memory. He constantly got the facts about his poems wrong, and not

just those of the small or minor poems. The Fenwick Notes wrongly date at least eleven poems written in the spring of 1802: the Fenwick date is in brackets, with page no., the most likely date in italics.

'Louisa' ('Town-End. 1805', 8)
　By Feb. 1802
'Alice Fell' ('1801', 1)
　March 1802
'The Sailor's Mother'
　('Town-End 1800', 9)
　March 1802
'To the Cuckoo'
　('Composed in the Orchard at
Town-End 1804', 13)
　March 1802
'To a Butterfly'
　('Grasmere Town-End. Written in
　the Orchard 1801', 1)
　March 1802
'The Sparrow's Nest'
　('The Orchard, Grasmere
　Town-End 1801', 8)
　March–May 1802
'My heart leaps up' ('This was written
at Grasmere Town-End 1804', 1)
　March–May 1802
'Written in March'
　('Extempore. 1801', 14)
　April 1802
'To a Butterfly' ('Grasmere Town-End.
　Written in the Orchard 1801', 1)
　April 1802
'To the Small Celandine'
　('Grasmere Town-End, 1805', 11)
　30 April–1 May 1802
'Resolution and Independence'
　('Town-End. 1807', 14)
　May 1802

An error in his 1836 date for the *Ode* immediately stands out: we know that he had in fact finished a version of his *Ode* by March 1804, not by 1806. The first complete surviving manuscript of the poem was written out in March 1804: DC MS 44 77^v–81^v, in the collection of poems put together for STC to take to Malta, probably assembled around 6 March and certainly by 18 March. See *P2V* xxi. All that the later

recollections tell us, perhaps, is that there was a gap of some years – in WW's recollection 'at least two', and possibly three in his figures '1803–06' – between the writing of the first stanzas of the poem and the rest of it. WW may only have been remembering that the poem had been started in one way, but finished in quite another way; he may, too, not be entirely accurate about the number of stanzas. In a manuscript of the poem in the so-called Beaumont Commonplace Book – which *may* precede DC MS 44 and which clearly derives from a rather different textual path – the poem appears without stanza three, with a few other small omissions and with some unexpected variant lines. The poem was entered in an unknown hand into a folio book kept by the Beaumonts for copies of poems or extracts from poems by WW and STC, which they generally – but not always – received in letters; and it was in use from either 1803 (*P2V* xviii) or 1804 (*P2V* 4) to 1807. Whatever the source of the Commonplace Book text of the *Ode* may have been, it derived from a slightly earlier stage of the poem than that transcribed in DC 44; and the question must therefore arise whether the third stanza was even, perhaps, the last written, and was therefore not yet in the text that supplied the copy for the Beaumont Commonplace Book. Many things may of course account for the non-appearance of a stanza in a copy: copyist's boredom, an instruction not to bother with the whole poem, a missing page in the text being copied. It does however suggest that whatever it was that WW wrote that morning in March 1802, stanza three *may* not have been part of it, if he *did* start the *Ode* that day; and that stanza three was perhaps written as late as 1802 or 1803 if the first part of the poem had actually been written in 1800. If we can get anything out of WW's recollections, we should therefore be looking for a starting date for the *Ode* 'at least' two years, and perhaps three, earlier than the date when the poem was finished (which we do not know); but given that it is unlikely that WW finished the poem to order in March 1804, *so as* to include it in DC MS 44, we might be looking for a completion date no later than sometime in the second half of 1803: so a starting date no earlier than 1801, and perhaps as early as 1800, is possible. The earlier it was finished, the earlier it may have been started. It is only fairly primitive human ingenuity which has concluded that the first four stanzas of the poem must have been written on 27 March 1802; and the remaining stanzas rather less than two years later, just in time for DC MS 44.

16   *P2V* 273, l. 76; *HaG* 259 (MS 1. was probably inserted into its 'Calais Book' (DWJ 137) in the winter of 1802).

17   *P2V* 578 (ll. 63–4), *P2V* 365 (ll. 73–4, DC MS 44); *BV* 170; see p. 171.

18   *HaG* 56 (ll. 315–16); *P2V* 272, 518 (l. 22).

19   *Dejection* 127 (ll. 289–94).

20   DWJ 111.

21   *P2V* 275, 519 (ll. 139–41: non-verbal variants Commonplace book).

22   *P2V* 275, 519 (ll. 126–31: verbal and non-verbal variants Commonplace book).

23   The autumn of 1800 has been a favourite location for the break: see pp. 6–10 and Preface note 31. Susan Eilenberg however structures her book around the divide between Coleridge and Wordsworth which she believes began in the winter of 1798–9 in Germany (Eilenberg 134–5).

24   STCCW xii. 746.

25   LWDW i. 348; DWJ 37.

26   DWJ 83.

27   *The Poetry of Coleridge*, ed. Richard Holmes (London: Harper Collins, 1996), p. 169; *Selected Poetry of Coleridge*, ed. John Beer (London: Dent, 1991), p. 81. Beer does, however, also give '4 April 1802 Sunday Evening' as a subtitle.

28   STCCL ii. 790–8; Jones calls it 'A Letter to Asra' (137).

29   The 4 October 1802 printing in the

Morning Post is the most explicit about the date; it has, as well as the new title *Dejection*, 'AN ODE, WRITTEN APRIL 4 1802': the addressee is 'Edmund'. The earliest datable text of any of the *Letter* poetry is in the letter which STC sent to William Sotheby on 19 July 1802, which has the title 'Letter written Sunday Evening, April 4' preceding it, and is addressed to 'Wordsworth' (see Appendix I). Even the partial text which STC sent to Sir George Beaumont on 13 August 1803 has the title '*Dejection: an Ode* (Imperfect) *April 4 1802*' at its head and is addressed to 'William'; the copy of the *Letter* written out by STC himself, for the Wordsworths, is preceded by 'A Letter to ——— / April 4, 1802. – Sunday Evening', and is addressed to 'Sara'. The title STC first inscribed in that manuscript was 'April 4, 1802'. Only then did he add the title 'A Letter'; and only at some point subsequent to that does he appear to have added 'to ———' to the manuscript. The other authoritative text of the *Letter*, copied out by MH (or MW: we do not know the date), lacks title, date, details and recipient, but is addressed to 'Sara'.

30   *Dejection* 115 (l. 116).

31   DC MS 41.

32   *Dejection* 115 (l. 128–9).

33   STCCL ii. 801.

34   *Dejection* 121 (ll. 201–3).

35   Holmes i. 312.

36   STCNB 1065 21.190. The other project was

> To write a <u>series</u> of Love Poems – truly Sapphic, save that they shall have a large Interfusion of moral Sentiment & calm Imagery on Love in all the moods of the mind – Philosophic, fantastic, in moods of high enthusiasm, of simple Feeling, of mysticism, of Religion – /comprize in it all the practice, & all the philosophy of Love – (STCNB 1064 21.189)

37   *Dejection* 125 (ll. 265–7).

38   STCNB 1142 6.8.

39 STCNB 1018 21.170.

40 The least characteristic is perhaps the poem of that name (STCCP 290). Ashton states that STC wrote the poem on 4 April and that this also 'was the day on which Wordsworth left Keswick to propose to Mary Hutchinson' (Ashton 201): but she also rather comically assumes that STC, as well as being ill in bed, stayed up all night (after writing a 338 line poem) persuading WW to propose. In spite of her own argument that WW proposed to MW the previous November, Barker concurs (287).

41 It is to me extraordinary that Jonathan Wordsworth should claim that the *Letter* should not only lament the hopelessness of STC's love for SH but also 'his increasing sense of exclusion from the Wordsworth household' (*BV* 154), or that he should also think that WW might have felt deeply criticised by the poem (171). A Wordsworth perhaps feels bound to be especially partial, biographically.

42 *P2V* 276, 519 (ll. 164–6: non-verbal variants Commonplace book).

43 DWJ 84. Barker assumes that the disheartening problem was MH's reaction to the idea of the Calais visit to see Annette (286); an example of what happens when a biographer focuses on one character at the expense of the concerns of the group.

44 LWDW i. 350.

45 LWDW i. 352.

46 DWJ 84.

47 LWDW i. 347.

48 LWDW i. 348.

49 *Dejection* 107–8.

50 These were lines 80–91 of the July poem, or perhaps lines 92–8. In October 1802, STC told Tom Wedgwood that the second passage (ll. 264–70) 'in the original followed the line – My shaping Spirit of Imagination' (STCCL ii. 875) and was corrected by Griggs ('nor do they follow, as Coleridge says, the line on imagination in the original draft of the poem'). STC might be given credit for knowing his own poem; this is a piece of evi-

dence for the slow growth of the poem over the summer of 1802, as on 29 July STC told Southey that at this point in the text there were 'a dozen Lines that would give you no pleasure' (STCCL ii. 831); this suggests that the lines in question (ll. 241–63) were written *after* 'the original' but before 29 July.

51 DWJ 89; e.g. 'Do you ask what the birds say?' and 'The Day-Dream'. Parts of the *Letter* are addressed to STC's wife (t'other Sarah), so it is just possible that it was those bits to which DW was referring; though unlikely, unless it were a poem like 'The Happy Husband' which he had read out.

52 See pp. 160–1.

53 Text from Commonplace Book: *P2V* 277, 520.

54 See Appendix II, ll. 52–60.

55 See pp. 31 and 56; STCCL ii. 830.

56 STC used the phrase in the title of his 1798 poem 'The Nightingale: A Conversation Poem, April, 1798'. Bate claims that 'the verse becomes more flexible, the idiom still more colloquial . . . it was with a half-humorous apology as if to say it was a "middle thing" between poetry and conversation' (Bate 47). But the crucial thing is not only the *reflective* quality of the verse (as Bate stresses) but its *reflexive* quality: it constantly constructs other minds and imaginations with which it is engaged, and with which it both differs and agrees.

57 *P2V* 273, 520 (ll. 64–70: non-verbal variants Commonplace book).

58 *P2V* 277, 520 (ll. 203–6: non-verbal variants Commonplace book).

59 *P2V* 363 (ll. 51–7: variants from DC MS 44).

60 *P2V* 363, 361 (ll. 42–50, 6–9: variants from DC MS 44).

61 *Dejection* 109 (ll. 39–43).

62 *Dejection* 109 (ll. 44–51).

Chapter Seven

1 Sir George and Lady Beaumont.

2 LLWMW 38.

3 LLWMW 63.

4 Pamela Woof suggests that 'ride' is a mistake for 'write' (DWJ 219) but WW

only seems to have started to write the poem after entering Raby Park, and it was probably forbidden for people to ride through the park except at walking pace. The slow speed of the horse could thus have permitted and provoked the poem, rather than the poem coming anyway and WW having to slow down to accommodate it.

5 DWJ 88–9.

6 The horse belonged to William Calvert, one of STC's neighbours in Keswick (and an old friend of the Wordsworths); he put his horse at WW's and DW's disposal for their journey to Eusemere, and for WW's to Bishop Middleham and back; see LWDW 346–7 and 347 n 1.

7 DWJ 84.

8 WW to STC, 16 April 1802 (DC); SH's copy is in DC MS 41.

9 *P2V* 102, 103, 447 (ll. 15–20: variants from DC MS 41).

10 LWDW i. 348.

11 See William Blake, 'The Rose', l. 4.

12 'Strange Fits of Passion', WWTP 367 (ll. 25–6).

13 DWJ 86.

14 See p. 60; LWDW i. 347.

15 See pp. 62–3.

16 DWJ 87.

17 DWJ 85.

18 LWDW 352.

19 LWDW 347.

20 *Dejection* 24 (ll. 29).

21 *Dejection* 24–5 (ll. 45–51).

22 STCNB 1159 6.88.

23 STCNB 1160 6.150.

24 STCNB 1161 6.89.

25 STCNB 1018 21.170; see p. 145.

26 *Dejection* 28 (ll. 144–7).

27 STCNB 1162 6.90.

28 *P2V* 566 (ll. 1–5: variants from DC MS 41).

29 *P2V* 75, DC MS 41; DWJ 88. Pamela Woof describes how 'incomprehension and mockery were . . . general reactions when the poem was published, much revised, 1807 (as shown in the publication of, for example, *The Simpliciad – a Satirico-Didactic Poem containing Hints for the Scholars of the New School*, anon. (1808); see esp. ll. 9–10, mocking

Poets who "With brother lark or brother robin fly / And flutter with half-brother butterfly" and ll. 17–20' (DWJ 218–19).

30 See *P2V* 404.

31 *BV* 153; *P2V* 75, 437 (ll. 1–5: variants from DC MS 41).

32 *P2V* 76, 437 (ll. 12–14, 18–25: variants from DC MS 41). In his Cumberland accent (see p. 240) WW would have pronounced the word 'childeren'.

33 DWJ 88.

34 *P2V* 215–16, 494 (ll. 3–6, 12–19; variants from DC MS 41).

35 Ll. 7–9.

36 DWJ 88.

37 DWJ 88.

38 STCNB 1163 6.91.

39 DWJ 88–9.

40 DWJ 89.

41 'Sunshine', 'field', 'sport' and 'lambs' are words which do not appear in the *Letter* (at least in its finished state) but are crucial in the 1804 version of the *Ode*. WW's own sorrow was certainly capable of communicating itself to DW; one wonders whether she had been re-reading the *Ode*, as well as listening to STC. However, perhaps surprisingly 'sad', 'sorrow' and 'sky' are all of them significant words in the *Letter* and none of them appears in the *Ode*. The words 'sorrow', 'lamb' and 'sky' are, however, all in 'To H. C.', suggesting how strongly it too was involved in this conversation of poems and ideas.

42 DWJ 89.

43 DWJ 89.

44 Jonathan Wordsworth makes the point (*BV* 163), but does not link it to DWJ 82; see pp. 64–5.

45 DWJ 92.

46 See *P2V* 274–5 (unrevised Commonplace book text), 428–9 and *Biographia Literaria*, ed. George Watson (London, 1967), chap. XXII, p. 262.

47 STCCP 286, l. 45.

48 It exists independently of the finished *Ode*, however, in DC MS 44.

49 *BV* 162.

50 See p. 25; DWJ 91.

51 DWJ 91.

52 See pp. 35–6.

53 Having got the poem as far as the proof stage of his 1807 volume, WW retreated into respectability and cancelled it. See *P2V* 528–30.

54 See p. 36.

55 *P2V* 528–30, 551–2 (ll. 1–4, 19–22, 38–45: between ll. 42 and 43, DC MS 40 and MS 41 both insert an extra line).

56 The barberry-tree is really a shrub [Berberis vulgaris] native to Europe, with small yellow flowers, succeeded by oblong, red, sharply acid berries; *P2V* 576 (ll. 9–13). For authorship, see *P2V* 576, WWTP 985 and *BV* 152 ('Wordsworth never published it . . . but it is undoubtedly his, and belongs almost certainly to the end of May 1802').

57 *P2V* 577 (ll. 16–18, 37–44); *LB* 65 (l. 39).

58 *P2V* 577 (ll. 45–50); *LB* 66 (l. 11).

59 *P2V* 577–9 (ll. 25, 45–6, 41–2, 89–90); *BV* 151; for ll. 5 ('nodded in the breeze') and 6 ('rustled in mine ear') see *LB* 201 (l. 28) and *LB* 179 (l. 17); see Chapter Six [note 17].

60 For a very different way of thinking about the poem, see *BV* 149–54, 166, 168–71; it has also been accepted as a genuine WW poem in *HaG* and *WWTP*. Computer analysis using the Qsum technique, however, strongly supports my suggestion of joint authorship. Jill Farringdon reports, in a letter of 28 July 2000, that using for comparison material from STC's *Dejection* and WW's 'The Leech-gatherer', a clear distinction appeared between its parts: 'Under analysis, the text fell into two parts, separating at (about) sentence 14.

And when my trance was ended
And on my way I tended
Still, so it was, I know not how . . .

The first half of the poem is indistinguishable from STC but separates from WW. The second half of the poem is indistinguishable from WW, but separates from STC.' See too Chapter Six note 11.

61 E.g. ll. 1–13.

62 *P2V* 579 (107–11).

63 STCCL ii. 830.

64 DWJ 92.

65 LWDW i. 335.

66 DWJ 92.

67 DWJ 92.

68 Ben Jonson in February and March (DWJ 66, 76, 81), Bishop Hall in February (DWJ 72). He would also copy out Marvell's 'Horatian Ode' later in the year (sometime after August): see p. 226 and Chapter Ten note 9.

69 *P2V* 252, 510 (ll. 19–22: text from DC MS 40).

70 DWJ 93.

71 DWJ 94.

72 DWJ 94.

73 DWJ 85; the Lesser Celandine is 'Common Pilewort'.

74 DWJ 86.

75 *P2V* 80 (ll. 23–4).

76 DWJ 89.

77 *P2V* 80–1 (ll. 9–16, 33–6, 49–53, 57–60). Cf. 'The Mask of Anarchy' (1819), stanza XCI: 'Rise like Lions after slumber / In unvanquishable number – / Shake your chains to earth like dew / Which in sleep had fallen on you – / Ye are many – they are few.'

78 *P2V* 83 (ll. 41–8).

79 *P2V* 68, 434 (ll. 69–70: variants from DC MS 44); *P2V* 118 (ll. 28–9).

80 *P2V* 67, 433 (ll. 38–40: variants from DC MS 44).

81 LWDW i. 350; DWJ 94.

82 STCCL ii. 812.

83 STCCL ii. 830.

84 Gill 201.

85 STCCL ii. 830–1.

86 STCCL ii. 800–1.

87 STCCL ii. 830.

88 STC's terrifying letter to WW of 30 May 1815 (STCCL iv. 572–6), saying what he had *thought* the poem would be about, often read as pure description – 'The most detailed, though not necessarily the most reliable, account of *The Recluse . . .*' (*BV* 352) – is actually an astonishing exercise in self-aggrandisement, summing up as it does so much of what *he* had wanted to do, and had failed to do.

89 *BV* 171.

Chapter Eight

1 Gill 201, Johnston 776.
2 Magnuson 309. See also Mahoney 194.
3 See pp. 151–4.
4 No other details can be established: DW left most of the Sunday and the whole of the Monday out of her journal as she was changing notebooks.
5 Only one other of his poems had had exactly this opening: 'There was a boy' of 1799.
6 DWJ 93.
7 DWJ 94. The fact that the sentence 'William was very nervous' (DWJ 101) was crossed out in the journal shows that it meant the kind of criticism which some later reader did not want preserved, Cf. Samuel Johnson's comment 'A tender, irritable and as it is not very properly called, a nervous constitution' (letter to Mrs Thrale 24 November 1783).
8 DWJ 95.
9 DWJ 95.
10 *Benjamin the Waggoner*, ed. Betz, p. 82 (MS 1): original draft written in 1806.
11 *Benjamin the Waggoner*, ed. Betz, p. 329 (1836 MS).
12 DWJ 95. DW is (understandably) mistaken. STC recorded in his notebook 'April 20, 1802 Tuesday Evening, ½ after 7 / Cut out my name & Dorothy's over the S. H. at Sara's Rock –' (STCNB 1163). When he returned to Keswick on the 25th, however, he 'got into a Gig with Mr Beck' (DWJ 91) so had no chance to improve his lettering. Neither WW nor DW had travelled up to Keswick since 20 April, so 4 May would have been the first time either of them could have seen the new initials. DW thought that STC had done it all that morning; but it would have been natural for him to do some extra work, deepening the inscription, before the Wordsworths arrived at midday. The letters were still not quite right: hence WW's next action.
13 *Benjamin the Waggoner*, ed. Betz, p. 82 (1806 MS1, l. 496); STC was thinking about it (under that name) in November–December 1806 as one of the subjects to be introduced into his projected

poem *The Soother of Absence* (STCNB 2950 11.102). See p. 239.
14 The later history of the rock is a tragicomic version of the Isis–Osiris myth:

In the late 1880s the water level of Thirlmere was raised, the old road blasted, and the Rock with it, to make way for a higher road and to find rubble for the dam. Fragments of the Rock of Names were gathered up by Canon H. D. Rawnsley, cemented into a small pyramid of stone, and placed above the new road. In 1984 there were new fears for the safety of the initials and they were fixed into natural slate in their original configuration (as early photographs make clear) and embedded into a rock-face behind the W Museum at Grasmere. (DWJ 191–2)

See Illustrations 1 and 2.
15 WW and STC walked past the rock together towards Keswick on 24 May; STC walked past on 12, 23 and 24 June; STC and WW came past together on 29 June, and STC went by on his own on 30 June. WW and DW went past it together on 9 July.
16 *Benjamin the Waggoner*, ed. Betz, p. 118 (ll. 55–8, 51–4, 47–8); the phrase also suggests the common wild viola tricolour 'Heartsease' or 'Love-in-Idleness': common, spontaneously generating itself.
17 'A Complaint', *P2V* 253 (ll. 5–6, 9–10).
18 DWJ 95.
19 DWJ 95–6. DW quoted STC's epigraph from the 'Ballad of Sir Patrick Spence' accurately, from her own reading in Percy's *Reliques of English Poetry*: she may have checked it when she got home, before writing her diary.
20 STCNB 1165 6.93; I owe the identification to Claude Rawson. The work was much translated, published and embellished: e.g. *Basia or, the Charms of Kissing*, from the Latin of Catullus and Secundus, tr. Thomas Tooley (London, 1719).
21 STCNB 1176 6.151.
22 DWJ 89.

23 *Dejection* 111 (ll. 58–66).

24 *P2V* 381 (ll. 66–8).

25 DWJ 96.

26 DWJ 97.

27 DWJ 76, 71.

28 DC MS 41 (ll. 1–2, 9–14).

29 See DWJ 227.

30 *Dejection* 142 (ll. 25–30).

31 STCNB 1105 6.59.

32 MH wrote out the only manuscript which exists of 'The Day Dream' on the last part of the second sheet of her copy of the *Letter*. She may simply have been using up the lower half of a page with another poem by STC of the right length (cf. DW's use of the sheet containing the 'The Full Moon in a Passion' – DC MS 40 – to write out another couple of poems). There is no way of dating the two sheets; she could have inscribed her copies at any time over the next thirty years. The fact that they survived among her own private papers (see *Dejection* viii, LLWMW 7) suggests that they were important to her. STC *may* have sent a copy of 'The Day Dream' to the Wordsworths, and they *may* have sent it on to Gallow Hill, around Friday 7 May, and it *might* have been accompanied by a copy of the *Letter*, together with a request that the poems be copied. On the other hand, the *Letter* is unique in lacking any trace of the complicated title with date; and 'The Day Dream' oddly enough lacks a title too. The copies were not being made with a view to the further transmission of the texts. They were, however, in 1802 the two poems which were most explicit in conveying STC's love for SH; I mentioned earlier the trouble there would have been if a perceptive Hutchinson brother had read such poetry, and made the connection with his sister which it invited. It seems likely that MH made her copies as discreetly as possible, of two dangerous texts, and that their appearance on the same sheet tells us nothing about when they arrived (or were written).

33 DWJ 97.

34 At the end of the month, for example, she noted 'I wrote out the poem on "Our Departure" which he seemed to have finished' (DWJ 103).

35 DWJ 97–8.

36 The poem would be a favourite of STC: see STCCL i. 154–5.

37 *P2V* 581 (ll. 17–18).

38 *P2V* 581 (ll. 23–7); *P2V* 128 (l. 126).

39 *P2V* 582 (ll. 32–6).

40 *P2V* 582 (ll. 42–4).

41 *P2V* 583 (ll. 50–4, 64–9).

42 *P2V* 319 (ll. 29–33: DC MS 41); see Appendix II.

43 *P2V* 581–2 (ll. 28, 18, 10, 1).

44 DWJ 98.

45 DWJ 98–9.

46 Holmes i. 321–2.

47 DWJ 99.

48 DWJ 99.

49 DWJ 100.

50 STCCL ii. 802.

51 See STCCL ii. 804.

52 DWJ 97, 98, 100.

53 See Chapter Three note 16.

54 DC MS 31. The transcription in DWJ 100 misreads the blotted and altered date as '16th May 1802', but the position of the entry directly opposite the journal entry for the 15th makes it clear that it too had been inserted on the 15th.

55 DWJ 100.

56 DWJ 101.

57 See, e.g., her journal entries for 9–14 June, which correspond to the long letter DW sent MH on 14 June (LWDW i. 361–4). The journal simply records: 'Lloyds called'. The letter says 'The Lloyds called in a Chaise, luckily we did not see them; we are determined to cut them entirely as far as Will goes; there is one chain about us, Priscilla, but she shall only drag us to Brathay about once a year' (LWDW i. 362). And whereas DW's journal entries about SC are either brief or (more often) non-existent, her letter of 14 June is malicious (LWDW i. 362).

58 DWJ 102.

59 DWJ 37.

60 STCCL ii. 832.

61 STCNB 1189 21.207.

62 *P2V* 126 (ll. 64–8).

63 See Appendix II.
64 DWJ 87.
65 See p. 154.
66 *BV* 171.
67 LWDW i. 365.
68 DWJ 103.
69 LWDW i. 355.
70 LWDW i. 365.
71 LWDW i. 366–7.
72 DC MS 41; *P2V* 323.
73 LWDW i. 367.
74 LWDW i. 364; see DWJ 70.
75 LWDW i. 367.
76 DWJ 23–4. The meeting was apparently on 13 September; JW met him later the same day. DW inserted her account in her journal on 3 October; something made her include it at that point, and it is probable that she did so on WW's suggestion.
77 DWJ 109.
78 FN 14.
79 See Chapter Six note 15.
80 See Heath 123.
81 DWJ 111; see p. 111.
82 They also had a problem with somewhere to stay in London on their way to France, and were not able to 'fix our time' until they had heard whether the rooms belonging to their old acquaintance the lawyer Basil Montagu were free (LWDW i. 367 & n.1); see Chapter Ten note 3 and p. 250.
83 DWJ 116–17.
84 *Biographia Literaria*, ed. Watson, chap. XXII, p. 272.
85 *P2V* 129 (ll. 136–8).
86 See *P2V* xxvii.

Chapter Nine
1 LWDW i. 364; DWJ 108.
2 *P2V* 587 (ll. 9, 11).
3 Gill says that 'Wordsworth dwells on the cottage, on the garden they have created' (Gill 205), but he is trying to make the poem a parallel (a leaving-Grasmere poem) to *Home at Grasmere* (which had marked their arrival).
4 LWDW i. 352.
5 DWJ 113–14; STCCL ii. 849.
6 See Chapter One note 14. The upstairs room was (and is) much lighter and more pleasant, but the roof is reported

to have leaked and the fire to have smoked: sufficient reason enough for a new bride to be given the downstairs room.
7 DWJ 91, 9, 12, 94, 97, 100; 9, 59, 60, 62, 83, 88, 97, 91–2, 89, 97.
8 DWJ 89, 96, 102, 118. 'Nailing up' trees may refer to the old habit of driving nails into fruit trees in the belief that they would fruit better; it is more likely to mean supporting drooping branches with wooden props.
9 DWJ 96, 102.
10 'Farewell, thou little Nook', *P2V* 588 (ll. 26–7).
11 DWJ 117; see the Preface note 11 for the variety of vegetables and fruit they produced.
12 'To a Butterfly', *P2V* 216, 494 (l. 11).
13 'We took home a great load of Gowans and planted them in the cold about the orchard' (DWJ 99): see DWJ 98 for a list of the plants and flowers they brought back. DW always appreciated help; back in October 1801 she had 'planted all sorts of plants, Tom helped me' – Sara and Mary's brother Tom, that is, who also 'brought me 2 shrubs from Mr Curwen's nursery' (DWJ 36). Wild plants would not of course cost anything.
14 See p. 36; *P2V* 588, 692 (ll. 21–4: variants from DC MS 41).
15 DWJ 102, 103.
16 LWDW i. 367, confirmed by DC MS 40, a fragment textually close to the first draft; the line was changed to 'Here with its primroses the steep rock's breast' (l. 53). WW and DW had been reading Spenser since 1801 (DWJ 38, 41) and in the spring of 1802 had read the 'Prothalamium' together on 25 April (DWJ 91). Spenser appeared in vol. ii. of *A Complete Edition of the Poets of Great Britain* compiled by Dr Robert Anderson.
17 DWJ 111.
18 *P2V* 587. The title 'A Farewell' was only given to it in 1827.
19 Nor did DW when she recorded bringing the plant home on 11 May (DWJ 98) or seeing it beside the Lake on the 14th (DWJ 99).
20 *P2V* 588 (ll. 28–9).

21   *P2V* 588 (ll. 34–6, 50, 56).

22   *P2V* 589, 692–3 (ll. 57–63: variants from DC MS 41).

23   *P2V* 581 (ll. 26–7).

24   DWJ 102. He regularly seems to have had an afternoon sleep: in his chair (17 April), outdoors (30 April), in the window seat (12 May), indoors (14 May), in the window seat (3 June); the bower would have an additional place in summer.

25   Cf. a recent biographer: 'The poem's ostensible subject, their garden, is heavily overdetermined by the real one, the realignment of erotic allegiances' (Johnston 780). What is 'real' to a biographer may be an imposition upon a poem.

26   *P2V* 588, 692 (ll. 44–5: variant from DC MS 41).

27   *P2V* 588, 692 (ll. 49–52: variant from DC MS 41).

28   *P2V* 589 (ll. 53–6).

29   Johnston 779.

30   See Johnston, however: 'As a farewell, it is addressed more to Dorothy than to Annette: the renunciation of the sister had, after ten years, become harder than renouncing the lover' (779). The poem has nothing at all to do with Annette.

31   LWDW i. 358–9. As late as April 1802, the nature of WW's visits to MH was still being concealed from RW: 'William is gone for a few days into the County of Durham' (LWDW i. 345) was how DW referred to the visit.

32   DWJ 233, DC MS 31: as Heath 144 pointed out, the names on what is now the first surviving page of the journal are heavily crossed through.

33   Johnston 779.

34   See Gittings and Manton 132–4.

35   LWDW i. 345.

36   LWDW i. 361.

37   LWDW i. 359.

38   LWDW i. 359.

39   LWDW i. 359.

40   Gittings and Manton 133.

41   LWDW i. 394. It is, however, just possible that STC was contriving to give her money too, this summer. She would borrow £20 from him in July, leaving him a note to draw on RW for the money after two months. But RW's accounts show that STC had still not done so by 8 October (LWDW i. 374 and n.2): we do not know if he ever did. DW had at times to resort to such strategies to ensure that RW paid her what she expected from him; she would do the same in December 1803, when she borrowed £20 from SH, leaving it to SH to recover the money from RW – who would obviously not fail to pay such a debt (LWDW i. 379).

42   DWJ 103.

43   LWDW i. 359, LLWMW 35.

44   LWDW i. 359.

45   DWJ 103.

46   DWJ 104.

47   DWJ 105.

48   DWJ 106, 108, 109, 112.

49   DWJ 107.

50   FN 56.

51   DC MS 41; *P2V* 204–5, 489. Paul Betz argues that the opening lines of *Benjamin the Waggoner* 'seem almost to be a companion piece' to 'The Sun has long been set', and suggests a date of 15 June 1802 for them (*Benjamin the Waggoner*, ed. Betz, p. 9); no manuscript material, however, supports the suggestion.

52   LWDW i. 362–3.

53   LWDW i. 363.

54   LWDW i. 363.

55   STCCL ii. 737; see e.g. pp. 164 and 191.

56   STCNB 1204 6.175; DWJ 108.

57   LWDW i. 362.

58   DWJ 108; on 12 May, however, STC had been put in the sitting room after an unexpected arrival at night (DWJ 98–9).

59   STCNB 1203 6.174.

60   STCCL ii. 802.

61   DWJ 109, 118.

62   Biographers of STC could use this information to develop the idea that SH was in love with him, though it may simply have been that SC did not like her husband getting letters (no matter what their contents) from an unmarried woman whom he admired, so that it was easier for SH to send letters to him via WW and DW, without there being any-

thing in the letters which would have made deceit necessary.

63 DWJ 109.
64 *Dejection* 32, 28, 31, (ll. 257, 164, 242–4).
65 See p. 194; STCCL ii. 832.
66 STCCL ii. 800.
67 See Chapter Four notes 14 and 15.
68 DWJ 109.
69 *P2V* 140–1, 460 (ll. 1–4, 5–8, 9–12).
70 See *Henry V* iv. i. 274–90.
71 DWJ 110.
72 DWJ 110.
73 DWJ 112.
74 DWJ 115.
75 DWJ 114.
76 DWJ 115. They returned the following year, and again she emphasised her sense of possession: 'I am writing in my own room. Every now and then I hear the chirping of a little family of swallows that have their abode against the glass of my window. The nest was built last year, and it has been taken possession of again' (LWDW i. 393).
77 *Benjamin the Waggoner*, ed. Betz, p. 44 (1806 MS1, ll. 8–9, 13–14); see too pp. 8–9.
78 DWJ 118.
79 DWJ 119.
80 DWJ 119.
81 LWDW i. 374.
82 DWJ 119.
83 STCCL ii. 808–9.
84 DWJ 120.
85 DWJ 129; 'she threw out some saucy words in our hearing' (DWJ 120).
86 DWJ 119.
87 See Chapter One note 104.
88 See LSH xxxviii, 23.
89 STCNB 973A 22.1.
90 LWDW i. 404.

Chapter Ten

1 DWJ 124.
2 WW may have got to France in October 1793: see Preface note 63.
3 DWJ 123; STCCL ii. 858; the rooms they had hoped to acquire from Basil Montagu (see Chapter Eight note 82) may not have materialised.
4 WW's sonnet 'Earth has not anything to shew more fair' (*P2V* 147), although dated 'Sept. 3, 1803' (the year altered to '1802' only in 1838) drew on what he saw on this departure from London, as DW's matching journal entry (DWJ 123) suggests; cf. 'composed on the roof of a coach, on my way to France Sep^br 1802' (FN 56). It may not have been written down before Calais. The return journey over Westminster Bridge was at six in the morning on 30 August and according to DW's journal 'It was misty & we could see nothing' (DWJ 125). WW may have finished work on the poem in London in September, hence the date: he may simply have wanted to give it a 'London' date.

5 STCCL ii. 849.
6 Four weeks may argue 'a real commitment to re-establishing contact with Annette and to getting to know Caroline' (Gill 208): they may have been forced upon WW and DW.
7 Between August and October 1802, he wrote around twenty-five sonnets. Six were connected with the Calais visit: 'Earth has not any-thing to shew' (*P2V* 147), 'Fair Star of Evening' (155), 'Is it a Reed' (156), 'Jones! when from Calais southward' (156–7), 'Festivals have I seen' (158–9), 'It is a beauteous Evening' (150–1).
Three are linked with the return to England from France: 'We had a fellow-Passenger' (161–2), 'Dear fellow-Traveller!' (162–3), 'Inland, within a hollow Vale' (163).
Two were connected with the return to London: 'O Friend! I know not' (164–5), 'Milton! thou should'st be living' (165).
Five may have been drafted in Calais: 'There is no bondage which is worse' (168–9), 'Where lies the Land' (137), 'With Ships the sea was sprinkled' (142), 'The world is too much with us' (150), 'Great Men have been' (166).
Three may have similar links with London: 'It is not to be thought of' (166–7), 'When I have borne in memory' (167), 'England! the time is come' (170).

Seven cannot be dated at all: 'Nuns fret not' (133), 'O gentle sleep!' (140), 'A flock of sheep' (140–1), 'Fond words have oft' (141–2), '"Beloved Vale!" I said' (148), 'Methought I saw the footsteps' (148–9), 'Calvert! it must not be unheard' (151–2).

8 DWJ 137: see DC MSS 38, 45, 47, 70. They had an ingenious fastening arrangement, in which the cover at one end was extended like the sealing flap on a modern envelope, with a short cord attached, so that the notebook could be tied up and kept closed in the pocket; the covers are of blue-green cardboard and the 62 leaves are of laid paper, with chain-lines running vertically, watermarked F D or F. WW started DC MS 47 as late as 1804, which suggests that they were kept for special occasions.

9 The republication of Marvell's poems in the 4th edition of 1776, edited by Captain Edward Thompson, included the first printing of the poem since the 1681 printing had been withdrawn, and all except two surviving copies issued without it. See too *BV* 416.

10 See e.g. DWJ 234.

11 'Great Men have been among us', *P2V* 166, l. 3.

12 DWJ 246.

13 See DWJ 249–50: the ring is now in the Wordsworth museum at Grasmere.

14 'There is a separate copy of this Calais section made probably for friends such as Mrs Clarkson' (DWJ 246).

15 The fact that '& dirt' is omitted in the manuscript copy of the journal suggests horse dung.

16 See 'To a Friend, Written near Calais, on the Road leading to Ardres – August 1st 1802 (DC MS 44: *P2V* 156). Longman MS gives the date as '7th' revised from '1st' (*P2V* 156). 1 August was a Sunday, and the day they landed in Calais, though DW thought it was 31 July (DWJ 124). WW may have taken his walk towards Ardres on the day of their arrival or the following day: certainly within the week.

17 *P2V* 156–7, ll. 2–4, 9–12.

18 *P2V* 156; *Gentleman's Magazine*. 72 (August 1802), pp. 769, 771.

19 *P2V* 158, 467 (ll. 5–8).

20 *P2V* 158 (ll. 9–11).

21 DWJ 124.

22 See note 7 above for sonnets possibly drafted in France.

23 Moorman i. 565; Gill 208.

24 Howard Brenton, *Bloody Poetry* (London, 1985), p. 30, which vividly (if maliciously) imagines Byron's reaction to her and to WW.

25 See STCCW iii. 1. 311–39. An untraced remark by Bonaparte about France ('*the best, greatest, and wisest nation of Europe*') quoted in STC's second essay (p. 331) may derive from something WW had heard and passed on.

26 DWJ 124.

27 Ll. 12–13, 6–12, 14.

28 One line identically repeated in the surviving journal (and then deleted) may be a simple error (she copied out her own line), but it *may* be an indication that DW was copying from another document when she wrote up at least this part of her journal (bold indicates deletion)

Romance was ever half so beau
tiful. **Romance was ever half so beau
tiful** Now came in view (DC MS 31:
    DWJ 125).

29 DWJ 246.

30 DWJ 124.

31 DWJ 125.

32 DWJ 125.

33 DWJ 125.

34 FN 21.

35 *P2V* 150–1, (ll. 9, 6–8, 2).

36 Ll. 10–11, 12, 14.

37 *P2V* 276.

38 *P2V* 161–2.

39 DWJ 125.

40 DWJ 125.

41 Gittings and Manton 207.

42 LWDW i. 282.

43 *P2V* 151 (ll. 10–11: from DC MS 44).

44 *P2V* 276 (ll. 182–3: variants from Commonplace Book).

45 He had discovered that it was stopping

opium which led to catastrophic physical effects; but these he attributed to his stomach in its natural state, without opium, rather than to withdrawal symptoms. Cf. his letter to SC of 16 November 1802:

> I have now left off Beer too, & will persevere in it – I take no Tea . . . & once in the 24 hours (but not always at the same hour) I take half a grain of purified opium, equal to 12 drops of Laudanum – which is not more than [an] 8th part of what I took at Keswick, exclusively of B[eer,] Brandy, & Tea, which last is undoubtedly a pernicious S[timulant –] all which I have left off – & will give this Regimen a *fair, compleat* Trial of one month – with no other deviation, than that I shall sometimes lessen the opiate, & sometimes miss a day. But I am fully convinced . . . that to a person, with such a Stomach & Bowels as mine, if any stimulant is needful, Opium in the small quantities, I now take it, is incomparably better in every respect that Beer, Wine, Spirits, or any *fermented* Liquor – nay, far less pernicious than even Tea. (STCCL ii. 884)

46 See Appendix II.
47 STCCL ii. 827.
48 STCCL ii. 825, 837.
49 STCCL ii. 846, 834–5.
50 STCCL ii. 837–8. WW and DW had paid 3/6 each in Patterdale, in April, for their evening meal, followed by 'rum and water, dry beds and decent breakfast': DW thought they had been charged 'one shilling too much' (DWJ 216).
51 STCCL ii. 838–9; LWDW i. 347.
52 STCCL ii. 840. The shepherds were right but STC had not climbed the highest Scafell peak: Scafell Pike is 3,210 ft., Helvellyn 3,118 ft., Scafell itself (which STC had climbed) 3,100 ft., Skiddaw 3,053 ft.
53 STCNB 1218n.
54 One modern critic takes STC to task for 'having apparently informed no one of

his hazardous itinerary – even then that must have been the First Law of Mountaineering' (Ruoff 184). But no shepherds would have downed crooks or started scouring the mountains for a lost poet, even if they had known a poet was missing. Cragfast sheep were another matter; see STCCL ii. 842.

55 STCCL ii. 842.
56 STCCL ii. 842–3.
57 STCCL ii. 841–5.
58 STCNB 1225 2.20.
59 STCNB 1225 2.20.
60 STCCL ii. 846, 848.
61 It seems to have become a kind of anthology of love experiences, and notebook entries record suitable candidates: see e.g. STCNB 1913 9.34, 1937 21.430, 2980 11.49. His feelings for SH naturally became a part of such a sequence of love poems: but so did his dejection. In Malta in 1805, he noted:

> Soother of Absence. Days & weeks & months pass on / & now a year / and the Sun, the Sea, the Breeze has its influences on me, and good and sensible men – and I feel a pleasure upon me, & I am to the outward view of all cheerful, & have myself no distinct consciousness of the contrary / for I use my faculties, not indeed as once, but yet freely – but oh [Sara]! I am never happy, never deeply gladdened – I know not, I have forgotten what the Joy is of <that> which the Heart is full as of a deep & quiet fountain overflowing insensibly, or the gladness of Joy, when the fountain overflows ebullient. – S.T.C. (STCNB 2279 21.473)

The 'Soother of Absence' here looks like yet another version of the *Letter* and *Dejection*, with SH the focus. By 1808, STC associated the word 'soothe' with SH, referring to 'her Face' as 'my soothing and beckoning Seraph' in a notebook entry also contemplating the projected poem (STCNB 3404 13.35).

62 STCNB 2224 22.15.
63 'In the S. of A. to describe Setting

allegorically, losing the way to the temple of Bacchus, come to the Cave of the Gnome, &c &c' (STCNB 2842 15.233).

64 STCNB 2950 11.102.

65 See too STCNB 3947 L.1 18.

66 STCNB 515 5–114(a).

67 STCNB 798 51/2.42.

68 DWJ 19.

69 DWJ 20.

70 *Dejection* 27, l. 135.

71 STCNB 7 1.18; DWJ 54.

72 STCNB 801 51/2.45.

73 STCNB 1156 6.147. Coburn remarks 'There is no such night recorded, and it is difficult to see . . . when it could have taken place with all five present' (1156n); it is actually impossible, not just difficult, to tell when a projected poem might have 'taken place'.

74 STCNB 1218 2.12(b); 1160 6.150.

75 *LB* 114 (ll. 22–31). Cf. too the end of the poem:

> Nor wilt thou then forget,
> That after many wanderings,
>   many years
> Of absence, these steep woods
>   and lofty cliffs,
> And this green pastoral landscape,
>   were to me
> More dear, both for themselves and
>   for thy sake. (ll. 156–60)

The word 'absence' is not common in WW's poetry of the period.

76 A ballad stanza of STC's, probably dating from 1802, is so determined to introduce 'Helvellyn' as a rhyme word that the central figure appears in four different versions in attempts to match it (O'Kellyn, O'Relhan, O'Rellian, Orellan):

> Where is the grave of Sir Arthur
>   O'Kellyn?
> Where may the grave of that good
>   man be?
> By the side of a spring, on the breast
>   of Helvellyn.
> Under the twigs of a young birch
>   tree!

(STCCP 326, 565; see too *The Complete Poetical Works of Samuel Taylor Coleridge*, ed. Ernest Hartley Coleridge, 2 vols (Oxford, 1912) [hereafter CPWSTC], i. 432 n.1). This is evidence from 1802 of the hold which Helvellyn had on STC's imagination; but, once again, it is of Helvellyn as a mountain where the *human* action is significant, not just the wildness: where 'each Thing has a Life of it's own, & yet they are all one Life', to adopt the language STC used in September 1802. That suggests what 'The Bards of Helvellin: or the Stone Hovels' (the bards perhaps living *in* the stone hovels) might have been like: a poem concerned with the poets' experience of the mountain as a place which both awed and impressed them but to which they also belonged; in which they could 'move, & live, & *have* their Being' (STCCL ii. 866).

77 STCCL ii. 864–5.

78 STCNB 1541 16.46.

79 STCCL ii. 865 n.1.

80 STCCL ii. 996.

81 STCCP 325 (ll. 64–9).

82 STCCL iv. 974.

83 Griggs makes them letters *to* SH (STCCL nos. 450 and 451), and Holmes appropriates them as 'a superb journal letter to Asra' (Holmes i. 328). On 10 August STC wrote to SH (STCCL no. 453) with details of his visit to Grasmere which would also have appeared in the third journal-letter, if he had ever finished it: she was not the only intended recipient of the journal-letters. STC had continued to insert entries into his notebook which would allow him to write up the third letter, and told SH on 10 August that he had 'half such another, the continuation of my tour, written' (STCCL ii. 848). But the third journal-letter was neither finished nor sent.

84 STCCL ii. 844.

85 In November 1799, STC and WW wrote a joint journal-letter which they sent back to DW at Sockburn; it only exists in the form of a copy made by MH, and ends 'Why were you not with us Dorothy? Why were not you Mary

with us?' (STCCL i. 545), showing that it was designed to be read by both. It was perhaps the first of the group letters, only SH being excluded (it is possible that STC had not yet met her).

86 STCCL ii. 835.

87 STCCL ii. 836.

88 *Dejection* 27, l. 133.

89 STCCL ii. 839.

90 STCCL i. 542–5.

91 STCCL i. 545.

92 STCCL i. 654–5; as reasons for not producing the work he claimed that what he had written 'would raise a violent clamour against me & my publisher' (i. 654), and that the letters had been lost (see Holmes i. 234). See too STCCL i. 645.

93 STCCL ii. 732.

94 STC himself sent truncated accounts of the journey to two other friends (Southey and Sotheby), neither of whom would therefore have needed the full versions (STCCL ii. 846, 858–9).

95 See STCNB 973A 22.1 and n., 1007 21.159, 1008 21.160, 1009 21.161, 1010 21.162 and nn. SH may even have retained STC's notebook no. 8 between March and November 1802: see STCNB 1261n.

96 STCCL ii. 841.

97 'I vainly strive / To beat away the Thought' appeared in the *Letter* (*Dejection* 29, ll. 169–70), but not in the version of *Dejection* sent to Sotheby in July (nor in the *Morning Post* in October).

98 Gill 206.

99 CPWSTC ii. 969.

100 Gill 206.

101 STCNB Volume II, 'General Notes', p. xxv; Coburn offers a number of other schemes. See too Preface note 75 and Chapter Four note 109.

102 STCCL ii. 958, 1013.

103 STCCL ii. 849.

104 STCCL ii. 849.

Chapter Eleven

1 *Dejection* 56 (l. 68); 'Marriages & Deaths of Remarkable Persons', *Gentleman's Magazine*, 72 (July–December 1802), 1224.

2 'Farewell thou little Nook of mountain ground', (*P2V* 587) (l. 18).

3 See p. 124.

4 WW and DW never seem to have contemplated returning to Grasmere before the wedding. The tidying up they had done in July was very clearly in the expectation that the next time they were in Town End, MH (now MW) would be with them. It would theoretically have been possible for them to have got back to Grasmere by the end of August, which would have allowed them a month at home before going over to Yorkshire (assuming that the wedding was fixed for October). But that never seems to have been contemplated. This, in its turn, suggests that the wedding date had *not* been fixed either; that they had simply decided to get married just as soon as WW and DW got up to Yorkshire. As it turned out, this would be nearly a month later than originally expected.

5 LWDW i. 376. Back in the spring they had suggested that the Hutchinsons might like to buy the gig belonging to John Olive when the latter was selling up: 'I wrote . . . to Sara about Mr Oliff's Gig' (DWJ 79).

6 LWDW i. 376 n 1.

7 LWDW i. 375–6. 'Paper Buildings' was in the Inner Temple. By 'fat' DW means that John's face was full and his figure filled out; see her remarks about MH (quoted below) when she met her later in the month.

8 It may not actually have been since 1778 or (more probably) 1787 that they had all been together; see too LWDW i. 540.

9 LWDW i. 376.

10 LWDW i. 376; STCNB 2537 17.95.

11 She believed she had 'caught cold' on 21 May (DWJ 101) and at the start of June was suffering from 'the most severe cold I have ever had in all my life' (LWDW i. 358). She was not really well again for the rest of the month, and was still too poorly to travel on 11 July (DWJ 119). In Calais in August she had another 'bad cold' (DWJ 124), this 'violent cold' in London, and then, at the end of the month, in Yorkshire 'con-

tinued to be poorly most of the time of our stay' (DWJ 126). These serious illnesses were in addition to the incidents of being not 'quite well' which her journal also recorded.

12 See Chapter Ten note 7.
13 Johnston 716, 787.
14 DC MS. WW's 'Michael' runs:

> . . . but whatever fate
> Befall thee, I shall love thee to the
>   last,
> And bear thy memory with me to
>   the grave. (*LB* 238–9, ll. 425–7)

15 Johnston 787. He implies that JW was desperately eager to answer a letter which he assumes would have arrived in Portsmouth: 'John sent a letter to Mary . . . on September 12, the day after he landed, having rushed from port to Richard's lodgings at Staple Inn' (787). There is no evidence of rush. JW dropped anchor on the 10th, saw Richard on the 11th, and added his postscript to DW's letter on the 12th.
16 LWDW i. 649: he would have needed especial inviting to the home of a married couple.
17 *LB* 238, ll. 423–5.
18 See pp. 63–4; Barker 255; Johnston 788.
19 LLWMW 142, 117; LWDW i. 377.
20 DWJ 126.
21 DWJ 126.
22 Her '*recollections*' of the Scottish Tour made with WW and STC in 1803 were written without any notes; see LWDW i. 421. See however Chapter Ten note 28.
23 Gill says that although she wore it, it was 'not on her second finger' (211): she says it was on her forefinger. It is not clear what the significance of the second finger would have been, and we do not (anyway) know which hand DW was wearing it on. Johnston asserts that WW put it on to her 'third finger' – the ring-finger, if her left hand – and gives the Gill biography as his source (788).
24 See DWJ 249–50.
25 Joanna was one of the witnesses – together with her brothers Jack and

Tom – on the Marriage Certificate; it would have been odd for George to stay behind.

26 DWJ 126.
27 DWJ 126.
28 Moorman i. 573 and n. 1.
29 See LWDW i. 375 and n. 2.
30 See p. 64.
31 DWJ 126.
32 DWJ 127.
33 DWJ 129.
34 DWJ 131–2.
35 DWJ 131.
36 DWJ 132.
37 DWJ 134.
38 DWJ 135.
39 DWJ 137.
40 Gittings and Manton 142–3.
41 DWJ 14.
42 Moorman i. 576.
43 See Chapter Ten note 24.
44 See Chapter One note 99 and Holmes i. 310.
45 STCCL ii. 876.
46 Woof, 'Wordsworth and Stuart's Newspapers', p. 183.
47 Johnston 789.
48 LWDW i. 615.
49 Johnston 788.
50 STCCL ii. 826–7.
51 Moorman i. 575.
52 STCNB 1250 21.214.
53 DWJ 249.
54 Holmes i. 333.
55 *Dejection* 50, 51, (ll. 21, 22, 40).
56 *Dejection* 54, 56, 60, 62, (ll. 48, 67–8, 129, 138).

Epilogue

1 LLWMW 49.
2 In 1843 he dated the sonnet 'October 3ᵈ. or 4ᵗʰ 1802' and continued 'Composed, after a journey over the Hambeton Hills, on a day memorable to me – the day of my marriage' (FN 22). Either he was starting to forget the date of his wedding day or he had done some prior work on the poem.
3 LWDW i. 381.
4 'Composed perhaps between around November 1802 and early January 1803' (*P2V* 586): a version of Milton's Sonnet VI, printed in Anderson's *Complete*

Edition of the British Poets, Volume V, p. 170:

Giovane piano, e semplicetto amante
Poi che fuggir me stesso in
  dubbio sono,
Madonna a voi del mio cuor
  l'humil dono
Farò divoto; io certo a prove tante
L'hebbi fedele, intrepido, costante,
De pensieri leggiadro, accorto,
  e buono;
Quando rugge il gran mondo,
  e scocca il tuono,
S'arma di se, d' intero diamante,
Tanto del forse, e d' invidia sicuro,
Di timori, e speranze al popol use
Quanto d'ingegno, e d' alto valor
  vago,
E di cetra sonora, e delle muse:
Sol troverete in tal parte men duro
Ove amor mise l'insanabil ago.

A literal translation of the original would run:

Since I am a young, unassuming
  and artless lover,
And do not know how to escape
  from myself,
I will make you, lady, the humble
  gift of my heart
In my devotion; I have proved it
  in many a trial
Faithful, brave, constant,
Graceful, wise and good
  in its thoughts.
When the whole world roars, and
  the lightning flashes,
[My heart] arms itself in itself, in
  perfect adamant,
As safe from chance and envy,
From fears, and from vulgar hopes
As it is eager for distinction of
  mind, and for real worth,
And for the sounding lyre, and for
  the Muses:
You will find it less hard only in
  that spot
Where love stuck its incurable sting.

5 STCNB 1575 21.296(a).
6 As early as July 1800 STC had referred to WW as 'such a lazy fellow' (STCCL

i. 611) in a letter to Humphry Davy, but that was almost certainly a joke about someone whose powers of application normally put STC to shame. The charge may, however, also record one of the real differences between them, of which they were both conscious: WW working comparatively slowly, STC either doing nothing at all or working with great rushes of enthusiasm. Jokes are very often based on versions of truths; and in 1803 it would especially have appealed to STC to characterise his friend as lazy.

7 STCCL ii. 1012–13.
8 Never reprinted by WW: STC's reaction may well have influenced him.
9 STCNB 1310 8.59, 1336 8.71.
10 STCCL ii. 958.
11 STCNB 1449 7.2; and e.g. 'A Man Happily made, but most unhappily thwarted, And oft there came on him – &c And sudden Thoughts that riv'd his heart asunder By the roadside, the while he gaz'd at flowers' (STCNB 1444 16.18); 'What? tho' the World praise me, I have no dear Heart that loves my Verses – I never hear them in snatches from a beloved Voice, fitted to some sweet occasion, of natural Prospect, in Winds at Night –' (STCNB 1463 7.16). The savage references to WW apparently made on the Scottish tour at STCNB 1471 7.24 – 'Friend . . . O me! what a word to give permanence to the mistake of a Life!', 'O Esteesee! that thou hadst from thy 22nd year indeed made <u>thy own</u> way & <u>alone!</u>' – are additions made c. 1812.
12 Lefebure believes that the quarrel was about STC's opium addiction (*BO* 378–9). See STCNB 1471n. for WW's and STC's daughter Sara's later opinions.
13 With the (subsequent) deletions restored: 'Cf. Carland Crags – O Asra wherever I am, & am impressed, my heart akes for you, & I know a deal of the heart of man, that I otherwise should not know' (STCNB 1451 7.4). The second time was a few days after his attack on WW:

This is Oct. 19. 1803. Wed. Morn. tomorrow my Birth Day, 31 years of age! – O me! my very heart dies! – This *year* has been one painful Dream / I have done nothing! . . . O Sara Sara why am I not happy! why have I not an unencumbered Heart! these beloved Books still before me, this noble Room, the very centre to which a whole world of beauty con- verges, the deep reservoir into which all these streams & currents of lovely Forms flow – my own mind so popu- lous, so active, so full of noble schemes, so capable of realizing them/this heart so loving, so filled with noble affections – O Asra! wherefore am I not happy! why for years have I not enjoyed one pure & sincere pleasure! – one full Joy! – one genuine Delight, that rings sharp to the Beat of the Finger! – ++all cracked, & dull with base Alloy! (STCNB 1577 21.297)

14 DWJ 132.

15 DWJ 133.

16 See Chapter Four note 75.

17 See *Gentleman's Magazine*, 72 (July–December 1802), 1223: '23. At Greta-hall, Keswick, the wife of T. S. Coleridge, esq. a daughter'.

18 STCNB 1333 8.69.

19 DWJ 136–7.

20 DWJ 137.

21 LWDW i. 335.

22 STCCL ii. 911–13, 915 ('I took no opium or laudanum'); Wedgwood, however, had given STC instruc- tions about what to omit in 'a system of Diet' (ii. 917).

23 STCCL ii. 913: see STCCL ii. 788 for STC's February 1802 plan for them to spend the summer together in France and LWDW i. 362 n. 3 for a June 1802 rumour of their plans to go to Montpellier.

24 *HaG* 383 (ll. 873–4 of MS. B).

Index

The following abbreviations are used in the index and in the endnotes:

SC   Sarah Coleridge
STC   S.T. Coleridge
MH   Mary Hutchinson (later MW)
SH   Sara Hutchinson
DW   Dorothy Wordsworth
JW   John Wordsworth (brother of DW and WW)
MW   Mary Wordsworth
WW   William Wordsworth

Earnest